THE

# GOVERNMENT OF ENGLAND

VOLUME II

# THE

# GOVERNMENT OF ENGLAND

BY

A. LAWRENCE LOWELL

PROFESSOR OF THE SCIENCE OF GOVERNMENT
IN HARVARD UNIVERSITY

VOLUME II

London
MACMILLAN & CO., Ltd.
NEW YORK: THE MACMILLAN COMPANY
1908

Set up and electrotyped. Published May, 1908.

Norwood Press
J. S. Cushing Co. — Berwick & Smith Co.
Norwood, Mass., U.S.A.

# TABLE OF CONTENTS

## VOLUME II

CHAPTER LIII



## PART VI.—THE EMPIRE

CHAPTER LIV



CHAPTER LV



CHAPTER LVI



CHAPTER LVII



CHAPTER LVIII



## PART VII.—THE COURTS OF LAW

CHAPTER LIX



CHAPTER LX



CHAPTER LXI



CHAPTER LXII



## PART VIII.—REFLECTIONS

CHAPTER LXIII

THE

# GOVERNMENT OF ENGLAND

VOLUME II

# CHAPTER XXXI

## ANCILLARY PARTY ORGANISATIONS

The Central Office.

In an earlier chapter ancillary organisations were described as handmaids to the party, which make no pretence of trying to direct its policy, but confine themselves to the work of extending its popularity, promoting its interests, and preparing the way for its success at the polls. Owing to the concentration of responsibility for political action in the cabinet, bodies of this kind are peculiarly numerous and highly developed in England, and some of them are older than any other party organisations now in existence. By far the most important, the Central Office of the party, has already been mentioned many times. It may seem strange to classify the Central Office under the head of ancillary organisations, because it is the chief piece of mechanism in the party; but the term is intended to denote that a body is ancillary to the party, not that it is ancillary to the main party organisation. The Central Office certainly falls under the definition already given, which, although unusual, is believed to be sound and to rest upon an essential distinction.

Its Organisation.

Historically and in its present character the Central Office is an extension of the whip's office, and as such it is under the direct control of the leaders of the party in Parliament. On the Liberal side the work is done in the name of the Central Liberal Association, composed of the subscribers to its funds, and containing several hundred prominent men scattered over the country.[1] But in fact the body never meets as a whole; its duties are performed by an executive committee, nominally chosen by the asso-

[1] It was formed in 1861. Ostrogorski, I., 146.

ciation, and really selected by the whips. The association publishes no minutes or records of its proceedings, and is practically little more than a convenient instrument to assist the whips in the transaction of their business outside of Parliament. In the Conservative party even the form of an association was abandoned at the time of the reconciliation with Lord Randolph Churchill in 1884. Since that year the leader of the party has consulted whom he will, and the work of the Central Office is arranged at a conference of three men, the leader, the chief whip, and the principal agent. The latter is, indeed, a highly important figure, the person through whose hands the main threads of the political machinery in the country lead. We have seen his connection with the National Union, and noted how, by having his own paid subordinates act as secretaries to the divisional unions, he kept in close touch for many years with the local organisations throughout the nation. This enabled the Central Office to serve as a link or buffer, as the case might require, between the local associations and the party leaders. That particular bond with the Union has now been broken, but the office still maintains its own agents over the country. Moreover, the principal agent plays a leading part in the work of the great political clubs in London, which has long been very effective. The Liberal Central Association has an officer of a similar kind, but he is not a personage of the same importance. Owing to the comparative dearth of rich men in the Liberal ranks the resources of their Central Office are much smaller than those of its rival, and it cannot support paid agents in the provinces. The chief officer has under his direct control only the staff in his headquarters in Parliament Street, and for his relations with the local associations he must rely on the National Liberal Federation and on such voluntary help as he may get from the agents employed by the local bodies.

Its Functions.

The Central Office has naturally nothing to do with formulating the policy of the party, except so far as the leaders may consult it about the effect a measure would be likely to have upon the voters. Its duty is simply to win elections; and as success at the polls depends much upon long and careful preparation, the Office is busy all the time, although its activity is, of course, most fast and furious when a dissolution takes place. The National Liberal Federation and the National Union of Conservative Associations are trying to do the same thing, and therefore, quite apart from the desire to keep them out of mischief, there is great positive advantage in coöperating with them. In each party the result has been achieved by housing the Central Office and the popular organisation together, and by having the secretary of one serve as honorary secretary of the other.[1] One of the obvious functions of both bodies, and hence one in which they have acted in concert, is the distribution of political literature. This is sent out by the ton in the form of periodicals, pamphlets, and stray leaflets almost innumerable. The Liberals issue each month a number of *The Liberal Magazine*, and their rivals print a monthly periodical called *Handy Notes on Current Politics.* The Conservatives publish also *The Constitutional Almanack* and *The Constitutional Year Book*, the latter a valuable political annual as well as a party handbook; while their rivals issue in the same way *The Liberal Year Book.* The pamphlets contain speeches, arguments on different subjects, hints for conducting elections, and other matter of the kind one might expect; while the leaflets, cheaply printed, and often reproducing political cartoons, make a coarser appeal to the prejudice of the masses.

**Publication.**

Another function of the Central Office is the suggestion of names to constituencies in search of a candidate. This is a matter which neither party has allowed to pass into the hands of a popular organisation; and it is a source of considerable influence, because a member of Parliament

**Recommending Candidates for Parliament.**

[1] Captain Middleton's successor was not honorary secretary of the National Union, although he continued to sit upon its council. This was a symptom of the unfortunate loss of harmony between the two bodies.

who owes his seat to the whips naturally feels a sense of loyalty to them. The Central Office never obtrudes its suggestions unasked, but when a constituency seeks advice it is always prepared to recommend two or three names. Men with parliamentary aspirations often apply for this purpose to the whips, and a list of them is kept, preference being given to those who are prepared to pay their own election expenses, or who have deserved well of the party, and especially to those who have already made a good fight for a hopeless seat.

Aiding in Election Expenses.

Still another important function is providing money for candidates who cannot pay the whole cost of their own elections. In accordance with the military principle of distracting the attention, and exhausting the resources, of the enemy, both parties bring forward candidates in as many constituencies as possible, even where the chance of success is small. But in England the expense of an election falls almost wholly on the candidate, the local partisans rarely subscribing much;[1] and it is not easy to find men who are willing to spend heavily with little prospect of success. In order, therefore, to enable a candidate to stand, it is often necessary to pay a part of his expenses, and this is frequently done even in the case of seats that are by no means hopeless. The hold which it gives over the members of Parliament who have received help has been referred to in an earlier chapter, while the influence it confers over many local associations need hardly be pointed out; but it may be observed that the practice favours the Conservatives on account of the larger funds at their command.[2]

The power of the Central Office is based to no small extent upon its financial resources. Formerly, under the

[1] Formerly considerable sums were raised for the purpose in Lancashire and Yorkshire by wealthy members of the party.

[2] The activity and ingenuity of the Conservative Central Office in devising means of reaching the electorate has been remarkable. One of the later agencies is that of travelling vans or wagons, which are used in places where meetings cannot be organised. A man drives the van and makes the speeches, while a boy looks after the horse and manages the lantern.

head of "secret service" the government received from the national treasury an annual grant of ten thousand pounds, which it used for party purposes without rendering an account. This was abolished in 1886, and since that time the war chest, as it is sometimes called, has been filled by private contributions. Rich men who subscribe large sums to help the party prefer to give them to the Central Office rather than to a local committee, both because it really does more good to the cause, and because there is a better prospect of reward. Even in the purest governments large gifts to the party do not go wholly without recompense. In England the cruder forms of paying political debts have been long outgrown; and to-day the public offices in the free gift of the government are few, while almost all of them, at least in the home administration, must be awarded for services rendered in Parliament. But the fountain of honour has not run dry. Titles and orders of knighthood are as much coveted as ever, and people are not shocked when these are conferred upon partisans. It is commonly said that a sufficient contribution to the party funds will bring a baronetcy, perhaps even a peerage, and the precise sum needed for the former is sometimes stated. Not that a man can stipulate for it; such an attempt would be repelled with indignation; but a payment made in faith is supposed to bring its deserts. When members of each party assert that their leaders never give a baronetcy in return for a contribution to the war chest unless the honour is otherwise merited, but that their opponents do so, one is led to conclude that the claim of a recipient, apart from his gift, is not always self-evident. But these matters rest largely upon surmise, for the Central Office renders no public accounts, and no one but the leader of the party, the chief whip, and often the principal agent, knows what sums have been subscribed or what use has been made of them. Resources of the Central Office.

A conspicuous form of ancillary organisation in England is the party club, which has been a force in politics for a

Political Clubs — The Conservatives.

long time.[1] The oldest of those still serving that purpose is the Carlton Club, founded in 1831 as a centre for Conservative activity. It fulfilled its object well, and became the meeting place of Tories who were ambitious or interested in politics. But as its membership was limited, and the men who wanted to belong to it were many, there came to be a long waiting list, and a Junior Carlton was founded. Even this does not supply the need, and in the region of the great clubs, that is, in the neighbourhood of Pall Mall, there are also the Conservative, the Constitutional, and the Junior Constitutional Clubs, besides the St. Stephen's Club opposite the Houses of Parliament, and the City Carlton, situated as the name implies down in the City of London. Party clubs of a similar kind exist also in the large provincial towns.

Their Functions.

The object of all these institutions is to make use, for party purposes, of the great part played by clubs in English social life. They are centres for the distribution, not the manufacture, of political opinions, for they make no attempt to guide the party, or to influence the policy of the leaders; but they do undoubtedly help to keep their members orthodox in their political creed, and prevent them from deserting the party fold. The six great Conservative clubs in the west end of London do also some active missionary work, in coöperation with the Central Office and under its direction. The political work of the Carlton Club, the most important of all, is really done at that Office, and, in fact, it has no separate political committee of its own. The others have political committees, but the principal agent of the party is the secretary of most of them. They organise lectures, lantern exhibitions and the like, among the Conservative workingmen's clubs over the country, and at times encourage them by the gift of a piano or some other attraction.

The political workingmen's clubs arose after the extension of the suffrage in 1867, and they have become very

[1] Ostrogorski discusses the clubs in Vol. I., pp. 143–45, 420–35.

numerous, especially among the Conservatives, often taking the place of a local party association. In fact the smaller ones are accorded the privilege of sending delegates to the Conference of the National Union on payment of one half the regular fee. Although the annual dues of such clubs must necessarily be small, they are supposed to be self-supporting; but in many cases their expenses would appear to be defrayed in part by gifts from the member of Parliament or candidate for the constituency. They contain a place for meetings and entertainments, rooms for reading, for cards or other games, and usually a bar. About a dozen years ago an ingenious plan was devised for increasing the interest in these clubs and the opportunities of their members. An Association of Conservative Clubs was formed, with Lord Salisbury as its president. It is supported and managed by the six great party clubs at Westminster; and it gives, free of charge, to any Conservative club that chooses to affiliate itself, lectures and prizes for debating, lends them boxes of books, and supplies them with club requisites at cheap prices. It confers on their members honorary membership in the seven hundred and fifty interaffiliated clubs scattered all over the country.[1] It has organised a cycling club; publishes a monthly gazette for a penny a number; and supplies the inevitable badge, which both appeals to the craving of poor human nature for marks of distinction, and promotes loyalty to the cause that the badge represents.

The Working-men's Clubs.

The workingmen's clubs have not proved of much use in fighting elections. They do not furnish a large body of active workers. On the contrary, the members are too apt to stay in the club-house playing cards when the constituency is being scoured for voluntary canvassers. In short, these clubs have not kindled enthusiasm for politics; but

Their Utility.

[1] The clubs of a different social position, such as the rich party clubs in London and the provincial towns, although members of the association, are naturally not among the interaffiliated.

that does not mean that they are valueless. No doubt the members, and in consequence many relatives and friends of the members, are kept faithful to their party allegiance. In fact the members are commonly required to sign an agreement to support the party and its leaders, or to resign when they cease to do so.

The Liberal Clubs.

Among the Liberals the party club has not been so fully developed, for they have relied less upon social influence of all kinds. They have been unfortunate also; their great meeting place in London, the Reform Club, founded in 1836, was sharply divided over the Home Rule Bill, and as neither side obtained control, but both Liberals and Liberal Unionists continued to be admitted, it ceased to be a real party club.[1] About that time, however, the National Liberal Club was founded, a huge concern with several thousand members, which serves as a rallying point for the party, and a place for meetings, but makes no pretence of exercising any corporate influence. There are other Liberal clubs of different kinds in London and in the provinces, but it is needless to dwell upon them as factors in politics, because their functions are similar to those of their Conservative rivals, although they are, on the whole, performed upon a smaller scale.

The Primrose League.

The most extraordinary of the ancillary party organisations in England is certainly the Primrose League. Founded by members of the Fourth Party in 1883, on the occasion when Beaconsfield's statue was unveiled, and named after what was supposed to have been his favourite flower, it seemed, with its mock-chivalric titles, a fit subject for ridicule; but it grew so rapidly that in a few years it was a powerful aid to the Conservatives, and a cause of anxiety to the Liberals. In 1887, when only four years old, it had over half a million members; in four years more it had a million, and by the end of the century about a million and a half. It contains members of both sexes, and of every rank in life. Its success as an

[1] Brooks', the old Whig club, has had a similar fate.

electioneering machine is, indeed, due to these two facts, for such is the nature of the English middle and lower classes that the upper ten thousand, and especially women of high social position, are most effective in winning votes.

**The Grades of Membership.**

To meet the needs of an organisation appealing to all classes, the constitution of the League is very complicated.[1] The members consist of knights, dames and associates; the knights and dames paying to the Grand Council an entrance fee and an annual "tribute" of half-a-crown, besides the dues that may be charged by their local "Habitation;" the associates having the same privileges, but paying only the local dues. The associates belong to the poorer classes, and form nine tenths of the members, while the knights and dames, who are nearly equal in numbers, are drawn from people able to pay more towards the support of the League. But their regular tribute is not enough, and in order to raise more money an Imperial Chapter for Knights and a Ladies' Grand Council were created, with annual dues of a guinea in each case. The League, however, rewards work as well as subscriptions; the knight, beginning as a knight-harbinger, may after a year of meritorious service "be elevated to the dignity of a knight-companion," a dame may be elevated to the order of merit, and an associate to the dignity of honorary knight or dame; while for special meritorious service in the cause there has been established a grand star of the League in five grades. For each of the ranks of membership, for all the dignities and offices, gaudy badges and clasps are supplied at remunerative prices; and that they are attractive to the masses is proved by the enormous numbers of them that have been sold.

**The Organisation.**

A local branch of the League is styled a Habitation. It is created by a warrant of the Grand Council, which may be withdrawn, and it must contain at least thirteen knights or dames. Its affairs are managed by an executive committee. Its meetings are presided over by a "ruling councillor" or "dame-president," and what is more impor-

[1] *Cf. The Primrose League Manual*, 1899.

tant it has officers called wardens, charged with the duty of recruiting members and canvassing all the voters within their respective districts. The Habitations are grouped under divisional and provincial councils, and there is held every year in London a Grand Habitation, consisting of one representative from each divisional council and two from each Habitation. It is a vast gathering which meets for mutual elation. Except for choosing auditors and a few members of the Grand Council, it transacts no business, but it listens to a speech by the Grand Master — usually the leader of the Conservative party — witnesses the presentation of banners to the local Habitations that have done the best work, and gazes at a platform filled with great ladies and lords of high degree. The whole management of the League is placed in the hands of the Grand Council, consisting in fact entirely of men, and so composed as to be practically a self-perpetuating body.[1] It appoints all the officers, controls all matters relating to the League, makes the ordinances, regulates the admission of members, issues the warrants for all Habitations and expends the funds. There is, indeed, a Ladies' Grand Council, but this has no power, and is specially forbidden to issue any circular, leaflet or other publication with the imprint of the League which has not been approved by the Grand Council. But after all the League is really managed by the vice-chancellor, who has charge of its permanent central office in London.

The Objects of the League.

Every member of the League must subscribe on his honour and faith a declaration that he will devote his best ability to the maintenance of religion, of the estates of the realm and of the imperial ascendency of the British Empire. These are the objects of the organisation which it professes to maintain quite independently of party politics. In its

[1] It consists of the Grand Master, the four trustees and the treasurer, of nine members elected by the Habitations in the nine provinces, twelve selected by the retiring Council, sixteen elected by the Grand Habitation, and eight coöpted by the Council itself.

publications it asserts constantly that it has been founded not to put any particular person or party in power, but to uphold principles, and that it would oppose any government, Conservative or Liberal, that threatened them. Naturally it goes on to explain that "at the present moment the Radical Party are attacking these principles." In fact it is nothing but a great electioneering machine for winning Conservative victories at the polls. Its propagandist labours are incessant, not only when elections are pending, but all the time. On the approach of an election, indeed, the local Habitations, for fear of infringing the provisions of the Corrupt Practices Acts, went for many years through the form of disbanding; but finding that there was no legal need of this, the Grand Council "decreed that they should not be dissolved nor suspended during election contests, but that the Ruling Councillors should place themselves and their Habitations entirely at the disposal of the election agent of the party which the League supports, so that the members of the League may work as organised bodies, and not simply as individual citizens."[1]

**Its Methods of Operation.**

Like other organisations, the League issues its monthly paper,[2] floods the country with leaflets, and wearies it with lectures. But far more important is its work in registration and canvassing, in which the dames are particularly effective, for an artisan will often tell a lady about his political opinions and his domestic affairs, when he would resent being questioned by a man. The members of the League get up meetings, distribute the party tracts, supply carriages at elections, and perform with enthusiasm all those unenviable services of the ward politician on which success at the polls largely depends. The chief source of the League's influence, however, is social, and in spite, it is said, of some cases of tactlessness, this is brought to bear as a rule with consummate skill. Rank and title have strong attractions for almost all classes of English

[1] *Primrose League Manual*, 1899, p. 59.
[2] *The Primrose League Gazette.*

people; and it is said that if the local squire or a peer can be induced to put himself at the head of a Habitation, its success is assured; if not, there is difficulty in making it succeed. The rich or noble members of the League give teas and receptions in their houses or parks; the knights and dames organise entertainments at a minute cost, with refreshments and dancing, or dramatic diversions, interspersed with some political instruction. The Liberals decry these things as playing upon the snobbish instincts of the masses, while the supporters of the League boast that it promotes "mutual intercourse with all classes," and "has knit together classes who were apart before, and whom it was the interest of agitators to keep apart."[1] The Liberals complain also that the League brings pressure to bear upon voters through their means of livelihood, by the fear of a tradesman's losing his customers, or a tenant his holding. The League repudiates the charge, and in its statement of principle there is a clause that, "Any attempt to gain members by threats of withdrawal of custom or favour, or by anything of the nature of what is popularly known as boycotting, is absolutely forbidden."[2] Pressure of this kind is not systematically, and probably not often intentionally, used; but the shopkeeper in a country town is no doubt sufficiently versed in human nature to be aware that the approbation of his rich neighbours tends to improve his trade.

Its Effectiveness.

That the Primrose League has been a valuable ally to the Conservative party no one would deny, but the degree of its efficiency is very hard to measure. It varies in different places, roughly in proportion to the influence of social rank. It is, on the whole, greater in the country than in the cities, in the South of England than in the North, and it is least in Scotland where the people have a sturdy independence that is far less open to social blandishments. Its power must vary also with the times. When politics are quiet, or when the issue turns on a sentiment of loyalty to the

[1] Lord Salisbury quoted in *Primrose League Leaflets*, Nos. 217 and 194.
[2] *Primrose League Manual*, 1899, p. 3.

government, or upon patriotic impulses, as at the election during the South African war, it counts for much; but when passions or personal interests are strongly stirred, the motives to which it appeals are faint. Its real work is not in convincing the strong, but in herding the indifferent; and in times of stress its exertions have much less effect upon the verdict of the nation.

**Women's Liberal Organisation.** As soon as the Primrose League had proved a success, and long before it had reached the enormous membership it attained later, the women in the Liberal party formed an organisation to secure similar benefits for their own side. In the dark hour after the general election of 1886 had overwhelmed the Home Rule Bill and Mr. Gladstone's ministry every organisation was encouraged, and in February, 1887, the Women's Liberal Federation was founded, with Mrs. Gladstone as president. Its constitution and method of operation were, however, copied not from the Primrose League, but from the National Liberal Federation, for it relied not upon social attractions, but upon appeals through speeches and pamphlets. It is managed by an executive committee, and has a Council composed of delegates from the local associations. There is also an annual meeting, but this is chiefly an opportunity to hear speeches, for the rules say that it is held "to discuss the policy of the Federation which shall not be alterable except by the Council."

**It Breaks in Two.** Curiously enough a dissension arose almost at the outset over the objects of the Federation. Some of the members wanted to place the parliamentary franchise for women among its fundamental aims; while others, although many of them wanted the franchise, felt that their main object ought to be the success of the Liberal party, and that it would be unwise to jeopardise this by insisting upon a question that was not a part of the Liberal programme. The Federation soon became sharply divided between these two groups, which strove together for five years. At first those who sought to place woman suffrage among their primary objects were in a small minority, but they increased rapidly in numbers, and in 1892 they succeeded in passing a decisive vote. Each side complained of unfair dealing by the other, and the dissension was so acute that the members and local associations opposed to including woman suffrage in the objects of the Federation seceded, and formed a new organisation, called the Women's National Liberal Association. Hitherto attempts at reconciliation have proved fruitless;[1] but the two bodies have avoided active hostility, and each has refrained from creating local associations in places already occupied by the other. They really represent very different attitudes toward public affairs. The relation of the Women's National Liberal Association to the Liberal party is that of an English wife, a true but subordinate helpmate. At its meetings men speak constantly; its resolutions are few, and are in harmony with the official policy of the party.

Character of the Women's Federation.

The Women's Liberal Federation, which is much larger, is, on the other hand, more independent, and its meetings have a more feminine character. The standing orders provide, not without cause, that "a member who speaks shall direct her speech strictly to the motion under discussion." The resolutions adopted are sometimes very numerous, and many of them relate to matters especially interesting to women. They are keenly debated, amendments are moved and a division is often taken. In 1899, for example, the Council adopted resolutions on Home Rule, Welsh disestablishment, reform of the House of Lords, and woman suffrage; thanked the Czar for his rescript on the Hague Conference; indorsed the sisterhood of nations, and international arbitration; resolved that this vote should be sent to the Czar, and to international meetings of women; passed several resolutions on temperance, education and labour legislation, and others on state regulation of vice, on the unequal treatment of the sexes, on London government,

[1] *Cf.* Rep. Ann. Meeting of the Council of the Women's Lib. Fed., 1899, p. 30 *et seq.*

slavery in Zanzibar, protection of birds, old age pensions, cottage homes, and vivisection. In the course of a debate on restricting the labour of women it interjected also a personal vote of confidence in its president. To party leaders who have suffered from the Newcastle Programme, such an array of resolves might give food for reflection on the possible effects of woman suffrage.

Their Work.

The women's liberal organisations do good work in registration and canvassing, and in prevailing upon men who are lukewarm to go to the polls. Sometimes this is done directly, sometimes through the influence of their wives; and it is said that in the North, where the people are more independent in character, the political influence of their wives is more marked. The women's organisations do educational work also, distributing the regular publications of the party, and printing a few leaflets of their own; but their social influence is much less than that of the Primrose League, because they make little attempt to use it, because the glamour of rank has less traditional power over the Liberals, and because the split in the party that followed the Home Rule Bill of 1886, by depriving them of many rich and titled people, left them at a great disadvantage as compared with their opponents in the number of members with a high social position.[1] English women take a peculiarly keen interest in public affairs, and they have become an important factor in politics; not as voters, for they are excluded from the parliamentary franchise, and in the local governments where a part of them have a right to vote they produce no marked effect; nor by the force of their opinions, which seem to have little influence on public men; but as party workers. If it be true that women are better fitted to live and work and die for a faith than to create one, then their political activity in England is directed aright, for their powers are exerted chiefly to make one or the other of the parties prevail;

[1] There is, however, a Liberal Social Council organised by ladies to bring the leaders and followers together at evening parties.

and it is not surprising that those powers are employed most fully on the side that professes to support the existing institutions of the realm.

Other Ancillary Organisations.

The Tories have another organisation on the same pattern as the Primrose League, and like it an electioneering body, though of far less importance. It is called the National Conservative League, is composed mainly of workingmen, and is organised by lodges. The Liberals had at one time a similar league which died out.[1] Then there are the societies formed solely to furnish speakers at public meetings. The earliest of them, the Eighty Club, takes its name from the year when it was founded by a group of ardent young Liberals. It was copied, as every useful instrument devised by one party is imitated by the other, and its counterpart among the Conservatives is the United Club. Besides these bodies there have been from time to time others, founded to emphasise some particular opinion without disturbing the unity of the party. Among them must be classed, on the Liberal side, the National Reform Union of Manchester, appealing to the more radical elements, and the Liberal League, which has tried to promote imperial sentiment within the party; but societies of that kind are apt to be either small or short-lived.

In this sketch of political organisations only bodies have been mentioned which are connected with the two chief parties in the state. They have evidently quite a different relation to public affairs from those belonging to the smaller independent groups. The Irish Nationalists and the Labour members have their own organisations, and the last of these will be described hereafter in a chapter by itself, but the question how they are managed and controlled has no direct bearing upon the position of the cabinet. One group, however, that of the Liberal Unionists, has really ceased to be a separate political entity; and its machinery, especially since the acceptance by the Council of Mr. Chamberlain's plan for preferential tariffs in 1904,

[1] *Cf.* Ostrogorski, I., 567–68.

has become in effect ancillary to the Conservative party. In many constituencies there are joint unionist committees, made up of representatives from the Conservative and Liberal Unionist associations. But the National organisations, though pursuing the same end, have been kept entirely distinct. It may be proper, therefore, to remark that the organisation of the Liberal Unionists is a partial copy of that of the Liberals. There is a federation for the Midlands, and a central office, but no federation for the whole country. There are also a Women's Liberal Unionist Association and a Liberal Union Club of public speakers. But the whole organisation is in the main a survival, a result of imperfect amalgamation.

Having surveyed the various forms of party machinery, we are confronted by the problem of their normal relation to the parliamentary form of government.

# CHAPTER XXXII

## THE FUNCTIONS OF PARTY ORGANISATIONS

The Subject to be Discussed.

If the system of a responsible ministry necessarily involves government by party, it determines also in large measure the functions of the party organisations. But here we must distinguish between the part played by parties in the life of the body politic, and the functions of the machinery within the party itself. The difference is like that between the influence of sea power on history, and the operation of the engines on a battleship. The two things are connected, but they are not the same; and the failure to keep the ideas distinct is responsible for much of the misconception that exists, especially in America, about the relation of parties to public affairs. Both the part played by parties in the government, and the action of organisations within the party, vary with the political conditions of each country, and it is the latter alone, in connection with the English parliamentary system, that forms the subject of this chapter.

Possible Functions of Party Organisations.

In a nation which is ruled by party the organisation might conceivably extend its operations as far as those of the party itself. It might in its conventions, or by its committees, frame all the legislation, direct the foreign policy, and regulate the internal administration, controlling it even in the minutest details. If we regard the cabinet as an organ of party, this is precisely what happens in England, for there is nothing in the whole range of party government for which a minister is not responsible. But when we speak of party organisations we do not usually mean to include the cabinet; we are thinking of the machinery of party outside the organs of government. Using the words in this sense, the party organisations are limited to a far narrower field. Leaving out of account the details of administration, and the appointment of subordinate officials, which do not fall within the proper sphere of parties, and with which in England they fortunately do not interfere, we may say that party organisations have in general three normal functions: (1) the formulation of party policy; (2) the selection of candidates for office; and (3) the effort to bring the public to their side and win a victory at the polls. In the United States, where the form of the institutions has caused a high development of party machinery outside the framework of government, the organisations exercise all three functions; but by reason of the nature of the parliamentary system, this cannot be true of the two leading parties in England.

**Formulation of Policy.**

We have seen that the Newcastle Programme proved a source of difficulty and weakness to the Liberal cabinet, and this was not an accident. It was not due to a casual rivalry of political forces, but resulted from the very position of a responsible ministry. In the chapter on the cabinet and the House of Commons it was pointed out that the existence of committees with real power to frame legislation would be inconsistent with the authority that must necessarily reside in the Treasury Bench. Now these two things rest upon the same principle. If the ministry is to be fully responsible for the whole course of legislation, and for the management of all public affairs; if it is to resign on any defeat on a matter of importance; then it must have power to select its own line of policy. The action of the ministers must appear, at least, to express their own earnest convictions. The House will not follow them unless they lead it, and they cannot speak to it with dignity and effect if their programme is manifestly forced upon them by others. All this applies with even greater force to a policy framed by a body outside of Parliament than to one that emanates from a committee of the House itself, because the outside body knows far less of the temper of the House, and takes little account of the feelings of its members. The Newcastle Programme created difficulty enough, and yet it did not go so far as to force upon the leaders a policy they did not approve, for it was supposed to embody only matters on which the whole party, including the leaders, were heartily in sympathy. The only complaint was that it brought too many such matters prominently forward at the same time, and made it awkward for the ministers to choose between them without causing disappointment. The situation it created was uncomfortable; but if the Federation were to go farther, if it were to discuss and vote upon doubtful points, and really try to decide what the policy of the party should be, the position would become intolerable. One can imagine a system in which both the ministers and the members of the party in Parliament should be absolutely pledged to carry out the orders of the organisation. The Caucus would then be a true outside parliament, and the House of Commons merely a machine to register its behests; but in that case the cabinet would be responsible to the Caucus, not to Parliament, and the present form of government would be entirely changed. So long, therefore, as government by a ministry responsible to the Commons endures, it is obvious that policy must be formulated by the cabinet alone, and that this is inconsistent with any serious effort to formulate it by means of a party organisation.

Selection of Candidates.

The local associations naturally select the candidates for Parliament, and by the choice of persons who share their own views they can exert a potent influence upon public policy. Nor is there any objection to this provided the pledges they exact from their representatives are not of such a character as to prevent the members of the party from acting solidly together. The national party organisations have never attempted to dictate the choice of candidates to the local bodies; and although the Central Office recommends names, it never attempts to force its favourites upon the constituencies. The selection of ministers is quite a different thing. In the United States the president is nominated by a party convention, because that is almost the only way in which it can be done. In England both of the party organisations have at times talked of taking part in the selection of the leader in Parliament, but the same objections that exist to a formulation of policy by them would apply with even greater force to any action of this kind. The ministers must be the leaders of the majority in Parliament, and they can lead only in case they possess its confidence. Assuming for the sake of argument, that a party convention is well qualified to select statesmen, it would not in most cases choose the same men who issue as leaders from the warfare of the House of Commons. Although it might take men of as much character, ability and wisdom, they would often not be the men who possess the confidence of the House. Lord Althorp, for example, would in all probability never have been a favourite with a convention, but he did have the confidence of the House of Commons; and similar instances could be taken from later times. The selection of the ministers to-day, and the securing of harmony among them, is the most delicate part of the parliamentary system, and it would become well-nigh impossible if they, or even if the Prime Minister alone, were chosen by a body of men other than that whose support the cabinet must command in order to remain in office.

**Carrying Elections.**

It would appear, therefore, that, besides the selection of candidates for the House of Commons by local associations, the only national functions that party organisations can perform in England, consistently with the parliamentary form of government as it has developed there, are those connected with the winning of elections. For this purpose the Conservatives, owing in part to larger pecuniary resources and the greater social influence of their prominent adherents, have been better equipped than the Liberals. Their machinery has been more complete, it appeals to a wider range of motives, works with a greater variety of tools, and is under a more vigorous and centralised control. The Liberals have inherited the ideas of the eighteenth century publicists and of the philosophical radicals. They have always had a tendency to conduct their campaigns on the assumption that man is essentially a rational being; while the Conservatives treat him as not less a creature of impulse and suggestion. Moreover, the popular organisation of the Conservatives makes less pretence of directing the policy of the party. So far as it purports to do this, it is a palpable sham, which deceives no one; whereas the resolutions of the National Liberal Federation are taken seriously by many people, and are certain whenever a Liberal government comes to power, either to hamper its action to some extent, or to cause some disappointment. The difference is no doubt due quite as much to the traditions of the two parties, and to the character of their members, as to the form of the organisations. But each of these things is at the same time both cause and effect, and for our purpose it is unnecessary to distinguish between the two. It is enough to point out that of the two organisations outside of Parliament, that of the Conservative party has been more in harmony with government by a responsible ministry.

Like all things that grow, the English government suffers constant change. For no consecutive hundred years has it gone without material alteration, and it may be that the present system is destined to be seriously modified in the near future. For the last fifty years the tendency has been for the parties to consolidate, and the power of the cabinet to develop, more and more. It may be that this will proceed to such a point that the responsibility of the ministers to the House of Commons will be almost replaced by the responsibility of the majority to the ministers. It is more likely that the process will be reversed. It may be that the Labour members, who increased so largely in the last election, will become more and more numerous, until they prevent the division of the House into two distinct fractions. Not being a party formed to sustain a ministry, they are more under the control of their organisation; and it may be that, as in Australia where they have been a political force for a longer time, they will cause what astronomers call perturbations in the orbits of the older parties. In these ways, or in others wholly unforeseen, the parliamentary system of government may change, and if so the position of the party organisations may change also, but while the present system lasts the organisations of the two great parties, however popular they may be in form, however bold in claiming authority, cannot profitably be more than ancillary bodies. The evolution through which they have both passed is not an accident. It is the result of that same process of adjustment which has made the whole English government a self-consistent organism.

# CHAPTER XXXIII

## THE LABOUR PARTY

The Underlying Forces.

In tracing the recent efforts to establish a direct representation of Labour in the House of Commons it is needless to go farther back than 1868, when the working-classes first obtained the franchise upon a large scale. Since that time two distinct forces, socialism and trade-unions, have been at work to bring Labour members into Parliament, and the history of the movement has turned on the varying political activity and the mutual relations of these two forces. Of the two, socialism has been the more aggressive; but the trade-unions have had a vastly larger membership, with far greater resources in money, and hence success in electing Labour candidates has depended upon securing their coöperation. Nor has this been given freely in support of socialistic plans, for the British workingman is not a theorist. He is little attracted by shadowy dreams of an ideal commonwealth, and is not easily provoked to class hatred. He has a practical, almost conservative, turn of mind, and is stirred to strong political feeling only by a sense of present grievance. When that has been remedied he falls again readily under the lead of those classes that have habitually conducted public affairs.

The Earlier Trade-Union Movement.

The part played by the trade-unions in parliamentary elections since the Reform Act of 1868 has gone through several phases.[1] After a couple of Independent Labour candidates had run in vain at the general election of that year, the Trade-Union Congress took the matter in hand

[1] For the political attitude of trade-unions in the past see Sidney and Beatrice Webb, "Industrial Democracy," 250 *et seq.*, 537 *et seq.*

and created a Labour Representation League, which brought forward, though without much success, thirteen candidates at the general election of 1874. There was a grievance at that time in the condition of the law relating to trade-unions and conspiracy, and when this was substantially removed by Parliament, the movement died out. An attempt to revive it a score of years later met with no response, and the attempt to elect Labour members to Parliament by joint action of all the unions in England slumbered until 1899. The different trades had not enough in common to make it easy for them to combine. The unions of a single trade, or of a single constituency, could act far more easily, and for twenty-five years they had the Labour field almost to themselves. A few of them, notably the miners' unions in Durham, Northumberland and South Wales, carried their candidates in some cases at every general election, and thus there has long been a small Labour group in the House of Commons.[1] But although this has had an organisation of its own, claiming to be independent of the two great parties, its members have been gradually drawn into closer and closer contact with the Liberal party. The local Liberal Associations have often abstained from making rival nominations, and have even adopted its representatives as their candidates. In fact its most conspicuous figure, John Burns, who entered Parliament in 1892 as more or less of a Socialist, became in 1905 a member of the Liberal cabinet. At present the men nominated by a single trade-union, or a local combination of trade-unions, belong in the House of Commons to what is known as the Liberal Labour Group, closely bound to the Liberals, and quite distinct from the Labour Party recently created

[1] An appendix to the Rep. of Conf. of Lab. Rep. Com., 1902, gives the number of Labour members elected to Parliament as follows: 1874, 2; 1880, 3; 1885, 11; 1886, 9; 1892, 15 (and at a by-election in 1894 one more); 1895, 12 (and at subsequent by-elections 3 more); 1900, 11. At the general election of 1906 there were 56. In 1900 and subsequently a part of the Labour members were put forward by the national organisations about to be described, and the rest became more or less closely associated with the Liberal party.

by a united movement of the trade-unions throughout the country which was renewed for the purpose.[1]

The Fabian Society.

Meanwhile several Socialist organisations had been formed. One of the earliest among them, the Fabian Society, founded in 1883, assumed its name to show that it relied for the triumph of its principles, not upon force, but upon the slow growth of opinion. Although in 1893 it began to advocate electoral activity by the Socialists and the trade-unions and has since taken part in movements of that kind, its work has been mainly of a missionary character, conducted by means of discussions and tracts. For this reason it has never sought to enroll a large quantity of members, and in 1906 it had only seven hundred and eighty-four names on its list.[2] Its greatest achievement lay, perhaps, in helping to remove extreme prejudices, by making the propertied classes familiar with socialistic ideas, and by preparing their minds for such collective experiments as the control of public utilities by local public authorities. But although there are a number of affiliated bodies bearing the same name scattered about the country, the importance of the society has gradually diminished of late years. While on good terms with the Labour Party, and represented upon its electoral committee, the Fabians appear to have little influence to-day with the workingmen.

The Social Democratic Federation.

Another Socialist organisation, of a very different kind, is the Social Democratic Federation, which held its first Annual Conference in 1881. Unlike the Fabian Society, it is composed essentially of people drawn from the working-classes,[3] and its structure is strictly federal in form. The members all belong to local branches, but pay threepence a month apiece which is sent to the Central Office. There are also affiliated bodies paying to the Central Office one

Its Organisation.

[1] One representative of a miners' union, Taylor, of Chester le Street, Durham, joined the Labour Party in 1906.

[2] Rep. of Conf. of Lab. Rep. Com. or Labour Party, 1906, p. 28. The report of the same body for 1901 (p. 5) gave the number as 861.

[3] It is, of course, a much larger body than the Fabian Society, and had in 1901, 9000 members. Rep. of Conf. of Lab. Rep. Com., 1901, p. 5.

shilling a year for each member, with power to send to the Annual Conference delegates who cannot, however, vote on important questions. By 1906 the number of branches and affiliated societies had slowly increased to one hundred and fifty-one. A national Conference composed of delegates from the branches is held each year to determine the policy of the party, and heated discussions sometimes take place. Here also is chosen an Executive Council of six London and six provincial members, which is by no means a mere administrative body, for the organisation of the Federation is in some ways highly autocratic. Subject to a right of appeal to the Conference, the Executive Council has power to expel a member of the Federation, or to dissolve a branch for action deemed "to be opposed to the objects and principles or general well-being of the Federation." [1] This power has, in fact, been used, a couple of members being expelled in 1903 for making public attacks upon the management of the organisation.[2] Nor is this all. No member of the Federation can become a candidate for any local public office without the consent of his branch, nor for Parliament without that of the Executive Council. He must submit his programme and election address for approval both to the local branch and to the Executive Council; he must be prepared to remain under the general guidance of the branch for local, and under that of the executive for parliamentary, action; and he must withdraw from the position to which he is elected when called upon to do so by the Executive Council. Moreover, in regard to Labour candidates not nominated by the Federation, the members or branches must act as directed by the Executive Council.[3] Naturally the managers of this body are not worried about the relations between the organisation and a future ministry of their party.

The Social Democratic Federation makes no appeal to physical force, although it is in close sympathy with the **Its Aims.**

[1] Rule 34. [2] Rep. of the 23d Ann. Conf. in 1903, pp. 7–15.
[3] Rules 38, 39, 41, 42.

revolutionary socialism of the Continent and talks about universal class war. The statement of its objects is comprehensive. It begins with "The Socialisation of the Means of Production, Distribution, and Exchange, to be controlled by a Democratic State in the interests of the entire community, and the complete Emancipation of Labour from the Domination of Capitalism and Landlordism." Such an emancipation, it declares, "can only be the work of the working-class itself," and in order to insure greater material and moral facilities for the working-class to organise and carry on the class war, it demands certain immediate reforms. Many of these relate to such matters as the hours and price of labour, old age and other pensions, public ownership of monopolies and public services; but they include also the abolition of the monarchy and of standing armies, and the repudiation of the national debt.[1] If the programme is as yet hardly within the range of practical politics, the Federation is tenacious of its principles. In character it is uncompromising, and this has produced an inability to coöperate with other people which has curtailed its influence. Of quarrels in its own ranks we have had a glimpse in the expulsion of members; the friction with other Labour organisations will appear in the history of those bodies.

**Relation to the Great Parties.** The attitude of the Federation toward the two leading parties in the state is well illustrated by the action of the Conferences of 1899 and 1900. At the first of these a resolution was adopted "That in the opinion of this Conference the organised vote of the Social Democratic Party in Great Britain should be directed solidly to the extinction of Liberal candidates by the votes being cast steadily on the Tory side up to and through the General Election"; and the Executive was instructed to take such steps as might be necessary to organise the vote so that it might be used against all Liberal candidates except those belonging to the extreme Radical Left. The resolution was

[1] *Programme and Rules*, 1906.

urged upon the ground that "wherever independent candidates had been run, they found themselves opposed by buffer candidates in the shape of the Liberals. Their only hope was to force the people who ran these buffer candidates, either to concede something to us, or to force them out of the way." The next year the policy was reversed before the general election took place, by a resolution "That in view of the collapse of the Liberal Party, it is impossible for the S. O. F. to carry out at the next election the electoral policy agreed upon at the last Annual Conference, and that, in the changed condition of affairs, the Socialist vote shall be concentrated on our own candidates when they are being put forward; and in other constituencies the vote shall be given only to those candidates who have opposed the capitalist imperial policy in South Africa," and who accept certain definite socialist measures. "Where both Liberal and Tory are supporters of the aforesaid capitalistic policy, Socialists should abstain."

**Election to Public Office.**

The Federation has sought to propagate its views, by meetings, by open air demonstrations, by leaflets, and by its weekly organ *Justice;* and it has tried to give them political effect by electing members of public bodies. On the councils of boroughs, districts, parishes, and on boards of guardians, in England and Wales it has, of late, succeeded in placing three or four score of its nominees, and at one time the mayor of West Ham belonged to the Federation; but although in 1906 it nominated eight candidates for Parliament, who polled together more than twenty thousand votes, it was, as on previous occasions, unable to elect a single member to the House.[1]

**The Independent Labour Party.**

The first organised effort to unite the forces of Socialism and of Labour was made at a Conference held at Bradford in January, 1893, where the Independent Labour Party

[1] W. Thorne, who was elected for South West Ham in 1906, is a member of the Federation. He was not, however, nominated by it, but by the Labour Representation Committee. Mr. Grayson, a pronounced Socialist, was elected for Colne Valley at a by-election in July, 1907.

was formed. The Conference was attended by delegates from many local Labour parties, from the Social Democratic Federation and from the Fabian Society.[1] A constitution and rules were adopted, in which the object was stated to be, "the collective ownership and control of the means of production, distribution, and exchange"; and the method of operation, "representation of the people in the House of Commons by men in favour of the object of the Party and rigidly pledged to its policy." [2] A programme for immediate effort was laid down demanding a universal eight-hour day; abolition of overtime, piece work, and employment of children under fourteen; provision for the sick, aged, etc.; free, unsectarian education of all grades; work for the unemployed; taxation to extinction of unearned incomes; and disarmament of the nations. The organisation was to be composed of branches which were to send delegates to the Annual Conference; and this in turn was to choose a National Administrative Council. The Council was expressly directed to carry out the decisions of the Conference, and not to initiate any new policy without a special Conference called for the purpose, but, of course, it became in fact the mainspring of the organisation. A parliamentary candidate could receive no financial help from the party unless he bound himself in writing to advocate the object and programme of the party, to sit in opposition in the House of Commons, and to act with the majority of the party. From time to time the constitution and rules have been amended in detail. The object has been stated in the grander form of "An Industrial Commonwealth founded upon the Socialisation of Land and Capital." The method has been enlarged to include the education of the community in the principles of socialism, and the representation of socialist principles on all elective bodies. The immediate programme has been extended to cover

**Its Organisation.**

[1] The Fabian Societies of London and of several provincial towns were represented.

[2] *Cf.* Rep. of Conf., 1893, p. 4; 1894, pp. 7, 13.

woman suffrage, triennial parliaments, second ballot, and municipal ownership of all such industries as the local bodies think proper, especially drink shops and hospitals. At the same time the control over elections has been centralised, for a special Conference must be called prior to every general election to determine the policy of the party thereat,[1] and no candidate can be nominated for Parliament without the approval of the Council.[2]

Growth of the Independent Labour Party.

Like all organisations of the kind, the Independent Labour Party seeks to direct its members and influence public opinion, by resolutions adopted at its Annual Conferences. These relate not only to subjects immediately touching socialism and the working-classes, but also, and especially of late years, to matters of general national policy. With the same object it issues occasional pamphlets, and for many years it published a monthly organ called *The News*, until it substituted therefor at the end of 1903 the weekly *Labour Leader*. The total membership of all the branches is considerable, but does not appear to have increased rapidly after the first few years. As early as 1896 the Council computed the members at more than twenty thousand;[3] while in 1901 the organisation paid affiliation fees to the Labour Representation Committee on a membership of only thirteen thousand,[4] and in 1906 on no more than sixteen thousand[5] although the interest of workingmen in politics was very great at that time. But the active membership of an organisation of this kind is a very imperfect measure even of its direct influence. A better test may be found in the candidates it has elected to public office. Now the

[1] In the case of by-elections the electoral policy is determined by the Council after consultation with the local branch.

[2] By an amendment adopted in 1906 the Council was enlarged to thirteen members, of whom seven were to be elected by local divisions, and the rest by the Conference. (Rep. of Conf., 1906, p. 36.) The branches now pay to the Council one penny per month for each member, and ten shillings for each delegate sent to the Conference in any year.

[3] Rep. of Conf. (I. L. P.), 1896, p. 11.

[4] Rep. of Conf. (I. L. P.), 1901, p. 31. Rep. of Conf. (L. R. C.), 1901, p. 5.

[5] Rep. of Conf. (L. R. C.), 1906, p. 28.

Success in Elections.

Independent Labour Party has tried to place its members on local councils of all kinds as well as in Parliament, and since 1897 it has printed a list of its representatives on public bodies in an appendix to the annual report of the Conference. Taking together county, borough, district and parish councils, boards of guardians, school boards and the like, in England and Scotland, they numbered all told in 1897 between two and three hundred. They increased slowly until 1905, when they ran up quite suddenly to nearly four hundred, in spite of the fact that school boards had been abolished in England. For Parliament, also, seats were won at last, although at the outset the results were disappointing. At the general election of 1895, the first that took place after it was formed, the party nominated twenty-eight candidates, five of whom polled over three thousand votes; but not one of them was returned, and even Keir Hardie, its president, who had been elected for South West Ham in 1892 before the party was organised, lost his seat. At the special Conference called before the election to determine the policy of the members it had been decided to support only avowed Socialists, and the delegates voted by an overwhelming majority to abstain from the polls altogether rather than cast any ballots for either Conservatives or Liberals. When the next general election took place in 1900 a broader policy was pursued, and a vigorous effort was made to coöperate with Labour organisations that were not strictly socialistic. At the special Conference it was agreed to support not only Socialists, but also other Labour candidates; and, where there were none, to leave each branch free to decide for itself what action to take so as best to promote the interests of Labour and Socialism at the polls. On this occasion the Independent Labour Party won its first parliamentary victory, in electing Keir Hardie. Six years later, at the general election of 1906, when the tide was running strongly in favour of all radicals, it achieved a far greater success, for no less than seven of its candidates, and sixteen of its members, were returned to the House of Commons; but this was done with the help of another organisation, which will be described in a moment.

Its Internal Struggles.

The Independent Labour Party has always been socialist, and yet it has aimed to secure the coöperation of workingmen who were not convinced Socialists. This has caused from the beginning a dissension between the more uncompromising elements in its ranks and those willing to waive drastic insistence on principles for the sake of tangible results. The difference of opinion appeared at the opening Conference over the very name of the organisation. A motion was made to adopt the title of Socialist Labour Party, but in order to appeal to the vast mass of workers, and not to the Socialists alone, this was rejected almost unanimously in favour of the title of Independent Labour Party. The same question was raised year after year, but the body has steadily refused to change its name. Partly, perhaps, in consequence of this, the Fabian Society and the Social Democratic Federation declined to join the organisation.

Friction with the Social Democratic Federation.

That two bodies, professing essentially the same faith, aiming at the same immediate end, and using much the same means, should work apart, was clearly unfortunate, and attempts have been made to bring them together. The obstacles have come both from questions of principle and from personal rancour. In 1894 the Council of the Independent Labour Party appointed a committee to confer with the Social Democratic Federation upon some plan for harmonious working relations.[1] The matter came before the Federation at its Conference in August of that year, when a delegate said that "the Independent Labour Party and the Social Democratic Federation had two different objects in view. The Social Democratic Federation were striving for the abolition of wagedom, the Independent Labour Party were striving to get better rations for the wage-slaves." A motion was then carried, "That

[1] These and the following statements are taken from the official reports of the Annual Conferences of the two bodies.

in the opinion of this Conference there can be no need for the separate existence of the Independent Labour Party on the ground that the proper place for conscious Socialists is inside a revolutionary Socialist organisation such as the Social Democratic Federation." A committee was, however, appointed for the purpose of defining the position of the two bodies, but, not unnaturally, it led to nothing. The next year the Independent Labour Party issued a circular suggesting the formation of a single Socialist party, to which the Federation after some correspondence replied that the present circumstances did not justify a hope of success in this direction.

In 1897 the differences in policy having apparently diminished, the matter was taken up again, and representatives of the two Councils met and agreed that it was desirable to unite in a single organisation. The question was then submitted to the members of both bodies, with the result that 5158 voted in its favour, and 886 against it. The Social Democratic Federation regarded the ballot as decisive, and prepared to act upon it; but this time the Independent Labour Party drew back. In view of the small proportion of members who had taken part in the vote, its Council laid the matter before the Annual Conference for 1898, deprecating a step that would suddenly dissolve the party and put its members into a new and doubtful position, and suggesting that federation would at this stage be more judicious than fusion. The Conference decided to take another general vote of the members on the alternative of federation or fusion. This gave a distinct, though small, majority in favour of federation, a conclusion which the next Conference ratified. The Social Democratic Federation, however, refused to agree to such a plan, on the ground that it "invites the continuance of personal friction, and the present perpetuation of waste." The negotiations caused bitterness and provoked a complaint, at the Conference of the Independent Labour Party, that the members were weary of the squabbles among the Socialists, and that it was the leaders who were keeping the two bodies apart. At this juncture the dissensions of the two bodies, although by no means healed, became overshadowed by the most effective movement for the separate representation of Labour in Parliament that has yet been devised.

**The Labour Representation Committee.**

**Its Origin.**

The Independent Labour Party grew out of the action of a trade-union congress, and the new movement sprang from the same source. The congress held in September, 1899, instructed its parliamentary committee to invite all coöperative, socialistic, trade-union and working-class organisations in England and Wales to unite in calling a special convention to devise ways and means for securing the return of an increased number of Labour members to the next Parliament.[1] Since the main object was the formation of a committee to promote the election of Labour members, the new organisation, taking its name from that body, became known as the Labour Representation Committee. The convention, which met at London in February, 1900, was attended by delegates from trade-unions, and from the Fabian Society, the Social Democratic Federation and the Independent Labour Party.

**Dissensions among the Socialists.**

Not unnaturally dissensions between uncompromising and opportunist socialism broke out at once. The first resolution as originally moved declared the need of representation in Parliament by members of the working-classes. Objection was made to the exclusion of persons not themselves workingmen, and after a debate the motion was amended so as to favour representation by men in sympathy with the aims and demands of Labour. This was merely a preliminary skirmish. The delegates of the Social Democratic Federation proposed a second resolution, that the representatives of the working-class movement in the House of Commons should form there a distinct party "based upon

[1] Similar action was taken at the same time by the Scottish Trade-Union Congress; and a special convention held at Edinburgh in January, 1900, took the same course as the convention at London in February, creating a Scottish Workers' Committee, which corresponds to the Labour Representation Committee in England, and has continued to the present day.

the recognition of the class war, and having for its ultimate object the socialisation of the means of production, distribution and exchange." The delegates of the Independent Labour Party moved and carried an amendment omitting all reference to class war and socialism. Thereupon *Justice*, the organ of the Federation, said in a leading article that the "resolution afforded the chiefs of the I. L. P. an opportunity for a display of that treachery to which we have unfortunately by this time become accustomed." The language seems to have given offence to the Council of the Independent Labour Party, which sent to the Council of the Federation a letter suggesting "that such attacks do not promote those friendly and harmonious relations between the two bodies which we desire to see established," and asking whether the article in *Justice* expressed the official attitude of the body. The Council of the Federation then passed a formal vote that it "accepts that statement as fully expressing their view of the conduct of the I. L. P. delegates at the Labour Representation Congress, and confirms it as an Executive Council." The members explained in their report to the next Conference that they had no alternative to replying as they did. Yet the Council of the Independent Labour Party voted to hold no further communications with them until such imputations had been withdrawn.[1] At the Conference of the Labour Representation Committee the next year the Social Democratic Federation again brought forward a resolution pledging candidates to recognise the class war, but it was lost, and in August the Federation formally voted to withdraw from the new organisation.[2]

In spite of these dissensions the convention called to

[1] Reports of Conferences of the Social Democratic Federation and Independent Labour Party for 1900.

[2] Further irritation came from a nomination by the Social Democratic Federation of a parliamentary candidate for a by-election at Dewsbury in October, 1901, without consulting the other Labour organisations, which was criticised as a breach of faith. (Report of Conferences of Independent Labour Party and Labour Representation Committee for 1902.) In fact the friction with the Social Democratic Federation has never passed away.

form the Labour Representation Committee pursued its way. It adopted a series of resolutions, which were recast three years later into the form of a constitution. This has been somewhat expanded from time to time, and the statements made here are taken from the revision of 1906. The Labour Representation Committee, or as it was renamed after the victory of 1906, the Labour Party, is described as a federation of trade-unions, trades councils, socialist societies and local Labour associations; and the trade-unions have joined so freely that at present the total membership of the affiliated bodies reaches almost a million.[1] The general direction is vested in the Annual Conference, to which the trade-unions and socialist societies are entitled to send one delegate for every thousand members, and the trades councils and local representation committees as many delegates as they pay for in fees.[2] But the current management is in the hands of an Executive Committee of thirteen members chosen at the Conference by the representatives of the various constituent elements in the party,[3] and a position of great influence is held by a secretary elected at the Conference and acting under the direction of the Committee.

Organisation of the Labour Representation Committee.

The object of the institution is, "to organise and maintain a Parliamentary Labour Party, with its own whips and policy"; and for that purpose, "to secure the election of Candidates for whose candidatures an affiliated Society has made itself financially responsible, and who have been selected by a regularly convened conference in the constitu-

Parliamentary Candidates.

[1] In 1906, 158 trade-unions were affiliated; 73 trades councils, that is, joint councils for the different trade-unions in a locality; two socialist bodies, the Fabian Society and the Independent Labour Party; and two local Labour representation committees, these last having been admitted only since 1905.

[2] Each of these bodies pays at least £1 10*s*., and for this it is entitled to send a single delegate, but it may send an additional delegate for every 10 shillings more that it pays. A ballot when demanded is taken by means of cards issued in proportion to the delegates to which an affiliated body is entitled, without regard to the number of delegates actually present.

[3] At present the delegates from the trade-unions elect nine of the members; those from the trades councils and local representation committees, one; and those from socialist societies, three.

ency." Hence the work of the Committee relates chiefly to candidates. These are nominated by the local affiliated bodies, and then approved by the Committee; but as good candidates are not always easy to find, and sundry conditions are prescribed for approval, the Committee has been in the habit of keeping on hand a list of persons of whom it has approval, and from whom the local bodies may, if they please, select a name. The conditions with which a candidate must comply in order to secure the indorsement of the Committee are stated in the revised Constitution of 1906 as follows: —

They must Obey the Party.

1. Candidates and members must accept this Constitution; agree to abide by the decisions of the Parliamentary Party in carrying out the aims of this Constitution; appear before their constituencies under the title of Labour Candidates only; abstain strictly from identifying themselves with or promoting the interests of any Party not eligible for affiliation; and they must not oppose any Candidate recognised by the Executive Committee of the Party.

2. Candidates must undertake to join the Parliamentary Labour Party, if elected.

As in the other Labour organisations, therefore, a candidate must pledge himself, if elected, not to act according to his own judgment, but to obey the decision of the party, at least on questions that affect the object for which the party exists. This pledge, together with the agreement not to promote the interest of any other party, was inserted in the constitution in 1903, because Mr. Bell, who had been chairman of the Conference in the preceding year, took part in the election of Liberal candidates for Parliament, and showed signs of pursuing an independent policy of his own. In order to make sure that the pledge is taken, the Committee has been in the habit of requiring candidates to sign the constitution before they are approved. Some men have been discarded because they were unwilling to do so;[1]

[1] *E.g.* Rep. of Conf., 1905, pp. 22–23. Among them was Mr. Bell, who thereupon joined the Liberal Labour Group in Parliament.

but the organisation feels that in order to be a force in politics it must keep its small body of representatives closely united and in fighting discipline. The pledge, however, is not the only means to that end; another is furnished by finance.

Financial Control over them.

Labour members in Parliament are not usually men of private wealth. In going there they must abandon their occupation, and cannot do so unless they are supported in some other way. Representatives of trade-unions have commonly received a subsidy from those bodies, but in a general organised movement like that of the Labour Representation Committee it was clear that the matter must be regulated in a more systematic way. In addition, therefore, to the ordinary assessments to carry on the movement,[1] the affiliated bodies are required to pay annually one penny for each of their members to form a parliamentary fund. Part of this is used to defray one quarter of the returning officers' charges for candidates, the rest of the election expenses being borne by the local bodies that make the nomination. But the chief object of the fund is the payment of a salary of two hundred pounds a year to each of the representatives of the party in the House of Commons. The number of members returned in 1906 was, however, so great as to put an unexpected strain upon the fund; for it appeared from the accounts of the Committee that the tax of one penny yielded only about four thousand pounds, a sum far too small, after deducting election expenses, to provide salaries of two hundred pounds apiece permanently for the thirty members of the party in Parliament.

Nature of the Party.

By means of the pledge the representatives of the organisation in the House of Commons have been made a united party; but outside of Parliament the Labour Representation Committee, or Labour Party, is not a compact body.

[1] The affiliated trade-unions and socialist societies pay 15*s.* a year for each thousand members or fraction thereof. The trade councils and local representation committees pay £1 10*s.*, and 10*s.* more for each additional delegate to the Conference.

It is hardly a federation, but rather an instrument for combining the political action of many independent organisations for a single purpose, that of electing representatives of Labour to the House of Commons. In local matters it takes no part, and even for national elections its sources of power are very limited. It has no local agencies, it has not even branches, for the affiliated bodies are almost all formed for quite different objects, and are not under its control. Its strength is chiefly moral, and to a small extent financial. It seeks to infuse political energy into the trade-unions, and by resolutions adopted at the Conferences it tries to guide popular opinion on many subjects. It indorses candidates, but, save for the promise of financial aid, the indorsement has only the effect of advice to affiliated societies and to workingmen, who need not follow it.

Its Success.

Yet the party, largely on account of its loose organisation and its lack of power to command, has proved politically by far the most successful of all the Labour movements. No doubt it has had good luck. Started just as the South African war brought the radical forces to their lowest ebb, its life has been hitherto spent on a constantly rising tide of prosperity. It met, however, with some success even at the outset. The general election of 1900 came before it was fully organised, but it elected two of its candidates, and they were reënforced by subsequent by-elections, for it carried another seat in 1902, and two more the year after. At this time the legal position of the trade-unions was greatly affected by the opinion of the House of Lords in the Taff Vale case, which held that they were liable to damages for wrongful acts done by their officials in the conduct of a strike.[1] The decision was given in 1901, and rightly or wrongly it certainly produced among the trade-unions a stronger sense of grievance and a more widespread political activity than they had known for years. Coming

[1] Taff Vale Ry. Co. *vs.* Amalgamated Soc. of Ry. Servants App. Cas., (1901), p. 426.

at a time when public sentiment was on the eve of turning against the administration, and combined with the aversion of workingmen to Chinese labour in South Africa and to Mr. Chamberlain's suggested tax on food, the decision gave a great impulse to the Labour Representation Committee. At the general election of 1906 it put fifty candidates in the field, and elected twenty-nine of them. Mr. Taylor also, who had been nominated by a trade-union of miners alone, signed the constitution after election; and thus there was formed in the House of Commons a group of thirty members pledged to act together, with a chairman and whips of their own. In recognition of the fact that the aim of creating a distinct representation for Labour in Parliament had been attained, the name of the organisation was changed to "The Labour Party."

The Labour Groups in Parliament.

The same forces that favoured the Labour Representation Committee helped also the candidates of trade-unions who were not associated with it, and hence there are now two groups of Labour members in the House; each with its own chairman and whips; both considerable, and not very unequal in size. Nominally their positions are very different, practically the difference is much less. One of them, known as the Liberal Labour Group, pursues its own policy in industrial questions, but is in other respects a fraction of the Liberal party. It has twenty-six members without counting Mr. John Burns, who belonged to the group before he entered the cabinet. The group has no organisation outside of Parliament, and its members are not pledged to act as a unit. The other group is the Labour Party, which professes to be wholly independent of all other parties, but really agrees with, and is inclined to support, the Liberals on matters that do not touch the special interests of Labour. Its members are, no doubt, more radical than the average Liberal. Many of them are Socialists, and the body has a socialist tone, yet it is not committed to socialism, nor from the nature of its task could it be. Like other English parties, its object is not to maintain a theory or principle, but to draw together for immediate united action large masses of men whose views differ greatly, and this condition governs its attitude. At present it cannot be frankly socialist, because if it were it would alienate many workingmen whose support it has been trying to gain.[1]

**Relation of the Labour Party to the Liberals at Elections.**

This same condition determines the relation of the Labour Party to the Liberals, especially at election time. It draws its adherents from both of the older organisations. In Yorkshire, for example, its followers have come mainly from the Liberals, while in Lancashire, where the weavers are on the whole Conservative, its forces have been recruited very largely from that side. It could not, therefore, call itself Liberal, if it would, because many former Tories, who are glad to take part in an independent Labour movement, would not be willing to vote for a Liberal. Nor does this cut off votes seriously from the other quarter if no Liberal candidate is in the field, for the bulk of the Radicals care very little whether a candidate is classed under the head of Liberal or Labour. Nevertheless, the Labour Party being really much nearer to the Liberals than to the Conservatives, some attempt is made to avoid nominating candidates to run against one another. It is not done systematically or thoroughly, and there appears to be little communication on the subject between the central offices; but there is something like a tacit understanding that it is not for the interest of the Liberals to set up a candidate where a Labour man would stand a better chance, and that, except for the purpose of testing the strength of their movement in a new field, it is unwise for the Labour Party to

[1] An example of the practical and conciliatory attitude of the party was given in 1905, when, to prevent overlapping of candidates, an agreement for mutual assistance was made with the Parliamentary Committee of the Trade Union Congress. This provided, among other things, that all Labour and trade-union candidates, approved by the Parliamentary Committee, and not standing on the platform of any other political party, should be supported by the Labour Representation Committee though not indorsed by it; and that the Labour Representation Committee should make it clear that their constitution does not require abstention on the part of electors in constituencies where no Labour candidate is running. (Rep. of Conf. of Labour Party, 1906, pp. 13–14.)

make a nomination that would be likely to give a Liberal seat to the Conservatives. At the general election of 1906, no doubt, candidates indorsed by the Labour Representation Committee were in many cases opposed to Liberals, but far less often than they were opposed to Conservatives, and in the two-member constituencies where they took the field there was almost always one Liberal and one Labour candidate who were not really antagonists.[1]

Whether the Labour Party will increase or lessen in the coming years, whether it will remain independent, or like the other Labour group will tend to draw closer to the Liberal party, it is not easy to foresee. The control of a political body over its followers, its ability to arouse enthusiasm and

Future of the Labour Party.

[1] Moreover, the candidates of the Labour Representation Committee were decidedly more successful against the Conservatives than against the Liberals. At the general election they contested in England and Wales thirty-three single seats. In one of these cases the only other candidate was a Liberal who won it. In twenty the Liberals made no nomination, and the Labour men carried fifteen of them against their Conservative opponents. In the other twelve cases, where both parties had candidates, the Liberals and Conservatives won five seats apiece, and the Labour men only two. The Labour Representation Committee contested also twelve double seats, nominating a single candidate in each case. In one of them the only other candidates were two Liberals, one of whom was defeated. In another both of the old parties nominated two candidates, and it so happened that both the Liberals were elected easily. In the remaining ten cases the Liberals and Labour men put forward one candidate apiece, while in four places the Conservatives made a single, and in six a double, nomination. In nine of the ten boroughs the Labour man was elected, having in one instance a Conservative, and in the rest a Liberal, for his colleague. In Scotland, where the Committee elected only two members, they came into more frequent conflict with Liberals. The four candidates indorsed by the Labour Representation Committee — in one double and three single constituencies, — were in every case opposed by a full list of Liberals and Conservatives. It is instructive to contrast with these figures others which show the relation to the Liberals of those Labour candidates who were not associated with the Labour Representation Committee. Some of them, having received a Liberal nomination, are classed in the election returns as Liberals, and of the thirty-three not so classed in England and Wales at the general election of 1906 (not including Socialists) only six were opposed by Liberals. Two only of the six were elected, and one of them immediately joined the Labour Party, while of the remaining twenty-seven all but five were elected, with the support, of course, of the Liberals. These facts show to what extent the independent Labour members have now come into the Liberal fold. Curiously enough, the connection is much less close in Scotland. There the half a dozen independent candidates were all opposed by Liberals, and were all beaten.

win votes, does not depend in England so much upon the attractiveness of its theories, or the excellence of its principles, as upon a belief that it can accomplish something. In this respect the Labour Party had rare fortune in the first session of the new Parliament. The government sought to remove the grievance felt by the trade-unions on account of the Taff Vale case by a Trade Disputes Bill, which provided that a union should be liable in damages only by reason of acts which its officials were authorised by the by-laws to perform. A rival bill, supported by the Labour Party, was also introduced, providing that trade-unions should in no case be liable for the tortious act of their officials. At first the government objected through the Attorney-General, that this was going too far, but after a few days it gave way. The Prime Minister, with several of his colleagues, helped by their votes to carry the second reading of the rival bill and agreed to modify their own bill accordingly. This appeared to be a great victory for the Labour Party, yet in reality the concession was made not to their demands, but because it was found that a large part of the Liberals had pledged themselves on the subject at the elections. The provision was, of course, a concession to Labour, but it was brought about by pressure of the voters on Liberal candidates, rather than by the action of the Labour Party as an organisation.

With the large majority behind the cabinet the Labour Party is not likely to force its hand during the present Parliament, or have many exploits to recount. And if at some future time it should hold the balance of power, it will almost be compelled to make common cause with the Liberals, and that without being able to display publicly the concessions that have been made as the price of its support. This suggests, indeed, one of the two factors that work against the permanence of the Labour Party as an independent group; the tendency in the English parliamentary system toward the absorption of third parties into the ranks of the Government and the Opposition.

The other great factor in the situation is the difficulty of maintaining harmony among the elements of which the Labour Party itself is composed. The ideals of the Socialists are by no means shared by the bulk of the members of trade-unions, and the latter do not take part keenly in politics unless they have a grievance. What is more, each of the organisations that seeks to brigade the Labour vote is managed by a few men, many of them with little experience of affairs, and often jealous and suspicious of the leaders in a rival body. Whether, when an immediate grievance is not felt, a sense of common interests will be strong enough among the working-class to overcome these obstacles, and perpetuate a distinct representation of Labour in the House of Commons, is one of the things that the future will disclose.

# CHAPTER XXXIV

## CANDIDATES AND ELECTIONS

Little Contest for Nominations.

A STRANGER who tries to search out the institutions of a foreign land is often perplexed because the people with whom he talks do not understand the difficulties that arise in his own mind. He asks why certain political forces do not produce the effects that he has witnessed under apparently similar conditions at home; and he gets no satisfactory answer, because those effects are precluded by an environment and by traditions which seem to his informants a part of the order of nature. They do not explain such things, for it never occurs to them that any explanation is needed. Mr. Kipling has illustrated the difficulty in his story of "An Error in the Fourth Dimension." Now, one of the matters that puzzles an American student of English government is the small amount of rivalry for nomination to Parliament. In the United States the nomination is often as hotly contested as the election itself, and by the ordinary electoral methods. In many constituencies, indeed, where the party majority is secure, it is the only real struggle that occurs, the nomination when obtained being equivalent to election. In England a seat in Parliament is much coveted, but one does not hear of aspirants for a nomination canvassing the organisations in advance, and trying to create for themselves a machine within the party machine. So far as these things take place at all, they are done in a very quiet way, on a very small scale, and there is rarely, if ever, an attempt to reverse the decision of the executive committee by carrying the fight into the larger body of the council. In short, nominations for the House of Commons are not keenly fought for, and this appears to arise, in the main, from the comparative lack of marked personal preferences in the selection of a representative, and from the limited range of possible candidates. Both of these matters require examination.

Its Causes.

Constituents Free from Strong Personal Preferences.

The voters are chiefly interested in the victory of the party to which they belong, in the accession to power of a ministry professing the principles in which they believe. The particular person who sits as their representative on a bench behind those ministers, though by no means a matter of indifference to them, is of less importance; and this is true not only of the voters at large, but also of the small group of men who take an active part in politics. They are not bands of liegemen following their chief in the hope of personal profit. He has no patronage in his gift, no favours from the government that he can distribute among them. He cannot even do much to promote the special interests of his constituency, because, except for such things as dockyards and barracks, the national treasury spends no money for local improvements, and private bill legislation is almost wholly removed from his control. His supporters can look to him for little but the small sums paid to party workers at the registration or election; the constituency can look for little but nursing; and these things will come freely from any candidate who has moderate wealth and an open hand. The local politicians like a man who is generous and popular; they like a man who creates a good impression, and especially a man of distinction of whom they can be proud; they are glad to have their member make a mark in Parliament, and they want him to be true to his party; but for the rest, their personal preferences are singularly far from strong, and certainly they are not a body of intriguers whose material or political prospects depend upon the selection of their own patron. The nomination is in the hands of a few men, but they are interested in general politics, and, apart from an occasional local friendship, their object is usually to win the seat for the party rather than to give it to a particular person.

Limited Range of Candidates.

So much for the position of the constituents; that of the possible candidates has still greater weight, for the choice is limited in many ways. In the first place, the sitting member has a strong claim to a renomination, a claim that, except in cases of positive personal offence or marked cleavage in political opinions, is almost invariably recognised by the local association. Now this covers a large part of the seats where the chance of election is good, because a man who has once sat in Parliament usually wants to stay there, and having carried the constituency at one election his party is on the average likely to carry it again at the next. Moreover, even a defeated candidate who makes a good fight has a certain prescriptive claim to stand again if he wants to, and his desire to do so will be roughly proportional to the prospect of victory. Many of the most promising seats have therefore permanent candidates.

Due to Claim to Renomination;

to the Expense Involved;

Another limitation upon the possible range of candidates arises from the expense involved. Save in the case of Labour men, who have behind them the whole force of a trade-union organisation, the cost of contesting a seat in Parliament falls almost wholly upon the candidate, and it is by no means trifling. First comes the yearly expense of registration, and then the expense of the election itself. Neither of them is small and in addition there is a constant outlay in nursing the constituency. This varies very much, but is in most cases considerable; in fact it is one of the motives for the common practice of nominating candidates long before a dissolution appears to be impending. The constituency likes to be nursed, while the habit gives the candidate a chance to make himself known, and to ingratiate himself with the voters, a precaution all the more important because he is often a stranger with whom at the time of nomination they are not acquainted. If we set down the cost of a contested election at from five hundred to a thousand pounds, and the average yearly outlay for registration and nursing at four or five hundred pounds, which are by no means large estimates,[1] it is evident that the number of men who care to pay the price for a seat in Parliament is not unlimited; while the number who are willing to incur that expense for the mere chance of a seat is still less. For it must be remembered that the prospect of any financial return is very small. The members of Parliament are not paid; they must live in London during the most expensive season of the year; few of them ever receive salaries as ministers or otherwise, and then, as a rule, only after long years spent in the House of Commons.

The result is that, apart from the Labour members, the House is mainly recruited from men who can afford the privilege. Radicals complain of this, clamouring for the payment of members, and for the transfer of electoral charges to the public treasury. But it has been pointed out that the people themselves prefer to elect rich men; that the cost of a seat is due more to the practice of nursing than to official charges at elections, and that this is quite as much the fault of the voters as of the candidates.[2] The central office of the party often helps, no doubt, to defray a part of the election expenses of candidates, especially where the chance of success is not bright, but that does not tend to bring in new elements, for the candidates so favoured are naturally of the same type as those who sit habitually in Parliament.

**to the Preference for Gentlemen;**

Nor is it merely wealth which confines the selection to members of a class. The electorate at large prefers that class. The English tradition of government by gentlemen has not lost its hold upon the mass of the people. This is not due to-day mainly to the local influence of the old county families, for although that has by no means disappeared, yet with the change in economic conditions the number of the landed gentry who can afford a seat in Parliament has much diminished. It is due to a spirit of deference, or snobbishness, which still lingers in spite of an industrial

[1] These estimates do not refer to Scotland and Ireland.
[2] *Cf.* "Payment of Constituents," *Progressive Review*, Sept. 1897.

revolution and the advent of democracy. It is most marked in the case of a title of any kind, or a connection with a noble house, which is always attractive; and it is helped by a jealousy of men of their own grade on the part of what are known as the lower and lower-middle classes. Even a workingman with political aspirations is said to find his worst enemies among his own fellows, unless, indeed, he is put forward as the candidate of a Labour organisation.

to the Choice of Non-residents;

It may seem a paradox to say that the habit of electing strangers, as well as residents, to represent constituencies tends to narrow the field of choice, yet it would appear to be true. The possible range of candidates for any one seat is, of course, enormously increased thereby, but the number of people who set their hearts upon obtaining the nomination for a particular constituency is diminished. A man is not confined to the place where he resides; if he meets with serious opposition there, his chance of success will be quite as good elsewhere, and hence instead of conducting a desperate struggle at home, he looks about for a constituency where his prospects both for nomination and election are favourable. Thus fierce contests for nomination do not occur between men whose only chance of sitting in Parliament depends upon getting control of the local organisation.

to the Lack of Political Stepping-stones;

Another condition that limits the supply of candidates for Parliament is the absence of a political pyramid with steps narrowing towards the top, such as exists in some other countries. A man frequently goes into the House of Commons without holding previously any elective office. This might, in fact, be considered the general rule. He does not habitually begin as a borough or district councillor, then become an alderman or member of the county council, and so on through various grades of public service before he goes to Parliament; and conversely there are not on hand a large number of men qualified by the proper apprenticeship to aspire to the nomination. Many members of the House have, no doubt, already served on local bodies, but the habit has not become so general as to make those places regular stepping-stones in a political career; nor does the practice appear to increase in a marked degree. In fact, the gap between Parliament and the local councils is so great that they are not likely to become nurseries of candidates.

**and to the Method of Nomination.**

Something must also be ascribed to the way in which party nominations are made. The candidate is usually selected by a small sub-committee, appointed for the purpose, whose recommendation is accepted without question by the local association. In the Liberal party this is not always done, and where the committee is in doubt between two or more persons, it often invites them to address on successive evenings the council or executive committee of the association, which thereupon selects one of them. The choice in such a case is made in the main not by canvassing and intrigue, but by competitive public speaking. This is the less demoralising method of the two; yet it has a bad effect, because many of the best men dislike it, and will not submit to it. The matter is more skilfully managed by the Conservatives. Among them, both in England and Scotland, a contest for nomination rarely, if ever, comes before the council of a local association. If the small committee is not able to decide among the persons suggested, if there are still two or more men who want to carry the question farther, outside influences are brought to bear to persuade all but one of them to withdraw. Some man prominent in the neighbourhood by his high social position, or his authority in the party, intervenes for the purpose; and there may be cases where it is necessary to appeal to the national leaders, but that is objectionable, because it raises expectations of a definite reward for compliance with their requests. In any event the disinterestedness of a man who withdraws naturally gives him a certain claim to future consideration. Such a method of selecting candidates obviously lessens the number of persons openly seeking to be chosen, and reduces to a minimum the struggle for nomination.

The Process of Selection.

The nomination is, therefore, really made in most cases by the members of a small committee. It might be supposed that they would have no difficulty in finding a suitable candidate, that the only embarrassment would be in choosing among a crowd of aspirants local and non-resident, but for the reasons already given, this is by no means always true. The candidate is, no doubt, often designated by existing conditions; he may be the sitting member, or the man who contested the seat at the last election; and sometimes in case of a vacancy there is a local man whose position gives him a decisive claim to the nomination. A man of that kind makes the best candidate, but he is often not forthcoming. A local man has usually made enemies as well as friends; his neighbours, who think they have as good a claim as he, are likely to be jealous of him, and often prefer a young scion of a noble house, or a successful barrister or banker from London. So that, although a stranger who does not belong in the place is sometimes decried as a "carpet-bagger," and tries to hunt up a ghost of some fanciful connection with it, yet there is, on the whole, no preference, or at least no strong preference, by the constituencies for local candidates. One even hears it asserted that they are at a positive disadvantage; and, in fact, something like one half of the members of Parliament are not local men.[1]

When there is no suitable local candidate, and no outsider who has a claim to the nomination, the committee is apt to consult the Central Office of the party, which takes care not to obtrude its advice unasked, but is always ready to make suggestions when they are wanted. It suggests invariably more than one name, both because it wishes the men who have signified their desire to stand for Parliament to know that the office is trying to find them seats, and still more because it is anxious to avoid the appearance of dictating candidates to the constituencies. The habit of consulting the Central Office is so general that many

[1] More than one half according to the estimate of Ostrogorski, I., 451.

members obtain their seats through its mediation, and sometimes, as we have seen, with its pecuniary assistance. That the voters of a provincial town should send to Westminster to seek for a candidate wholly unknown to them seems strange to those accustomed to the intensely local spirit produced by democracy in some other countries. Like the absence of sharp contests for nomination, it is due to the habit of electing non-residents, to the limited range of candidates, and to the fact that the people who control the nomination usually care more about the success of their party than about the personality of their representative. That personal qualities are not, however, without effect upon the voters, may be seen in the two-member constituencies, where on a close vote one nominee of each party is not infrequently elected, the colleague of the candidate at the head of the poll running enough behind to be beaten by the favourite on the other ticket. At the general election of 1900, for example, this happened in four out of the twenty-three two-member boroughs.[1]

**Scarcity of Independent Candidates.**

Independent candidates who stand against the nominees of the party associations have usually been few of late years. Leaving out of account for the moment candidates nominated by the Labour men, Socialists and Irish Nationalists, who belong to distinct political organisations, and also an occasional Scotch Crofter, the instances in Great Britain where there have been more than two candidates for one seat show a marked diminution since 1885. At the general election in that year there were thirty-two such additional candidates; but eleven of them polled less than two hundred votes apiece and fifteen more did not have votes enough to affect the result, so far as appears from the figures, although it is of course impossible to assert positively that they did not affect it. At the general election of 1886, which turned on the question of Home

[1] In another two-member borough, Bolton, only one Conservative and one Liberal were nominated, these two men having defeated at the previous election two other candidates, Conservative and Liberal.

Rule, feeling ran high, and party lines were sharply drawn. In three constituencies the Conservatives and Liberal Unionists having failed to reach an agreement, both of them nominated candidates,[1] and in another, two Liberals were in the field; but in none of these four cases does the result appear to have been affected. At the next three general elections of 1892, 1895 and 1900 taken together, there were in all only ten such additional candidates, five of whom polled less than one hundred votes apiece, another less than two hundred, while of the remaining four, who had a substantial vote, not one appears from the figures to have affected the result of the election. In these three general elections, therefore, a candidate of this kind was nominated on the average for only one seat out of one hundred and seventy, and in most cases he had no real support. The question of fiscal reform, on which the Conservative party was sharply divided, brought forward a larger number of third candidates in the election of 1906. In nine places, apart from the Universities, a Liberal was opposed both by a Unionist Free Trader and a Unionist Tariff Reformer; and the result in three of them was to give the seat to the Liberal. There were also four cases where, besides the Unionist and the Liberal, there was a third candidate who called himself a Liberal or an Independent, but in none of them did his presence apparently affect the result. These figures make it clear that, save in those exceptional periods when one of the two great parties is suffering from internal dissensions such as befell the Liberals in 1886 and the Unionists in 1906, the cases where Independent candidates stand against the regular party nominees are now very few.

The Cause Thereof.

The fact is that since politics in England turn upon public questions, and the issues are framed by the party leaders in Parliament, the intelligent elector votes not so much for Mr. X or Mr. Y, as for the Ministry or the Opposition, and hence he rarely cares enough about the personal opinions

[1] In two of these cases the Liberal Unionist did not poll three hundred votes.

or discretion of any candidate to jeopardise the success of his party by encouraging the nomination of a third person. In this way the parliamentary system produces in England the same restraint upon a multiplicity of candidates that is brought about in America by more elaborate and highly disciplined party organisations. Moreover, the chief cause for independent nominations in the United States does not exist in England. A member of Parliament having few opportunities to procure favours for himself or his supporters cannot provoke resentment by the unscrupulous use of a machine in the distribution of patronage; and therefore one does not hear of third candidates brought forward without regard to a difference in political opinions simply as a protest against political jobbery. England has little that resembles either of two correlative types of men common in American public life, the spoilsman and the reformer.

**Labour Candidates.**

In dealing with third candidates nothing has been said about those that are most common, because they belong to quite a different category. The Irish Nationalists, for example, are an entirely separate party in the state. They are not dissident Liberals, but a real third party fighting for their own programme, and as such they do not come into a discussion of the nomination of independent candidates. To some extent this has been true of the Labour organisations also, but their position has not always remained the same. In the preceding chapter we have noted how the Liberal party has tried to bring them into its fold, to arrange that Liberal and Labour candidates should not stand against one another, and in many cases it has been able to do so. Its success, however, has varied from time to time. Not counting the candidates of the Social Democratic Federation and others who came forward under the name of Socialists, there were in 1885 four Labour candidates standing against Liberals; in 1886 there were none; in 1892 there were fourteen, and in 1895 they rose to twenty-four. In 1900 they fell again to three, but in 1906, the increased activity of the Labour organisations, and especially the formation of the Labour Representation Committee, with its cardinal principle of independence, brought the number of such conflicts to thirty-two; and this in spite of many other instances where the Liberals abstained from nominating any opposing candidates. The Labour men usually poll a vote so substantial that in about one third of the cases where Liberal and Labour candidates have stood against one another during the last twenty-five years the result has been to give the seat to a Conservative. But after a period of independent activity on the part of Labour organisations, the danger of losing seats to the Conservatives tends to bring about either a coöperation with the Liberals or a decline in power.

**Socialist Candidates.**

The purely Socialist bodies have worked upon a much smaller scale, the largest number of their candidates who have stood against Liberals being found in 1906, when they were seven in number.[1] Moreover, they have rarely cast votes enough to affect the result of the election.

**Proposals for a Second Ballot.**

In this connection it may be worth while to note the suggestion of copying from the Continent the principle of election by a majority instead of a plurality, with a second ballot in case no one obtains that majority. The plan would, in the opinion of many people, prevent the nomination of a third candidate from giving the seat to the common enemy, and therefore it has received no little support among Liberals. Bills to carry it out have more than once been brought into Parliament.[2] A motion in favour of the principle was actually adopted in the House of Commons, on April 5, 1895, by a vote of 132 to 72;[3] and in 1897 the matter was taken up by the National Liberal Federation. During the summer the Executive Committee circulated among the affiliated associations a memorandum entitled, "The Second Ballot," which contained some in-

[1] In that election two more stood against Labour men when there was no Liberal in the field.

[2] Two such bills were introduced in 1894, and one in 1895. There were provisions for the same object in earlier bills, in 1872 and 1882, for example.

[3] Hans. 4 Ser. XXXII., 1115.

formation on the practice in foreign countries, together with many arguments on both sides. A resolution in favour of the system was then moved at the meeting of the General Committee in December and carried by a large majority; but the subject was never brought before the Council, for the reason, no doubt, that opinion upon it was not sufficiently uniform. That Liberals should perceive a possible advantage in the plan is natural, because they suffer more than the Conservatives from third candidates put forward by Labour men and others, who would, as they believe, rally to the Liberal candidate on a second ballot. But it can hardly be doubted that the system would make third candidates more common at the first ballot, for a Labour organisation in making an independent nomination would run no risk of giving the seat to the Conservatives, while it would have a chance of showing its own strength, and perhaps of forcing the Liberals to support its candidate at the final vote. It is by no means clear also that the friction, and the sense of political independence among the extreme elements, developed by the more frequent nomination of third candidates for the earlier ballot, would not have in the end a far stronger tendency to sow dissension than any forced concentration on a second ballot could counteract. It would seem that on the Continent the system, instead of consolidating the parties, has encouraged a multiplicity of factions, and thus promoted that disintegration of the legislative chamber into groups which has injured parliamentary government.[1]

**The Conduct of Elections.**

Any one setting out to describe the electoral campaign in England is as much puzzled as the judge who tries an election petition to know when the electoral period begins. For our purpose it may be said to begin, or rather to be perpetually in progress, in the annual work of registration.

**Registration.**

In a former chapter we have seen how registration is left mainly to the voters themselves, and that means to the party organisations, for unless one side has a great superi-

[1] *Cf.* Lowell, "Governments and Parties," II., 108–11.

ority in numbers, success is likely to depend on the votes of the well-disposed, but indolent, careless or zealless electors, and they cannot be trusted to get themselves registered. The local party association must do it for them, and in order to be sure that it is serving its friends and not its foes it must make a canvass of the constituency. Where the association is active this is done very thoroughly,[1] the political opinions of every voter being ascertained as far as possible, together with his claims to be on the list, and any objections that can be raised to his qualifications. For such a purpose the services of unpaid canvassers do not appear to be very valuable, and it is customary to hire a great number of persons, a fact that explains a large part of the cost of registration.

Once a year the revising barrister holds court to decide all questions about the register. In practice he occupies a judicial position, merely passing upon claims and objections according to the evidence that is laid before him, and that evidence is presented by the paid secretaries of the local associations. Their aim is naturally to get as many of their own side on to the register and raise objections to as many of their opponents as they can. To illustrate how far this is carried, the writer happens to have at hand an announcement of the sittings of the Revision Court for Liverpool in 1898, from which it appears that the total number of claims and objections to be brought before the court was 13,102 out of a total electorate of about eighty-four thousand. The secretaries of the local organisations nominally come before the court as counsel for the claimant or objector, but in reality they act for the political parties. Like counsel in a lawsuit, they make agreements which are virtually conclusive, although they may be in the interest of the local associations rather than the individuals affected. In Glasgow, for example, a leaflet was issued by the party organisations in May, 1899, reciting an agreement that for the next five years all lodger claims should be adjudicated

[1] *Cf.* Ostrogorski, I., 175 *et seq.*

by the city assessor, and that all parties should accept his decision as final and unite in asking the court to carry it out.

Uncontested Seats.

Except for an effort to cultivate the acquaintance of the voters, and to win their affection by nursing, the active work of a candidate often ends with the registration, because no opponent is nominated. This is due chiefly to a peculiar feature of the English electoral law. In other countries a vote is always taken at every election, even if there is only a single candidate in the field, and it is taken at the public charge. Under these circumstances a political party can make a nomination with little or no outlay, and can then put as much effort into the contest as it chooses. But in England if only one person is nominated he is declared elected without a ballot, whereas if two are nominated, a vote must be taken at their joint expense. Now the cost in such a case is usually borne by the candidate himself, unless he can induce the Central Office of his party to defray a part of it; and therefore a man hesitates to accept a nomination where the chance of election is small. This is the more true because by contesting a seat without success a man gains little or nothing beyond a claim to be recommended for a better place on another occasion. Hence the number of uncontested seats at a general election is usually large. Quite apart from Ireland, where it is useless for the English parties to nominate candidates in Nationalist strongholds, and apart from the Universities, which stand by themselves, there were one hundred and nineteen, or one fifth of all the county and borough seats in Great Britain, uncontested at the general election of 1895, while in 1900 there were one hundred and sixty-one, or considerably more than a quarter. By far the greater part of the unopposed candidates were Conservative, because the nomination for hopeless seats is mainly a question of expense, and the Conservatives have more rich men than the Liberals. They have also a larger central fund with which to help candidates, and they use it to carry war into the enemy's country. At the general election of 1906 the enthusiasm and hopefulness of the Liberals were so great, that, except for the Universities and the seat of Mr. Speaker, they contrived to have a free-food candidate of some kind in every constituency outside of Ireland; and thus the number of uncontested county and borough seats in Great Britain fell to twenty-nine.

The Contest.

No man accepts a nomination for Parliament unless he is ready to expend the money and effort to make a good fight, and therefore a contested election means a very vigorous contest. When the time is reached at which the judges trying an election petition are likely to say that the electoral period begins, the character of the struggle undergoes a change. This point may come at a by-election when the writ is issued; at a general election it may come when Parliament is dissolved, or perhaps when a change of ministry takes place which must shortly involve a dissolution; but whenever it comes, a change in the method of operation comes also. From the moment the electoral period opens, the candidate is required by law to appoint an agent, who must disburse all the election expenses and file an account of them. How far these returns are trustworthy has already been discussed, but there can be no doubt that nursing the constituency, winning popularity by open-handed charity, must be suspended, or at least it must be done with extreme caution. A letter to the local newspaper that a certain candidate has been accused of corrupting the electorate, but that he has merely given five pounds to a poor widow who is not a voter, may gain for him credit without risk, but such things cannot be carried far.

Lectures.

In another way the nature of the struggle changes when the election period begins; the making of converts becomes a less important object, and urging lukewarm followers to the polls a more important one. Hence those agencies, like lectures, which are directed chiefly at proselyting play little part. In the days when the Liberals, and still more the Radicals, believed that political opinions in a democratic state were based upon reason, lectures were freely used, but although they were adopted to some extent by the Conservatives, they have steadily lost ground in English public life.[1] People much prefer hearing or reading what the leading statesmen on the two sides may say about current issues, to listening to some unknown speaker who expounds in a partisan spirit facts that are sure to be denied by his opponents. The political lecture is not a search for truth, but an *ex parte* argument usually made by an inferior man. Not unnaturally, therefore, it is going out of fashion, and it is certainly out of place at election time.

**Party Literature.**

One of the forms of activity that does not diminish during a general election is that of distributing party tracts. They are of sundry kinds, from the single leaflet cheaply printed on a half sheet of paper, to pamphlets containing arguments on special subjects or the speeches of prominent statesmen. All these things are published in enormous quantities by the national party organisations, and in order not to violate the Corrupt Practices Acts, they are sold at election time to the local associations or the candidates at cost price; but their influence, at least during that period, may be doubted. The longer pamphlets are probably little read, except by speakers or others who must be posted about facts and prepare themselves to meet objections. In every country pamphlets of this kind are used, but the vast quantities of single sheets scattered like leaves in autumn are peculiar to English elections. The professional agents, however, are of opinion that it is useless to distribute them in bunches, because they will be thrown away, that it is much better to select the one appropriate to a particular class of men and send it alone. Occasionally, no doubt, a statement cleverly put, or a striking cartoon, may have no little effect;[2] but in order to catch attention in the excitement of

[1] *Cf.* Ostrogorski, I., 399–406.

[2] Such a one issued by the Liberal Unionists in 1895 is said to have had an influence in the election. The subject was the recent Home Rule Bill which retained the Irish members in the House of Commons, and the leaflet

an election, the parties work upon a broader scale. Posters with short appeals to prejudice, selfishness or humour, are exhibited on walls, in shop windows, on grass plots, and wherever ingenuity can suggest and good nature permit; while doggerel verses set to familiar airs are devised to charm the ear.

Public Meetings.

Another perennial method of agitation is that of public meetings. They are certainly valuable when an election is not in progress, for to use a commercial metaphor they are an effective form of political advertisement. They quicken the party pulse in the neighbourhood, especially if any of the speakers are men of note; and it is sometimes said to be important for a constituency to have a statesman of cabinet rank speak in it every little while. Moreover, they furnish an excellent means of bringing the views of the leaders before the public, because their speeches on these occasions are very fully reported in the press all over the country. Public meetings are also a regular accompaniment of electoral contests, although their value at such times is very much doubted by the professional agent. He says that in order to give them every appearance of success they are attended by the active party workers who might be more profitably employed in other ways. Naturally the people who go to them do not require conversion, and amid the hubbub of an election such gatherings are hardly needed to keep the party from oblivion; but they are useful in giving the candidate a chance to be seen, and above all they are part of the machinery for arousing enthusiasm, or the semblance of enthusiasm. Men are fond of magnifying their sentiments by the contagion of numbers, and as a prominent organiser has remarked, even the Indians have a war

had a picture of an Irishman sitting in one chair marked "Dublin," with his feet in another marked "Westminster." John Bull, standing beside him, says, "Don't you think you ought to be satisfied with a seat all to yourself, and not occupy my chair also?" To which the Irishman, pointing to the chair his feet are in, replies, "Shure you can sit down there, and I'll make a bit of room for you; but you mustn't be after expecting a chair to yourself."

dance before going to battle. So meetings go on at elections all the world over, nominally to educate the public, really to raise the courage of the partisans. In connection with them one hears a good deal of an English custom which appears to savour of public education, and that is "heckling," or asking the candidate questions after his speech has been made. But in fact the questions are not genuine, at least outside of Scotland, where the practice got its name. They are not propounded by honest seekers after truth; nor are they the means commonly used to extract pledges from the candidate. They are merely attempts to entrap him, or turn him into ridicule, and are commonly prepared by his opponents, often by the agent of his rival. They are sometimes full of humour, and serve the purpose of testing the cleverness and good temper of the candidate and his quickness at repartee.

**Heckling.**

**Breaking up Meetings.**

The meetings are not in fact always public, for in some cases they are not open to every one who chooses to attend, but are restricted to the holders of tickets which are issued freely only to the adherents of the party. The reason for such a precaution is the fear that otherwise opponents will come in large numbers, prevent the speaking by an uproar, or even storm the platform and capture the meeting for their own side. Nor is this an imaginary danger, for such things have been done over and over again, and one sometimes hears a party taunted with being afraid to hold an open meeting. Even where admission is only by ticket a mob of the other party has sometimes forced the doors and broken up the gathering. One reads the next day that the windows of the hall were smashed, the furniture broken, and that sundry public men, whose names may be household words, were forced from the platform and escaped by a back door or through a window. Of course these outbreaks always purport to be unpremeditated, the result of a fortuitous concourse of people incensed at the expression of opinions which they do not approve; but it may be observed that their conduct meets with little or no censure even from the leaders of their party.

Aston Park in 1884.

The most celebrated case occurred on Oct. 13, 1884, at Birmingham, which Lord Randolph Churchill proposed to contest at the next general election. With Sir Stafford Northcote he was to address a monster meeting arranged in his interest at Aston Park, and tickets of admission were given out in immense numbers until the committee, learning that many of them had found their way into the hands of Radicals, stopped issuing them. Thereupon, to use the graphic language of Mr. Winston Churchill,[1] "A few workingmen — a mere handful of trampled toilers — spontaneously, with no help from their party, inspired by no other emotion than zeal for freedom and Reform, organised a counter demonstration. The place of meeting was selected, by an unlucky coincidence, just outside the walls of Aston Park; and there also it happened that, on the appointed day, a cart containing ladders and other useful appliances drew up." The wall was scaled, a breach made from within, and a mob of fifteen thousand men poured through. In the riot that followed, the chief speakers were chased by an angry crowd, and barely escaped from its hands. The matter was brought before the House of Commons by an amendment to the address, and attempts to fix the responsibility for the disturbance were made in a debate which any one can read with interest in Hansard.[2]

The Reason for these Outbreaks.

Breaking up a public meeting by violence seems contrary to the fundamental principles of popular government and the sense of fair play. But in England it is not done from a general dislike of the expression of hostile opinions. There is never any attempt to destroy a newspaper that prints unpopular doctrines. During the South African war, for example, when so-called pro-Boer meetings were constantly attacked, the freedom of the press was completely

[1] "Lord Randolph Churchill," I., 362.
[2] 3 Ser. CCXCIII., 543 *et seq.*

respected. The fact is that Englishmen regard an ordinary political meeting as a demonstration, rather than a place for serious discussion, and as such they think it fair game for counter demonstration. This view does not seem to be a mere survival from the roughness of the old hustings, since it shows no marked signs of dying out. Nor is the practice of breaking up meetings condemned by average public opinion, for if it were, a little determined action on the part of the police, a few arrests followed by severe sentences for rioting, would quickly put an end to it.

But by far the most effective form of political activity at election time, much more profitable than party literature or public meetings, is the personal canvass of the electors. The ground has already been well surveyed in the course of the registration, but this does not avoid the need when the election comes of going over it again, and in the case of the boroughs very systematically. As the employment of paid canvassers at elections is illegal, an army of volunteers, both men and women, give their services. That they always act from purely disinterested motives, that they are not overpaid at the registration, or occasionally receive tokens of gratitude at a subsequent time, it would be rash to assert. This subject has already been touched upon when the election laws were discussed. But, apart from any mercenary workers, there is a great host of wholly unpaid canvassers, who act solely from devotion to the cause or friendship for the candidate. Canvassing.

Where the canvass is well done, the polling districts, into which the borough is divided by law, are sub-divided into blocks, with canvassers assigned to each. They are armed with canvass books, ruled with spaces for the house, the name of the voter, his registration number, whether he is for or against the candidate or doubtful, his present address if he has moved, and any other remarks, such as whether he will come to the polls of his own accord or a carriage must be sent to fetch him. Every voter who can be found is seen once, and the doubtful ones more frequently, often as many as a dozen or a score of times. For although the chief object is to discover a man's affiliations, and if favourable, to get him to vote, yet the arts of persuasion are by no means wholly neglected. It is deemed important to note the voter's occupation and connections in order to bring the right influence to bear upon him, that of his church or minister, for example, that of some alderman, or if he is a publican that of the brewer who controls his business. There appears, however, to be little effort on the part of employers, whether individual or corporate, to put pressure upon their workmen or to solicit their votes. So far as one can hear, instances of this kind are rare and excite strong disapprobation, especially in the North where the sense of personal independence is strong; but a feeling of loyalty to a kind employer is often strong enough to prevent his political faith from being altogether without effect upon many of his men.

Its Accuracy and Effectiveness.

The object of the canvass is, of course, to set at naught the provisions for secrecy in the Ballot Act, and sometimes men are unwilling to state how they intend to vote. This is particularly true of small tradesmen who are afraid of offending their customers; but as a rule the voters have no strong objection to expressing their opinions, at least to the canvassers upon their own side. For this reason it is much easier to determine accurately the number of one's supporters than of one's opponents, and a shrewd agent credits the men reported as doubtful almost entirely to the enemy. After a thorough canvass a good agent is said to know within five per cent how many votes his candidate will receive, while the margin of uncertainty about his opponent will be at least two or three times as large. On the whole the canvass is in most cases surprisingly close, and it brings out a fairly large vote. In the counties in Great Britain between seventy-five and eighty-three per cent of the registered electors, on the average, actually cast their ballots; in the provincial boroughs the average is a little larger; while for the metropolitan constituencies it is lower, running from sixty-five to seventy-eight per cent.[1] When we remember that this does not include the uncontested seats — which represent in an ordinary election not far from a quarter of the voters, and presumably those places where political feeling is on the whole least keen — the proportion of votes cast does not seem very large; but, on the other hand, the non-residents, who must often find it hard to be present, form a considerable fraction of the electorate, and the long period before the register comes into effect cuts off many persons that have moved away in the interval. Among the contested seats there are, of course, a number in which the result is not really in doubt, and it might be supposed that in such cases the candidate would make no greater effort, and incur no more expense, than is needed to insure his return. But this is true only in part, because the size of the majority is telegraphed all over the country, and compared with the results of previous elections. It is published with the comment that Mr. X has gained or lost so many votes given for Mr. Y or for himself on the last occasion, a statement that affects his reputation for success in politics.

The Candidate.

The candidate himself canvasses personally very little at the present day. The ancient custom whereby he visited all the electors in the borough, asked after their children

[1] The average percentages for the elections of 1895, 1900 and 1906 were approximately as follows:—

| | 1895 | 1900 | 1906 |
|---|---|---|---|
| English Counties | 81.0 | 77.2 | 83.5 |
| Welsh Counties | 76.5 | 62.8 | 78.4 |
| Scotch Counties | 79.4 | 75.7 | 79.9 |
| Metropolitan Boroughs | 70.1 | 65.1 | 77.8 |
| English Provincial Boroughs | 82.6 | 78.8 | 85.2 |
| Welsh Boroughs | 86.6 | 72.3 | 85.7 |
| Scotch Burghs | 71.9 | 72.0 | 82.9 |

These figures are not exact because in the two-member constituencies the returns do not give the number of electors who vote, but only the number of votes cast.

and solicited their votes, has become an impossibility with the growth in size of the electorate. But it is still important that he should be known, that he should be something more than a name that stands for a party; for among the ignorant and indifferent voters even the slightest personal acquaintance may be decisive. Workmen have been heard to say that they should vote for such a candidate because he had sent them Christmas cards. In fact it is chiefly on account of his being better known in the constituency that a local man has an advantage; and it is for the same reason that a prominent statesman, a cabinet minister, for example, whose personality has impressed itself upon the public mind, is a stronger candidate even than a local man. The easiest means of bringing himself into notice is furnished by the meetings where he speaks, and where he can attract popular attention by engaging in a sort of tournament with his rival, each answering the other, although at different meetings. The candidate also visits the party headquarters, at the polling districts in a borough, or at the principal towns in a county division, where he meets, if not the mass of voters, at least the principal workers who are canvassing among the voters. In short, the candidate seeks to make himself as conspicuous as possible.

His Pledges.

In the course of his campaign, at public meetings, by deputations, or by appeals in the press, he is asked his opinion on political questions of all kinds, and is requested to pledge himself upon them. Some of these matters are of vital consequence, others are mere fads, while others again are mainly of local significance. The candidate often cannot avoid, if he would, a direct statement, and it is commonly said that a member goes to Parliament pledged up to the eyes on every subject. But in a government that runs as strictly as the English on party lines the pledges of the individual member are less important than they might appear. A candidate naturally will not, and cannot, pledge himself against any policy to which the leaders of his party are already committed; and as for any other question, if the ministers do not take it up, the pledges of the candidate are well-nigh immaterial, because no bill on a contentious subject has a real chance of being enacted unless it is made a government measure. This leaves only questions with which the ministers may be forced to deal during the course of Parliament without having taken a definite stand at the general election. A striking example of a lack of precaution on the part of the government, and its effect, was furnished in 1906 in connection with the demand of the trade-unions that their funds should be exempted from liability in suits for civil injuries. As the cabinet did not declare what sort of a measure it would introduce, and failed to warn its followers against committing themselves to any specific policy, many of them promised during the election to support the claim of the trade-unions. The result was that, after their bill had been brought in, the ministers found a large part of the Liberals already pledged, and were obliged to abandon their own plan and adopt that of the Labour Party. But cases of that kind are not very common. In the main they must relate to matters unforeseen, upon which pledges are not very likely to have been given.

The Election Day.

The excitement of one to three weeks of speaking and canvassing culminates on the day fixed for the poll. Men, women and children displaying the colours of their party shout for its candidate; and he, accompanied often by his wife, drives about, visiting the committee rooms or showing himself to the populace. Carriages — and with the recent progress of civilisation, automobiles — lent by rich friends, ply busily, taking voters to the polls, and one may see an equipage with a coronet upon the panel containing perhaps a workman in his blouse. Meanwhile the election agent and his subordinates are hard at work. Voting cards have previously been sent to the men who appear on the canvassers' lists as supporters of the candidate, and these are returned by the voter to representatives of the party at the polls. They are then sent to the committee room to be compared with the lists, and carriages are despatched for those electors who have failed to vote. At last the strenuous day comes to an end, the polls are closed, the votes counted, the result declared, and a crowd of followers cheer the victor, who thanks them for their confidence, and says what would naturally be expected; while the defeated candidate replies to somewhat less vociferous cheers with equally appropriate and conventional remarks.

# CHAPTER XXXV

## THE STRENGTH OF PARTY TIES

STATISTICS are proverbially deceptive. If used as a mechanical road to knowledge, they are apt to lead astray. They do not save the need of sound judgment; but if applied with discretion, they are indispensable as a means of discovering truth. This is peculiarly the case with those political phenomena of which all men know enough to talk glibly, and few know enough to form trustworthy opinions. Unless he corrects his impressions by statistics, an observer in every country is likely to be misled in regard to the influence of party; for he is acutely conscious of the things that strike him as wrong, of the instances where party is abused for purposes that seem to him improper, and on the other hand, he scarcely notes the cases where it is used for objects that he deems right. Its power in such matters may be immense, and yet he pays no attention to it, not because it is occult, but because it is obvious and natural. The American reformer who denounces the tyranny of the machine, seeks, if not a mere arm-chair critic, to create another machine, which, though based on higher motives, and aiming purely at the public good, is quite as intolerant, if not despotic, as the one he is trying to combat.

**Errors of Observation.**

The danger of error is especially great for a foreign observer, who is almost always impressed in any country by the strength of party. In his own land he understands to some extent the play of forces, but abroad he sees at first only their effects. He perceives that these are often irrational, that many things are done in the name of a party which appear to be solely for its own benefit, and even inconsistent with the principles it professes; and he concludes that party is a blind force based upon prejudice or cupidity. In this way he is liable to misunderstand the phenomena that he sees. He is prone, also, to imagine that the force which he has found at one point is equally active in all directions; but such an assumption is highly unsafe. In America, for example, party has far more influence at elections than in subsequent legislation, while in England, as we shall see, that is not the case.

Strength of Party Ties in English and American Elections.

The comparative strength of party ties at elections in different countries is hard to gauge, because no sufficient statistics have been compiled. To judge, however, from a cursory examination of results, it would appear that the permanent hold of party upon the voters is quite as great in England as in the United States. The proportion of constituencies that have steadily elected candidates of the same party through a long series of years may be taken as a test, although a very rough one. Since the Reform Act of 1885, about forty per cent of all the constituencies in the United Kingdom have adhered without change to one party; whereas this has been true during the same period of about thirty-five per cent of the congressional districts in the United States. For America, indeed, the figures cannot be made strictly accurate, because the districts have been laid out afresh after every decennial census, and the statistics must, therefore, be treated as merely approximate. Moreover, certain parts of each country are in such a political condition that they can hardly be regarded as typical. The persistence of Nationalist victories in Ireland cannot fairly be taken into account in estimating the strength of party allegiance with ordinary British voters; and the same thing is true of the vote of the "Solid South" in America. If, therefore, we leave out Ireland, and omit the Universities also, we find that a little more than one third of the county and borough seats in Great Britain have remained continually in the hands of the same party since the Reform Act of 1885; while in the United States this has been the case in only about one quarter of the seats in Congress north of Mason and Dixon's line.

Another rough test is the fluctuation in the total vote cast in national elections. Now, at the presidential elections since 1880, the largest popular majority polled by the Democrats was in 1892, when they cast seven per cent more votes than the Republicans; and the largest Republican majority was in 1904, when they polled fifty per cent more votes than the Democrats. Adding these together, we get a change of fifty-seven per cent. At the general elections in England since 1880 the Conservatives[1] have never polled in the United Kingdom over fifteen per cent more votes than the Liberals, and the Liberals never over thirty-two per cent more than the Conservatives.[2] Added together, these make a change of forty-seven per cent. The figures include, of course, no votes for the uncontested seats, because no votes were cast there; and, in fact, it is not clear how those seats can be taken into account. Attempts were made after the last three elections to compute the number of persons who would have voted for the two parties in the uncontested constituencies if they had been contested.[3] The estimates were

[1] Including the Liberal Unionists.
[2] The figures are approximately as follows: —

| | Conservatives | Liberals | Liberals (including Labour men and Socialists) |
|---|---|---|---|
| 1885 . . . . . | 1935.216 | 2156.952 | |
| 1886 . . . . . | 1423.765 | 1241.357 | |
| 1892 . . . . . | 2056.737 | 1921.614 | 1981.554 |
| 1895 . . . . . | 1780.753 | 1657.856 | 1698.245 |
| 1900 . . . . . | 1676.020 | 1503.652 | 1520.285 |
| 1906 . . . . . | 2308.391 | 2899.330 | 3045.157 |

If the votes for Nationalist candidates were counted as Liberal from 1886 to 1895 it would change the relative proportions of the parties, and make the fluctuations somewhat less; for it would very much reduce the size of the largest Conservative majority, and increase the largest Liberal majority by only two per cent.

[3] The *Liberal Magazine*, August, 1895, and November, 1900; the Liberal "House of Commons Poll Book," 1906.

based chiefly upon the results of former elections in those places, modified by the general trend of the polling elsewhere; and the figures obtained naturally increase the size of the popular majority for the winning party, but hardly enough to reach the fluctuations in America. These tests are very imperfect, but so far as they go they would seem to show that party allegiance is as strong among the voters in England as in the United States.

**Strength of Party in Legislative Bodies.**

The influence of party on legislation, the extent to which the votes follow party lines in Parliament and in the various American legislative bodies, can be measured with far greater accuracy, because elaborate statistics have been collected for the purpose. They were compiled by tabulating, throughout a session, the number of members of each party who voted on each side of every question on which the individual votes are recorded. The process was applied to the division lists of the House of Commons, and to the yea and nay votes in both Houses of Congress, for a number of sessions; also to the yea and nay votes in single sessions of the Legislatures of several states.[1]

**Statistics for the House of Commons.**

In selecting the sessions of the House of Commons for examination an attempt was made to avoid those in which a change of ministry occurred, or which were for any other reason abnormal. The ones selected were 1836, 1850, 1860, 1871, 1881, 1894 and 1899.[2] It was not always easy to classify all the members of Parliament under their respective parties,

[1] For the statistics in full, the writer must refer to his paper on "The Influence of Party upon Legislation in England and America," in the Report of the American Historical Association for 1901. The statistical summaries, and a part of the text of this chapter, are taken from that paper.

[2] For 1836, 1850, 1860, 1871, and 1894, the printed division lists were used. For the other two years, 1881 and 1899, they were not within reach of the writer at the time the tables were made up. For 1881 the figures were taken from the Parliamentary Buff Book, compiled in that year from the division lists by Mr. T. M. Roberts; and for 1899 the lists of divisions were taken from Hansard. Unfortunately, it was impossible for the writer to procure absolutely complete lists for any of these years except 1881 and 1894. For each of the others one or more divisions are omitted from the lists; but as the number of these does not exceed seven in any year, the possible error is very small, so small as to be hardly perceptible in the percentage of results.

especially on account of the habit that prevailed among Peelites and others, during the third quarter of the century, of styling themselves Liberal-Conservatives. Of these men some had really become Liberals and some Conservatives; but the task of classifying them is rendered less difficult by the curious psychological fact that many of those who disliked to call themselves by a party name were unusually constant in going into the lobby with the party whip. A more serious difficulty arose in dealing with certain semi-detached groups of members. Ought the Radicals or Nationalists, for example, to be classed at any particular time as Liberals or not? It was evident that this would affect the result, for they did not vote with the Liberal whips as steadily as the other members of the party, and hence to exclude them would increase the apparent amount of party voting, and to include them would diminish it. In deciding this matter the writer was guided by the prevailing attitude of the group during the session in question. The Radicals were, in fact, classed throughout as Liberals. The Home Rulers, or Nationalists, on the other hand, were classed as a separate party in 1850, 1881 and 1899, while in 1894, both sections of the Nationalists were treated as members of the Liberal party.[1] In the remaining sessions considered, the Irish members do not appear as a distinct group. On the other side of the House the Peelites were excluded in 1850, while the Conservatives and Liberal Unionists were counted together as one party in 1894 and 1899.

The results were condensed into summaries, or tables, which are reproduced in the note; but in order to make them clear it is necessary to explain that a party vote of any party is arbitrarily defined as one in which more than nine tenths of those of its members who voted in the division were on one side of the question; and, conversely, a non-party vote as one in which a tenth or more of the members voting were found on each side, that is, a vote

[1] It makes, in fact, no difference in the results whether the small body of Parnellites are counted in 1894 with the Liberals or not.

where at least one tenth of the voting members of the party split off from the rest.[1]

Increase of Party Votes since 1850.

The tables show a very great change in the proportion of party votes in the House of Commons from 1836 to the end of the century; a change that is not spasmodic but gradual, and therefore due not to accidental but to permanent causes. In 1836 the percentage of divisions where both parties cast party votes on opposite sides was 22.65. This diminished

Definitions and Symbols.

[1] In the following tables a party vote is indicated by an asterisk; a non-party vote by a dagger. Now for every division the attitude of both the leading parties must be taken into account, and hence there are for every vote two marks, one for each of the two chief parties. The first mark refers to the vote of the Conservatives, the second to that of the Liberals; and thus the symbol,*†, for example, means that the Conservatives cast a party vote in the division in question, while the Liberals did not. But it sometimes happens that the majority in both parties are on the same side. Clearly such cases ought to be distinguished from those where they are on opposite sides; and hence wherever either party casts a party vote on the same side of a question as the majority of the other party, the two marks are enclosed in brackets. To use the illustration already given, the symbol (*†) shows that the Conservatives cast a party vote, while the Liberals did not; but that the majority of both parties were on the same side. Where neither party cast a party vote it seemed needless to distinguish the cases in which the majorities were on the same and on opposite sides. All such cases are, therefore, indicated together by the symbol ††. The actions of the smaller political groups are not noticed in these summaries, because to include them would either produce a false impression, or make the symbols extremely complex.

Meaning of the Tables of Statistics.

The first of the tables, or summaries, printed here gives the number of each of the different classes of votes for each of the sessions examined; but in order to bring the results into a form more convenient for purposes of comparison, the second table, or summary, gives in four columns, for the several sessions examined: (1) the number of occasions where there were party votes of both parties on opposite sides; that is, true party votes, indicated thus, **; (2) the occasions where one party cast a party vote, and the other party did not, but where the majorities of the two parties were opposed, and these include, of course, both *† and †*; (3) the cases where this happened, but the majorities of both parties were on the same side, that is (*†) and (†*); and (4) the number of instances marked ††, where neither party cast a party vote. Each of the columns is followed by another giving the percentage, an arrangement which shows at a glance the comparative extent of party voting in the different sessions examined. From the second table there have been omitted all votes which were nearly unanimous so far as the two chief parties are concerned; that is, where more than nine tenths of both parties voted on the same side. These are the cases marked (**) in the first table. Their number in the sessions of the House of Commons examined never exceeds seven, except in 1881, when it reaches the enormous figure of 212, these being cast on questions brought forward by the Home Rulers, and opposed almost solidly by Conservatives

in 1850 to 15.89, and in 1860 to 6.22. It then rose in 1871 to 35.16; in 1881 to 46.73; in 1894 to 76.03; falling a trifle in 1899 to 68.95. This last fall, by the way, is counter-

and Liberals alike. Such votes must obviously be left out of account in estimating the percentage of party voting in any session.

The tables, or summaries, so made up, are these: —

TABLE I

| | YEAR | ** | (**) | *† | †* | (*†) | (†*) | †† | TOTAL |
|---|---|---|---|---|---|---|---|---|---|
| Conservatives and Reformers | 1836 | 41 | 5 | 25 | 21 | 36 | 11 | 47 | 186 |
| Protectionists and Liberals with Radicals (Peelites and Repealers not counted) . | 1850 | 51 | 7 | 41 | 45 | 53 | 22 | 109 | 328 |
| Conservatives and Liberals . | 1860 | 16 | 3 | 16 | 34 | 47 | 15 | 129 | 260 |
| Conservatives and Liberals . | 1871 | 90 | 7 | 36 | 42 | 30 | 10 | 48 | 263 |
| Conservatives and Liberals (Irish Home Rulers not counted) . . . . . . . | 1881 | 93 | 212 | 12 | 18 | 37 | 21 | 18 | 411 |
| Unionists and Liberals (with the Irish Nationalists) . . | 1894 | 184 | 4 | 10 | 9 | 27 | 2 | 10 | 246 |
| Unionists and Liberals (Irish Nationalists not counted) . | 1899 | 242 | 6 | 64 | 14 | 13 | 10 | 8 | 357 |

The following figures give an idea of the relative strength of parties in the sessions examined, although owing to changes in membership they are not, of course, perfectly accurate throughout the session: —

*1836*, Conservatives, 260, Reformers, 395; *1850*, Protectionists, 217, Peelites, 104, Liberals, 297, Radicals, 21, Repealers, 18; *1860*, Conservatives, 305, Liberals, 348; *1871*, Conservatives, 263, Liberals, 385; *1881*, Conservatives, 242, Liberals, 337, Home Rulers, 60; *1894*, Conservatives, 268, Liberal Unionists, 49, Liberals, 272, Anti-Parnellites, 72, Parnellites, 9; *1899*, Conservatives, 337, Liberal Unionists, 66, Liberals, 185, Anti-Parnellites, 71, Parnellites, 11.

TABLE II

| YEAR | ** | % | *† †* | % | (*†) (†*) | % | †† | % | TOTAL |
|---|---|---|---|---|---|---|---|---|---|
| 1836 | 41 | 22.65 | 46 | 24.86 | 47 | 25.97 | 47 | 25.97 | 181 |
| 1850 | 51 | 15.89 | 86 | 26.79 | 75 | 23.36 | 109 | 33.96 | 321 |
| 1860 | 16 | 6.22 | 50 | 19.46 | 62 | 24.12 | 129 | 50.19 | 257 |
| 1871 | 90 | 35.16 | 78 | 30.47 | 40 | 15.63 | 48 | 18.75 | 256 |
| 1881 | 93 | 46.73 | 30 | 15.88 | 58 | 29.15 | 18 | 9.05 | 199 |
| 1894 | 184 | 76.03 | 19 | 7.85 | 29 | 11.98 | 10 | 4.13 | 242 |
| 1899 | 242 | 68.95 | 78 | 22.22 | 23 | 6.55 | 8 | 2.28 | 351 |

balanced by the great increase, in 1899 over 1894, in the divisions where a party vote was cast by one party alone, but the majorities of the two parties were on opposite sides; and a corresponding decrease in the percentage of cases where the majorities of the two parties were on the same side. The column of divisions where neither side of the House casts a party vote tells the same story. The percentage of these divisions in 1836 was 25.97. It increased until 1860, when it reached 50.19; then diminished every ten years until 1894, when it was only 4.13; and finally almost vanished in 1899 with 2.28.

It would appear, therefore, that the amount of party voting in the House of Commons diminished after the Reform Bill until about the middle of the century, and since that time has increased steadily. The figures place the lowest point at 1860, but it occurred in reality somewhat earlier, for this is a case where the attempt to group the parties is misleading. In the summary for 1860 all the members of the House have been classed as Conservatives or Liberals, whereas in 1850 they have been classed as Protectionists, Peelites, Liberals and Repealers, and in computing the amount of party voting only the Protectionists and Liberals, as the two principal parties, have been taken into account. The fact is that in 1850 the House was so broken into independent groups that it is impossible to divide it wholly, as in 1860, into supporters and opponents of the ministry. The disintegration of parties was, indeed, greater in the years that followed the repeal of the Corn Laws and the fall of Sir Robert Peel in 1846, than at any other period since the Reform Bill of 1832, and hence it is at this time that taking, not the two chief parties alone, but all the members of the House, party government was really at its lowest point.

**Decrease of Defeats for the Ministers.**

The change in the amount of party voting, indicating, as it does, the strength of party cohesion, and the control of the leaders over their followers, finds its expression also in the rise and fall of the number of defeats for the government in the different sessions of Parliament. The exact tale of defeats in any particular session is, of course, largely a matter of accident, and is, moreover, liable to be swelled to an inordinate degree when, as in 1868, a ministry is struggling for existence without a majority in the House. Still, in the long run, it varies inversely with the strength of the hold that the Treasury Bench has over the party; and the table in the note, giving the total number of government defeats in the House of Commons in each session since 1847, certainly shows, though with some fluctuations, that they have tended to diminish steadily from the middle to the end of the century.[1]

[1] TABLE III

*Number of divisions in which the government whips were defeated in different sessions of Parliament*, 1847–1906

| SESSION | GOVERNMENT DEFEATS | SESSION | GOVERNMENT DEFEATS |
|---|---|---|---|
| 1847–48 | 3 | 1859: | |
| 1849 | 2 | First session | 4 |
| 1850 | 12 | Second session | 2 |
| 1851 | 13 | 1860 | 7 |
| 1852: | | 1861–62 | 10 |
| Before Lord Derby came in | 1 | 1862–63 | 13 |
| After Lord Derby came in | 2 | 1863 | 13 |
| 1852–53: | | 1864–65 | 12 |
| Before Lord Aberdeen came in | 1 | 1865 | 10 |
| After Lord Aberdeen came in | 15 | 1866 | 3 |
| 1854 | 15 | 1867 | 9 |
| 1854–55 | 12 | 1868 | 18 |
| 1856 | 15 | 1869 | 2 |
| 1857: | | 1870 | 6 |
| First session | 1 | 1871 | 7 |
| Second session | 7 | 1872 | 11 |
| 1857–58: | | 1873 | 6 |
| Before Lord Derby came in | 1 | 1874 | 2 |
| After Lord Derby came in | 5 | 1875 | 0 |
| | | 1876 | 1 |
| | | 1877 | 1 |
| | | 1878 | 0 |
| | | 1878–79 | 4 |
| | | 1880: | |
| | | First session | 0 |
| | | Second session | 2 |

Cases where their Followers Voted against them.

Another piece of evidence that leads to the same conclusion is to be found in the extent to which the members of the dominant party have voted against their own ministers. A majority of the party in power went into the lobby against the government whips in 1836 four times; in 1850 twelve times; in 1860 three times, while on three more occasions the party was evenly divided. In 1871 it occurred eight times; in 1881 twice; in 1894 twice, if the Nationalists are not counted in the ranks of the Liberals, and five times if they are included; and finally, in 1899, when the Conservatives were in power, it not only did not happen at all, but never did so much as one fifth of the Unionists who took part in a division vote against the government. During the middle period of the century it was not uncommon for a cabinet to be saved from defeat at the hands of its own followers by the help of its opponents. Now such a thing has become extremely rare. Nor is this due to the fact that cabinets for fear of defeat have grown cautious, and left questions open more than formerly. On the contrary, with the decay of legislation by private members' bills, the proportion of divisions in which the government whips

TABLE III — *Continued.*

| Session | Government Defeats | Session | Government Defeats |
|---|---|---|---|
| 1881 . . . . . . . | 3 | 1891 . . . . . . . | 3 |
| 1882 . . . . . . . | 3 | 1892 . . . . . . . | 0 |
| 1883 . . . . . . . | 7 | 1893 . . . . . . . | 3 |
| 1884 . . . . . . . | 5 | 1894 . . . . . . . | 1 |
| 1885: | | 1895 . . . . . . . | 2 |
| Before Lord Salisbury came in . . | 5 | 1896 . . . . . . . | 1 |
| After Lord Salisbury came in . . | 1 | 1897 . . . . . . . | 2 |
| | | 1898 . . . . . . . | 0 |
| | | 1899 . . . . . . . | 0 |
| 1886: | | 1900 . . . . . . . | 0 |
| First session . . . | 7 | 1901 . . . . . . . | 1 |
| Second session . . | 0 | 1902 . . . . . . . | 1 |
| 1887 . . . . . . . | 1 | 1903 . . . . . . . | 0 |
| 1888 . . . . . . . | 2 | 1904 . . . . . . . | 2 |
| 1889 . . . . . . . | 1 | 1905 . . . . . . . | 1 |
| 1890 . . . . . . . | 1 | | |

are tellers has increased. In 1836 it was less than one half, but in the sessions of 1894 and 1899 it was not far from nine tenths; and that this progress, though somewhat irregular if observed from year to year, has been on the whole continuous is made evident by comparing a series of sessions together. Taking the years from 1851 to 1860 inclusive, the government whips were tellers in 69.90 per cent of the divisions; and in the years 1878 to 1887 in 81.81 per cent.

**Tendency the Same in Both Parties.**

The tendency towards greater party cohesion in England is not confined to any one party, for although the Liberals have always been more independent than the Conservatives, and less willing to follow implicitly the guidance of their chiefs, yet the change of which we are speaking has not been less marked in their case. Their proportion of party votes, while always smaller than that of the Conservatives, has in fact borne to it a ratio not far from constant.[1]

A marked political change extending over many years is not accidental; and the causes of the increase in the amount of party voting are to be sought partly in the special

[1] If we take these proportions, computed for the years under consideration, upon the basis already explained, they may be summarised as follows:—

TABLE IV

| Year | Number of Divisions | Conservatives | | | | Liberals | | | |
|---|---|---|---|---|---|---|---|---|---|
| | | * | % | † | % | * | % | † | % |
| 1836 | 181 | 102 | 56 | 79 | 44 | 73 | 40 | 108 | 60 |
| 1850 | 321 | 145 | 45 | 176 | 55 | 118 | 37 | 203 | 63 |
| 1860 | 257 | 79 | 31 | 178 | 69 | 65 | 25 | 192 | 75 |
| 1871 | 256 | 156 | 61 | 100 | 39 | 142 | 55 | 114 | 45 |
| 1881 | 199 | 142 | 71 | 57 | 29 | 132 | 66 | 67 | 34 |
| 1894 | 242 | 221 | 91 | 21 | 9 | 195 | 81 | 47 | 19 |
| 1899 | 351 | 319 | 91 | 32 | 9 | 266 | 76 | 85 | 24 |

The falling off in the percentage of party votes among the Liberals in 1899 was due, of course, to their being in Opposition instead of being in power; and the fact that the party votes of the Conservatives did not show a corresponding increase after they took office, is, no doubt, to be attributed to their very large majority, which is always a stumbling-block in the way of party discipline.

conditions of English history during the period, and partly in the normal development of the parliamentary system.

**Historic Causes of Increased Party Voting.**

The feelings aroused by the agitation for the Reform Bill of 1832 kept party spirit in a state of activity for some years. Party lines at that time were not, indeed, so clearly drawn, and the members of a party were not so closely united, as at the present day. The Whigs and Radicals were far from a homogeneous body, and the Whig ministers were often sustained in resisting the demands of their Radical supporters by the help of Tory votes. Still the Reform Bill had brought a new meaning into politics, and the Conservative reaction that followed the first successes of the Liberals seemed destined to result in two fairly well-balanced parties confronting each other permanently and succeeding each other in power. But this condition of things did not last long. Neither parties nor opinions were thoroughly consolidated. Events were moving too fast for that; and the repeal of the Corn Laws was followed not only by a split in the Conservative ranks which never healed, but also by a general loss of party cohesion. This was the time when Lord Palmerston, having been forced out of the ministry at the end of 1851, for expressing, on his own authority, approval of the *coup d'etat* in France, had his "tit for tat with John Russell," as he said, and "turned him out" on the Militia Bill within two months.[1] For some years Lord Palmerston and Lord John Russell, like the leaders in a continental parliamentary government, were alternately turning one another out and sitting as colleagues in the same cabinet. During the fifties three different ministries were driven from power by the desertion of a part of their own followers. The parties were, in fact, in a state of confusion. The protectionist Conservatives were constantly in a minority, while the Liberals depended for a working majority, and hence for their tenure of office, upon the sufferance of the Peelites. The last two groups, indeed, long maintained a separate existence, yet they hardly dif-

[1] Ashley, "Life of Palmerston," I., 334.

fered in opinions from one another more than their members did among themselves; and since they had together an assured majority in Parliament it was possible for them, and especially for the Whigs who stood midway between the Peelites and the Radicals, to indulge in domestic differences without permanent danger to their principles or their supremacy.

As it takes two to make a quarrel, so no party can be maintained in fighting discipline unless it has another party to combat, strong enough to be a serious menace to its tenure of power. This the Liberal party did not have for more than a score of years after Peel's downfall in 1846. During the earlier part of that period one half of the former Conservative party was friendly, while the other half was impotent; and the same conditions that made strictly concerted action unnecessary for the Liberals made it useless for their opponents. In the course of Lord Palmerston's second administration, however, the Peelites disappeared as a separate body, being absorbed for the most part into the ranks of the Liberals; while the death of that statesman, in 1865, removed a great obstacle to reform, and opened a new chapter in the history of party. The change was not evident at once, for the election of 1868 placed so large a majority in Mr. Gladstone's hands that he could afford to neglect small numbers of dissentients on his own side of the House. Then came the golden age of Liberalism, when its principles could be worked out without too much regard to the exigencies of party warfare. But it did not last long, and before it passed away Disraeli had built up a formidable Tory party, a process that was not completed until some years after the Reform Acts of 1867–68 had brought a new element into the electorate. Until 1874 the Conservatives never obtained a majority in the House of Commons. They came into office, indeed, on three occasions, but only as stop-gaps while the majority were adjusting their differences and drawing together for a fresh lease of power. Since 1874 there has always been an Opposition that could appeal with confidence to the public for support whenever the ministers quarrelled among themselves, or lost their control over public affairs.

That the Liberal split over the first Home Rule Bill did not, like the quarrel among the Conservatives after the repeal of the Corn Laws, result in a general weakening of party ties may be attributed partly to the fact that, the measure having failed, the question remained unsettled; partly to the democratic nature of the electorate, which increased the influence of party as a political force; and partly to the normal development of the parliamentary system.

Organic Causes of Increased Party Voting.

It has already been pointed out that the parliamentary system in England sprang from the strife of political parties, and has tended to make them stronger by constraining the member of the House of Commons to support his leaders on all matters which they treat as questions of confidence. The system reacts upon the ministers also. Since the cabinet may be overturned at any moment, so that its very life depends upon incessant warfare, it must try to keep its followers constantly in hand; and since every defeat, however trivial, even if not fatal, is damaging, it must try to prevent any hostile votes — an effort which explains in part the much larger average attendance at divisions to-day than in the first half of the last century. Thus from the side both of the private member and the responsible minister there is a pressure in the parliamentary system towards more strict party voting. The tendency has been increased by the wide extension of the franchise under the Acts of 1867–68 and 1884. In a small and highly educated electorate, and still more within the walls of a legislative chamber representing such an electorate, it is possible to perceive the finer shades of politics, to appreciate the value of compromise, or even to bear with temporary coalitions, and hence party lines may be somewhat vague. But a democracy prefers broad contrasts, sharply defined alternatives, clearly marked issues and the frank opposition of party leaders. It understands better the struggle between the two front benches than the particular bearing of the measures debated. Unless matters of local interest are involved — and these the English practice almost eliminates — a democracy is prone to support the party, with comparatively little regard for matters of detail.

A high percentage of party voting appears, therefore, to be a natural result of the English parliamentary system, and with variations of degree, may be expected to continue in normal times so long as that system retains its character. If it should ever happen that the authority of the cabinet on the one side, and of the electorate on the other, became predominant, and Parliament should thus lose much of its importance, a general election might be nearly equivalent to the periodic choice of a commission of government. If so, the fiction of an entire agreement on all public questions might not be necessary, and the members of a party might be more free to express their individual differences; but in that case parliamentary government would have lost its character.

Common Belief that Force of Party has not Increased.

A discussion of this subject would be incomplete without an attempt to explain the opinion, commonly held among members of Parliament, that party lines are not more rigid than they were formerly. Independent voting, we are often told, has not become less frequent. That such an impression is erroneous is proved by the figures, but that it should be held is significant. The truth is that the degree to which a man is sensible of constraint, the bitterness with which he complains of tyranny, or conversely of laxity in discipline, depends not upon the amount of authority actually exerted, but upon the relation which that bears to the amount he thinks ought to be exerted. The outcry against theological domination comes not in an age of faith, but when scepticism is rife; and the same principle applies to political parties. It is, indeed, noteworthy that in 1894, when the division lists ran on party lines far more closely than at an earlier time, the periodicals were filled with laments over the breaking up of the House of Commons into groups, and with gloomy forebodings of a collapse of parliamentary government from a failure to maintain party cohesion Nor were these views entirely unwarranted. The parliamentary system in its present form requires a party discipline far more strict than it did fifty years ago, and perhaps more strict than will always be possible. Yet a member of the House of Commons may be unconscious of party pressure, and of a gradual increase of that pressure, so long as it is natural, continuous and evenly distributed. As Sir Henry Maine remarked in speaking of party: "The difficulty which Englishmen in particular feel about it is very like that which men once experienced when they were told that the air had weight. It enveloped them so evenly and pressed on them so equally, that the assertion seemed incredible." [1]

**Attitude of the Private Member.** The attitude of a thoughtful man towards his party is well expressed in Mr. Lecky's "Map of Life." [2] "A member of Parliament," he says, "will soon find that he must select a class of subjects which he can himself master, while on many others he must vote blindly with his party." And he adds: "Every member of Parliament is familiar with the scene, when, after a debate, carried on before nearly empty benches, the division bell rings, and the members stream in to decide the issue. There is a movement of uncertainty. The questions 'Which side are we?' 'What is it about?' may be heard again and again. Then the Speaker rises, and with one magical sentence clears the situation. It is the sentence in which he announces that the tellers for the Ayes or Noes, as the case may be, are the Government whips." It may be observed that Mr. Lecky explains the practice of voting blindly with one's party by a conscious inability to form an intelligent opinion upon the question at issue; but that it is by no means confined to such cases is perfectly evident.

**Causes of the Common Impression.** The impression that members of the House of Commons are as independent of party as ever is based largely upon the presence in almost every Parliament of two or three

[1] "Popular Government," 98–99. [2] pp. 131–32.

persons, whose seats are secure, and who, from temperament or ambition or disappointment, constantly attack their leaders and occasionally vote against them. Members of this kind are, however, very few, and their conduct rarely has a perceptible effect upon the course of public affairs. The impression is fostered, also, by the fact that debate was formerly left mainly to the ministers and a handful of their most active opponents, the country squire who had the privilege of writing M.P. after his name rarely speaking, and fulfilling his whole duty by walking through the lobby on important divisions. Now most members are anxious to have their constituents look upon them as active at Westminster, and hence the number of men who take part in debate has increased very much, while every man who rises to his feet seeks to make it appear that he is uttering his own personal opinions. The effect is perplexing to the stranger on his first visit to the gallery. He hears so many men on both sides of the House speak freely of the faults of a measure, urge amendments and criticise the position of the ministry, that he begins to think the result of the division really doubtful; but when the tellers bring in their report he finds that the government has obtained not far from its usual majority. One might argue that the authority of party appears in the division lists greater than it really is, because a member who will not vote against the whips, will often, if he objects strongly to a measure, abstain from voting altogether. But a man who from party motives abstains from a vote he would otherwise cast is yielding a half obedience to his party, so that even in these cases the record of the division furnishes an indication, although not an exact numerical measure, of the control of the party over its adherents. Strangely enough, the very fact that private members take a larger share in debate has helped, by consuming the time of Parliament, to diminish the opportunity of passing private members' bills, and hence of passing any bills without party pressure. It has thus actually tended to increase the proportion of divisions in which the government whips are tellers and the votes are cast on party lines.

**Proportion of Party Votes in Congress.** Turning from Parliament to the legislative bodies of the United States, we find quite a different array of figures. Five Congresses were examined, those elected in 1844, 1862, 1886, 1896 and 1898, and in each of them all the sessions of both branches were studied. From the summary of results, given in the note,[1] it is clear that no such continuous tendency has been at work, as in the House of Commons. The proportion of party votes changes very much from

[1] For the full tables of Yea and Nay votes, and the method in which they were compiled, the reader is referred to the original article in the "Report of the American Historical Association" for 1901. The summary of results is as follows:—

TABLE V

| | ** | % | *† †* | % | (*†) (†*) | % | †† | % | TOTAL |
|---|---|---|---|---|---|---|---|---|---|
| Twenty-ninth Congress (elected in 1844) | | | | | | | | | |
| Senate: | | | | | | | | | |
| First session . . . | 30 | 15.54 | 81 | 41.97 | 19 | 9.84 | 63 | 32.64 | 193 |
| Second session . . . | 18 | 16.66 | 55 | 50.92 | 9 | 8.33 | 26 | 24.07 | 108 |
| Both sessions . . . | 48 | 15.95 | 136 | 45.18 | 28 | 9.30 | 89 | 29.57 | 301 |
| House: | | | | | | | | | |
| First session . . . | 36 | 7.89 | 199 | 43.64 | 30 | 6.58 | 191 | 41.89 | 456 |
| Second session . . . | 31 | 18.34 | 65 | 38.46 | 25 | 14.80 | 48 | 28.40 | 169 |
| Both sessions . . . | 67 | 10.72 | 264 | 42.24 | 55 | 8.80 | 239 | 38.24 | 625 |
| Thirty-eighth Congress (elected in 1862) | | | | | | | | | |
| Senate: | | | | | | | | | |
| First session . . . | 27 | 6.98 | 152 | 39.28 | 60 | 15.50 | 148 | 38.24 | 387 |
| Second session . . . | 5 | 3.16 | 33 | 20.88 | 28 | 17.72 | 92 | 58.23 | 158 |
| Special session . . . | | | | | 1 | 16.66 | 5 | 83.33 | 6 |
| All sessions . . . . | 32 | 5.81 | 185 | 33.58 | 89 | 16.15 | 245 | 44.46 | 551 |
| House: | | | | | | | | | |
| First session . . . . | 150 | 36.49 | 126 | 30.67 | 33 | 8.03 | 102 | 24.82 | 411 |
| Second session . . . | 24 | 14.46 | 69 | 41.57 | 13 | 7.83 | 60 | 36.14 | 166 |
| Both sessions . . . | 174 | 30.15 | 195 | 33.79 | 46 | 7.97 | 162 | 28.08 | 577 |

one Congress, and even from one session, to another, but it does not follow closely any fixed law of evolution. It is,

TABLE V — *Continued.*

| | ** | % | *† †* | % | (*†) (†*) | % | †† | % | TOTAL |
|---|---|---|---|---|---|---|---|---|---|
| Fiftieth Congress (elected in 1886) | | | | | | | | | |
| Senate: | | | | | | | | | |
| First session . . . | 33 | 23.41 | 49 | 34.75 | 19 | 13.47 | 40 | 28.37 | 141 |
| Second session . . . | 111 | 66.48 | 23 | 13.77 | 11 | 6.59 | 22 | 13.70 | 167 |
| Special session . . . | 1 | 100.00 | | | | | | | 1 |
| All sessions . . . . | 145 | 46.93 | 72 | 23.30 | 30 | 9.71 | 62 | 20.06 | 309 |
| House: | | | | | | | | | |
| First session . . . | 13 | 12.08 | 51 | 34.22 | 35 | 23.49 | 45 | 30.20 | 149 |
| Second session . . . | 14 | 16.09 | 38 | 43.67 | 10 | 11.49 | 25 | 28.73 | 87 |
| Both sessions . . . | 32 | 13.55 | 89 | 37.71 | 45 | 19.06 | 70 | 29.66 | 236 |
| Fifty-fifth Congress (elected in 1896) | | | | | | | | | |
| Senate: | | | | | | | | | |
| First session . . . | 116 | 69.47 | 28 | 16.77 | 9 | 5.39 | 14 | 8.38 | 167 |
| Second session . . . | 12 | 10.71 | 61 | 54.46 | 15 | 13.39 | 24 | 21.43 | 112 |
| Third session . . . | | | 9 | 20.45 | 16 | 36.36 | 19 | 43.18 | 44 |
| All sessions . . . . | 128 | 39.63 | 98 | 30.35 | 40 | 12.38 | 57 | 17.65 | 323 |
| House: | | | | | | | | | |
| First session . . . | 30 | 85.71 | 3 | 8.57 | 2 | 5.71 | | | 35 |
| Second session . . . | 47 | 49.47 | 35 | 36.85 | 5 | 5.26 | 8 | 8.42 | 95 |
| Third session . . . | 7 | 20.00 | 10 | 28.57 | 3 | 8.57 | 15 | 42.86 | 35 |
| All sessions . . . . | 84 | 50.91 | 48 | 29.09 | 10 | 6.06 | 23 | 13.94 | 165 |
| Fifty-sixth Congress (elected in 1898) | | | | | | | | | |
| Senate: | | | | | | | | | |
| First session . . . . | 22 | 33.33 | 26 | 39.39 | 2 | 3.03 | 16 | 24.24 | 66 |
| Second session . . . | 26 | 35.14 | 18 | 24.32 | 6 | 8.11 | 24 | 32.43 | 74 |
| Both sessions . . . | 48 | 34.29 | 44 | 31.43 | 8 | 5.71 | 40 | 28.57 | 140 |
| House: | | | | | | | | | |
| First session . . . . | 48 | 60.76 | 14 | 17.72 | 5 | 6.32 | 12 | 15.19 | 79 |
| Second session . . . | 21 | 34.42 | 20 | 32.78 | 6 | 9.83 | 14 | 22.95 | 61 |
| Both sessions . . . | 69 | 49.28 | 34 | 24.28 | 11 | 7.85 | 26 | 18.57 | 140 |

indeed, much less in the first of these Congresses than in the last, and, no doubt, it tends on the whole to increase; yet great fluctuations have taken place, sometimes between two sessions of the same Congress. It has often happened, for example, that the proportion of party votes has been twice as large in one session as in another. The most striking case occurred in the Fifty-fifth Congress elected in 1896. Here the percentage of party votes in the first session of the House was 85.71, and in the third only 20; while in the Senate it was 69.47 in the first session, and in the third it disappeared altogether. Wherever this happens, and in fact wherever the number of party votes is especially large, it is because of some one particular measure on which the parties take issue. In the Fifty-fifth Congress it was due to the Dingley Tariff Bill, which the Houses had been called together in a special session to consider; and in the same way the 66.48 per cent of party votes in the Senate in the second session of the Fiftieth Congress was almost entirely caused by the Mills Tariff Bill, or rather by the Senate substitute therefor.

In Parliament contentious legislation is now conducted in the main by one party and opposed by the other, and hence the proportion of party votes is nearly constant. In Congress this is by no means true, and the quantity of such votes depends largely upon the presence of some question on which the parties happen to be sharply divided. On other subjects party lines are less strictly drawn. In short, in England the parties frame the issues; in America at the present day the issues do not, indeed, make the parties, but determine the extent of their opposition to each other in matters of legislation. In general the statistics for Congress show that whereas during the middle of the century the amount of party voting there was at least as great as in Parliament, and while in particular sessions the English maximum has been exceeded, yet on the average, party lines are now drawn distinctly less often than in the House of Commons.

Single sessions of the legislature were also examined for five of the larger northern States, three of them being among those in which party politics might be expected to be most acute.[1] But in New York alone among the States considered was the quantity of party votes considerable. Here the proportion ran in the Senate from twenty-two to thirty per cent, and in the Assembly from forty-five to fifty per

In the State Legislatures.

[1] These three States (New York, Ohio, and Illinois) are controlled sometimes by one party and sometimes by the other. The other two (Massachusetts and Pennsylvania) have large and constant Republican majorities. From a feeling that the condition in the sessions first examined in New York and Pennsylvania might be abnormal, another session was taken in each of those two States. Full lists of the votes in detail may be found in the article already mentioned. A summary of the results obtained is as follows:—

TABLE VI

| | ** | % | *† †* | % | (*†) (†*) | % | †† | % | TOTAL |
|---|---|---|---|---|---|---|---|---|---|
| Massachusetts, 1899 | | | | | | | | | |
| Senate . . . . | 1 | 1.05 | 23 | 24.21 | 7 | 7.37 | 64 | 67.37 | 95 |
| House . . . . | 3 | 6.12 | 19 | 38.78 | 3 | 6.12 | 24 | 48.98 | 49 |
| New York, 1894 | | | | | | | | | |
| Senate . . . . | 73 | 30.67 | 56 | 23.53 | 81 | 34.03 | 28 | 11.76 | 238 |
| Assembly . . . | 115 | 50.44 | 34 | 14.91 | 49 | 21.49 | 30 | 13.16 | 228 |
| New York, 1899 | | | | | | | | | |
| Senate . . . . | 50 | 22.52 | 62 | 27.93 | 63 | 28.38 | 47 | 21.17 | 222 |
| Assembly . . . | 93 | 45.36 | 42 | 20.48 | 43 | 20.97 | 27 | 13.17 | 205 |
| Pennsylvania, 1895 | | | | | | | | | |
| Senate . . . . | 12 | 6.42 | 44 | 23.53 | 81 | 43.53 | 50 | 26.74 | 187 |
| House . . . . | 6 | 1.15 | 52 | 9.96 | 139 | 26.63 | 325 | 62.26 | 522 |
| Pennsylvania, 1899 | | | | | | | | | |
| Senate . . . . | 1 | 1.25 | 7 | 8.75 | 30 | 37.50 | 42 | 52.50 | 80 |
| House . . . . | 7 | 3.32 | 31 | 14.69 | 69 | 32.70 | 104 | 49.29 | 211 |
| Ohio, 1900 | | | | | | | | | |
| Senate . . . . | 20 | 15.15 | 21 | 15.91 | 56 | 42.42 | 35 | 26.52 | 132 |
| House . . . . | 18 | 10.17 | 16 | 9.04 | 55 | 31.07 | 88 | 49.72 | 177 |
| Illinois, 1899 | | | | | | | | | |
| Senate . . . . | 8 | 5.44 | 25 | 17.01 | 69 | 46.94 | 45 | 30.61 | 147 |
| House . . . . | 16 | 12.5 | 28 | 22.05 | 43 | 33.85 | 40 | 31.49 | 127 |

cent. In the other State legislative bodies the proportion was much smaller. In none of them was it more than sixteen per cent, and in several cases it was less than two per cent. Moreover, a part of these votes were cast in the election of officers who have no possible connection with public policy.

Fewer Party Votes in America Due to Independence of the Executive;

The greater prevalence of party votes in England is due, of course, to the relation between the executive and the legislature. If a member of the majority in the House of Commons refuses to support an important measure on which the cabinet insists, and if enough of his colleagues share his opinion to turn the scale, the consequence must be a change of ministry or a dissolution; while under similar circumstances in America no such dire results will ensue. The measure will simply be lost, but the member can retain his seat undisturbed till the end of his term, and the administration will go on as before. Hence the difficulty in carrying out party platforms, and the discredit into which they have fallen. Moreover, a platform, however elaborate, can cover only a small part of the questions that arise in Congress. The general public are interested in few things, and these alone find a place in the platform. For the rest, even the moral compulsion that attaches to a party declaration of faith is lacking, and therefore it is very difficult to bring about party cohesion in such matters. The system of committees in American legislative bodies tends also to remove measures from the field of party politics, for the committees to which bills are referred are always composed of members of both parties. No doubt it sometimes happens in Congress, in the case of a tariff bill, for example, that the majority and minority of a committee virtually meet separately, so that the bill when reported is a pure party measure; but this is an exceptional procedure even in Congress, and in many of the State legislatures it is entirely unknown. The work of the committees is usually in the nature of a compromise; and if, as is often the case, the report of a committee is unanimous, or if the divisions among the

and to the System of Committees.

members do not run on party lines, it is obviously impossible to treat the bill when reported as a pure party measure. In Parliament, on the contrary, the great legislative committee is the cabinet, and every bill it introduces is of necessity a party measure, so far as its own side of the House is concerned. If seriously opposed, the resistance is almost certain to come from the other side, so that the fight is likely to be conducted on party lines. With the present tendency to leave the initiative to the government, this is getting to be true of almost all important questions. But the conditions in the United States effectually prevent such a result, and party issues can in the nature of things cover only a small part of legislation.

All this applies with still greater force to the States. The parties in America are essentially national. They exist primarily to elect the President, and only in a secondary degree to elect State officers. Hence they are divided mainly on national issues, and it is difficult for them to take sides upon questions of State legislation without provoking differences that cut across the regular party lines and offend a certain number of their adherents. Thus it happens that the members of most of the State legislatures are elected by parties which have comparatively little connection with the questions they are called upon to decide. The same cause, and a similar use of committees, produce like results in the English borough councils, for they are usually elected on party lines, but not usually divided upon them in their actual work; and it is noteworthy that in a provincial borough council the absence of party voting is a source of pride. To say that there is politics in the council is a term of reproach, as it is in America, because it commonly implies personal politics rather than a difference of opinion on public policy.

**Why an Impression to the Contrary Prevails.**

A party cannot exert in America the same direct pressure upon the members of legislative bodies as it does in Parliament where the ministry is responsible; and hence it is tempted to resort to other means of consolidating its authority and maintaining political cohesion. The most obvious means is patronage in the form of appointments to public office, and that is one of the reasons why it is more difficult to get rid of the spoils system in America than in England. This brings us to another problem, that of explaining the prevalent impression that party is less powerful and despotic in England than in the United States. But first we must repeat that the amount of irritation produced by partisan dictation depends, not upon the extent of that dictation, but upon the question whether it is felt to be justifiable or not. A very strenuous exertion of party pressure for a legitimate end will not cause as much complaint as a far smaller pressure for an improper purpose. Few sensible people object to a caucus of members of Congress to determine the attitude of a party upon the currency; but every one resents the appointment of a grossly unfit postmaster who happens to have a "pull" on an influential politician; and herein there is a great deal of confusion between the party and the machine, because people do not comprehend the relation that the machine bears to the party, or the class of matters with which it deals.

**Action of the Machine.** It is often said that in State legislatures the boss, or the caucus, dictates the action of the party on pending measures, and then carries it into effect by a party vote, so that legislation is really the work of the machine. That this is an error is proved by the statistics. If it were true, Pennsylvania, boss-ridden as she was at the time covered by the figures that have been given, ought to have had in her legislature a long series of party votes; but, in fact, she had almost none. It is not true, because in the first place the machine rarely controls more than a part of the members of the party, and in the second place the machine meddles little with general legislation. It knows that an attempt to dictate to its followers on such questions would only weaken its authority; and hence it confines its attention to the distribution of spoils, to laws that bear upon electoral machinery, and to such bills, public or private, as affect directly the persons from whom it draws its revenue. It has, indeed, been pointed out that the very position of the boss depends upon the fact that parties exist for public objects, while he exists for private ones[1]; and this is so well recognised that the great corporations which desire to obtain either selfish legislation, or protection against unscrupulous attack, subscribe impartially to the campaign funds of both political parties. That is the aspect of public life which provokes an outcry from reformers. It is what Minghetti, writing for Italy, called the undue interference of parties in affairs that ought to lie outside their field.[2] Parties in America are not, as a rule, despotic on public questions, because they have little cohesion; but their influence, or rather the influence of the machine, or of the individual politician, is freely exerted in things quite apart from those issues of public policy which form the only rational ground for party activity. In short, the boss is not a prime minister who directs policy, but an electioneering agent and a private bill and office broker.

**Why Parties in Parliament are not Despotic.**

A comparison of England and America shows, therefore, that the influence of party upon legislation is, on the whole, much greater in England, but that it is more closely confined to public measures. All this does not mean that the majority in the House of Commons can do whatever it pleases without regard to the wishes of the minority. To some extent that is the case, but it would be a great mistake to suppose that the parliamentary system in England is developing into mere party tyranny. There is another side to the shield, for the very fact that the government must avoid defeats often makes it cautious, if not timid. It cannot disregard the opinions of the minority, because they are often shared by many of its own followers, and the vote of a small fraction of its own side of the House added to that of the Opposition may be fatal. The same forces that lead

[1] "The American Boss," by Judge Francis C. Lowell, in the *Atlantic Monthly*, September, 1900.
[2] *I Partiti Politici*, chap. ii.

a member of the party to sacrifice his personal opinions to party necessity lead the cabinet to modify its policy in deference to the protests of a little band of supporters. Nor are the ministers affected only by a fear of defection on the benches behind them. They must consider the general public opinion outside, which determines ultimately their tenure of power. They cannot afford to make a ruthless use of their majority in Parliament to force through their plans, and it is worth their while to be conciliatory so far as they can do so without offending their own party. They often make changes in their bills to meet suggestions coming from both sides of the House; and sometimes they take up quite a different line of action after a debate has revealed an unexpected current of opinion.

**Relation of the Two Front Benches.**

The relation between the two front benches is, indeed, an important matter, little understood by the public. Occasionally the leader on one side will beckon to the leader on the other, and they will retire to one of the rooms behind the Speaker's chair to arrange some minor point that has led to misconception. Here explanations can be given more freely than in public, and if an agreement is reached, the leader of the Opposition, on returning to his seat, will let his followers see that a compromise has been made and there will be no division on the question. Personally the relations between the statesmen on opposite sides are usually friendly. An outgoing minister will inform his successor about the condition of affairs in his department, and offer to help him so far as he can. The members of the two front benches are, in fact, in a position similar to that of barristers representing the parties to a suit in court. They are not carrying on a civil war for life and death, but conducting a case in accordance with the amenities of the profession, and those amenities are as little appreciated by the world at large as the etiquette that prevails among lawyers. If two prominent opponents happen to drive to the House of Commons in the same carriage on the eve of a momentous debate it provokes criticism, just as Mr. Pickwick's ire was roused when his counsel met the counsel of the plaintiff with a friendly greeting. If, therefore, the parliamentary system involves party despotism, it is a despotism tempered by many powerful forces both within and without the dominant party.

English Parties are Instruments of Government;

The friendly relations between the opposing leaders, their willingness to help each other in personal mishaps, and their reluctance to push issues to extremes, causes men with a more dogmatic philosophy to complain of the unreality of the parliamentary system. In truth the parties in England are not, as they are over much of the continent of Europe, collections of men bound together by their faith in a fixed political creed; but rather instruments of government, representing general political tendencies, and ready to govern the nation in accord with those tendencies so far as circumstances will permit. In a sense, and by no means necessarily a bad sense, they are opportunist. The function of statesmen in a democracy is quite as much to precipitate, to crystalise and to formulate, as to create, public opinion. The proximate aim of the two great parties is to get into power, and hence they no longer stand for abstract principles without regard to their popularity. They urge only measures for which there is at least a reasonable prospect of securing immediate support; and if a policy proves permanently unpopular it is abandoned. While keeping in touch with certain essential elements in their ranks — the Conservatives, for example, with the Church and the landed interest, the Liberals with the Nonconformists and the men of radical views — both parties tend to approach the political centre of gravity. All this has its good and its bad side; the bad is self-evident, consisting in the substitution of success for principle as the aim and end of public life, while the good side is found in the fact that political leaders strive to carry out so much of their policy as is attainable, instead of clinging obstinately to ideals which cannot possibly be realised. Such conditions tend to promote, on the essentials of government, a popular

and Close to the Political Centre of Gravity.

accord from which no leading statesman is far estranged; and they tend to eliminate irreconcilable and revolutionary elements in the state.[1]

**Party Leaders Frequently Change Sides.**

In singular contrast with the strength of party as a force in legislation, and with the high proportion of votes on party lines in the House of Commons, there is another phenomenon which appears at first sight wholly inconsistent therewith. It is the large number of English statesmen in the nineteenth century who have changed either their party, or their principles, in the course of their career. Except for Lord John Russell, Mr. Disraeli,[2] Lord Salisbury and Mr. Balfour, it may be said that almost all the most famous ministers from 1832 to the end of the century did one or the other. Sir Robert Peel twice carried measures of the highest political moment against the convictions he had earlier held. Lord Palmerston was long a Conservative minister, and still longer a Liberal one. Lord Stanley and Sir James Graham both changed sides, the latter with kaleidoscopic rapidity. Mr. Gladstone from a high Tory minister became the most famous of the Liberal premiers. Lord Hartington and Mr. Chamberlain both passed from leading positions in Liberal cabinets to powerful influence in Conservative ones. Yet in most of these cases the change was made without reproach, and often with only a brief loss of authority. Usually the change was connected with a split in the party, but in some cases, like those of Stanley and Graham, it was virtually an individual secession.

**Why such Changes are Possible.**

Now, such transmigrations of party leaders are not really inconsistent with the strictness of party ties. If the parties were based on irreconcilable differences of race, or of politi-

[1] Dr. Redlich, who was much impressed by this aspect of English public life, remarks that the really great common interests of the nation are withdrawn from party conflicts, which turn on different views, not of fundamental principles, but of concrete questions. This truth he embodies forcibly in the paradox that England possesses her system of party government by a parliamentary cabinet because she has no parties in the continental sense. *Recht und Technik des Englischen Parlamentarismus*, 157–58. In the translation "Proc. in the House of Commons," I, 128–29.

[2] This refers only to Disraeli's parliamentary career.

cal or religious creed, a change of party would be apostacy, and would entail a forfeiture of public esteem. But, as English parties are really instruments of government, a statesman acts with one or the other of them, not because he is bound to it by an inflexible conviction, but because, on the whole, he thinks the balance of right is on its side; and, therefore, some event may well occur, some new question may arise, which causes a difference of opinion with his former friends, and makes the balance incline the other way. So long as he belongs to a party he must act with it, he must sacrifice smaller questions to the general result, but when he cannot agree with its policy as a whole, he must break away and go free. He is no longer bound to sacrifice his opinion on any point for the sake of harmony; and hence it is proverbial that when a minister resigns from the cabinet his differences with it appear to expand, and he is found opposing his colleagues on many points on which he would have been silent had he remained in office. With a rigid system of two parties, however, he must soon return to the fold, or join the other party, or lose his authority altogether. At any one moment there can, if the parliamentary system works normally, be only two parties; but formed as they are for practical ends, each is under strain, the different elements of which it is composed pulling to some extent apart. Every little while the strain becomes greater than the force of cohesion, the tie snaps, and a fraction of the party breaks off, to be absorbed in time by the other party, unless it is so feeble as to be eliminated from public life altogether. If the seceders are believed to have acted fairly by their former colleagues, and if some grave misunderstanding does not arise, the secession is not regarded as treasonable, but as the result of the fissiparous nature of politics. In short, it is the very fact that parties are groups of men bound together, not by the common possession of irreconcilable prejudices, but for the purpose of carrying on the government, that enables the members to sacrifice the smaller questions of detail to the general unity; and it is the same fact that makes it possible for a leader to change sides without necessarily abandoning his principles or playing false to his faith. With the greater strictness of party in the House of Commons, with the sharp frontiers and the disappearance of debatable ground between the parties, it may well be that such transitions will be more rare in the future, but far from being inconsistent with the strength of party in the parliamentary system, they arise in a sense from the same cause.

# CHAPTER XXXVI

## POLITICAL OSCILLATIONS

The Nation Oscillates between the Parties.

WHERE, as in many of the continental countries, the parties are based on religion or race, or on fundamental differences in political points of view which are absolutely inconsistent with one another, the voters are very constant in their fidelity, and hence the parties fluctuate little in size for long periods of time. The same cause preserves the solid phalanx of Irish Nationalists. But in Great Britain and in America, where the parties are not separated by an impassable barrier, and neither is very far from the political centre of gravity, ordinary current questions suffice to detach many persons from the body with which they voted at the last election, and therefore the party fluctuations are large and rapid. In fact there is an oscillation in politics so nearly regular that men have come to call it the swing of the pendulum. The results of any particular election can, no doubt, be explained by a reference to the circumstances under which it took place, to the nature of the issues presented, to the popularity of the leading men, and to the thriving or depressed state of trade at the moment; and yet if political oscillations are repeated regularly for a considerable length of time, we are justified in concluding that they are due to some enduring cause, and that the way in which the immediate issues are shaped is itself a result of that cause. Not that any such tendency to oscillation is paramount. At most it is only one of many factors in politics, and like other factors will produce its normal effects only so far as it is not counteracted by other forces. Oscillations that might occur with regularity in ordinary times will, of course, be entirely interrupted whenever some overmastering question arises, and therefore one ought not to expect them when the nation is grappling with an unusually momentous problem, or is in the throes of a great war. They are, however, important enough to merit observation if they have a sensible effect on current politics in tranquil periods.

**Slow Periodic Oscillations.** Now there appear to be in England two distinct kinds of political fluctuation, which may be compared with the changes of the seasons and the alternation of day and night, or with ebb and flow of the tide and the waves that ruffle the surface of the sea. Without going back to the times of violent commotion, it is evident that the long, slow fluctuations have existed in England at least since the death of Queen Anne. **Their History.** From that date the country was predominantly Whig, and was ruled by the Whigs, for more than a generation. Then, after a period of uncertainty, the Tories got the upper hand, and with a few short intermissions retained power from the accession of Lord North in 1770 until the ministry of Earl Grey in 1830. The turn of the Whigs, renamed Liberals, came once more, and they remained the dominant party for well-nigh a generation and a half. The only serious break in their ascendency was the administration of Sir Robert Peel from 1841 to 1846, for although the quarrels among the Liberals three times enabled Conservative cabinets to take office, no one of these had the support of a majority either in Parliament or in the nation. Again there was a period of uncertainty, lasting this time about a dozen years, and then from the Home Rule Bill of 1886 until the election of 1906 the Conservatives were the leading party in the state. A real change in national opinion had taken place, and during a score of years the undercurrent was just as distinctly Conservative as it had been Liberal earlier in the century. The weight of the leaders of thought in the country had unmistakably shifted. In the sixties it was almost safe to assume that an English man of science or letters was a Liberal; in the nineties he was in most cases a Unionist. Nor was the change wholly due to the Home Rule Bill. A close observer might have seen it coming before such a measure was thought possible. He might have seen it among the students at Oxford, for although the prevailing tone at the university is always Conservative, yet a band of unusually vigorous Conservatives developed among the undergraduates there long before the Home Rule Bill; and in the same way a change of national opinion in favour of the Liberals was predicted from the attitude of the younger university men several years before the election of 1906.

**Their Causes.**

The causes of slow fluctuations of this kind are not always patent. The occasion, and one of the sources, of the change in 1886 was, of course, the Home Rule Bill. Another source was the Eastern question which detached some people a number of years earlier. But a more deep-seated cause was the fact that the Liberal party had worked out its original problems, and for the time its mission was fulfilled. Democracy had been achieved; local government in great part reformed; universal education established; many outworn abuses swept away; and the theories of the philosophic radicals, with their principles of individualism and *laissez-faire,* which furnished in the past the intellectual motive power of the party, had been carried to the breaking point. The doctrines thought out by Adam Smith and Bentham, elaborated by John Stuart Mill, Cobden, Buckle and a host of other men, and put into systematic form after they were dead by Herbert Spencer, had spent their force, and a reaction set in.[1] Then socialistic doctrines from the Continent, backed by sympathy for the toilers and the poor and a desire to give them immediate help, began to appeal strongly to many Radical minds. All this tended both to weaken the party as a whole, and to split it into sections with widely divergent views. At the same time the imperial sentiment, with its vision of

[1] In his "Law and Opinion in England" Professor Dicey has analysed with great clearness these movements of thought and their effects on legislation.

a greater Britain, for which the earlier theories had no place, appealed strongly to popular imagination.

Moreover, as energetic youths are wont to seek their fortune in strange lands, so they find that in public life and in the realm of thought their best chance for distinction lies in following new paths not yet crowded with men of established reputation; and thus in the early eighties there was a large opening for young Conservatives of ability. The inclination of men to accept new ideas that are suited to the age, and to weary of them when they have run their course; the natural history of the rise, growth and decay of opinions, which in dress we call fashion, and in the field of thought we call epochs; these things belong to the province of social psychology, but they lie at the base of the slow fluctuations of party that have occurred throughout the story of English parliamentary government.

**Rapid Electoral Oscillations.**

The rapid party oscillations are of more recent origin. They began with the Reform Acts of 1867–68, which in placing the borough franchise on a really wide basis, almost doubled at a stroke the total voters in Great Britain and created working-class electors in large numbers. These acts, and their complement in 1884, which extended the franchise in the counties, have brought about a distinct tendency toward a change of party at each general election. From 1846 to 1874 the Liberals had an uninterrupted majority in the House of Commons, but since that time political history has been far more chequered.

**Their History.**

The first election after the Acts of 1867–68 gave a large majority to the Liberals, and Disraeli's ministry resigned; at the next election in 1874 the scale turned in favour of the Conservatives; at the third, in 1880, the Liberals were again successful. At the fourth, in 1885, the Liberals still outnumbered the Conservatives, but the total forces which had hitherto opposed them were almost exactly equal to their own, and it was only by winning the support of the Irish Home Rulers that Mr. Gladstone was enabled to carry on the government. The election of 1886, following the defeat of his Home Rule Bill, gave the control to the Conservatives and Liberal Unionists, who may be regarded from that time as a single party. Victory next passed to the Liberals in 1892, and returned to the Conservatives in 1895. The election of 1900 was held under the stress of war, a condition that always strengthens for a time the hands of the existing government, and the Conservatives obtained nearly as large a majority as before. Finally the election of 1906 brought the Liberals back to power in overwhelming force. Thus of the eight general elections since the one that followed immediately upon the extension of the franchise in 1867–68, all but two have resulted in a change of the majority in the House of Commons; and of those two one did not give a majority to either of the great parties, while the other was held under the excitement of war. For a score of years after 1886 the Liberals were in power, it is true, only once, and then with very little margin to spare; but it must be remembered that the undercurrent was setting against them. The ebb of the tide may prevent a wave from reaching as high a point as if there were no tide, but it does not prevent the tide from having waves upon its surface. The fact that the Liberals obtained a majority at all during the period of greatest Tory ascendency, while the feeling about Home Rule still ran high, is, indeed, a striking example of the way the political pendulum swings.

**Causes of Rapid Political Oscillations.**

The tendency to a change of party at each general election may be ascribed to a variety of causes.[1] The most obvious is that every elected body represents its constituents very imperfectly. Representative government has neither proved a panacea for all social ills, nor worked to the entire satisfaction of the voters. Now, what is true of the whole elective body is true also of the parties within it. The

[1] The same tendency exists in America, and the writer has attempted, in a careful, though perhaps somewhat fanciful, examination of the results of elections in the several States, to show that it is due to a revulsion against the party in power. "Annals of the Amer. Acad. of Political Science," July, 1898.

majority in Parliament does not reflect exactly the views of the party that elected it, nor can the cabinet represent fully all the varying shades of opinion among its followers. In short, when a party comes to power, much of its action is guided or retarded by a fraction of its members, and this gives rise to discontented elements within its ranks. Hence there are always a number of people who feel that the men they supported do not really express their sentiments, and who are ready at the next election to vote for the other party, or to stay away from the polls altogether.

Something also must be attributed to the theory suggested by Sir Henry Maine to account for the frequent rejection by the Swiss people of laws passed by their representatives. He pointed out that a man may very well approve of a policy when set forth in general terms, and yet find when it is actually embodied in a statute that it contains "much that is likely to disturb his habits, his ideas, his prejudices, or his interests."[1] Whether this is the explanation of the Swiss phenomenon or not, the principle has an application in England where a man who dislikes a law may stay at home or vote for the opposing candidate at the next election, and thus desert his party for doing the very thing he helped it to do.

Another potent cause of political oscillation results from the drift towards paternal government. The great increase in the functions of the state, the widespread faith in the possibility of regenerating the world by legislation, of manufacturing what my friend Mr. Joseph Lee has called "righteousness by statute"; these things, coupled with the exigencies of political warfare, have led the people to expect, and the parties to promise, more than any government can perform. The hopes that cannot be fulfilled lead naturally to disappointment, and the public, which always clamours for a scapegoat, throws the blame upon the party in power, and turns to its rival, only to move round again in the same old circle.

[1] "Popular Government," 97.

Analysis of the Changes.

At an ordinary election about one quarter of the constituencies change sides, but naturally they are not always the same ones, because few constituencies feel the effect of the rapid oscillations sufficiently to change their party at every election. From 1895 to 1906 only 27 have changed precisely as the majority in Parliament itself has changed. The total transformation in the membership of the House of Commons is, therefore, the result of many forces affecting the constituencies in different ways, some feeling one force, some another, some feeling no force strongly enough to change sides, while many are moved quite irregularly by local or other influences in harmony with, or contrary to, the general current of the time.[1]

Table of Changes by Constituencies.

[1] A table of the results of the oscillations in the county and borough constituencies of Great Britain, since the year 1885, shows at a glance the fluctuations that have taken place :

TABLE VII

| | | | |
|---|---|---|---|
| 1886. | 14 turned Liberal, | 156 turned Conservative. | Total changes, 170. |
| 1892. | 100 turned Liberal, | 17 turned Conservative. | Total changes, 117. |
| 1895. | 14 turned Liberal, | 112 turned Conservative. | Total changes, 126. |
| 1900. | 42 turned Liberal, | 30 turned Conservative. | Total changes, 72. |
| 1906. | 246 turned Liberal, | 4 turned Conservative. | Total changes, 250. |

In this table only the general elections have been taken into account, the by-elections being disregarded. The two-member boroughs are counted as two separate constituencies, and the labour men, crofters and other members of that kind have been classed as Liberals, while the Liberal Unionists have been classed with the Conservatives. The results are rough, for they take account only of the member elected, although he may have received a minority of the vote, the majority being divided between the two other candidates.

It will be observed that the election of 1900 was anomalous. A good many constituencies changed sides, more than half as many as usual; but they changed in both directions in nearly equal numbers. The war counteracted the swing of the pendulum; while in 1906, either an accumulated tendency, or perhaps a combination of the slow and rapid oscillations, caused a remarkably large change.

It may be interesting to classify the different constituencies according to their susceptibility to change. An analysis of the general elections in the 560 county and borough constituencies of Great Britain for the six general elections from 1885 to 1906 inclusive, shows that 197, or more than one third, remained unchanged throughout the whole period. Of these 108 were constantly Liberal, 88 Conservative, and one (the Scotland Division of Liverpool) Irish Nationalist. Nearly as many more felt wholly or in part the effect of the slow oscillation, and of that alone. Fifty-five felt it

Kinds of Constituencies that Change Sides.

If we try to discover what kind of constituencies are most susceptible to the forces that produce oscillations in politics, we find them less easy to classify than one might suppose. Among the seats, for example, where the changes have been exactly in accord with those of the majority in the House of Commons, one finds metropolitan boroughs, manufacturing towns large and small, seaports, county divisions engaged mostly in manufacturing and mining, an old shire town, and a number of county divisions devoted wholly or mainly to agriculture; in short, places of every nature. A careful analysis of the different kinds of constituencies, and a tabulation of the results in each of them, does not lead

fully, turning Conservative in 1886, and remaining so continuously until 1906, when they again became Liberal. Others felt the movement in only one direction; twenty-five turning Conservative in 1886, and remaining so permanently; and eighty-four beginning the period as Conservative, and becoming Liberal for the first time in 1906.

The effects of the rapid oscillations are more complex and more difficult to classify. Twenty-seven constituencies followed, as we have seen, the exact transformations of the majority in Parliament, changing sides at every election. Curiously enough, the North West Division of Lanarkshire did precisely the reverse, the result there in 1906 being due to a division of the vote between the Liberal and Labour candidates. Eleven others changed in nearly the same way as the majority in the House, becoming Liberal, however, in 1900 instead of 1906. Many more felt the tendency to rapid change partially. Fifty constituencies, for example, changed sides for a single election, swinging back immediately afterward to their former allegiance; and except so far as one of these two changes was made in the anomalous election of 1900, they were all in accord with the change in the majority in Parliament. Fifteen of these constituencies were, in fact, Conservative only from 1895 to 1900, and 13 only from 1900 to 1906. Twenty-five more went over in the same way to the Conservatives at the election of 1895, and returned to the Liberals in 1906. This also was in accord with the party complexion of the House of Commons, and considering the character of the election of 1900 was in effect a single oscillation. Fourteen other constituencies changed more frequently, and always, except at the election of 1900, in accord with the swing of the political pendulum. Finally, a number of seats felt to some extent both the slow and the rapid oscillation. Fourteen Conservative constituencies, for example, became Liberal for the single Parliament of 1892–95, went back to the Conservatives, and then became Liberal again in 1906; while three became Conservative in 1886, and then became Liberal again for the same Parliament of 1892–95 alone. This leaves only fifty-two, or less than one tenth, of the constituencies that have changed irregularly, sometimes in accord with the prevailing tendency, sometimes, under the pressure of local or other influences, in a contrary direction.

to any very definite conclusions.[1] Certain differences can, indeed, be observed. The dockyards, for example, are highly versatile, their politics turning on questions of employment by the state; but they form a small and peculiar group by themselves. One may observe, also, that the constituencies which have remained permanently Liberal are found chiefly among the manufacturing boroughs and the divisions of counties busy largely with manufactures and mines; while those, outside of London, which have remained steadily Conservative are made up largely of the agricultural divisions of counties. Still, there are manufacturing towns that have been Conservative throughout the period, and agricultural districts that have been as persistently Liberal; and there have been more of each of these classes of constituencies that have changed sides several times. Except, indeed, for the fact that the county divisions devoted to manufactures and mines have been rather exceptionally constant in their politics, there have been no such marked variations in the frequency of change as to justify any generalisations about the relative sensitiveness of the different kinds of constituencies to the fluctuations of political opinion.

The percentage of seats of each kind that have remained true to one party, or that have changed once, twice, three or four times, is, on the whole, surprisingly uniform; and the obvious conclusion is that England is to-day politically homogeneous. The motives that affect one part of the country appeal to the other parts also; those to which people living in the cities are open, touch the rural population as well. These conditions are due partly to the growth of a cheap newspaper press, and partly to the con-

[1] With the help of Dr. E. D. Fite, now of Yale University, the county divisions were arranged in five classes according to their proportion of agriculture or manufacturing and mining; while the boroughs were classified as large and small manufacturing towns, seaports, dockyards, holiday resorts, old shire towns, and districts composed of groups of towns. The metropolitan boroughs were classed by themselves. In all of these cases the results of the last five general elections were tabulated.

tinual kneading of the body politic by the political parties, which prepare the public mind for the reception of current impressions, and exploit quickly each new phase of public life in every hamlet of the kingdom.

**Class of Voters that Change Sides.**

Although the different kinds of constituencies are not unlike in their susceptibility to change, it does not follow that this is equally true of the various classes of voters within them; and it would be instructive to learn what sort of people are responsible for the overthrow of one party and the victory of its rival. The result may be brought about either by the mere abstention of electors who voted with the majority on the previous occasion, or by their actually voting for the other side. The first of these is probably common among all classes of the population, but not the second. In default of figures taken at successive elections from a number of polling districts, selected with a view of isolating particular kinds of voters, the best evidence on the subject is the opinion of the party organisers who make a business of knowing how the registered electors vote. According to these men, the voters that change sides come mainly from the working-classes and the small shopkeepers. The regular members of a party, they tell us, may stay away, but rarely vote for the other side, and in England almost all people of education or means are members of a party. Apart from a great schism, like that which followed Mr. Gladstone's championship of Home Rule and tore rents in every rank in life, or like that caused by the fiscal question, the upper and middle classes appear to shift in politics very little.

**Universities Change Little.**

University graduates certainly seem to be, as a rule, very constant to their party. The seats for Oxford and Cambridge do not indeed furnish a fair test, because the men who take orders keep their names on the books to a disproportionate extent, and hence the vote for a member of Parliament measures chiefly the opinion of the clergy of the Church of England. A change in the politics of the young men at those universities has already been referred to as the precursor of a change in national sentiment; but it reaches only a small part of the registered graduates, and is valuable as an indication, rather than for its direct effect on the university electorate. The ecclesiastical character of the voting list does not, however, apply to the universities in London and Scotland; yet from 1886 through 1900 they returned at every election Conservatives or Liberal Unionists, who were either unopposed or had an overwhelming majority. In 1885 London University elected a Liberal, and the vote for the seat of Edinburgh and St. Andrews was close; but thereafter no one not allied with the Tories had a chance of winning at either place until 1906, when a Liberal was defeated for London by only thirty-four votes, and the candidates put forward by Liberals and free-trade Unionists polled a very fair vote at both of the Scotch Universities. It would seem clear, therefore, that university graduates, while not proof against change, are little affected by the rapid oscillations coming at successive elections.

The City of London.

The elections for the City of London point with equal clearness to the fact that the money interests shift little in politics, for the City has long been overwhelmingly Conservative, and from 1885 to 1906 no Liberal attempted to contest a seat there. That many manufacturers, and people belonging to the upper middle class, who had been Liberals, joined the Unionists in 1886 is undoubted, but in the estimation of persons well qualified to form a judgment these classes are constant in their politics in ordinary times.

Evidence from Metropolitan Boroughs.

The opinion held by men actively engaged in party organisation that the voters who change sides at successive elections belong mainly to the poorer end of the social scale, receives some confirmation from a study of the London boroughs. Most constituencies contain voters of many kinds, but in a great city the rich and poor are segregated in different quarters. A vast metropolis, divided like London into sixty districts for the election of members of Parliament, gives exceptional opportunities to compare the results in places inhabited by distinct classes of people, and there can be no doubt that in London the working-class constituencies have shown, on the whole, a greater tendency to political oscillation than the others.

A Possible Danger.

If it be true that the voters who, by changing sides, determine the results of an election belong to the poorer classes, and especially if, as is sometimes asserted, they turn against the government because it has not fulfilled their expectations, then the position is unfortunate; for it means that the parties will be tempted more and more to outbid each other for the favour of those voters. Such a temptation is a danger in any state, but above all in a parliamentary government, where the control of party over legislation is strong enough to enable the leaders to carry out their promises, and to make them effectively responsible at the polls for a failure to do so.

## CHAPTER XXXVII

### THE EXISTING PARTIES

Absence of Broad Contrasts in Policy.

IN less self-complacent times philosophers delighted to portray the impression that the world of their day would produce upon an intelligent but unsophisticated Persian sage. If such a one should casually stumble upon current English politics, and try to discover the essential differences in principle between the two great parties he would be sorely perplexed. "From their names," he might say, "I suppose that the Liberals are the party of progress, and the Conservatives are opposed to all change. I have, indeed, heard that an extension of the franchise was once brought about in some unexpected way, that I never understood, by a Tory ministry; but surely the other organic changes, the reform of county government in 1888, for example, must have been made by the Liberals, and resisted by the Conservatives as harassing legislation. No! How strange. Perhaps it is on social problems, the burning questions of the age, that the parties are divided. Liberals, no doubt, favour, and Conservatives denounce, labour laws and half-socialistic experiments such as municipal trading. What? Am I wrong again? Both parties profess to approve of these things, and in fact it was formerly the Liberals, rather than the Conservatives, who disbelieved in the protection of labour? Yet I cannot be mistaken in thinking that measures on such subjects must have been introduced by one party and opposed by the other; and that a party with sincere principles must consistently support or oppose all measures of a similar character. Is the difference between the parties religious? Ah! That I can understand. The Conservatives, perchance, want to extend their Established Church over Scotland, and the Liberals are pledged to disestablish it in England. No! Well, the Conservatives are called the Imperialist party. The Liberals, as Little Englanders, probably want to reduce the empire by abandoning some of the British possessions, while the Conservatives proclaim a policy of annexation by conquest, or at least are anxious to force the colonies into closer union. You say that both parties talk about a common political organ for the whole empire, and neither has been able to think of one? How very odd. There are boats that cross the Channel, are there not? I think I had better begin my observations in some country where politics are less hard to comprehend." So the sage would consult Bradshaw, brush up his French, and depart.

**Not Inconsistent with Frequent Party Votes.**

We have seen that the strictness with which party lines are drawn in Parliament, and the frequency of party votes there, do not imply fundamental differences of principle. On the contrary, if the differences lay very deep, the party in power would not resign in favour of the Opposition when beaten upon a question that did not touch those principles. If in 1852 or 1855, for example, the Conservatives had stood for a revolutionary policy, it is incredible that the Liberals would have given place to them on account of a defeat on a bill to reorganise the militia, or to change the law of conspiracy to murder. But if the cabinet did not quit office when defeated on questions that are not fundamental, its followers would split more readily on those questions, for they could do so without putting their main object in jeopardy. It is, indeed, because the parties are not separated by a wide gulf, that one of them can, without shock to the state, take charge of the government when the other gets into difficulties; and it is the constant fear of such a change of administration that makes the party in power act as a unit and shun any defeat. Thus the very conditions that make party votes frequent, and hence make the attitude of the parties on pending measures very definite, arise from the fact that their general principles are not sharply opposed, and are, therefore, often obscure. In some continental nations, where the creed of the parties is clearly defined, their relation to current questions may be confused. In the United States, on the other hand, where the parliamentary system does not exist, both the principles of the parties, and their stand on particular measures, are at times indistinct. But in England the opinions of the two front benches on all important bills are unmistakable, while their general political principles are not easily described with precision.

A few years ago there were three parties in Parliament: the Conservative, which had absorbed, or become amalgamated with, the Liberal Unionists; the Liberal; and the Irish Nationalist. But at the last election the Labour members became so numerous that for the time, at least, they must be regarded as a fourth party both in the state and in the House of Commons. An attempt will be made here to describe first the policy for which each of these parties stands, and then the elements in the community of which each is composed.

**The Classic Theory of Parties.**

The classic theory of parties in England is well stated by May at the beginning of the chapter on the subject in his "Constitutional History." "The parties in which Englishmen have associated," he says, "have represented cardinal principles of government, — authority on the one side, popular rights and privileges on the other. The former principle, pressed to extremes, would tend to absolutism,— the latter, to a republic: but, controlled within proper limits, they are both necessary for the safe working of a balanced constitution. When parties have lost sight of these principles, in pursuit of objects less worthy, they have degenerated into factions." The same idea is expressed by the familiar contrast drawn between a party of progress and a party of order; and it has a close analogy with Macaulay's description of the two eternal parties which bear to one another forever the relation of the fore and hind legs of a stag, both equally needful, but the same pair always in front — Macaulay himself belonging, of course, to that pair.

These conceptions would be all very well if every political issue could be brought within the formula of authority on one hand, and popular rights on the other, and if every man took the same side on every question according as it fell into one or other of these categories. They would be all very well if progress in human affairs, like that of a stag, took place in only one direction at a time, and the same party was always in favour of movement in whatever direction it might be. But unfortunately this is not true. A man or a party may desire progress, or change, in ecclesiastical or temperance legislation, and not in fiscal or foreign policy; and from a philosophic point of view we do not help matters by calling our opponent bad names, and saying that he wants to progress backwards. Now there are periods in the world's history when things are moving so rapidly under a common impulse, that people are divided into the sanguine who are inclined towards every movement proposed, and the cautious who distrust them all. The transition from older conditions to the modern industrial state gave rise to a period of this kind over a great part of continental Europe during the second and third quarters of the last century. In a lesser degree the same thing occurred in England also; but it is not a necessary, or indeed a normal, state of affairs.

The Liberals and Conservatives until 1874.

From the period of agitation that preceded the Reform Bill,[1] the mission of the party, which took soon afterwards the name of Liberal, was to bring the political system into accord with the changes that had come over the nation. It extended the franchise to the middle classes, especially in the new industrial centres, reformed the poor law, the criminal law, municipal government and the civil service, passed laws for the improvement of public health, established general elementary education, gave greater freedom

[1] The best description of earlier party movements is still to be found in George Wingrove Cooke's "History of Party."

to trade-unions, removed grievances of Dissenters, disestablished the Church in Ireland altogether, enlarged and complicated the local government, and created a system of central control. It may be said also to have been the main factor in taking away the restrictions on trade, for although the most important measure in that direction, the repeal of the Corn Laws, was carried by Sir Robert Peel, he did it only with the help of the Liberals, and against the bitter opposition of the bulk of the Tories. Meanwhile the other party, which had taken the name of Conservative, acted fairly well the part that the title implied. Still it would be a great mistake to suppose that the Conservatives were opposed to all change, or all constructive legislation. Quite aside from Peel's action on the Corn Laws, he created the Metropolitan Police in 1829, eleven years before the Liberals set up a general county police; and throughout this whole time the Conservatives were quite as friendly as the Liberals to factory acts for improving the condition of the working-classes.

**After 1874.** The period when the Liberals could claim anything approaching a monopoly of progress, drew near to its close when the Conservatives won their victory at the election of 1874; and it came to an end largely because the Liberals had worked out their chief problems. They had brought the state in its most important aspects into accord with modern conditions; the things still needed to complete the work were of minor consequence, and hence the momentum of the party had become very much reduced. Moreover, the Conservatives under the subtle lead of Disraeli had adopted progressive ideas, a tendency confirmed later by the adhesion of the band of militant Radicals that broke away from Mr. Gladstone at the time of the Home Rule Bill. In some ways the principles of the Conservatives underwent no greater change than those of the Liberals, for in their task of breaking down the old barriers that cramped the growth of industry, the Liberals had accepted the doctrine of *laissez-faire*, but when the time came for constructing new barriers against the evils caused by unlimited competition, that doctrine became a hinderance. Gradually the Liberals abandoned it, and of late years the parties have vied with each other in advocating not only factory acts, but measures to provide employees with compensation for accidents, to furnish better dwellings for the working-classes, to improve public health, to better local government, and in short to regulate everything with a view to hastening the millennium and putting it to the credit of the party in power.

**Present Tendencies of the Parties.**

The two great parties are separated to-day by no profound differences in general principles or political dogmas. But this does not mean that they are not marked by distinct tendencies, and still more by a tradition of tendencies. There is a theory held by the Liberals — although denied by their opponents — that they are more democratic, that they have more trust in the people, and more real sympathy with the workingmen. After enfranchising the middle class, and winning its support, they felt that any further extension of the suffrage must have a similar result. They considered the lower strata of society as their protectorate, or at least within their particular sphere of influence, and they still regard an alliance between the Conservatives and any fraction of the working-classes as unnatural. This feeling is shared by the Labour leaders, and one sometimes hears them say that the Liberals favour labour legislation from conviction, the Conservatives only to get votes. Nevertheless that belief is by no means universal among workmen, many of whom have been said to support the Conservatives on the ground that owing to their control of the House of Lords they are really the most effective party in enacting labour laws.

There is another theory to the effect that Liberals believe in peace, retrenchment and reform, and are less inclined than the Conservatives to an aggressive foreign policy. There is truth in this; although foreign policy depends to a great extent upon the personal views of the minister who has the principal charge of it. Lord Palmerston was notoriously aggressive in his relations with other nations; and it would be unsafe to predict a more bellicose or submissive tone at Downing Street whenever a change of cabinet takes place. In regard to retrenchment or economy, it is certain that national expenditure has increased very rapidly, and if the Liberals have been more cautious in spending money, they have followed the Tory lead, although like the hind legs of the stag, at some distance.

Again there is a theory that the Liberals give greater weight to local opinion, that they have more regard for the wishes of Scotland, Ireland and Wales, and that they are generally more favourably disposed toward local control. This also is not without foundation, but it is hardly a general political principle, and was certainly not applied in the case of the recent Education Bill.

On the other hand, there is a theory that the Conservatives have more respect for existing institutions, and dread to disturb venerable things. The impression is partly true, partly a tradition, and to some extent exaggerated. It was, in fact, the Conservatives who swept away, by the County Councils Act of 1888, the local government of the counties by justices of the peace, certainly a venerable institution, and if not in harmony with the spirit of the age, by no means moribund or indefensible. It was they, a dozen years earlier, who recast the judicial system, making the greatest single change in the courts that had been made for centuries. The Conservatives, no doubt, talk far less about attacking institutions, and the same act raises less of a storm if done by them than if done by the Liberals. The vested interests of the country are, indeed, more affected by a dread of what the Liberals may do than by what they have actually done.

All these tendencies have some effect in shaping the policy of the parties, and in determining their position on current questions; but the differences are in degree rather than in kind, and are liable to present strange shapes under the stress of party warfare.

The Land, the Church, the Publicans and the Nonconformists.

The most marked and permanent tendencies in which the parties differ are found in their attitude toward certain powerful interests in the community. The Conservatives tend strongly to favour the claims of the Church of England, of the landowners and now of the publicans, while the Liberals are highly sensitive to the appeals of the Nonconformist conscience. These again are tendencies, and must not be stated in too absolute a form. In 1870 the Liberals, by not going far enough in framing the first great Education Act, offended bitterly a large fraction, perhaps a majority, of their Nonconformist supporters. In 1875 the Conservatives enlarged the rights of tenants at the expense of the landlords, in the Agricultural Holdings Act; and in 1888, by taking from the justices of the peace the county administration, they deprived the owners of large landed estates of a great and ancient privilege. Nevertheless these tendencies are persistent, and have not lost their strength in recent years. They are illustrated by the Agricultural Rates and Rent-charge Acts,[1] which relieved land and tithes of a part of their burden, and caused the Liberals to complain of doles to the squire and the parson. They are shown also by the struggle over the Licensing Act of 1904, which gave the publicans a certain security of tenure in their licenses; and they appear most clearly in the Tory Education Act of 1902, and its counterpart, the Liberal bill of 1906.

The Aims of the Irish Nationalists.

The principles of the other two parties in the House of Commons are more definite, and can be described in a few words. The Irish Nationalists pursue what they believe to be the interests of the Irish people as a distinct nation. They want to abolish all coercion acts; to have the police and the schools managed according to their own views; they want the land transferred from the holders of large estates to the farmers; but above and behind all they want the largest measure of independent self-government for Ireland that it is possible to obtain. They are ready to act

[1] 59–60 Vic. c. 16; 62–63 Vic. c. 17.

with any party so long as it holds out a fair prospect of conceding a considerable part of their demands; but neither promises nor threats can make them forget their final object for one moment. After the Liberals adopted Home Rule they supported them generally against the Conservatives, because such a course gave the best prospect of reaching their end. They have no intention, however, of becoming permanently a section of the Liberal party, no matter how much it may rule Ireland in accordance with Irish ideas. They are utterly opposed to accepting good government as a substitute for self-government.

**The Principles of the Labour Parties.**

The principles of the various bodies that aim to procure a direct representation for labour in Parliament have already been described in the chapter that deals with their organisation, and it is only necessary here to remind the reader that the Social Democratic Federation and the Independent Labour Party are both frankly socialistic, with the difference that the former maintains an uncompromising attitude, while the latter, as a means to reach its ultimate goal, is willing to act with persons who do not fully accept its doctrines. The general election of 1906 brought the Social Democratic Federation only one member in Parliament, and he, together with the more numerous representatives of the Independent Labour Party, was included in the wider ranks of the new "Labour Party." This last body, founded upon the idea of common action by persons whose social theories are not wholly the same, is naturally based upon compromise, and therefore sets forth in its constitution no object beyond that of maintaining a direct representation of labour in Parliament. But the resolutions passed at its annual conferences are more precise, and may be taken to express its policy. They have comprised from time to time measures of various kinds for improving the condition of the working-classes; a more complete extension of democracy, including woman suffrage and the payment of members; local veto on the sale of liquor; and the application of socialistic principles in certain directions, such as municipal trading, free meals for school children, old-age pensions, and "taxation designed to secure for the community all unearned incomes derived from what is in reality communal wealth." [1]

Their Dilemma.

The Labour Party professes to stand primarily for the interests of the working-classes; and herein lies its immediate strength, and a permanent cause of weakness. The strength comes from its appeal to the direct interest of the most numerous class of voters in the country. The weakness flows from the same source. It is the weakness that affects labour movements as a whole throughout the world, and results from the fact that no system of ethics avowedly founded on the interests of one class, no matter how just its claims at the moment may be, can permanently retain the admiration of mankind. Labour leaders everywhere are placed in a dilemma. If they contemplate applying their aspirations to all people, they become socialists, and realize their utopia by reducing everybody to one condition. This is ethically consistent, but in England has not approved itself as practically expedient, even to the working-classes. If they do not do this, if they take the working-class alone into consideration, their scheme is essentially based on coöperative selfishness. The Labour Party in England could not adopt the first of these alternatives if it wanted to, for it would lose the major part of its support. It is, of course, tinged with socialism, but it is not thoroughly socialist. It advocates, therefore, the principles in regard to duration, pay and protection of labour, which are believed by workingmen the world over to be for their advantage, and it acts in close accord with the trade-unions as the chief organised representatives of labour. It seeks also to extend their privileges, and in fact these bodies have obtained, under the Act of 1906, a power coupled with a freedom from legal control which is extraordinary.

Their Tendency.

On general moral and political questions that do not immediately affect the labour problem, on such matters

[1] *E.g.* Rep. of Conf., 1906, p. 58.

as temperance, education, foreign policy and the relations with Ireland, the labour members tend strongly to take the view of the more radical element among the Liberals, and in the past a Conservative organiser has sometimes been heard to lament that the Labour leaders were Radicals first and Labour men afterwards. Most of the Labour members who sat in the House of Commons for any considerable length of time before the election of 1906, have, indeed, been gradually drawn closer to the Liberal party. Their views have become enlarged with the wider horizon, they have learned the necessity of compromise, and their principles are not carried so much to extremes. They form the nucleus of the Liberal Labour Group in Parliament, composed of those representatives of labour who are not willing to pledge themselves to remain wholly distinct from the two great divisions of the House, and to obey the decisions of the Labour Party. The Group acts independently on purely industrial questions, holding to that extent the same principles as the rest of the Labour men. But it forms in other ways a true left wing of the Liberal phalanx. How far the same process will in time affect the Labour Party, now that it has become a compact and not inconsiderable body, is one of the interesting questions of the future.

The Liberal Labour Group.

It is noteworthy that in spite of their socialistic tendency, in spite of the avowed intention to benefit workingmen at the expense of accumulated property, the great increase of Labour members in Parliament has caused little alarm, except among a part of the Conservatives. People say that it is quite proper for them to urge the interests of their class; that personally they are sensible men, whose conduct in the House has been correct; that with experience their demands will become more moderate; and that as the immediate grievance about trade-union funds has been removed, workingmen are likely to show less independent activity in politics.

Almost steadily since the wars of Napoleon the greater part of the peers and land-owning gentry have been Tory;

The Membership of the Parties.

but for a while this was far more than counterbalanced by the accession of strength that came to the Liberals from the middle classes enfranchised in 1832. By the Acts of 1867 and 1884 the suffrage was extended to the workingmen, and to the surprise of the Liberals they were soon divided between the parties not very unequally. About the same time changes took place in the political relations of the older classes of voters. Since the Reform Act of 1832 the Liberal party in Parliament had been composed of two elements that were never completely fused; the aristocratic families and their adherents, known as the Whigs, who stood for a moderate type of Liberalism; and the members drawn from the middle class, with a temper often distinctly Radical, who had scarcely been represented in the House of Commons at all before the Reform. As this last element gained influence the Whigs became uneasy, until first the Eastern question in 1876–78, and finally the Home Rule Bill drove many of them over to the other side. Thus in 1886 the Liberals lost most of the people of title, wealth or fashion, who had belonged to their party. Nor was the migration confined to that class. Formerly the manufacturers and merchants in the new industrial centres were normally Liberal. But as they accumulated wealth, and especially as their children inherited that wealth, the situation changed. Social aspirations awoke, while their political attitude, instead of being militant and aggressive, became defensive, and inclined them toward the party by tradition Conservative.[1] Here again the Home Rule Bill served to precipitate a tendency that had been maturing, and drew people of this kind away from the Liberal fold.

The Conservatives.

At the election of 1906, party ties were again unsettled; but it may be said that the Conservatives, including the Unionist Liberals, still comprise by far the greater part of the people of title, wealth, fashion or leisure; nearly all of the clergy of the Established Church; and a large majority

[1] Ostrogorski (I., 267) speaks of this transformation.

of the university graduates, of the members of the bar, and of the richer merchants and manufacturers. The clerks, also, and other employees, who live upon small fixed incomes and are by nature the most unchangeable of men, belong in the main to the Conservative party. The rest of the middle class, including the tradesmen or shopkeepers, appear on the whole to be not unevenly divided, although their politics varies much from place to place; and until the last election the same thing might have been said of the workingmen, with a preponderance in the long run in favour of the Liberals. It may be observed, however, that the influence of the Labour leaders and of the trade-unions, when not used to elect a distinct candidate of their own, is thrown almost wholly on the Liberal side. Different explanations of this are given, and they are significant. The Liberals, and the Labour leaders who are associated with them, ascribe it to the fact that the more intelligent workingmen belong to their party; a statement which appears to be in part, at least, correct. Conservatives, on the other hand, attribute the result to their own negligence in allowing the trade-unions, when first formed, to be captured by their opponents. This also contains much truth. The Tories have not encouraged workingmen to take a prominent part in politics, or to come forward as parliamentary candidates even under the Tory banner; and, in fact, there have been no Conservative workingmen in the House of Commons. The party expects men of that class to follow, not to lead, and it is not surprising, therefore, that Labour leaders should be drawn into another field.

**The Liberals.** The Liberal party contains normally a small fragment of the rank and wealth in the United Kingdom, a somewhat larger share of the professional and commercial classes, about one half of the middle class — if we omit the clerks — and at least half of the workingmen. From the religious standpoint its affiliations are noteworthy. Although the influence of the Established Church is thrown on the Conservative side, many Churchmen, and even a few of the clergy, are Liberal, but the religious support of the party comes from the Dissenters. The Wesleyans are, indeed, divided; but the other Nonconformists in England and Wales are heavily Liberal, contributing largely to the strength of the party and colouring its policy. Apart from the Irish Nationalists, the Catholic Church has no sensible effect upon the English political groups. In Scotland religion has much less connection with politics, just as it has little effect on social position. The Episcopal Church has no doubt a fellow-feeling with the Church of England, and tends to be Conservative, but it casts a small vote; and although the clergy of the Church of Scotland feel the same way, neither that body nor the Free Kirk can be said to be closely bound to one of the parties, or to exert any strong influence on either side.

The Labour Party.

The Socialist and Labour organisations that nominate candidates for Parliament appeal, of course, to the working-classes, and the real strength of the movement that has elected Labour members to the House, whether they belong to the Labour Party or to the Liberal Labour Group, lies in the trade-unions. Yet it would be a mistake to suppose that all trade-unionists, and still more that the bulk of the working-class, are associated with the movement. Nor, on the other hand, is the support of a Labour candidate at the polls confined to workingmen. When he is standing alone against a Conservative, and there is no third candidate, most Liberals of every class usually vote for him. But the actual membership of the Labour organisations is drawn exclusively from workingmen, and so long as they profess to represent the special interests of Labour this must almost necessarily be the case.

Geographical Distribution of Parties.

Geographically Great Britain is by no means sharply divided between the parties. Conservatives, Liberals, and to a lesser extent Labour men are scattered over every part of it; and yet the political distribution is far from uniform. The more deferential population in the South of England has on the whole a larger proportion of Conservatives than that of the North. For the same reason Scotland is a stronghold of Liberalism; while Wales, partly because it wants to disestablish the Church of England, is Liberal also.

The political contrast between the North and the South is based upon a difference of temperament, but is not the only geographical division to be found in politics. Any one who looks at one of the coloured charts of the British Isles issued after a general election can hardly fail to observe that the blue squares indicating Conservative victories are especially massed about a diagonal line running from the southeast to the northwest. The causes of this are many, and often local. London as the centre of wealth is inclined to be led by the Tories in National matters, and as the capital of the empire it tends naturally to be imperialist in politics. The Home Counties are normally Conservative from the nature of the population. Birmingham and the adjoining parts of the midlands have been Unionist largely through the influence of Mr. Chamberlain; while Liverpool and a large part of the employees in the cotton mills of Lancashire have long been Conservative. The southwest corner of Scotland also is distinctly less Liberal than the rest of that kingdom; and Ulster is heavily Conservative, because all people in Ireland who are not Nationalist are thrown almost perforce into the arms of the Unionists. To the west of the Conservative belt is Wales, with its firm Liberal attachments, and it may be noticed that Cornwall, Devonshire and their neighbours incline far more to the same side than the rest of the South. On the other side of the Tory belt lies East Anglia, and a number of adjoining counties, in which Liberal sentiment is far from weak; and finally to the north are Yorkshire, Durham, Northumberland and Scotland, all strongholds of Liberal ideas.

Alone among the parties in the House of Commons that of the Nationalists is based upon race; and it is rendered still more incapable of expansion, and impervious to impres- Ireland.

sions from without, by the fact that it is virtually a geographical party. Irish votes are an important factor in a number of English constituencies, but the Scotland division of Liverpool is the only one where they have ever been numerous enough to elect their own candidates, and there they win easily at every election. Save for that division the Nationalist members are entirely confined to Ireland, where, apart from a couple of seats in Dublin, the party, or a section of it, is practically certain to carry almost every constituency outside of Ulster. A study of the elements in the Nationalist party, therefore, while highly important in relation to certain aspects of popular government, sheds no light on the nature of the English political parties.[1]

[1] The Welsh members have often had a leader and whips of their own, but in reality they are only a fraction of the Liberal party.

# PART III.—LOCAL GOVERNMENT

## CHAPTER XXXVIII

### AREAS OF LOCAL GOVERNMENT

**The Older Subdivisions.**

All local administration is necessarily based upon a geographical subdivision of the country, which must be known before the action of the different local bodies can be understood. Now of all parts of the political machinery in England, this is historically the most confused, and although the system has been much simplified of late years, yet the past has bequeathed so many anomalies to the present that it is impossible to avoid some explanation of the stages that local government has gone through. At the time of the Norman Conquest England was divided into shires, hundreds or wapentakes or rapes, and townships, each with functions and organs of its own. Of these the shires or counties, while changing their form of government, have always retained their importance. As the Plantagenet kings extended the royal power by means of the itinerant judges, the county court became the centre through which their authority was exerted; and at a later time, when, after a number of experiments in maintaining order in the realm, justices of the peace were created under Edward III., the county was the area of their jurisdiction. With the expanding needs of the times their powers were gradually increased by an ever lengthening list of statutes, until the whole government of the county, administrative as well as judicial, was placed in their hands. Appointed by reason

**The Shire.**

of their landed interest and their standing in the shire, they presented an aristocratic type of local self-government.

The Hundred.

The hundred had a very different history. Little needed and therefore well-nigh neglected by the Crown on one side, and weakened on the other by feudal practices and the encroachments of the manor, it became unimportant. Like most ancient British institutions, it was not abolished, nor did it disappear altogether. It lingered as a shadowy territorial division, but lost vitality to such an extent that when in the nineteenth century administrative areas intermediate between the county and the smallest units were needed, they were recreated quite regardless of the old hundreds.

The Township and Parish.

The township, or vill, in its ancient shape met a similar fate, but in another form it has survived to the present day. For a time it was very nearly absorbed by the manor, and might have disappeared with the decline of feudal customs, had not the activity of the Church given a fresh impetus to local life. The division of the inhabited parts of the country into parishes, which began in the Anglo-Saxon times, is said to have been completed by the reign of Edward III., long before the manors fell into decay. In area the parish was, in the main, the ancient township; but in the thinly peopled counties of the north it often covered far more than one township, while in the south a single township might include more than one parish. Moreover, the boundaries were not such as to prevent the lines of a parish from intersecting those of a county. Nor was this of much consequence, because the parish was not an administrative subdivision of the county. Many parishes, indeed, like the counties themselves, had outlying portions not contiguous with the rest. But while the motive force in the formation of the parish came from the Church, neither its government nor its functions were, in later times at least, wholly ecclesiastical. The ruling body came to be a mass meeting of all the inhabitants or freemen, called the vestry because it met in the robing room of the priest attached to the village church, or sometimes the common vestry to distinguish it from a representative body that had sprung up in some places and was known as the select vestry. It elected a number of officers, and chief among them the churchwardens. This organisation lasted until the re-casting of local administration in the nineteenth century, and thus while local self-government in the county, where the larger affairs were conducted, was aristocratic, for small matters, in the parish, it was democratic. The parish had long performed some civil functions; and when the monasteries, which had played a chief part in the support of the poor, were dissolved, and economic changes, by dislocating the conditions of labour, had made the question of pauperism a burning one, the Tudor monarchs laid the burden of poor relief upon the parishes. The statute of Elizabeth provided that each parish should elect overseers of the poor, the churchwardens to be among them *ex officio*.

The Borough.

Meanwhile the boroughs had grown up with a local life of their own, and had become separate units of local government, subordinate, indeed, in most cases to the justices of the peace for many purposes, but by no means administrative subdivisions of the county. A borough was not of necessity within a single shire; still less did its area coincide with that of a parish. It might well cover parts of several parishes without including the whole of any one of them. It arose from economic causes, and its boundaries might intersect all existing political lines. It obtained by charter from the Crown a right to regulate certain of its internal affairs, but except in cases where the authority of the justices of the peace was in whole or in part excluded, its territory remained under the ordinary local administration, so that its inhabitants were subject not only to its own officers, but also to the justices of the peace and the parish vestry within whose jurisdiction they happened to reside. The charters were far from uniform, and hence the municipal organisations presented a great variety of pattern, often that of a close, self-perpetuating, corporation quite independent of the great body of citizens.

The New Areas.

Such in its outlines was the condition of local government in England when the era of reconstruction began after the Reform Act of 1832.

The Poor Law Union.

One of the first subjects to engage the attention of the reformed Parliament was the care of the poor, which had fallen into a very bad state. The giving of outdoor relief had become so general that it was used to eke out the wages of able-bodied men, and a large part of the agricultural labouring class had been virtually pauperised. Acting upon the advice of a royal commission, Parliament determined to put an end to outdoor support of this kind, by giving assistance only in the workhouse in all but exceptional cases. Although the ordering of relief had passed largely into the hands of the justices of the peace, the parish, with its overseers who administered the relief, was still the natural geographical basis for the care of the poor. But as the parishes were very uneven in size, and as a rule too small to work economically, it was decided to group them into larger districts known as unions. Such a combination of parishes, which had been permitted by an Act of 1782, formed, therefore, an essential part of the great Poor Law Amendment Act of 1834. Commissioners were appointed under the Act with very extensive powers of control over the local officers; but their first duty was to form the unions themselves. In doing so they considered mainly the convenience in administering the poor law. A number of parishes near to a market town or other centre were grouped together, with little regard to any other unit of local government. Nor did this lead to any immediate difficulty, because the work of the union was quite independent of that of other local bodies, and was under the direct supervision of the commissioners in London. The result, however, was that the unions included both urban and rural communities, and often overlapped the boundaries of the counties; in fact, nearly one third of them did so.[1]

[1] Unfortunately also the grouping was done before railways had been built.

The Guardians.

The relief of the poor in the union, coupled later with other powers, was entrusted to a new authority created for the purpose and called the board of guardians. The justices of the peace were guardians *ex officio*, while the rest were elected on a complicated plan designed to give peculiar weight to property. All owners of land and all ratepayers were entitled to vote, and they had from one to six votes apiece, according to the amount of property which they owned, or on which they paid rates as occupiers. But a man, if qualified, might vote both as an owner of land and an occupying ratepayer, and hence might have as many as twelve votes.[1] This system of plural voting was adopted for other local authorities that were created later, and lasted for sixty years until it was abolished in 1894. Thus the Poor Law Act of 1834 introduced both a new local area, and a system of representation which, if not wholly new, differed from anything existing in the other organs of English local government.[2]

The Highway and Burial Districts.

The next year an act was passed requiring the appointment of a surveyor by every parish that maintained its own highways,[3] and this, by the way, had by no means always the same area as the parish for other objects.[4] The act provided, also, that such parishes might, at their own request, be united for the maintenance of highways, with a common surveyor acting for them all. At a later time the policy of joint management was carried farther, and the justices of the peace in quarter sessions were given compulsory powers to combine parishes for the purpose under a highway board.[5] Now the highway districts so formed had no connection with the poor law unions, and,

[1] By § 40 of the Act (4–5 Will. IV., c. 76) occupiers had only three votes; but this was changed to six votes, and the scale was made the same for owners and occupiers, by 7–8 Vic., c. 101, § 14.

[2] The plural vote for owners was copied from a regulation for voting at vestry meetings made a few years earlier, by 58 Geo. III., c. 69, § 3.

[3] 5–6 Will. IV., c. 50.

[4] Odgers, "Local Government," 173–74.

[5] 25–26 Vic., c. 61; 27–28 Vic., c. 101. §§ 13–14 of this last act provide specially for the creation of highway districts overlapping county boundaries.

in fact, seldom coincided with them.[1] The subject of cemeteries was treated in a similar way. Under a series of acts beginning in 1852, parochial areas — not necessarily identical with any other kind of parish — were empowered to provide burial grounds, and elect burial boards to take charge of them; and again these places were allowed to combine and form a distinct set of local government districts.[2]

**Sanitary Districts.**

Another class of territorial divisions designed to meet a special need resulted from the epidemic of cholera in 1847 and 1848, which brought to public attention the defective sanitary condition of thickly settled places. By an act passed in the latter year a General Board of Health was created with power to set up a local board of health in "any city, town, borough, parish, or place," which petitioned for it, or where the death rate was high. The General Board was expressly given power to determine the boundaries that might be most advantageously adopted for the area in question, and to make them different from the existing political divisions. In a borough the local board of health was to be the council; but if the borough formed a part only of the sanitary district, the council was to choose its share of the members of the board, while any part of the district not covered by a borough, or the whole district, if no borough were included therein, was to elect members of the local board of health by the same system of plural voting whereby guardians were chosen in poor law unions.[3]

**Improvement Act Districts.**

Meanwhile, by various special acts applying to particular places, a number of improvement act districts were created, under improvement commissioners with sanitary and other powers. But it is needless for our purpose to follow all the different local bodies, conservancy boards, port sanitary authorities, and the rest, that were set up during the middle period of the nineteenth century. It will suffice to mention

[1] Odgers, "Local Government," 175.

[2] *Cf.* Odgers, 186–89. Wright and Hobhouse, "Local Government," 64–65, 67.

[3] 11–12 Vic., c. 63, and see 21–22 Vic., c. 98.

the statute which brought to its culmination the policy of creating for a fresh need a new agency working in a new district.

School Districts.

The Elementary Education Act of 1870 [1] in providing for the first time schools under public management, required the formation of school boards wherever elementary education was deficient, the election to be conducted by the method of cumulative voting, a device hitherto untried in England and designed to insure the representation of minorities. Each borough was to be a separate school district, and so was each parish or part of a parish outside of a borough; but the Education Department was given the usual power to combine parishes into united school districts as they saw fit. In places where schools enough existed already under private management, school boards could also be formed at the option of the voters, for the purpose of passing and enforcing by-laws to compel attendance. This last object was carried out fully by the Act of 1876,[2] which provided that wherever school boards did not exist, the borough council or the poor law guardians should appoint school attendance committees to enforce the universal compulsory attendance introduced by that Act. Thus the Education Acts brought in to some extent new districts, and wholly new authorities, chosen on a brand new plan, while the duty of compelling children to go to school was thrown in part upon existing local bodies.

Chaos and Simplification.

With the Elementary Education Act of 1870 the confusion of local areas and authorities reached its highest point. The country was now divided into counties, unions, and parishes, and spotted over with boroughs and with highway, burial, sanitary, improvement act, school, and other districts. Except for parishes and unions, none of these areas bore any necessary relation to any of the rest, and each of them was under an authority of its own, often wholly independent of all other organs of local government,

[1] 33–34 Vic., c. 75. [2] 39–40 Vic., c. 79, § 7.

and sometimes selected upon a plan quite peculiar to itself. The policy pursued up to this time had been that of providing for each fresh need, as it arose, a special machinery adapted for that particular need. Such a creation of *ad hoc* authorities, as they have been commonly called, caused little practical inconvenience so long as the different bodies working within the same territory were not too numerous; while the intersection of boundaries did not become intolerable until the lesser local authorities were made subordinate to the greater. Moreover, there is an obvious justification in a special agency set up to meet a certain want in a particular place, which does not apply when the same agency is extended universally over the country; and it may be observed that in 1871 the only modern organs of local government that covered the whole land were the boards of poor law guardians, all the others — local boards of health, improvement commissioners, school boards, and the rest — having been established hitherto only in places peculiarly in need of them. Now in 1872 it became necessary not only to add to the local organs, which were already very numerous, but also to spread another network of authorities over the whole kingdom; and although the confusion of areas and authorities was by no means actually reduced, an effort not to increase it is distinctly perceptible.

**Public Health Acts of 1872 and 1875.**

The greater knowledge of the causes of disease, and the growing interest in sanitary questions, gave rise to a desire to extend throughout the land some of the provisions made for thickly settled places by the Act of 1848. This was done by the Public Health Act of 1872,[1] which divided the whole country into urban and rural sanitary districts. The urban districts were to be the boroughs, with the council acting as the sanitary authority, and, outside of the boroughs, the improvement act districts, with the improvement commissioners exercising the same powers, as well as the local government districts created under the Act of 1848, where these functions were vested in the local board of

[1] 35–36 Vic., c. 79.

health.[1] So far no substantial change was made; but the act went on to provide that any poor law union, or any part of a union, not included in an urban district, should be a rural district, and here the sanitary authority was the board of guardians — the members, however, who came from a portion of the union outside of the rural district being forbidden to take part.[2] These provisions were repeated in the great Act of 1875, which codified the law of public health.[3] Thus the rural districts were conterminous with the rural parts of poor-law parishes and unions, because, with rare exceptions, those districts were composed of whole parishes, or all the rural parts of parishes, and they were entirely included in the unions. The Act also placed the management of the rural sanitary districts in the hands of the same persons who represented the district on the governing body of the union. But while the new rural districts were thus fitted into the existing geography of parishes and unions, the boroughs and other urban sanitary districts, remaining untouched, cut across the parish and union lines without remorse, and the old county lines were disregarded by every other local area.

**The Creation of County Councils, and the Act of 1888.**

The Public Health Acts of 1872 and 1875 had taken care in creating rural sanitary districts not to make confusion worse confounded, but they had done nothing to lessen the existing complication; and little was attempted in that direction until it was proposed to bring the counties into the sphere of representative government by giving them elective councils with some control over lesser local bodies.[4]

[1] For the exceptional cases where the borough did not coincide in area with an improvement act or local government district, see Glen, "Law of Public Health," 12 Ed., 37–40. These cases have now almost wholly disappeared.

[2] The sanitary authority consisted, therefore, of the guardians elected by that part of the union included in the district, and the *ex officio* guardians residing, or owning property, there. (11–12 Vic., c. 63, § 9.)

[3] 38–39 Vic., c. 55.

[4] A somewhat feeble effort to simplify local government in a minor matter was made by the Highways and Locomotives Act of 1878 (41–42 Vic., c. 77), which provided that so far as possible highway districts should be made to coincide with rural sanitary districts, and that when this was

This was done by the Local Government Act of 1888,[1] which provided that every county should have an elective council on the pattern of a borough council, and transferred to that body all the administrative functions hitherto exercised by the justices of the peace.[2] A commission had been appointed the year before to consider the best means of adjusting boundaries so that no union, borough, sanitary district, or parish should be in more than one county; and the object was carried out in part by a provision of the Act of 1888 that every urban sanitary district — including every borough, not an administrative county by itself — should belong wholly to the county which comprised the largest part of its population.[3] The county councils were, moreover, directed to take the report of the commission into consideration, general powers being given to them, and to the Local Government Board, to alter the boundaries of the various local divisions.[4] But experience has shown that a merely permissive power has little effect against the tenacity with which local patriotism clings to existing conditions; and in this case the provision in the Act does not appear to have been much used, for a return made in 1893 [5] shows that two hundred and twelve parishes, and about one third of the rural sanitary districts and poor law unions, were still in more than one county.[6] A large part of this confusion was, however, removed by the last great act on local government.

the case, the rural sanitary authority might become the highway board. But such an arrangement seems rarely to have been effected. Odgers, 176.

[1] 51–52 Vic., c. 41.

[2] Except the control of the police which was, and still is, vested in a joint committee of the council and the justices of the peace (§ 9).

[3] § 50 (b).

[4] §§ 53–54, 57–60.

[5] Com. Papers, 1893, LXXVII., 491.

[6] Of the 613 unions, 176 were in more than one administrative county, while 60 more were partly in an administrative county and partly in a county borough. In only 53 cases did a union not include a rural sanitary district, and when it did not it usually included the whole or parts of more than one urban district or borough. In fact unions coincided with a borough or urban district in only 12 cases, and with a rural district in only 104 cases.

As the Act of 1888, passed by a Conservative ministry, created county councils on a democratic basis, so the Act of 1894,[1] passed under a Liberal cabinet, carried the same principle into the smaller units of local government. *Ex officio* members and plural voting were swept away, and the authorities for parish, sanitary district and union were henceforth to be chosen on a simple and nearly uniform system of representation. At the same time the authorities themselves were reorganised, and the areas under their control were brought into more harmonious relations. The Act of 1894.

The Act begins with the rural parish,[2] creating a parish council wherever there are more than three hundred inhabitants, and elsewhere a parish meeting of all the voters, and conferring on these bodies, among other things, the civil powers of the old vestry. The sanitary districts are then taken up. These are renamed more simply urban and rural districts, or collectively county districts; but except for the change in the method of representation, the act alters their organisation in substance very little. The urban district continues to elect separately its district council and its quota of guardians for the union; while in rural districts these two offices are still discharged by the same persons. But whereas by the earlier law the board of guardians, so far as its members represented the rural district, was the authority thereof, by the Act of 1894, the two bodies were made legally distinct; the persons, however, remaining the same; so that even when the district covered the whole of the union, the board of guardians and the rural district council, although composed of precisely the same people, transact their business separately and keep separate sets of records.

[1] 56–57 Vic., c. 73.

[2] In boroughs and urban districts, where the population is more dense, the powers of the principal local authority are of necessity greater than in rural areas, and hence there is less need of the triple division of local government. The parish is, therefore, far less important in urban places, and the Act of 1894 left it untouched, save for a provision (in §§ 33–34) which empowered the Local Government Board to transfer many of its functions to the council of the borough or district.

**Its Effect on Local Areas.** The Act of 1894 wrought a drastic change in rural areas, bringing the boundaries of counties, districts, and parishes almost wholly into line at a stroke, and thus making the district a true subdivision of the county, with the parish in turn a subdivision of the district. It provided that, where part of a parish was within, and part outside, a county district, each part should become a separate parish, and that the same thing should happen to a rural district that stretched into two counties; unless in either of these cases the county council should for special reasons otherwise direct.[1] The changes were made automatically by the Act itself; but they involved subsidiary adjustments, both by the county councils and the Local Government Board, which became, therefore, exceedingly busy for a time with questions of areas and boundaries.[2] The Act swept away another *ad hoc* division, by abolishing highway boards and transferring their powers to the district councils. Burial boards, on the other hand, were not abolished by the Act, and the area of poor-law unions was not directly affected, but provision was made for absorbing the powers of the former, and they diminished rapidly in number.[3] The Education Act of 1902 having since abolished the school boards, and vested their functions in the councils of the counties and larger boroughs, the only *ad hoc* districts of importance that now remain are the unions, and in these the authorities are not *ad hoc* in the rural parts of the country.

**Existing Local Divisions.** At last something like a systematic subdivision of the country for local government has been evolved out of the chaos which, strangely enough, had been deliberately created by the legislation of the two middle quarters of the nineteenth century. Although still blurred by some anom-

[1] §§ 1 (3), 24 (5), 36. The case of an urban district or borough that overlapped the county boundary had already been provided for by the Act of 1888.

[2] The Appendix to the report of the Local Government Board giving a list of the changes of local areas fills in 1893 seven pages, and in 1895 seventy-two pages.

[3] Odgers, 188–89.

alies, it is now possible to sketch the normal pattern of English local administration in comparatively simple outlines.

Counties and County Boroughs.

The whole country is divided into counties[1] and county boroughs, the larger towns being for administrative purposes counties by themselves.[2] Each of these divisions is governed by a single body called the council, composed of representatives popularly elected by wards, and of additional members, called aldermen, chosen by the council itself. The details are slightly different in the counties and county boroughs, but the general principles are the same; and in the latter the county powers are simply vested in the same council that governs the borough in other respects.

Boroughs, Districts,

The county is subdivided into boroughs and urban and rural districts, each of which is governed by a council formed on the same plan as a county council, save that in the district councils there are no additional members, or aldermen, elected by the council itself.[3] The functions of these councils differ very much, those of the boroughs being the most, and those of the rural districts the least, extensive. For that very reason the boroughs and urban districts, and of course the county boroughs, although usually divided into wards for electoral purposes, can hardly be said to be subdivided for local government, the powers of urban parishes being insignificant. The rural districts, on the other hand, are divided into parishes which possess

And Parishes.

[1] This is properly called the administrative county to distinguish it from the ancient county or county at large, from which it differs by the exclusion of the county boroughs, and by the changes in boundaries made in consequence of the Acts of 1888 and 1894. The county at large still exists for elections to Parliament, and in some cases for judicial purposes and for the militia, although as a general rule these last two matters follow the changes made in the administrative county. (51–52 Vic., c. 41, § 59.) There are in England and Wales only fifty-two counties at large, but in consequence of divisions for purposes of local government there are sixty-two administrative counties, only half a dozen of which now coincide in area with the counties at large.

[2] This privilege was intended for boroughs which had, or should thereafter attain, a population of 50,000, although some smaller places were included in the list because they were already counties of themselves. (51–52 Vic., c. 41, §§ 31, 54, and Sched. 3; *cf.* Wright and Hobhouse, "Local Govt." 2 Ed., 24–26.)

[3] 56–57 Vic., c. 73, §§ 23–24.

real functions, and were intended, at least, to take an active part in local administration; those with more than three hundred inhabitants having elected councils, and the rest transacting their business in mass meeting.[1]

London. The metropolis does not fall into this system of local government, but is organised on a plan of its own. The City of London, with its ancient limits, retains its old institutions, independently of the vast town that has grown up around it; while the rest of the metropolitan area is under a county council, created at the same time, and on the same general pattern, as other county councils. The territory over which it rules was divided in 1899 into boroughs, with councils to which the powers of the former parish vestries have been transferred;[2] and thus London is treated as a borough of the second degree.

Poor-law Unions. Cutting athwart this checkerboard of local areas the only important cross division remaining, that of the poor-law unions, covers the whole country with another network of lines. The members of the board which rules the union are still called guardians, and in the urban parts of a union they are separately elected, while in the rural parts they are simply the members of the rural district council elected there.

Anomalies. Described in this way the scheme of English local government may not seem complex, but in fact it is less simple than it appears, because there are in many places divers peculiarities and exceptions, under ancient local customs and special local acts, which mar the symmetry of the plan. Moreover, the areas, though simplified, are not laid out upon any uniform geographical pattern. Divisions of the same order are very unequal in size, for they were originally

[1] In the past there have been many kinds of parishes (Odgers, 44–48. Wright and Hobhouse, 1–8. Redlich and Hirst, "Local Govt.," II., 161–70), but now there are only two of any real importance, the poor-law or civil, and the ecclesiastical, parish. By two distinct series of acts the parishes of both kinds have been so changed that in most cases the ecclesiastical no longer coincides with the civil parish. The former is under its own vestry and church-wardens, who have no civil powers.

[2] 62–63 Vic., c. 14.

formed for immediate convenience or by political accident. Nor do they always conform to the object they were intended to serve. A number of the urban districts, for example, had at the census of 1901 less than one thousand inhabitants, and one of them had only two hundred and nineteen. Clearly these are in no true sense urban, or thickly settled places. Some of them became local government districts before 1872 because that was the only way they could get the benefit of the sanitary legislation of the time, and then they were turned into urban districts by the mechanical operation of subsequent statutes. Others, no doubt, sought to be made urban districts to avoid absorption by neighbouring urban districts, just as districts have obtained charters as boroughs to escape annexation by an adjoining borough. But if the plan of local government is still not wholly symmetrical, and if the form of organisation does not in all cases correspond with the true character of the place, historic traditions have in the main been so far preserved, and the habit of common public activity has been so far acquired, that for the most part the local bodies are full of a vigorous life.[1]

**Growth of Urban Population.**

One thing more remains to be noticed which has a bearing upon the whole English political system, and that is the growth of urban at the expense of rural communities. The population living in the metropolis, in the boroughs, and in the urban districts of England and Wales, is more than four times as great as that which dwells under a strictly rural form of government, and the proportion tends constantly to increase.[2] In short, England is becoming more and more a collection of cities, and this has already wrought a marked change in the character and political temperament of her people.

[1] This, as will be observed hereafter, is not generally true of the parishes.
[2] By the census of 1901 there were 666 rural districts with a population of 7,471,242; 1121 urban districts (including boroughs) with 20,518,205; while London had 4,536,063; and this, with 545 in sundry castles and small islands not included in any district, made up the 32,526,075 people of England and Wales.

# CHAPTER XXXIX

## BOROUGHS.[1] — THE TOWN COUNCIL

The Laws Governing Boroughs.

THE flood of reform that carried away many old abuses in the thirties, reached the boroughs in 1835. With a statute of that year the modern history of the English town begins,[2] and in fact the form of government then established has since been little changed. In other respects the law was amended often, until in 1882 the various statutes were consolidated in the Municipal Corporations Act of 1882[3] which governs all the provincial boroughs at the present day.[4] That Act, with its amendments, regulates the organisation, and to some extent the powers of the boroughs; but they derive by far the greater part of their functions from other sources, and especially from the Public Health Acts. These confer many important powers and duties on all urban sanitary authorities, placing them in the case of boroughs in the hands of the borough council.[5] A number

[1] Formerly a borough that sent members to the House of Commons was also an area of local government; but an addition to a municipal borough does not affect the constituency for Parliament; and hence by successive changes it has come about that many municipal boroughs no longer coincide with the parliamentary boroughs of the same name. The two have now no necessary connection. It may be noted also that except for the City of London, which alone among British towns has retained its ancient institutions, the word "city" has no significance in English municipal government. Formerly it meant that the place was, or had been, the seat of a bishop, but of late the title has been granted to several large boroughs *honoris causa*.

[2] The corresponding Scotch act was passed in 1833. [3] 45–46 Vic., c. 50.

[4] The boroughs left untouched by the Act of 1835 were either brought under the general law, or lost their privileges, in 1883 (46–47 Vic., c. 18); and by the Interpretation Act of 1889 (52–53 Vic., c. 63, § 15), a borough is now defined for municipal purposes as "any place for the time being subject to the Municipal Corporations Act, 1882."

[5] Almost all the exceptions have been abolished. *Cf.* Glen, "Law of Public Health," 12 Ed., 1899, 37–40.

of other statutes of a general nature also give powers of various kinds, and then there are a series of adoptive acts whose provisions a borough may accept or not as it pleases.

But statutes that apply, or may apply, equally to all municipalities by no means exhaust the subject, for alongside of the general public acts Parliament has never slackened the practice of passing special local acts for particular places. Except in the case of the metropolis these have been passed almost always, if not invariably, on the petition of the place itself. Occasionally they have affected the form of town government in some minor point, but in the main they have related to the grant of powers not universally conferred; and in fact a large part of those public functions commonly known as municipal trading have arisen in this way. In order, therefore, to know the law governing any particular borough, it is necessary to study both the general statutes and the many local acts affecting that place alone. Nevertheless, the local acts have as a rule followed precedents very closely, and what is more, the general direction of municipal progress has been much the same all over the country, so that not only are all the boroughs organised on a common pattern, but their powers and activities are in the main alike so far as they extend.

**Creation and Enlargement of Boroughs.**

By the Act of 1882 the King in Council may grant a charter of incorporation under the Act to any place, on a petition by the inhabitants thereof;[1] but while no limit of population is prescribed by the Act, and the boundaries may be fixed at pleasure by the Crown, size is naturally one of the facts taken into consideration in granting a charter. The annexation of populous suburbs by an existing borough is not less important than the creation of a new borough,

[1] 45–46 Vic., c. 50, §§ 210–18. Although the Crown has not lost its Common Law right of granting a charter of incorporation to a borough, it cannot confer the powers contained in this Act, and among them perhaps the power of taxation, except in accordance with the Act itself. Rutter *vs.* Chapman, 1, M. & W., 1.

and it may be brought about either by a private act, or by a provisional order of the Local Government Board confirmed by Parliament.[1] The principles applied in these two methods of procedure are very much the same. One borough, for example, is never merged in another without its own consent, and it is significant that the desire of a municipal body to preserve its independent existence is very strong even where the interests of the inhabitants would appear to be identical with those of the larger neighbour. The result is that a closely built unbroken town is often composed of a couple of boroughs, as in the case of Manchester and Salford, Liverpool and Bootle, Rochester and Chatham, Newcastle and Gateshead. This rule is not extended to a suburb that is not a borough, and hence a populous district adjoining a great town often applies for a charter of its own in self-defence. Annexation to a borough usually brings to the suburb, with enlarged public service, an increase in rates the dread of which provokes strenuous opposition on the part of the inhabitants. The facts considered in deciding such cases are the convenience and economy of common water supply, drainage and other public works, and the excellence of the government of the suburb. A number of annexations are made every year, and these with the grants of new charters swell the steady growth of the municipal population. There are now about three hundred and fifty boroughs in England and Wales, and they contain very nearly one half of the people of the kingdom outside of the metropolis.

The Electorate.

The qualifications for voting at a municipal election, for being enrolled as a burgess as it is called, are less complex than in the case of the parliamentary franchise. They consist in the "occupation, joint or several, of any house, warehouse, counting house, shop, or other building" of any value, or of land of ten pounds yearly value, for the twelve

[1] Local Govt. Act, 1888 (51–52 Vic., c. 41), § 54. For this subject see Redlich and Hirst, I., Book II., Part I., Ch. ii., an excellent chapter by Mr. Hirst.

months preceding July 15, and residence during that time in the borough or within seven miles thereof.[1] The rates, or local taxes, assessed upon the property must have been paid; but in fact few persons forfeit their right to vote by a failure to pay the rates, because of the universal practice of compounding, that is the payment by the landlord of the rates upon a group of small tenements in consideration of a reduction in the assessment.[2]

As usual in English election laws, the term "house" or "building" does not imply a whole structure, but means any part of a house or building which is separately occupied; and thus every one who hires an apartment, store, or workshop, however small, is entitled to vote. The municipal differs from the parliamentary franchise in boroughs chiefly in the fact that it does not include lodgers[3] — who form, however, in most places, a small fraction of the parliamentary register — that it includes occupiers of shops renting for less than ten pounds a year,[4] and far more important that it includes unmarried women and widows who possess the requisite qualification.[5] On the average the electorate for the borough council is about one eighth larger than that for Parliament,[6] the difference consisting

[1] Rogers on "Elections," 16 Ed., I., 176 *et seq.* In the case of land or building of the value of £10, only six months' residence is required, and by Acts of 1885 and 1891 absence of not more than four months on duty, or by reason of letting one's dwelling-house, does not prevent enrollment.

[2] The receipt of public relief is, however, a disqualification. But this does not apply to medical assistance, or the payments of school fees.

[3] Freemen also have no votes as such in the ancient boroughs where they still exist.

[4] That this is by no means always unimportant is clear from the fact that in Cardiff, for example, the number of buildings (including offices) rated at or under £10 was 4882 out of 32,418 buildings rated (Cardiff Year Book, 1900, p. 87).

[5] The Act of 1882 (§ 63) says that with reference to the right to vote the masculine gender includes women; but it has been held that this does not remove the disability of marriage at Common Law. Curiously enough the disability has been taken away by statute in the case of parish voters, although a husband and wife cannot qualify on the same property. Rogers, I., 187–88.

[6] See a return to the London County Council on Feb. 4, 1898, p. 13, giving the total percentages for fifty-nine large English boroughs.

mainly of the women voters. But the figures vary a good deal in different places. In Manchester and Bradford, for example, the excess of municipal voters is larger than this,[1] while in Cardiff and the administrative county of London it is much less, in the last case, at least, on account of the large number of lodgers on the lists.[2]

How nearly Universal.

It may be observed that the municipal suffrage is not universal, nor on the other hand is it confined to residents. Leaving out women, the registered voters form as in the case of Parliament about one sixth of the population, or more than three quarters of the men of voting age. Making allowance for those who fail to register through negligence, the proportion of men excluded is not very large. It consists mainly of servants, of bachelors living with their families, and of men who have migrated within sixteen months of the election. Such people have not a large stake in the community, but neither are they the poorest and most thriftless class. The slums, as one constantly hears, are not now disfranchised. On the other hand, men of affairs, who live in the suburbs and carry on business in the borough, are entitled to vote there, without, of course, losing their right to vote in the place of their residence also; and they form an excellent body of voters. How numerous they are it is impossible to ascertain with certainty, because they are not recorded separately in the registration lists. They are not nearly so many as they would be in most American cities, with wide outskirts of wooden houses reaching far into the country, and their number must vary much from place to place. In Birmingham the writer was told that they formed a trifling part of the register, in Glasgow that they ran into the thousands.

Scotland.

The municipal franchise in Scotland is not, indeed, ex-

[1] It is about one fifth in each of them. Handbook of Manchester, 1899, pp. 347–48. Year Book of Bradford, 1897–98, pp. 199, 207.

[2] Cardiff Year Book, 1900, pp. 85–86. Register of Voters in London for 1900, prepared for the L.C.C., January, 1900. This was before the franchise for the County Council of London was extended in 1900 to include lodgers and service occupiers.

actly the same as in England. Save for the inclusion of unmarried women, of peers, and of persons residing more than seven miles from the borough, it is almost identical with the parliamentary franchise.[1] But there is an important difference between the English and Scotch electorates, both parliamentary and municipal, which comes from the Scotch practice of assessing only a part of the rates upon the occupiers, and not allowing compounding of that part by the landlord. The result is that a very large number of the less thrifty people are not on the voting lists. In Glasgow, in 1892, 28,152 persons, a number equal to about one quarter of the registered voters, were excluded in this way, and in such a case the provision is tantamount to a considerable property qualification.[2]

**Elections.** The only municipal offices now filled by a vote of the burgesses are those of borough councillors and elective auditors. The latter, normally chosen on the first of March, are not in fact officers of any great consequence; and hence the sole important election is that of the first of November in each year, when the voters choose councillors, who are the legal centre and source of the whole government in the borough. The procedure for nomination and election is copied, in the main, from the rules for parliamentary elections.[3] The secret ballot prescribed by the Ballot Act is applied, and there are similar provisions forbidding corrupt and illegal practices, regulating expenses,[4] and creating a

[1] 63–64 Vic., c. 49, § 23; 3 Edw. VII., c. 34, § 2.

[2] Com. Papers, 1893, LXXVII., 1199; *cf.* Shaw, 41–42. In Glasgow in 1896 there were 122,678 municipal voters registered, of whom 20,437 were women. Bell and Paton, "Glasgow," 63. The proportion of persons excluded by non-payment of rates varies a good deal in the different Scotch towns. In Dundee, for example, it is much larger than in Glasgow; in Aberdeen much less.

[3] 45–46 Vic., c. 50, Parts III., IV., and Sched. III.; 47–48 Vic., c. 70. *Cf.* Rogers on Elections, Vol. III.

[4] These are fixed at £25, with 3*d.* more for each registered voter above five hundred. The expenditure of municipal authorities in holding the election is defrayed by the borough (45–46 Vic., c. 50, Sched. V., Part II.). The candidate is not required to appoint an election agent, but must make a return of his expenses.

court for the trial of disputed elections.[1] The most venal class of electors for Parliament, the ancient freemen, have as such no votes in municipal matters, and bribery is uncommon, although a case where it is widespread occasionally comes to light. In 1902 a lamentable state of things was revealed at Shrewsbury, where it appeared that, in the ward for which the election petition was presented, more than half of all the registered voters were bribed to support the successful candidate, although they did not all vote for him; and the witnesses asserted that the custom had persisted steadily for a generation.[2] As in the case of parliamentary elections it would seem that corruption is apt to affect a large part of the electorate if it exists at all; and in the great cities one hears nothing of it. The contest in most places is hardly fierce enough to raise a strong temptation to bribery, while nursing, in the form of subscriptions to clubs and charities, is done on a minute scale compared with that often practised by candidates for Parliament.

**The Action of Parties.** The part played by the national parties in municipal elections varies a good deal in different boroughs. In most English towns the candidates are nominated and supported by the party organisations of the place; and the paid secretaries or active members in the local party associations encourage this. With the long and uncertain intervals between elections to the House of Commons they feel the need of exercising their troops in order to maintain discipline, and while their ardour is less than in parliamentary contests, they generally do more or less hard work in borough elections.[3] In fact, when the candidates are brought forward as Conservatives or Liberals, the nomination and canvassing are conducted by the regular party machinery. That was, indeed, one of the principal objects of the Birmingham Caucus, which was copied in other towns though applied to

[1] This consists of a barrister appointed by the rota of judges selected for the trial of parliamentary elections.

[2] Com. Papers, 1903, LV., 505.

[3] A manual on this subject has recently been published by J. Seymour Lloyd, entitled "Municipal Elections, and How to Fight Them."

municipal purposes less thoroughly. Sometimes the names of the national parties are discarded, and the terms "Moderate" and "Progressive," taken from the London County Council, are used instead. In London these divisions tend to run close to the national party lines; for although a Liberal is not always a Progressive or a Conservative always a Moderate, and a member of one national party may actually stand for the council on the opposite side, still the two lines coincide on the whole very nearly,[1] and the party organisations lend their aid to no small extent in the contest, a condition that appears to be more pronounced in provincial boroughs.

Even in towns where the candidates are avowedly put forward by the political organisations, and this is true in the greater part of the boroughs, every burgess does not invariably vote with his party. But the exceptions are not common enough to prevent the result from being regarded as a test of party strength, although the vote for borough councils is so light that the majority of the council not infrequently belongs to one of the parties, while the members of Parliament belong to the other. Of course national questions are not really at issue, and with the modern attitude of the Conservatives toward social problems, there is no necessary connection between national and local policy; for while the Liberals are on the whole more inclined to favour the extension of municipal functions, in some places the Conservatives are the more progressive body in local matters, and in many more it is impossible to draw any distinction between the parties on that basis. Sometimes national questions play a prominent part in electioneering speeches; more often platform oratory turns on local issues. Sometimes the more important matter of the fitness of the candidates is publicly discussed, but this is apt to give rise to an interchange of personalities that has a bad effect.

**Third Candidates.**

Third candidates are not common. A dozen years ago ratepayers' associations, formed to protest against the in-

[1] For a further discussion of this subject see pages 231–32 *infra*.

crease of local taxation, arose in several boroughs, but they were composed of men who carried little weight, and, obtaining no vigorous popular support, soon faded away. The prevalent sentiment of the day was in favour of greater communal activity, which involves increased expenditure; and neither these associations, nor the casual independent candidates, could point to any general maladministration which would furnish a basis for a genuine non-partisan movement. At the borough elections in London in November, 1906, and the County Council election of the following March, an extraordinarily successful agitation against the growth in the rates was carried on by the "Municipal Reformers"; but they did it by absorbing the Moderates, and making themselves one of the two great parties in the local politics of the metropolis. The Labour men and the Socialists, also, have often nominated candidates in many towns, and the former have gained representatives slowly, but steadily, on borough councils. They have done so, however, not so much in triangular contests, as by prevailing upon one of the leading parties not to oppose their candidates. The Socialists have been less successful. Except for the working-class suburb of West Ham in the east of London, where they controlled the council for a short time, they have not elected many of their own nominees, although the authorities of the boroughs are everywhere leavened by a spirit that would have been thought highly socialistic fifty years ago.

Non-party Boroughs.

Political habits of thought once acquired exert an influence far beyond the conditions that justified their existence, and thus it has happened that municipal elections in England are based for the most part on the division of the nation into two parties with which they have no rational connection. But this is not the case in every town. There are a few boroughs large and small, notably Brighton in the extreme south, and Newcastle in the far north, where the elections are not conducted on party lines at all, and any attempt to introduce party politics is resolutely frowned upon. This is true also of most of the large Scotch towns, such as Edinburgh, Glasgow, Aberdeen, Dundee and Perth, where a custom prevails of making nominations in open ward meetings.

The boroughs in which the elections are not fought on party lines are by no means noted for a lack of interest in national politics, and it is not easy to see why the practice should be observed in them rather than elsewhere. It appears to be a matter of tradition, for there is little tendency to change it. These towns retain their custom, but do not incite other boroughs to copy them. They are proud of the usage, and boast of it; and yet it may be doubted whether it is as important as one would naturally be inclined to suppose. Such places are well administered, but not conspicuously better governed than the better class of boroughs where nominations are made on party lines. One hears at times statements that party politics are the curse of borough government, but this refers to the use of party for personal instead of public ends; and, on the other hand, one sometimes hears a sly remark that party politics give the borough politician something to talk about on the platform, when he might otherwise be criticising the permanent officials, who ought to be screened from public view. The bearing of this side of the question will appear more fully hereafter, as will also the fact that party counts for much less in municipal government than the mere study of elections might seem to indicate.

**Many Seats Uncontested.**

All the larger boroughs, and many of the smaller ones, are divided into wards, among which the seats in the council are apportioned.[1] As a rule — although by no means an invariable one — each ward is represented by three councillors, and since they serve for three years, one of them retiring each year, the voters in a ward are usually called

[1] The division into wards is based upon local taxation as well as population, and thus a certain weight is given to property. 45–46 Vic., c. 50, § 30 (10). For the relations of population and property in the wards of Glasgow see Bell and Paton, "Glasgow," 63.

upon to elect only a single representative at the annual election. This is an important matter, because it affects seriously the political activity of the voters, and the popular interest in municipal elections. The general English custom of continuing in office any man who has done nothing to forfeit public esteem is followed in local affairs. A councillor is, therefore, almost always renominated by his party or body of supporters. But there is no strong motive for nominating an opponent unless he has a fair chance of success. An Englishman does not care to be set up only to be knocked down. He earns no claim to political reward by leading a hopeless contest for a seat on a borough council, and the seat itself is not a stepping-stone to higher public office. Nor is the desire to keep its followers in battle array sufficient to make the party organization insist on marshalling them on every occasion. If a popular vote took place in any event it would be natural for each party to have a candidate in the field; but that is not the fact. As in the case of Parliament, no poll is held unless more candidates are nominated than there are seats to be filled, and hence an opponent does not come forward unless he means to conduct a serious fight. The result is that in many a ward there is no contest, especially when the sitting member is ready to stand again. The number of uncontested seats varies, of course, a great deal. In one hundred and three boroughs and urban districts, large and small, taken at random at the elections of 1899, decidedly less than half the seats in the aggregate were contested, while in thirteen of these places there was not a single contest.[1] Nor does there appear to be any marked difference in this respect between large and small towns, or between the places where the

[1] The figures, which are taken from newspaper clippings, give 302 seats contested out of 667. But they are not quite accurate, because in some cases the number of wards contested was obtained, in others only the total number of candidates and vacancies. The results are, however, accurate enough to give a very fair idea of the proportion of seats contested. Shaw gives some figures for elections a few years earlier. "Mun. Govt. in Great Britain," 48–50, 51 note.

nomination is made on party lines and those where it is not.

Smallness of the Vote Cast.

Not only are many wards wholly uncontested, but even where a poll is taken the vote is light. It is habitually much smaller than in parliamentary elections, not much more, perhaps, on the average than two thirds as large. At the elections for the London County Council in 1901 and 1904, for example, the proportion of registered voters who cast their ballots was not far from forty-five per cent;[1] and even in 1907 when the public interest was great, and the Progressive majority in the council was beaten, it was only about fifty-two per cent; while at the parliamentary elections for the London boroughs it was fifty-five per cent in 1900 and seventy-six per cent in 1906. The same thing happens constantly in the provincial towns. In seeking an explanation of the small vote in borough elections one is usually told that the richer people take little part, but that class by itself does not form a large fraction of the electorate, and the size of the vote implies a good deal of apathy or contentment in municipal affairs throughout the body politic. Now if only one half of the wards in a borough are contested, and only one half of the voters in these go to the polls, it follows that no more than one quarter of the total electorate actually take part in the election.

The Council.

The borough council is not composed of representative members alone. It consists of the mayor, aldermen and councillors sitting together as a single body.[2]

Councillors.

The councillors are elected by popular vote in the manner already described, and their number varies roughly in proportion to the size of the borough. It runs from nine in the smallest towns to one hundred and three in Liverpool. It must, however, as a rule be a multiple of three, because the councillors are elected for three years, one third retiring

[1] In 1901, 40.8 per cent of the total registered electors voted, and in 1904, 45.7 per cent; but on the first occasion five, and in the latter two of the districts were not contested. "London Statistics," 1904–5, 182.

[2] The composition of the council is regulated by 45–46 Vic., c. 50, §§ 10–16.

each year. To be eligible as a councillor one[1] must either be registered as a voter, or being otherwise entitled to be registered must reside within fifteen miles of the circumference of the borough and possess a certain amount of property or pay a certain sum in local taxes.[2] The qualification for serving on the council is thus wider than for voting, because it includes people of some little means living more than seven and not over fifteen miles from the town. In accordance with the usual English tradition, councillors are not required either by law or by custom to be residents of the ward for which they are elected. So slight, indeed, is local jealousy or social envy that a working-class ward will often choose as its representative a man who lives in the richer part of the town, or in the suburbs, and thus the councillors are drawn from the more comfortable portion of the community out of proportion to its commercial strength.[3] In pursuance of another valuable tradition they are constantly reëlected. Many members of borough

[1] Until 1907 women were ineligible, the provision in the Act of 1882, § 63, giving them only a right to vote. Beresford-Hope *vs.* Lady Sandhurst, 23 Q.B.D. 79. But this has been changed by 7 Edw. VII., c. 33, and the corresponding Scotch Act, c. 48.

[2] In a borough with less than four wards he must possess real or personal property of £500, or be rated on land and buildings of the annual value of £15. For boroughs with four or more wards these amounts are doubled. The only special disqualifications for the office of councillor are an interest in any contract made on behalf of the council, holding an office or place of profit in its gift, and in the case of a borough, but not of other local bodies, being in holy orders or the minister of a dissenting congregation.

[3] In his paper on "The British Municipality," in the Report to the National Civic Federation on Public Ownership and Operation (1907), Professor Goodnow points this out very forcibly, and gives some striking figures on the subject. He shows (pp. 44–45) that of the 137 members of the council in Liverpool (including aldermen) only 25 live in the wards they represent, while, of the remaining 112, 50 live outside the city limits, and 44 others in the six richest residential wards; that of the 80 aldermen and councillors representing the twenty working-class wards only 8 live in those wards, and 53 in the six richest residential wards. Taking up other towns he finds, for example, that 51 of the 78 members of the council in Glasgow live outside their wards, that the same is true of 32 out of the 48 elected members in Leicester, while 68 of the 118 elected members of the London County Council live outside of their districts. Later (pp. 52–53) he shows that this is no less marked in the case of the members of the principal committees of the council in Liverpool.

councils have been long in service, and this, with the fact that the position is not a stepping-stone to higher public functions has great advantages. The council is not a means to an end, but an end in itself, while the members stay there long enough to see, and be responsible for, the consequences of their actions.

Aldermen.

The aldermen are in number one third as many as the councillors; but although selected in a different way, and holding office for a different term, they are from a legal point of view simply members of the council like the rest, with one trifling exception. They act as returning officers for the wards to which they are assigned.[1] That is their only privilege at law. Otherwise they are simply a more honourable grade of councillor, and the special honour is primarily based upon the longer tenure of office. They are chosen for six years instead of three, one half of them going out every third year. The qualifications also are the same as in the case of councillors, for it is provided that a person shall not be chosen alderman unless he is a councillor or qualified to be one. They are elected by the council itself on November 9, that is immediately after one third of the council has been renewed by the popular election of that year.

Selection of Aldermen.

One possible advantage in having aldermen might be the opportunity it affords of placing on the council men of special knowledge or usefulness, who have not been, or for some reason are not likely to be, elected by popular vote. In some other local bodies this is done not infrequently, but in the boroughs the aldermen have long been taken almost exclusively from the members of the council itself, the choice of an outsider, although not wholly unknown, being rare.[2]

The motives for selection vary not a little from town to

[1] This assignment may be quite independent of the alderman's residence, or of the fact that he has hitherto represented a ward as a councillor.

[2] It is naturally done when suburbs have been annexed and made into new wards, *e.g.*, Bradford in 1899, and Newcastle in 1904. When a councillor is chosen alderman he vacates his office of councillor and a new election is held in his ward.

town; but two of them call for special notice — party and seniority. The latter always has weight, for whether the aldermen are taken within the ranks of a party, or from the members of the council as a whole, seniority gives a strong claim for consideration, and in fact it is usually the chief ground for preference among the councillors eligible by the custom of the place. In some boroughs, indeed, in Manchester, Derby and Cardiff, for example, the aldermen are said to be selected almost entirely in the order of length of service in the council.[1]

**How Far on Party Lines.**

The influence of party in the choice of aldermen is a more variable force. In the few English towns where party is disregarded altogether in the nomination of councillors, it cannot, of course, be brought into the elections made by them. But quite apart from these cases, there are borough councils elected on party lines which refuse to make the choice of aldermen a party question. There are others, apparently more common, where the minority is given a share of the places, sometimes less, sometimes more, than their numerical proportion; and others again where the dominant party insists on electing all the aldermen from its own side. Naturally, although by no means fortunately, this last condition occurs most often where the parties are nearly evenly balanced, for a party that has a large majority can afford to be generous, whereas one that has only a small preponderance needs all the votes it can obtain to make its control of the council secure. It has happened, in fact, not seldom that a party which had less than half of the elected councillors has been enabled by the votes of the aldermen who do not retire,[2] to elect the new aldermen from its own adherents, and thus prolong its power. As the men so chosen hold office for six years, and the other half of the aldermen do not retire for three years, a very large or long-continued popular majority is required to

[1] In Carlisle there is a curious habit of electing as successor to an alderman the senior councillor from the same ward.

[2] The retiring aldermen have no votes: 45–46 Vic., c. 50, § 60 (3).

change the complexion of the council. For this reason it has been urged that none of the aldermen ought to be entitled to vote at the election of their own order.[1] In many places another custom is not inappropriately followed. It is a common habit to confer as a compliment the first vacancies that happen among the aldermen upon the mayor and his predecessors who have passed the chair.[2]

**Actual Influence of the Aldermen.**

While the aldermen have no important legal powers not enjoyed by the other members of the council, their influence is much greater, for they are the members who have served longest, and they hold the most of the chairmanships upon the committees. In some towns, indeed, these posts are reserved exclusively for them, and everywhere one is struck by the fact that they are on the whole the leading figures in the council. The influence naturally conceded in a body of this kind to seniority and experience is enhanced in an English borough council by the fact that as a general rule, apart from a change of party in the council, retiring aldermen are reëlected so long as they are willing to serve.[3] This may not be in accord with the strict theory of representative government, but it has substantial advantages. It insures the presence in the governing body of men of long experience; and in fact it is not uncommon to find in a town council a few men who have served there continuously for twenty-five or thirty years, or even more. It conduces to stability in administration; and it relieves a small and valuable portion of the council from the need of

[1] *E.g.* Rep. of Com. on Amalgamation of London, Com. Papers, 1894, XVII., 1, Qs. 10,072–74.

[2] In order to keep out of sight a discussion that had better not be made public it is the custom in some places to call a private informal meeting of the members of the council before November 9, and take an informal ballot there for mayor and aldermen. Then, unless sharp party dissensions have arisen, the successful candidates may be elected without debate, or even unanimously, at the regular meeting of the council in spite of decided differences of opinion.

[3] It is not an invariable rule. In Carlisle and Oldham, for example, an alderman is not reëlected, on the principle that after serving his term of six years he ought to go back to his constituents for approval. But this is not considered by most observers to work well.

popular election, with that personal criticism which too often accompanies it in an English town and which many of the older men, conscious of faithful work, as they are, dislike to undergo. Nor from the standpoint of popular government is it irrational, for, with the habit of selecting aldermen almost entirely from the senior councillors, these men must have proved at several elections that they have acquired and retained the confidence of their constituents. They never lose the feeling that they are responsible to public opinion for the whole course of their public service, and this with an honourable man is a far better thing than immediate responsibility to a small popular electorate.[1]

The Mayor.

The first business of the council at the meeting on the ninth of November is the election of a mayor, for the term of one year, from among the aldermen, councillors or persons qualified to be such.[2] The mayor is a justice of the peace for the borough during his term of office, and for one year thereafter; but this is the only duty of importance that he performs apart from the council, of which he is both a member and the chairman.[3] In practice the mayor is almost always chosen from the members of the council, and from the members who have served for a considerable length of time. In a large city the writer has heard the fact that the mayor had been on the council only nine years

His Legal Position.

[1] The bailies in a Scotch burgh occupy by no means the same position as the aldermen in England. They are not additional members of the council, nor do they hold an office distinct from that of other members, and the election of a councillor to the post creates no vacancy. They are simply ordinary councillors who are selected to act as magistrates during their period of service on the council (63–64 Vic., c. 49, §§ 5, 57–58). The elevation to the dignity of bailie does not remove them from popular election, or lengthen their term of office, except that in some places the bailie appears to be transferred to the long term from his ward, his colleagues therefrom going out sooner in consequence. Moreover, it is not the habit in Scotland to reëlect the bailies.

[2] 45–46 Vic., c. 50, § 61. The outgoing aldermen can vote.

[3] He appoints an auditor from the council; he passes upon the validity of nominations of councillors; he acts as returning officer at parliamentary elections for the borough (if not a county); and at municipal elections if the borough is not divided into wards.

before his election referred to as something quite unusual there.

**Party in his Election.** As in the case of the aldermen the extent to which the election is made on party grounds varies a great deal with the tradition of the particular town, and it changes from time to time. After the ninth of November the press publishes every year a list of all the newly chosen mayors with a statement of the party to which they belong, but party is not really a factor in the selection of such universal consequence as this might lead one to believe. Nor does it play so large a part in the case of the mayor as in that of aldermen. There are few boroughs where he has been invariably chosen by the majority from its own partisans, although there are many where this is usually done. It is not uncommon to elect a mayor occasionally from the minority; in some places the selection is, by agreement, made alternately from the two sides; and there are a number of towns where the council professes to choose without regard to party lines. The fact is that apart from a personal desire for the office, there is little object in conferring it on a party man. The mayor does not ordinarily shape the policy of the council, his election creates no vacancy, and therefore does not strengthen the forces of the majority, and he has no patronage in his gift.

**Limited Number of Candidates.** What is more to the point, it is not always easy to find a member of the party who is willing to accept the office. With this is connected the fact that a mayor is not usually reëlected. In a few towns a second term is customary, and occasionally the position is held even longer. But, as a rule, the mayor is changed every year, not because the desire for the place is so general as to lead to rotation, but because it is an expensive luxury which few men can long afford. The honour of the post is highly prized, and the pomp and circumstance surrounding it are imposing. The mayor, exalted in a few of the biggest cities with the title of Lord Mayor, is clad in robes, or uniform, with a gold chain about his neck, and represents the borough on all ceremonial occasions. When royalty visits the town in connection with any civic celebration he is usually knighted, and at the Queen's jubilee, on the fiftieth anniversary of her coronation, the mayors went in a body to London, and all received the honour of knighthood. But if the dignity of a mayor is great it is also costly, for he is expected to entertain on behalf of the town at his own expense. He gives every year a reception, well supplied with refreshments and wine, at which in the large cities twenty-five hundred people may be present; and he extends his hospitality to distinguished strangers who visit the town at any time. No one but the mayor himself knows, of course, what he spends, but men in a position to form an estimate, compute his expenses in different places at sums running from five hundred to four or five thousand pounds, the amounts varying roughly in proportion to the size of the town. In most places he has no salary at all; in others he receives from a hundred pounds in a small town, to twenty-seven hundred pounds at Liverpool, that being the largest salary the writer has found; but in no case does the salary cover the amount which he expends. Under these conditions the number of men who aspire to the honour is not unlimited, and in fact one hears at times of a difficulty in finding a member of the council willing to undertake it. This in itself helps to explain why the pressure for the mayoralty is not greater, and why the party in power is inclined to be generous in accepting candidates from the minority. It explains also the occasional instances where a mayor has been selected outside the council. This has usually occurred in the case of a peer living in the neighbourhood, who has been elected for the lustre of his title, and with a view to hospitality at his castle.

Actual Influence of the Mayor.

By a universal custom, embodied in the standing orders of the borough, the mayor is *ex officio* a member of every committee of the council. This would appear to give him a controlling influence over the whole administration, but his time is so filled with consultations about the course of affairs at council meetings, with giving audiences to people of all kinds about every sort of grievance, with ceremonial duties, and with presiding on innumerable occasions of a public and charitable nature, that he has usually little time for committees or for his own private business. The amount of attention he pays to the administrative work of the town varies no doubt in different places and with different men. Sometimes he really attends many committee meetings, and exerts a great deal of influence on the course of affairs; sometimes his position is almost purely ornamental. To draw a general portrait from inquiries made in a considerable number of towns, it may be said that as a rule he attends those committees alone of which he was a member before his election to the chair, and that, while from personal experience and standing he is usually a man of weight, he does not as mayor ordinarily have much influence on the general policy of the council or the conduct of its work. Mr. Chamberlain's administration of Birmingham when mayor, from 1873 to 1876, is always cited as an example to the contrary, but his power is universally admitted to have been quite exceptional, and no second instance of the kind is ever mentioned.[1]

**The Council at Work.**

After the mayor and aldermen have been elected a borough council divides as a rule little on party lines. Sometimes they crop out again in the appointment of committees and of the most important permanent officials, but for the rest they are usually almost forgotten. It is, indeed, commonly said that the members enter the council as political partisans,

**Party.**

[1] In Scotland the provost, who corresponds to the English mayor, and occupies a similar position, is elected by the council for three years (63–64 Vic., c. 49, § 56). He is not usually reëlected, although there are exceptions to that rule in the smaller burghs. The office is on the whole more valued than that of mayor in England, and the holder exerts more frequently a decided influence on municipal administration. The councils of the five largest Scotch burghs contain, beside the mayor, bailies and councillors, a dean of guild elected not by popular vote but by the surviving remnants of the ancient merchants' guilds; while in Edinburgh and Glasgow there is also a deacon convener who represents what is left of the trade guilds. These dignitaries still sit in the council with all the rights of membership.

but after election they drop their politics, and devote their time to municipal duties. There are three reasons for this. The first is the absence of a general system of spoils in the distribution of patronage. The second is the fact that the parties are not often sharply divided on questions of municipal policy. In London, which is large enough to have a political tide of its own, the parties in the county council have been really divided on local policy; the Progressives being in favour of extending the sphere of public administration and municipal trading, by undertaking freely the direct management of agencies which affect the whole community; while the Moderates believe in leaving such matters much more in private hands. Under these circumstances the parties are often opposed to each other on a question like that of erecting a building by contract or by the works department of the council, of leasing the tramways to a company or operating them directly, and of establishing a line of municipal steamboats on the Thames. Such a division of parties is occasionally found in provincial boroughs. A few years ago it was true in Leeds, where conditions were curiously reversed, the Conservatives being the progressive body in the council. It was true also in West Ham, where the line of cleavage came between the Socialists and the Moderates, the former, in 1899, holding a caucus before the meeting of the council to determine the action to be taken on the questions to come up. But clearly marked differences between the parties on municipal policy are not common in English boroughs. Even where the Liberals tend to be on the whole more progressive than the Conservatives, some of the latter usually agree with them, and more frequently no line of separation of this kind can be drawn at all; so that while at election time there may be a good deal of talk about efficiency or economy on one side or the other, these distinctions generally disappear when the council is at work. Sometimes the members of a party in the council hold a caucus upon an important matter that will be brought forward, but they rarely adopt binding resolutions. In short there are a few boroughs where votes on party lines are frequent; in many more they are uncommon; while in others, about equally numerous, they are, except for the elections already described, practically unknown.[1]

Committees.

The third reason for the small prominence of party in the actual work of the council is its internal organisation by means of a great number of committees. It must be remembered that the borough has no distinct executive organ, the whole administrative labour being imposed upon the council. But a large assembly cannot attend to this directly, and hence the councils have resorted to the obvious device of forming committees, each entrusted with the oversight of some branch of the administration. Only one of them is prescribed by statute. That is the watch committee, charged with the maintenance of the police force;[2] but the Act of 1882 empowers the council to appoint committees for any other purposes that it thinks fit,[3] and the right has been freely used.

The number of committees runs from half a dozen to more than a score, depending not on the size of the town, but rather on the extent of jurisdiction of each committee. Where this is large sub-committees are appointed for different departments or branches of administration, the whole being under the control of the main committee which is responsible to the council. While the number and names of the committees differ from town to town, their organisation, their functions, and their relation to the council are singularly uniform throughout Great Britain; and thus, although the system rests, not upon general statutes, but upon local custom, it is possible to give a description of it

[1] In the Scotch burghs, where the councillors are not nominated by the political parties, and in the few English boroughs which follow the same practice, there are, of course, no party votes in the council.

[2] 45–46 Vic., c. 50, § 190.

[3] *Ibid.*, § 22. Under the provisions of various statutes, some committees, those on Education and on Libraries, for example, contain additional members, not on the council.

which is applicable everywhere.[1] Now an elaborate system of committees tends to break up party lines, because both parties are always represented in a standing committee, and the differences of opinion therein on concrete questions do not often coincide with distinctions of party, so that party divisions in the committees are very rare; and because the members, being in the habit of working together, tend to agree and present a united front in the council, except when some unusually important matter of policy is involved. In fact it is not uncommon for a dissenting member to say that he will raise no opposition in the council unless some one else does so. This is true even where the strongest party in the council is given a majority of the members of all the committees, and that is very far from being always the case.

**Choice of Committees.** The Act of 1882 says that the council shall appoint the committees, and in accordance with the ordinary English habit this is done directly by the council itself, the practice of delegating the power of appointment to the chair being quite unknown. In some cases the lists are really arranged at a party caucus, and in a few towns the representatives from each ward present their own condidates, but more commonly the nominations are made by a committee of selection, or general purposes committee, which habitually contains the chairmen, or at least representatives, from each committee. As a general rule, indeed, the committees are to a very great extent permanent in membership; and, subject to the principle that every member of the council must have his fair share of places, they are practically able to fill their own vacancies.

**Chairmen of Committees.** In England the chairman is almost always, though not quite universally, chosen each year by the committee it-

[1] The only substantial variation from the type which the writer has met in studying a considerable number of towns, large and small, is in Perth, where instead of the ordinary committees the whole council is divided into two groups, with a number of different conveners, or chairmen, for different matters. As the council contains only twenty-five members, each group is about as large as a committee in most borough councils; and there are a few sub-committees for particular branches of work.

self, and this is usually prescribed in the standing orders of the borough. But in Scotland, curiously enough, a different custom prevails, the chairmen, or conveners as they are called, being elected by the council. Where party spirit runs high, the chairmen are sometimes taken wholly from the party in power, but it is more common to give a few of these places to the minority, or even to disregard party altogether. The general habit of retaining the chairmen in office has, moreover, a strong effect in mitigating the influence of party in the selection; for it is the prevailing habit to reëlect them, unless there is a strong personal reason for making a change. The standing orders of Brighton provided a few years ago that no chairman should serve more than two successive years, and there are a few instances where the chairmanship of the watch committee goes by a sort of rotation; but such cases are very rare.[1] Reelection as long as a man is willing to serve is the regular custom, and one hears frequently of chairmen who have held the position for a dozen years, or more. Under such conditions it is natural that experience should lend weight to their authority. The influence of a chairman with his committee depends, of course, largely on his personal force, but as a rule it is great, and in extreme cases one hears that the work at committee meetings is all done at the head of the table.[2] To prevent the control of the town government, therefore, from falling into a very few hands, it is common to provide by the standing orders that no one shall hold more than one or two chairmanships.

**Work of Committees.**

The work of the council is really done through its committees, for almost everything that comes before it is either brought up in the form of a report from a committee, or is referred to a committee for consideration; and the standing committees have a vast amount of work to do. Subject

[1] The London County Council adopted a general habit of changing the chairmen each year.

[2] The standing orders commonly provide that the chairman shall be *ex officio* a member of all the sub-committees.

to ratification or control of their acts by the council, they manage the various departments of the public service and prepare the plans for any change or enlargement. The gas committee, for example, in a borough that owns the supply of gas, is virtually in the same position as an executive or managing committee of a gas company. Now many of the cities having gone extensively into municipal trading, there are often similar committees for water supply, electricity, tramways, baths and wash houses, dwelling houses, not to speak of such matters as streets and police which are universal. In a large city each of these committees is really managing a huge business, which involves a great deal of work and responsibility, and sometimes the employment of large numbers of men. The committees meet every week or two, their sittings, as a rule, not being open to the public. In fact there are obvious objections to discussing the details of administration with open doors, and in Birmingham where reporters were admitted to the meetings of the watch committee the practice was found so inconvenient that the real business was done the evening before at a sub-committee containing all the members of the committee, the regular meeting the next day merely adopting formally the conclusions reached. But the committees keep full minutes of their proceedings, and this, which is generally prescribed by the standing orders, gives the council an effective means of control over their work.

Relation of the Committees to the Council.

The duties of the council consist mainly in supervising, and when necessary ratifying, the work of the committees. The statute of 1882 provides that "the acts of every such committee shall be submitted to the council for their approval," [1] and this has been sometimes taken to mean that the minutes of the committees must from time to time be submitted in full to the council for ratification. A provision to that effect is not infrequently found in the standing orders, but it is more common in the larger towns to submit

[1] § 22. The watch committee is given special powers by the same statute, §§ 190–91.

only an epitome of the minutes or proceedings of the committee, together with any recommendations for action on the part of the council, and in fact this is sometimes specially authorised by local acts. The minutes, or the epitome of proceedings, are habitually printed in the agenda for the council meeting, which is distributed among the members, and usually given to the press, several days in advance. It forms a bulky pamphlet, but although everything in it must be confirmed by the council, the operation takes less time than one might suppose. The mayor simply reads out the numbers of the paragraphs in their order, and if no objection is made they are deemed to be approved. In that way several pages of a committee's proceedings are often approved in a minute, and discussion is concentrated on a few matters of which notice has been given beforehand to the town clerk. The habit of preparing and printing a very full agenda thus enables the council to maintain a good deal of oversight of the city administration without consuming an inordinate amount of time upon details.

The four quarterly meetings prescribed by the Act of 1882 being, of course, insufficient, the council meets in most boroughs once a month, and in a few towns fortnightly or even more frequently. At these meetings by far the greater part of the proceedings and recommendations of the committees are approved without comment. The number of objections raised is not large, and the cases where they prevail are smaller still. A cursory examination of local newspaper reports of the meetings of fifty-three borough and district councils, large and small, taken at random a few years ago, would seem to show that on the average there were in a council not more than three cases a year where anything in the reports of committees, of sufficient importance to attract the attention of the press, was amended or referred back. The number of such cases is usually greater in large towns, but it is always small, and while the ratification by the council can by no means be regarded as a mere form, the real administration of affairs is left substantially in the hands of the committees.

The report of a committee is presented by its chairman, who explains it, defends it, sometimes even accepts amendments or withdraws some recommendation without consulting the other members of the committee. In short he acts like a minister in charge of a bill. The comparison is, in fact, highly appropriate, for the chairman, like a minister, answers questions relating to his department even on matters not touched upon by the minutes or report; and in some towns the standing orders specially provide that any member of the council shall have a right to address questions to him. As in the national government, the practice must tend to promote a sense of constant responsibility for the state of the administration, but it magnifies also the position, and hence the influence, of the chairman.

# CHAPTER XL

## BOROUGHS. — THE PERMANENT OFFICIALS

BEHIND the council and its committees, little seen by the public, but carrying the main burden of the public work, stand the permanent officials. Here again the statutes give little idea of their functions, or even of the offices they hold, and in fact the only officials mentioned in the Act of 1882 are the town clerk and the treasurer. The Act, however, goes on to provide that the council shall from time to time appoint such other officers as it may think necessary, and we are therefore not surprised that the permanent officials vary from place to place in number, titles and attributes. Nevertheless we always find, under some name or other, besides the town clerk and treasurer, a surveyor or engineer, a medical officer of health,[1] a chief constable, and save in boroughs with less than ten thousand inhabitants, a clerk of the education committee or superintendent of schools. The number of other officers depends very much upon the extent to which the borough has embarked in municipal trading. Where it undertakes to supply its people directly with the conveniences of life, we find engineers or managers of water works, gas works, electric lighting, tramways, public baths, markets and so forth. Each of these officers is, of course, at the head of a staff of subordinates who carry on the work of the department under his orders.

The position of the permanent officials may be conveniently discussed under three heads: the method of their Their Selection.

[1] By the Public Health Act of 1875 (38–39 Vic., c. 55, § 189) the council is required, as urban sanitary authority, to appoint this officer, and also a surveyor.

selection; their duties; and their relation to the political governing body of the borough. The officials at the head of any department are elected by the council. Their subordinates are usually appointed either by the council, or by the committee in charge, on the recommendation of the permanent chief; while the workmen and other employees are engaged by the officials, or by the foremen at the works. But it is only of the chief officials that it is necessary to speak here.

The prevalent English custom of selecting men for any post in public or private life by means of an advertisement and the submission of testimonials is applied in the case of municipal officers. When a vacancy occurs in the position of a town clerk or borough surveyor, for example, it is the general, although not invariable, habit to advertise for a successor; and this is sometimes done even in cases where the councillors have really made up their minds to promote a subordinate already in the service of the borough. If a promotion of that kind is not made, and a clerk, engineer or other officer is appointed from outside, a man is usually selected who is employed in a similar public office elsewhere — either at the head of a department in a smaller place, or as a subordinate in a larger one. In this way municipal service tends to become a career by itself. A town clerk, for example, must always be a solicitor or barrister by profession, and occasionally a person in private practice is selected, but it is far more common to take a man who is already engaged in municipal work, and has therefore had experience in the particular class of duties he is called upon to perform. In short, a town clerk usually enters the public service as a young man in a subordinate capacity, often as an articled clerk in a town clerk's office, and works his way up. It is rare that a solicitor is put into one of the higher posts in a borough from private life, and rarer still that a town clerk, or one of his assistants, goes back into private practice. The same thing is true of the engineers. It is not common to appoint a borough engineer on account of his reputation in general practice; or for a man who has seen service as an engineer of a town to go back into any other kind of work. In short, municipal engineering tends to become a distinct profession. The transfer of officers, and especially of town clerks and their assistants, from place to place is no doubt one of the chief reasons for the uniformity that prevails throughout the country in matters regulated not by statute but merely by local custom.

**Party in Selection.**

Politics enters into the appointment of the permanent officials to some extent, especially in the case of the town clerk, who is the most influential of them all. In fact it may be said that the town clerk is commonly, and other officials are occasionally, selected by the majority in the council from their own political party. Not that the practice is abused by the appointment of persons unfit for the place. The attempt in such cases is to find a really good man who belongs to the party; or, as the matter lies in the minds of the councillors themselves, between men equally fit, a partisan is given the preference. Nor does this have the bad effects that might be feared, because the officials abstain wholly from party politics, and because, although party motives may have affected the choice of a man, they never lead to his discharge if the majority in the council happens to change.

In short, there are no spoils, or rather nothing of the practice that renders spoils a blight, that is, the removal of office-holders to make room for partisans. So long as an English borough official does his work well, he is retained regardless of party. An exception of the kind that tends to prove the rule occurred in West Ham in 1899. The Socialists obtained a majority in the council, and forthwith turned out the borough surveyor. His discharge made no small stir among the municipal engineers of the country; but an inquiry into the circumstances led the writer to believe that the removal was really made on personal rather than political grounds. The surveyor seems to have been lacking in tact, and had become very unpopular with members of the council.

The Duties of the Officials.

The Town Clerk.

The town clerk has precedence among the officials, and is, in fact, the principal figure in the permanent service of the borough. By the Act of 1882 he is given the custody of the charters, deeds and records, is charged with the rendering of accounts to the Local Government Board, and with a number of important duties connected with elections; but these form a very small part of his work. He combines the functions of town clerk and borough solicitor, for besides keeping the records of the town, and of the meetings of the council and its committees, he does all the legal business of the corporation except the argument of cases in court — this last being, of course, the province of a barrister. He must be familiar with the long list of public and private acts that apply to the borough, together with the decisions that interpret them. He must be prepared to give advice upon legal questions, and to instruct counsel when lawsuits arise. He drafts all private bills to be laid before Parliament, prepares the evidence in their support, and goes up to London to attend the hearings. His position as clerk and legal adviser gives him a great influence with all the officers and members of the council, an influence extending far beyond the domain of law into general business management; and while the work of each of the other officers is limited to his own special department, a good town clerk has to a greater or less extent an eye on everything. In short, he fills the place of guide, philosopher and friend to every one connected with the government of the borough.

The Other Officials.

The treasurer is the disbursing officer, the banker, for the council; but he has little or nothing to do with appropriations, or with the financial policy of the town.[1] The chief constable is at the head of the police force, acting under the control of the statutory watch committee. The medical

[1] "The treasurer of a borough has no duty except to pay on the orders of three members of the council, countersigned by the town clerk . . . the treasurer is a mere machine as regards finance." Evidence of Mr. E. O. Smith, town clerk of Birmingham; Rep. of Com. on Mun. Trading, Com. Papers, 1900, VII., 183, Qs. 1819–20. But the treasurer may be consulted about financial and banking operations.

officer of health has the obvious duties, and under or with him are an inspector of nuisances and a public analyst. The surveyor has charge of the paving and maintenance of streets, and in many places of the construction and care of public buildings as well. Of the engineers or superintendents of the various municipal undertakings carried on by the town, such as water, gas, electric lighting, baths, markets or tramways, it is unnecessary to speak, further than to say that, as a rule, whatever the titles of these officers may be, they are really the head managers of their departments, and not merely professional advisers.[1] The position of the officials connected with education will be discussed in a later chapter.

**The Position of the Officials.**

The traditional position of permanent officials in England, and their relation to their political chiefs, have been described in an earlier chapter, and they apply to municipal government.[2] It is often said that the council determines the general policy to be pursued, while the officials carry it out in detail,[3] and this describes, no doubt, the legal situation, but it is very far from expressing the actual influence of the officials upon the administration of the borough. In the first place no sharp line can be drawn between policy and details; and then an official who has in any degree the confidence of his committee will always influence them very largely about the general policy of his

[1] Sometimes there is also a consulting engineer. Occasionally, as in the case of the supply of gas at Manchester, there is a secretary to the committee in charge and an engineer at each of the two gas works, no one of whom is really the general manager of the business; but such an arrangement is exceptional and not generally regarded as wise.

[2] A good deal of light is thrown on the position and actual influence of borough officials by the evidence contained in the report of the Commission on the Amalgamation of the City and County of London (Com. Papers, 1894, XVII., XVIII.); but the impressions of the writer have been acquired mainly by personal inquiries from officials and members of the council in a considerable number of boroughs of different size in all parts of the country.

[3] Redlich and Hirst ("Local Govt. in England," I., 350–51), who have dwelt upon the importance of the officials more than any one else, repeat this statement in a slightly different form; and although they point out that it is not accurate, they seem to regard it as more nearly so than it appears to the writer.

department. His position is like that of a permanent undersecretary of state. The members of the council, like the ministers, assume the responsibility for what is done. They are expected to shield the official from blame, and naturally take the credit for good management. He enjoys, therefore, with a large share of real power, freedom from attack, and a permanent tenure of office in consideration of self-effacement. At a meeting of a society of engineers he may read a paper on his work in the town, but otherwise he will never speak in public as if he were doing anything himself. In some ways, no doubt, his position differs from that of a permanent undersecretary. It is not so generally understood, and hence he is not quite so well protected from public criticism. Moreover, he is often placed under men of much smaller caliber, who are for that reason more sensitive about having people suppose that they are in the hands of their subordinates. He is usually more careful, therefore, to avoid the appearance of leading his committee; and in fact one observes that the smaller class of councillors are often unaware how much they are really guided by the officials. Still, after making allowance for minor differences of this kind, it is not inaccurate to say that in general the chairman of a committee plays a part not unlike that of a minister with the official as his permanent undersecretary.

**Their Means of Influence.**

None of the officials, save the town clerk, is ordinarily present at meetings of the council, and with rare exceptions, none of them, save the clerk, ever speaks there. The clerk, indeed, is supposed to express his opinion only in answer to a question; but being the legal adviser of the council he has many chances to state his views, and not infrequently makes a remark which affects the course of debate. In Scotland, or at least in Glasgow, other officials may be seen sitting at the long table in the centre of the council chamber, by the side of the conveners of their committees, to prompt them in their statements about the departments; but this almost never happens in England. The real work, however, is done in the committees, where the officials appear freely whenever matters affecting their departments are under consideration, urge their projects, and expound their views. In fact, in well-regulated towns the business of the committees is mainly prepared by them, and their opinions habitually prevail. There are, of course, councillors who think they know as much as the expert, but they are commonly suppressed by their more experienced colleagues, and cause no serious trouble. Even if an engineer cannot, for financial or other reasons, induce the committee to do what he wants, he can almost always prevent it from doing a thing that he does not approve. If a proposal is made which he thinks unwise, he will tell the committee that he cannot recommend it; that while he will, of course, execute loyally any directions that may be given him, he cannot assume the responsibility for the proposal; and that if the members wish it carried out they must take the responsibility of passing a vote to that effect, and putting it upon the records. Owing partly to the respect in England for expert knowledge, and partly to the fact that the councillors retain their positions for long periods of time so that they are very sure to reap the blame for errors they insist on committing, it is constantly asserted that a committee will almost never take the responsibility of passing a vote of this kind.

The official has thus a direct influence on the committee itself, where he always appears, unfolds his plans, and explains what he wants. Moreover, he can do this without the disturbing effect of a public hearing, for, as we have seen, committee meetings are not as a rule open to the public, and every one knows how much more uncompromising members of representative bodies become when reporters are present. But if his direct control over the committee is not enough he can usually increase it by a little preparation in advance. It is a very common practice for the official to go over with the chairman beforehand the questions that are to come before the committee; and as the chairman is usually much the most influential member of the committee, the matters that have been agreed upon between him and the official will in all probability be adopted by the committee. The chairman then makes it his business to see that they are confirmed by the council. In this way the official impresses his views on the chairman, who in turn impresses them on the committee, and this body carries them through the council. Thus the motive force behind the council is to be found mainly in the permanent officials, whose power, being unseen, is little understood by the public. In fact, the real influence of an official sometimes depends upon his skill in avoiding the appearance of directing, and in making the councillors believe that the plans proposed are in great part their own suggestion.

**Extent of their Influence in Different Places.**

Naturally enough, the amount of power exercised by the permanent officials is not the same everywhere. The weight attached to their opinion varies from place to place, and in some towns there is more tendency than in others to interfere with the details of administration in their departments. Sometimes one is told that the relation of a surveyor, engineer or superintendent to his committee resembles very closely that of the general manager of a company to his directors;[1] sometimes one hears that he has less independence in substance as well as in form. A great deal must depend upon the tact and force of character of the official himself, and one may find two heads of departments in the same town who stand on quite a different footing with their committees.

Then the personality of the town clerk counts for much. Where he is a strong man, and uses his power to support the other officials, he can raise their authority to no small extent. A great deal depends also upon the general traditions of the place, and these vary in different towns, and in different parts of the country. Thus one observes that the officials have, as a rule, more authority in large than in small places; and on the whole more in the north than in the south of England. Of course none of these things can be

[1] In Glasgow especially each department is managed very much like a distinct concern.

measured by statistics. In each case it must be a matter of opinion what the precise influence of the officials may be; and yet one often gets a fairly definite impression of their comparative power in any particular town. One cannot fail to perceive, for example, that it is, or has been, greater in Glasgow, Liverpool, Birmingham or Bradford, than in Manchester, in Bristol or in London under the County Council.[1] This difference explains to some extent the shortcomings in the last three places; and in fact the writer, after studying a number of English cities, was led to imagine that the excellence of municipal government was very roughly proportional to the influence of the permanent officials. That influence, be it observed, is by no means confined to matters where purely expert knowledge is required. A very small fraction of the time of a town clerk is devoted to questions of law, or of a surveyor to engineering problems. By far the greater part of their work is administrative, and it is not too much to say that the administration of a typical English borough is conducted by the officials. Bagehot's quotation from Sir George Cornwall Lewis about the functions of cabinet ministers, can be applied to the committees of a borough council. It is not their business to work the departments, but to see that they are properly worked.

**Benefits of their Influence.**

The merits of English municipal government have been commonly attributed to the concentration of power in the hands of the council, but in its essence the system is virtually that of management by committees; and such a system, by its very nature removed in details from public observation, is singularly open to abuse. There is probably no method of government that in bad hands lends itself more readily to inefficiency and corruption than administration

[1] At the time of the investigation in 1897 into the falsification of accounts in the Works Department of the London County Council, one of the complaints made was that the manager had little freedom of action without interference by his committee (L.C.C. Rep. of Com. on the Works Department, XXXIV., XLVI.). This impression is confirmed by looking through the evidence printed with the report. A new departure was made under the succeeding manager, who became the real head of the department.

by committees, and none that is less sensitive to healthy criticism. But it works very well where, as in the English borough councils, the committee acts under the guidance of upright and capable experts. Under these circumstances the officials, who really administer the city, find support, protection and permanence of tenure; while at the same time they are prevented from becoming bureaucratic, and are kept in touch with public opinion.

Dangers that threaten it.

The traditional position of the permanent officials seems to be very firmly established in the British towns. The deterioration in the caliber of the councillors, which has been slowly going on in most of the larger places, has not as a rule made any change in it, because the natural tendency of a smaller type of man to interfere more in details has been offset by a growth in the mass of business that makes it very hard for a councillor to grapple with the facts. This comes from the increase in population and the extension of municipal functions, and is, therefore, likely to continue. A lowering in the caliber of the council may, however, involve a serious danger, for men who are not accustomed to dealing with affairs on a large scale are prone to look askance at high salaries. At present the officials are fairly well paid, and although they earn less than they might in private practice, the permanence of tenure so far makes up for this that there has been no great difficulty in getting good men. But it is not certain that this will continue. When Mr. Chamberlain, more than thirty years ago, carried through in Birmingham the purchase by the city of the gas and water works, he is said to have told the council that if they were not prepared to be generous in their salaries to their experts, they had better not enter upon a policy of municipal ownership. More recently he has said in a speech at Glasgow that if ever corruption creeps into the cities of Great Britain it will be when the higher officials are paid less, and lower employees more, than the market value of their services;[1] and the time will never come when this warning will not be sound.

[1] Local Govt. Journal, Nov. 13, 1897, p. 730.

# CHAPTER XLI

## BOROUGHS. — POWERS AND RESOURCES

Sources of Authority.

THE reader will remember that the powers of borough councils are derived from three distinct sources; first, the Municipal Corporations Act of 1882 with its amendments; second, the Public Health Acts and other statutes of a similar kind, which apply to, or may be adopted by, all urban districts, and sometimes rural districts also; and third, special, private or local acts. The first and last of these classes confer authority on the borough council as such, the second on the council in its capacity of local sanitary authority;[1] but in speaking of the boroughs this distinction is not very important, except for the fact that the control of the central government over local administration is on the whole greater, and is exercised in a somewhat different way, in the case of powers vested in the local sanitary authority, a matter that will be explained when we come to deal with central control.

Powers of Borough Councils under General Laws.

A very small part of the authority essential in any city government is conferred by the Act of 1882. It covers little except the power to adopt by-laws, to erect buildings for public use, to keep up borough bridges, and to maintain a police force.[2]

[1] The Local Govt. Act of 1888, which transferred the administrative functions of the justices of the peace to the newly created county councils, stands in a position by itself, for it conferred the same powers upon the councils of the county boroughs named in a schedule to the Act, and made some adjustments in the case of smaller towns. The actual enlargement in the powers of the county boroughs produced by this Act were not, however, great. The Education Act of 1902 is also anomalous. It vested the whole or a part of the control over public education in the councils of boroughs with more than 10,000 people, and in those of urban districts with a population of 20,000.

[2] By the Local Govt. Act of 1888 (51–52 Vic., c. 41, § 39) the right to maintain a separate police force was taken away from boroughs with less

The authority given by the Public Health Act of 1875 is far more extensive.[1] It includes such things as maintaining sewers; making, paving, lighting and cleaning streets; taking measures against infection and epidemics; providing fire engines, hospitals, pleasure grounds, markets,[2] water for private as well as public use,[3] public baths and wash-houses, dwellings and lodging-houses for the working classes;[4] contracting, with the consent of the Local Government Board, for the purchase of a gas company's rights; and applying for provisional orders to supply gas if there be no company, or to take land compulsorily to carry out any of the purposes of the Act — for land in England is so sacred that it can almost never be taken for public use without a private act, or provisional order confirmed by Parliament, in each particular case.

By later statutes local authorities, including boroughs, are given power to maintain cemeteries,[5] museums, gymnasiums and public libraries;[6] to obtain provisional orders for supplying electric light,[7] and for constructing and owning, but not for running, tramways.[8] They are further authorised to provide allotments of land for labourers' gardens;[9] to close houses unfit for human habitation; to clear out, by means of provisional orders, large unhealthy areas, and

than 10,000 people. The Act of 1882 authorised trustees under local acts for paving, lighting, supplying water, gas, etc., to transfer their powers to the borough council, and that has been done. But these powers are not conferred by the Act itself.

[1] No attempt is made here to trace the history of the grant of these powers, and the references are merely to a few of the principal statutes now in force.

[2] Provided this does not interfere with any existing privilege of keeping a market. 38–39 Vic., c. 55, § 166.

[3] Provided again that the borough cannot furnish water within the limits of a company which is giving a proper and sufficient supply, § 52.

[4] By adopting the Baths and Wash-houses Acts and the Labouring Classes Lodging-houses Acts. *Cf.* § 10.

[5] Public Health (Interments) Act, 1879, 42–43 Vic., c. 31.

[6] By adopting the Museums and Gymnasiums Act, 1891, 54–55 Vic., c. 22, and the Public Libraries Act, 1892, 55–56 Vic., c. 53.

[7] Electric Lighting Acts, 1882, 45–46 Vic., c. 56; 1888, 51–52 Vic., c. 12.

[8] Tramways Act, 1870, 33–34 Vic., c. 78.

[9] Allotments Acts, 1887, 50–51 Vic., c. 48; 1890, 53–54 Vic., c. 65.

rehouse the working classes displaced thereby.[1] Moreover, by another series of acts the local authorities are empowered to furnish technical instruction, and schools for science and art;[2] and finally, by the Education Act of 1902, the county boroughs are placed in control of all schools managed by public authority, while the smaller boroughs and larger urban districts are given charge of elementary schools.[3]

Under Private Acts.

Such are the principal powers conferred upon the borough councils by general statutes, but they by no means cover the whole ground, because the boroughs are all the time seeking and obtaining fresh authority by means of private acts of Parliament. This is especially true in the field of municipal trading. Even where, as in the case of supplying gas or electric light, the right can be acquired by provisional order, the borough, believing that it can obtain directly from Parliament better terms or more extended powers than the government department will grant, often proceeds by private bill. In the case of tramways the statute does not permit the grant by provisional order of authority to operate, yet many boroughs have been given power to do so by private acts. The same thing happened at an earlier date in regard to the municipal management of water works and gas works, for the experiment was tried in a few places under private acts before a general statute was passed on the subject. Boroughs are, in fact, constantly engaged in promoting or opposing private bills in Parliament that affect their interests. The proceedings are costly, but until 1872 the council had no right to defray the charges out of public money. Now, however, the expense of opposing a bill can always be defrayed out of the borough treasury; and the cost of promoting a bill can be paid in the same way, with the approval of the Local Government Board and the consent

[1] The statutes on this subject, and on the provision of dwellings and lodging-houses for the working classes, were consolidated in the Housing of the Working Classes Act, 1890, 53–54 Vic., c. 70.

[2] Technical Instruction Acts, 1889, 52–53 Vic., c. 76; 1891, 54–55 Vic., c. 4. Schools for Science and Art Act, 1891, *ibid.*, c. 61.

[3] For the details of this subject see the chapters on Education.

of the municipal voters given at a meeting called for the purpose.[1]

Audit of Accounts.

Among the powers of supervision given to the Local Government Board is that of auditing the accounts of almost every kind of local authority except the borough councils. The examination is conducted by means of district auditors, appointed by the Board, who have power to refuse to sanction any expenditure unauthorised by law, and throw it back upon the persons who have ordered the payment. This is called the power to disallow and surcharge, and it involves an appeal to the Board itself, which can remit the repayment of the item, and that in fact is usually done where the payment was made in good faith for a reasonable object.

But the audit of the Local Government Board does not extend to the provincial boroughs, and the sole provision made by law for the examination of their accounts is the one contained in the Municipal Corporations Act of 1882, directing that there shall be three auditors; two elected by the burgesses, called elective auditors, who must not be on the council; and one appointed by the mayor, called mayor's auditor.[2] There is no requirement that these men shall be professional accountants, and as a rule they are not. Very little interest is taken in their election, they cannot undertake a really thorough examination of the accounts, and in short the institution has been freely called a farce.[3] In the larger boroughs, at least, professional auditors are, in fact, regularly employed by the finance committee, or by the committees in charge of the great departments; but this is not obligatory, and the boroughs object strenuously to being brought under the audit of the Local Government Board, which they regard as vexatious. There are a number

[1] Borough Funds Act, 1903, 3 Edw. VII., c. 14. By the Borough Funds Act, 1872, 35–36 Vic., c. 91, the approval and consent were required in the case of opposing as well as of promoting a bill; and the consent was that of owners and ratepayers, with votes in proportion to property according to the scale then in use for the lesser local authorities.

[2] 45–46 Vic., c. 50, §§ 25–27, 62.

[3] *Cf.* Rep. of the Com. on Mun. Trading, Com. Papers, 1900, VII., 183, Qs. 1713–67, 1806–8, 1827, 1847, 2026–48, 2470–72, 3863–66, 3900.

of small expenses, not strictly legal, incurred for such purposes as antedating a little an increase of salary, decorating the town for a royal visit, and perhaps some petty junketing, which would be disallowed and surcharged by the auditors of the Board. The second Committee on Municipal Trading devoted its whole attention to this matter, and reported that, while in a large number of cases the ratepayers are as fully informed about municipal undertakings as the shareholders of an ordinary company, there are some instances to the contrary; and they recommended that the boroughs should be obliged to appoint, with the approval of the Local Government Board, professional auditors empowered to probe matters to the bottom.[1]

Sources of Revenue.

Except for the fact that the support of the poor still remains in the hands of the union with its poor law guardians, and that in the smaller towns the parishes are rated directly by the county for certain expenses connected with education, police and other matters that are managed in those towns by the authorities of the shire, the whole financial administration of the boroughs is vested in their own councils. The revenues and expenditures, like the powers, of the council as such and as local sanitary authority, are indeed kept apart, but the distinction is not for our purpose important. There is a borough fund and a district fund, and the borough rate is made separately from the district rate, the reductions of assessment on railways, canals and agricultural land not being the same in the two cases;[2] yet these differences have no vital bearing on the municipal finance.

[1] Com. Papers, 1903, VII., 1.

[2] In urban districts, railways, canals and almost all agricultural lands are rated at only one quarter of their ratable value, on the ground that they obtain very little benefit from sanitary expenditure. Public Health Act, 1875, § 211; *cf.* 53–54 Vic., c. 17; 54–55 Vic., c. 33. By the temporary Agricultural Rates Act, 1896, continued to 1910 by 1 Edw. VII., c. 13, and 5 Edw. VII., c. 8, all other agricultural land everywhere is rated at only one half its value for all local purposes, except in the case of rates laid for its special benefit, the loss to the local authority being made up from the national treasury.

The revenues of boroughs are derived from rents of property; from tolls, fines and licenses; from profits of industrial undertakings, like gas, electricity, and the like; from local taxation in the form of rates; from subventions by the national government; and from loans. The amount of land and buildings owned by a borough is sometimes large. Glasgow, for example, draws an income of more than fifty thousand pounds a year from municipal property known as the "common good"; and in a few places, like Doncaster, the receipts of that kind are so great that it has not been necessary to levy any local rates at all. The next source of revenue, tolls, fines, license fees collected by the town, and the like, furnish as a rule comparatively small sums of money; while the profits of industrial enterprise, which vary, of course, very much in different boroughs, will be discussed in the chapter on municipal trading. This leaves the three chief sources of revenue which are open to all boroughs: rates, loans and national subventions.

**Local Rates.**

English local taxation, by whatever authority it is levied, is exclusively in the form of a rate assessed upon the occupier of land.[1] It would seem that the Act of Elizabeth was not intended to be so confined, and in a few places stock in trade was formerly rated also; but this was forbidden by statute in 1840, and since that time the rates have been levied only on the present enjoyment of rights in land.[2] They are assessed to the occupier, not the owner, unless he happens to occupy his own land;[3] and they are

[1] In Scotland the rate is divided between the occupier and the owner, the part assessed upon the latter being usually payable whether the property is occupied or not.

[2] *Cf.* First Rep. Com. on Local Taxation, Com. Papers, 1899, XXXV., 733. The ratable interests in land include, besides lands and buildings, mines, tithes and sporting rights.

[3] The owner of small tenements habitually compounds for the payment of his tenants' rates, and may be compelled to do so. In such cases he is allowed to deduct a percentage of the rate that the occupier would be charged, and he is allowed a further deduction if he is assessed upon the tenements whether occupied or vacant. 32–33 Vic., c. 41, §§ 1–13, 16; 38–39 Vic., c. 55, § 211.

based upon the net annual value of the land in its existing condition. The net annual value is obtained by estimating the gross rent at which the property is let, or might reasonably be expected to be let, and deducting therefrom the probable annual cost of repairs, insurance and other expenses of keeping it in order, an amount that appears to be fixed in different towns from one fifth to one tenth of the gross rent.

**Effect on Vacant Land.**

It will be observed that unoccupied land or buildings are not assessed at all;[1] and that in the case of occupied land the valuation is based not upon its capital or salable value, but upon its rental value in its existing condition, so that a garden in the heart of a city is taxed only at its rental value as a garden. In fact, under the Public Health Acts it is assessed in the general district rate for sanitary purposes at one quarter of its ratable value as a garden; and under the Agricultural Rates Act at one half of that value for all other purposes. In this way the tax laws encourage the holding of land unbuilt in the cities or their suburbs, and there is an inversion of the doctrine of taxing heavily the unearned increment. So far as taxation is concerned, a man who owns a tract of open ground, needed for building, can afford to keep it vacant, either with a view to speculating upon an increase in value with the growth of the town, or because he enjoys the luxury of a garden about his house. To that fact, coupled with the slow progress made until very recent years in methods of rapid urban transit, is no doubt largely due the congestion of the towns. The sudden change, indeed, from solid blocks of houses to open fields, which although less marked than it was formerly, still characterises most English cities, contrasts strongly with the penumbra of detached residences that stretch, more and more sparsely, far into the country in America.

**The Commission of 1896.**

Complaints of the method of local taxation have been loud for some time, partly on the ground that it tends

[1] *Cf.* Encyclopædia of Local Government Law (1907), V. 333.

to keep land out of the market, partly on account of a feeling that the landowner does not bear his share of the public burdens. In 1896 a royal commission was appointed to inquire into the whole subject, and its reports are a mine of information. They are largely concerned with the relations of national and local finance; with the difference between beneficial expenditure, where the burden ought to be borne in proportion to benefit, and onerous charges, which ought to be borne in proportion to ability and cannot, therefore, fairly be defrayed from rates alone; and they discuss at length the share of each of these kinds of burdens that ought properly to fall upon agricultural and urban land. In its final report[1] the commission deals with the taxation of site values, and concludes that a separate estimate of the annual value of site and building would be difficult, that to levy on the site a special additional rate would be unjust, and that an attempt to tax vacant land on its capital value would be a misguided effort to insert a new principle in a system of taxation based upon a wholly different plan. This last proposition was accepted even by the five members who signed a special minority report on the subject of site values.[2] These members recommended, however, that sites and buildings should be assessed separately, with a higher rate upon the former; and while rejecting the suggestion of a tax on uncovered land based upon its capital value, they urged that any such land which is intended to be let, or could be let, with a covenant for immediate building, should be rated at the rent it would fetch for that purpose.

Land in England is a sacred heirloom that is rarely offered for sale. Few men, either in town or country, own the freehold of the house in which they live. Great tracts of urban land belong to peers or other rich men, who let them on long ground leases, but would never think of selling a single house lot outright — a condition especially marked in the towns that have grown up in modern times.

[1] Com. Papers, 1901, XXIV., 413, pp. 43–44.

[2] *Ibid.*, p. 149.

Hence an Englishman thinks and speaks habitually not of the capital value but of the rental value of land, and this is deemed an easy thing to estimate. Land can hardly be said to have a market value; and a suggestion that it should be taxed as capital is met by the answer that it is more fair to tax it upon the actual revenue it produces, than on some problematical price that it might bring if sold.

**National Subventions.**

It has long been the practice for the national government to help the local authorities by contributions from the treasury, made partly to relieve the ratepayer, and partly to stimulate local effort by grants conditional on efficiency. So far as the sources of revenue are concerned the matter was simplified by the Local Government Act of 1888,[1] which substituted for sums granted annually by Parliament, permanent subventions from the proceeds of special taxes. These were a fraction of the receipts from the probate duty, and the whole net receipts from the local taxation licenses to sell liquor, to act as auctioneer, tobacco dealer, pawnbroker and so forth, or to keep armorial bearings, carriages, male servants, dogs and guns. In 1890 certain additional taxes on spirits and beer were added,[2] and in 1894 the new estate duty took the place of the probate duty.[3] The money is paid to the counties and county boroughs, and inscribed in what is known as the Exchequer Contribution Account. Part of it is used by these bodies directly, and the rest is distributed by them among the lesser local authorities. But while the new system changed the sources, it did not alter the objects of the grants, which remain of a miscellaneous character, including such things as a portion of the cost of officers of poor law unions, the maintenance of pauper lunatics, one half of the salaries of medical officers and inspectors, and one half of the pay and clothing of the police. Besides the Exchequer Con-

[1] 51–52 Vic., c. 41, §§ 20–27.
[2] 53 Vic., c. 8, § 7; 53–54 Vic., c. 60, §§ 1, 5.
[3] 57–58 Vic., c. 30, § 19.

tribution Account, which amounts for the United Kingdom to about ten million pounds a year, the national government makes a still larger grant for the support of public education, the total subventions being equal to about one quarter of the sums raised by local rates. Moreover, the government has made since 1896 a further special contribution in relief of agricultural land.[1]

Loans. The expenditure required for lasting public improvements in the form of buildings, sewerage plants, water works, parks and the like, are so great that no city at the present day can do its work without borrowing money in large amounts; and this necessity is made still greater where the borough undertakes to supply its inhabitants with commodities such as gas, electricity and transportation. Provision has, therefore, been made for raising loans, subject to the supervision of the central government. A borough, for example, can with the approval of the Treasury borrow money to erect public buildings.[2] As local sanitary authority it can, with the sanction of the Local Government Board, borrow for the purposes of the Public Health Act;[3] and in fact each statute that confers power upon the council contains a provision for the loans needed to carry it out. Parliament has gone farther. It has made itself a lender on a grand scale by creating a board of Public Works Loan Commissioners, to whom it has intrusted large sums to be lent to local authorities.[4] In 1887 these amounted to more than thirty-seven millions of pounds, and they are constantly increased by fresh grants from the funds in the hands of the National Debt Commissioners.

Not only do the loans of local bodies require in all cases the consent of some department of the central government, but careful provisions are made for repayment. A sinking

[1] *Cf.* Note 2 on page 185, *supra.*
[2] Municipal Corp. Act, 1882, 45–46 Vic., c. 50, § 105.
[3] Public Health Act, 1875, 38–39 Vic., c. 55, §§ 233–34.
[4] *Cf.* Public Works Loans Act, 1875, 38–39 Vic., c. 58; Nat. Debt and Local Loans Act, 1887, 50–51 Vic., c. 16.

fund must be maintained which will extinguish the debt in sixty years at the longest;[1] and on that point there are constant dissensions between the Local Government Board and the local councils, the former insisting on a short period, while the latter contend that this throws an excessive burden upon the existing ratepayers for improvements that are in the main a benefit to posterity. Herein lies one of the reasons why boroughs seeking special powers often prefer to proceed by private bill instead of by provisional order; for they hope to obtain more favourable terms from a private bill committee than from a government board.

By statute, loans can be contracted only for permanent works, and it is provided that those made under the Public Health Act shall not in the aggregate exceed the assessable value for two years, that is, twice the net income of all the land in the borough. But the rule may be relaxed by the Local Government Board,[2] and it does not include all the loans that a borough is entitled to make, notably those authorised by special local acts. In fact, the municipal debt of England has rolled up like a snowball during the last half century.

**Rapid Increase of Rates.**

It might be supposed that when local taxation is levied upon the occupier there would be a controlling interest in the community to restrain expenditure, and this happens in the rural districts, where the rates are keenly felt by the farmer. But in the cities it is not so, partly no doubt because the landlords compound for the rates of the poorer classes, who form a large fraction of the voters.[3] As Odgers remarks: "No one works harder than an Englishman to make money, yet no one submits more passively to having his money taken from him. . . . The ordinary

[1] The period is only twenty years when the act does not otherwise prescribe. Local Loans Act, 1875, 38–39 Vic., c. 83, § 13. For workingmen's dwellings the maximum is now eighty years. 3 Edw. VII., c. 39.

[2] Public Health Act, 1875, 38–39 Vic., c. 55, § 234.

[3] Mr. Smith, Town Clerk of Birmingham, estimated that seventy or seventy-five per cent of the municipal voters of the city were compound householders whose rates were paid by the landlord. Rep. of Com. on Mun. Trading, Com. Papers, 1900, VII., 183, Q. 1949.

ratepayer looks on a rise in his rates in the same way that he looks on an increase in the rainfall. Both are matters to be grumbled at; but in neither case does he inquire into causes, and he considers the one as irremediable as the other."[1] The ratepayers all over England have certainly not shown interest enough to go to the polls in large numbers; and in fact, so far as a stranger could observe, the prevalent feeling until the late elections in London was one of condemnation for municipal parsimony, with the natural result, a gradual growth of expenditure.

The steady increase of both rates and loans has long attracted attention, and has given rise to elaborate parliamentary reports. Two of them are especially noteworthy, those prosecuted by Mr. Goschen in 1871, and by Mr. Fowler in 1893.[2] From these reports it appears that the total amount of money raised by local rates in England and Wales increased from the beginning of the century until about 1817, and then, owing largely to the reform of the poor laws in 1834, it diminished until near the middle of the century, when it began to increase again at a constantly accelerated rate. Yet on account of the growth of the country in wealth and population, and the consequent advance in the net annual value of land, the change in the amount raised by local taxation did not for a time involve a much heavier burden on the ratepayer. In fact the average number of shillings in the pound of the total rates had fallen very greatly, and in 1841 was not much more than half of what it had been in 1803. About the middle of the century the average rate began to rise, but not very fast at first, and in 1891 it was 3*s.* 8*d.* as against 4*s.* 5¼*d.* in 1803, and 2*s.* 7*d.* in 1841. Naturally the changes had not been the same everywhere. The cost of local administration had grown much more rapidly in the towns than in the country; and while the ratable value had, up to 1891, increased in the rural districts faster than the expenditure, in the urban districts the expenditure

[1] "Local Government," 30–31. [2] Com. Papers, 1893, LXXVII., 1, 233.

had increased faster than the ratable value, in spite of the enormous gain in the latter. Since Mr. Fowler's report both expenditure and rates have marched with long strides. In the dozen years from 1889–1890 to 1901–1902, the total expenditure of the local authorities in England and Wales, apart from loans, rose from forty-eight to eighty-seven millions of pounds, and the average rate from 3*s.* 8.2*d.* to 5*s.* 3.8*d.* in the pound.

**Increase of Local Debt.**

The aggregate local debt meanwhile has been keeping pace. In 1874–1875 it was ninety-two millions of pounds, in 1889–1890 it was nearly two hundred millions, and in 1901–1902 it had grown to three hundred and forty-three millions, or not far from half the size of the whole national debt,[1] only about one half of it having been borrowed for undertakings that might be supposed to yield a revenue. The tendency that has prevailed is shown forcibly by a small table printed each year in the report of the Local Government Board.[2] In this it appears that from 1874–1875 to 1901–1902 the population of England and Wales increased thirty-seven per cent, the ratable value of property sixty-one per cent, the amount of money raised by local rates one hundred and forty-one per cent, the outstanding loans two hundred and seventy per cent, and the subvention for local purposes from the national treasury six hundred and forty-five per cent.

**Actual Weight of Taxation.**

The growth of both rates and debts has naturally been greater in the boroughs than in the rural districts, and the burden of taxation in English cities is certainly not light to-day.[3] In order to form a more definite impression on

[1] Rep. of the Local Govt. Board, Com. Papers, 1904, XXV., App. P.

[2] *Ibid.*, p. cciv.

[3] For some purposes the rates are limited in amount. Thus the rates under the Technical Instruction Act, 1889, 52–53 Vic., c. 76, and the Public Libraries Act, 1892, 55–56 Vic., c. 53, cannot exceed in each case one penny in the pound, and a similar limit is placed upon expenditure under the Museums and Gymnasiums Act, 1891, 54–55 Vic., c. 22. The Education Act, 1902, 2 Edw. VII., c. 42, fixes the limit for secondary schools in non-county boroughs at one penny, and for county councils at twopence. But these provisions are exceptional, and not very important.

the subject the writer has tried to make a comparison with the conditions in his own city of Boston, not habitually one of the worst governed, but perhaps the most extravagant, of American cities. At first sight any common measure seems out of the question, because English rates are assessed on the rental value of land alone, while in America local taxes are based on the capital value of both land and personal property. But in fact the proportion of local expenditure borne by land is not far from the same in the two cases. In the year 1902–1903 seventy-five and one half per cent of the aggregate revenue derived from taxation in the county boroughs of England and Wales was supplied by rates,[1] while in Boston in 1903 the tax on real estate supplied seventy-three and one half per cent of the income.[2] A comparison, therefore, of the burden laid upon land in those places gives a fair impression of the relative weight of local taxation. Now the total average rates in the county boroughs at the time was 6*s.* 10.6*d.* in the pound, or thirty-four and one third per cent of the net rental value.[3] In Boston, on the other hand, the tax on the capital value of real estate, after deducting the part of the state tax that is clearly not a local charge, was $14.134 on every thousand dollars, which would be equivalent to the burden in the English county boroughs if the average net rent in Boston after paying taxes and repairs were four and one quarter per cent of the capital value, certainly not a high return. The comparison is not exact, because vacant property in England is not rated, and there is a reduction

[1] From the Report of the Local Govt. Board (Com. Papers, 1904, LXXXI., 1003) it appears that the receipts of county boroughs from tolls, fines, etc., were £373,182, the Exchequer Contribution Account including subventions for police were £1,635,964. The amount paid by the Treasury for the support of public education in the county boroughs is given nowhere, but if we assume that the grants are in proportion to population these boroughs received £2,709,074. The three sums added together make £4,718,220 as against £14,442,836 raised by rates.

[2] The rest of the income being derived from the tax on personal property, from the corporation, bank and poll taxes, and from licenses. *Cf.* Statistics Dept. City of Boston, Special Pub. No. 13.

[3] Com. Papers, 1904, LXXXI., 1003, p. 40.

when the landlord compounds, while land without buildings upon it pays very little. Still it would seem that the burden of local taxation in Boston is not very different from that of the average county borough, and it is probably less than in the larger English cities where the rate is usually higher than in smaller towns.[1]

Any one who presumes to estimate with precision the comparative merits of any government must either possess a marvellous knowledge of the subject in all its bearings, or place great reliance on superficial impressions. The first thing that strikes an American in England is the excellence of the paving in the streets, and although one sometimes hears complaints on this score in a provincial town, it is evidence rather of a high public standard than of any serious defect. The streets are also well lighted, and they are fairly clean, a matter in which the climate is a hindrance. The regulation of street traffic by the police, especially in London, is amazing; and in other respects the order maintained is on the whole good, although the prolonged series of murders in the open by Jack the Ripper a score of years ago did, no doubt, indicate a lack of efficiency in the poorer parts of the metropolis. The occasional failure to protect strike breakers from violence shows, also, a weakness which is unfortunately too common in many countries. That the police have not everywhere been altogether free from corrupt influences, especially in the matter of enforcing the

**Efficiency of Administration.**

[1] The rates for 1906 in the ten largest boroughs of England and Wales were as follows: Birmingham, 7*s.* 4*d.*; Bradford, 8*s.* 4*d.*, Bristol, 7*s.* 10*d.*; Kingston-upon-Hull, 7*s.* 10½*d.*; Leeds, 8*s.* 8*d.*; Liverpool, 7*s.* 8⅞*d.*; Manchester, 8*s.* 0⅛*d.*; Nottingham, 7*s.* 6*d.*; Sheffield over 8*s.* (in this case the Municipal Year Book does not give the poor rate; the borough and district rates amount together to 6*s.* 6½*d.*); West Ham, 10*s.* 8*d.* In the various parishes that make up the County of London the rates vary a great deal. In one case alone they were in 1906 less than 6*s.* In most of the parishes they were more than 7*s.*; in many cases more than 8*s.*; in several more than 9*s.*; and in the three parishes of Poplar they were 12*s.* In Boston, also, taxes have increased. For this same year, 1906, the rate, after deducting the purely state tax, was $14.89 per thousand of capital value, which on the basis of an average net return of only four and a quarter per cent on all real estate would be equivalent to an English rate of seven shillings in the pound.

license laws, is certainly true,[1] and there was a bad scandal on this subject in Manchester a few years ago.[2] Complaints, moreover, about the evil effect of having persons who are interested in breweries or public houses serve on the watch committee are very common.[3]

The water supply and the sewerage in British towns are good, as appears from the fact that the death rate, while not extraordinarily low, is by no means high as compared with other cities under modern administration. On the other hand, the amount of overcrowding is still such as to be a physical and moral danger to the community, and one cannot help feeling that if more wisely and firmly attacked in its causes it might be very much reduced. Public education, which was in a very deplorable state forty years ago, is now in good condition and constantly improving. A great deal has been done also in providing those things which are the luxuries rather than the necessities of city life, parks and open spaces, libraries, baths and wash-houses; although it must be added that, except for these last, the result while good is not remarkable. Until the last few years rapid transit and electric lighting were very backward, owing mainly to a conflict between the systems of private and municipal ownership; but the discussion of this question must be postponed to the chapter on municipal trading.

On the whole, if one may venture to express a general opinion, without its being taken too seriously, it would seem that municipal administration in England to-day is throughout efficient, solid and businesslike, rather than brilliant. There are few glaring shortcomings, and few extraordinary

[1] Some of these cases are referred to in the minority report of the commissioners on the liquor licensing laws. Com. Papers, 1899, XXXV., 1, pp. 158–62.

[2] An inquiry and report was made by J. S. Dugdale, Q.C., and the evidence taken was printed.

[3] Both the majority and minority of the commission on liquor licensing laws recommended that such persons should be disqualified from serving, and the minority said that the evil aimed at amounted to a gross scandal. Com. Papers, 1899, XXXV., 1, pp. 21, 162.

successes; few failures that furnish the world lessons in what to avoid, and few great achievements which the world will seek to imitate.

Absence of Corruption.

The English towns have, as a rule, been singularly free from corruption. Any one with a taste for scandals can, of course, find them, as he can in any form of business, however high its general tone may be, for it is impossible to prevent the occasional election of a dishonest man who may find a chance to do a dishonest thing. There have been cases of contracts in which a member of the council has been interested, and one of these came to light some years ago just in time to prevent an alderman in a large city from being chosen mayor. There have been also cases of jobbery involving councillors and sometimes officials, but they have been uncommon and on a small scale. Nothing in the nature of systematic corruption has existed, unless the combination of mismanagement and jobbery recently exposed at Poplar was a case of that kind.[1]

Employment of Labour.

The same thing is true of the abuses connected with municipal labour. In some places members of the council recommend workmen for employment — although on personal rather than on political grounds — and occasionally this has been carried so far as to be unfortunate, but as a rule pressure of that kind does not seem to be serious, and more often it is so slight that the permanent official at the head of a department can practically disregard it. He has

[1] From Davy's official report (*The Times*, Nov. 9, 1906) it appears that in thirteen years the number of persons receiving outdoor relief multiplied fivefold, largely it seems in pursuance of a socialistic policy. Relief was given without any labour test, and this caused an enormous increase in the amount expended, until the Local Govt. Board ordered an inquiry, when pauperism suddenly dropped one half. People over sixty years of age were given relief regardless of the earnings of the other members of the family, and in fact one of the progressive guardians admitted that the poor rates had been used as a means of granting old age pensions. The inmates of the workhouse were maintained in luxury previously unknown, with a supply of beer furnished under a medical pretence, but stopped when the inquiry began. There was also evidence of jobs in awarding contracts, and of some bribery.

Since this chapter was written scandals have been brought to light in West Ham in 1907.

usually a free hand also in discharging workmen for incompetence, indolence or insubordination; although one meets with instances where employees are protected by councillors, who bring cases of discharge before the committee, or even before the council. The freedom of an official in such matters depends, of course, a good deal on his personal force, and the practice is sometimes different in two departments in the same town. Anything, however, like a systematic use of patronage in the employment of workmen to help the electoral prospects of a party or an individual seems to be almost, if not entirely, unknown.

Wages Paid.

This is a danger that depends upon the wages paid. If they are substantially larger than a man can earn for similar work in private concerns, employment by the city becomes a privilege which is almost certain to foster spoils. Now the boroughs have hitherto paid as a rule little if any more than the market rates. Wages in England, especially in the larger towns, are regulated to a great extent by the trade unions, and it is the regular custom in many places to pay the trade-union, or standard, rate of wages. The standing orders of some boroughs provide, indeed, that those rates shall be paid by all contractors doing work for the city; and at one time the London County Council, in its desire to play the part of a model employer of labour, carried this policy so far as to deter the best class of contractors from making bids.[1]

Amount of Work Done.

But if the boroughs do not pay substantially higher wages than private firms, their treatment of workmen is often more indulgent, and one hears not infrequently of the difficulty in getting a full day's work. Without formal action by the trade-unions, the policy of workingmen in England has tended to lessen the amount of work done in a day, with a view to increasing the demand for labour. This has been particularly marked in the case of the bricklayers, whose tale of bricks has decreased in a most startling way. The tendency is even stronger in public than in pri-

[1] *Cf.* Rep. of the Com. on the Works Dept., 1896–97, pp. vi, viii.

vate employ, and it has been sometimes expressed by the term "corporation stroke."

**The Danger Involved.**

As yet these things have not attained very serious proportions, but they involve a danger which would become menacing if the employees of a city should combine to carry elections and better their own condition. Except, perhaps, in West Ham when under the control of the Socialists, this has not happened, but with the vast growth in the number of men employed it has certainly become possible, and many people are of opinion that the municipal employees ought to be disfranchised, a measure which has been partially adopted in the colony of Victoria, in the case of the state railways.[1] Of late years the number of Labour members on the borough councils has increased, and although they bear in general the reputation of being personally intelligent and faithful councillors, although they are not elected as spokesmen of the municipal employees, yet they look at things from the point of view of their own class, rather than from the single standpoint of the general welfare. While they do good service as intermediaries between the council and its employees, and ward off unreasonable demands by the workmen, they are after all the representatives of the trade-unions, and as such they tend to throw their influence on the side of higher wages or shorter hours.

**Decline in the Caliber of Councillors.**

Not only have the Labour members increased, but on the whole the quality of the men elected to the council has declined. This is not true everywhere. In some places one is told that there has been no change. But one often hears that the prosperity of a town was built up by large merchants who sat on the council, and that such men either come into it no more, or much less than in former days. There can, in fact, be no doubt that the average standing of the councillors has gone down. The men of

[1] The railway employees there were deprived of their votes in the regular constituencies, and given a few representatives of their own, so that they cannot bring direct pressure to bear on the other members. Victoria Const. Act, 1903, §§ 12, 25–27; Com. Papers, 1903, XLIV., 109, pp. 7–8.

wealth, of large affairs, the leading citizens, have been gradually replaced by people with perhaps as much public spirit and as good intentions, but with an experience less broad and of a smaller caliber. This is due in part to social centralisation, the attractions of London, and the decline of interest in provincial affairs. It is due also to the nature of electoral contests in the boroughs. Many a man who would be perfectly willing to give his time in the council, shrinks from an election in which he must try to curry favour, while disagreeable things are said about him on the platform or in the press. Parliamentary contests are largely confined to one social class, and the prize is tempting; but neither of these things is true of the borough councils. It is the old story of democracy, where a man is not sought out for office, but must fight for a chance to serve the public; and if, as in the English boroughs, this leads to no political preferment, it requires civic virtue of a very high order.

Causes of Efficiency.

After all the criticisms of English municipal administration have been made, no one can deny that it is upright and well conducted in a remarkable degree, in spite of the fact that the leading citizens are to some extent deterred from taking an active part. Its good qualities would seem to be due in the main to three factors. The first of them is the nature of the electorate, the extension of the franchise to suburbans who carry on business in the town, and coupled with this the willingness of the voters to elect men that do not reside in their ward. The second is the institution of aldermen, which allows a man who has served the town faithfully, and acquired experience in municipal affairs, to remain in the council without submitting to a reëlection. One is told that in this way many valuable councillors are retained who would be unwilling to throw themselves again into an electoral contest. Thus a number of the senior members of the council have been kept from retiring, and even if not of the largest caliber when first elected, they have attained a position of prominence, have become proud of the good name of their town, and perpetuate the administrative traditions.

The third factor is the position of the permanent officials. Their professional character insures efficiency, their effacement shields them from any temptation to achieve a cheap notoriety, and their permanence relieves them from the need of doing personal favours to retain their posts. They carry on the current administration, in most cases they suggest the improvements, and their presence is a bulwark of integrity. A dishonest councillor can hardly defraud the town, or make corrupt profits from contracts, without the connivance of an official who has an even stronger motive for honesty. The former, if a man without self-respect, risks little but the loss of his career on the council, but the official if exposed would be ruined. He would certainly forfeit his post, and would find it almost impossible to get another place where he could earn a livelihood. It has, in fact, happened, where a council contained men not too scrupulous, that the officials, with the town clerk at their head, have stood together and resisted successfully the perpetration of jobs.

# CHAPTER XLII

## LONDON

Recent History of London Government.

LOCAL administration in the metropolis has passed during the nineteenth century through a chaos of areas, authorities and rates, similar to that which prevailed over the rest of the country; and if the condition was less deliberately produced, but rather in the nature of an inherited malady, it took a somewhat more aggravated form, and the recovery has been less complete. London owes its vast growth to two distinct forces, which are combined to the same extent in no other city of the modern world. It has long been at once a great commercial and political centre, formed by the union in one metropolis of the old mercantile City of London and the national capital at Westminster. Around these two foci there has grown up a huge town, with its various kinds of business and social activity on the whole more concentrated in definite localities than is the case in most other large cities. But the political organisation has by no means kept pace with the social evolution, and long after London had become a great city it continued to be governed by a number of quite distinct local authorities, many of them instituted for the administration of purely rural communities, and all quite independent of any central body.

The Metropolitan Police.

The first important step toward the single management of matters of common interest was the creation by Sir Robert Peel in 1829 of the metropolitan police, still familiarly nicknamed from their founder "bobbies" or "peelers." This was in no sense a measure of self-government, for the force was placed, and remains to-day, under the charge of a board strictly subordinate to the Home Secretary.

Nor was it quite universal, because the old City has always retained an entirely separate police force of its own.

The Metropolitan Board of Works.

The next step was taken in 1855, mainly in consequence of the attention drawn to sanitary matters, the crying need of a system of drainage and the obvious impossibility of constructing main sewers without a central authority. In that year the Metropolitan Board of Works was established with power to construct main drains, improve streets and bridges, manage the fire brigade, and exercise some other functions which were enlarged from time to time.[1] The area included was the whole urban region of the day, but the scope of the Board's functions was very small, the other municipal duties being left, or placed, in the charge of many local bodies. These were the Corporation of the old City, nearly a score and a half of vestries for as many large parishes, more than a dozen district and other boards for groups of smaller parishes, and, not wholly conterminous therewith, some thirty boards of poor-law guardians and other special authorities.

The Metropolitan Board of Works did a great deal that was useful. It began and nearly completed a system of sewerage, which, if not perfect, has remained substantially unchanged. It built the greater part of the embankments along the Thames, and it laid out a number of new streets to make room for traffic in the narrow congested thoroughfares. But the Board was organised on what was later decried as a bad plan. Instead of being elected directly by the people, its forty-six members were chosen by the City Corporation and the various vestries and district boards. Now the popular interest in the vestries and boards was so slight that after a time the proportion of voters who took part in their election was ludicrously small. The Board of Works came into the hands of inferior men, fell in popular esteem, and finally lost the respect of the public altogether by the exposure of jobs whereby some of its

[1] For a history of the Board see Sinzheimer, *Der Londoner Grafschaftsrat.*

officers, and at least two of its members, had made corrupt profits out of dealings in land.[1] This happened just as Parliament was about to create elective county councils all over England, and London was included in the scheme.

Creation of the County Council.

The Act of 1888 abolished the Metropolitan Board of Works, transferred its duties to the new London County Council, and, with some exceptions in favour of the City, added also the powers given to the councils in other counties.[2] The area of the Council's jurisdiction, thereafter known as the administrative county of London, was the same as that of the Board of Works, and it has remained almost unaltered to the present day, although the urban population has now spread far beyond those limits. The most striking fact, indeed, about the movement of population in London has been the steady decrease of residents in all the central districts; the most rapid growth being found in the region, outside of the administrative county, but within the far larger area of the metropolitan police, called in the reports of the Registrar General the "Outer Ring of Greater London." At the census of 1901 the administrative county, with 118 square miles, had a population of 4,536,541, while the greater London under the metropolitan and city police, with 693 square miles, had 6,581,372 people; and thus nearly one third of the inhabitants of the metropolis are now outside of the administrative county.

Creation of the London Boroughs.

The Act of 1888 did not change the existing vestries and district boards, but a feeling became general that further reorganisation was imperative, and it was not lessened by the fact that all the vestries did not bear a spotless reputation. People assumed commonly that with its enormous size London could not, like other towns, be placed under a single authority; that its government must be based upon a federal system of some kind; and the Commission on the Amalgamation of London, appointed by the Liberal

[1] Rep. of Com. on Met. Board of Works, Com. Papers, 1888, LVI., 1.
[2] Local Govt. Act, 1888, 51–52 Vic., c. 41, §§ 40–45, 77, 88–90, 113–17.

ministry in 1894, was of this opinion.[1] But there was a difference of opinion between the political parties on two points: the amount of power to be vested in the County Council, then controlled by the Progressives, and how far the ancient privileges of the City, which was in the hands of the Conservatives, should be spared. The Liberal cabinet went out of office before it could give effect to its views, and the subject was then taken up by the Conservatives. Their policy was embodied in the London Government Act of 1899, which left the privileges of the City untouched, and divided the rest of the county into twenty-eight boroughs, partly old and partly new areas of local government, but all with new powers and governing bodies. Since that time a new Metropolitan Water Board has been created in 1902, while in 1903 the School Board was abolished and its powers transferred to the County Council.

**Existing Authorities.**

At the present time London is governed by the County Council and the Metropolitan Asylum Board, whose authority extends over the whole administrative county; the Commissioners of Metropolitan Police, whose authority does not include the City, but extends far beyond the county; the Metropolitan Water Board and the Thames and Lea Conservancy Boards, whose powers also are by no means limited by the county boundaries; the Corporation of the City and the councils of the twenty-eight metropolitan boroughs, whose authority — save for certain powers of the City — is confined to their own borders; thirty-one boards of guardians with areas that do not necessarily coïncide with any others; two sick asylum boards and four poor-law district boards, appointed jointly by certain boards of guardians; and finally a large number of old vestries in the City whose functions are insignificant.

**The City of London.**

By far the most picturesque of all the local bodies in England, preserving more than any other, in its Lord Mayor's show and the banquets of its guilds, the pageantry of

[1] Com. Papers, 1894, XVII., 1, pp. 12–13.

former times, and the only one still retaining a semblance of its ancient form of government, is the City of London. Partly because they are old, partly because some of them are very rich, but chiefly because too much of their revenues has been lavishly spent in sumptuous feasts instead of being devoted to public uses, the guilds have been severely criticised by radical reformers; and proposals are constantly made to abolish their privileges, and bring the City under institutions common to the whole metropolis.

Yet there is a reason why the City of London should be administered differently from any other place. It is not an ordinary town, to be governed for the benefit of its inhabitants. It has, in fact, few residents[1]; and they have been steadily diminishing. At the beginning of the nineteenth century they numbered one hundred and twenty-eight thousand. But a hundred years later, in 1901, the census showed that they had fallen to less than twenty-seven thousand. Moreover, a large proportion of these residents must inevitably be janitors or care-takers, with their families, who are simply employed to live there to look after other people's property. The one square mile within the limits of the City is the financial centre of the world, and under venerable forms it is governed by the people who carry on their business there; for although the guilds still possess certain imposing political functions, the government of the City is really vested in the representatives of the men who occupy rooms for commercial purposes, irrespective of their membership in a guild.

The Guilds. The London guilds, or livery companies as they are commonly called, have survived from the time when the control of industry and local government was organised on the basis of common occupations. They are now divided into twelve greater and sixty-seven minor companies, representing among them the old merchant and trade guilds. A few of them own large estates in London and elsewhere, and they now use a great part of the revenues

[1] That is people who dwell and sleep there.

for educational and other purposes, chiefly for technical instruction. Formerly the guilds really conducted the municipal government, and until 1867 no one could vote who did not belong to one of them; but this is no longer true, the electors being about three times as numerous as the members of the guilds; and in fact while the liverymen still retain the right to vote for members of Parliament they have as such no longer the franchise for municipal elections. Collectively the liverymen, meeting together with the mayor, sheriffs and aldermen in the Court of Common Hall, have a few functions of greater apparent than actual importance. They elect the sheriffs, the chamberlain or treasurer of the City, two bridge masters and four auditors — none of them politically very important officers — and they nominate two candidates for Lord Mayor, of whom the aldermen select one. But the mayoralty is not a position of great administrative consequence, and the nomination is practically limited to aldermen who have not already passed the chair. Moreover the election of aldermen is a matter over which the Court of Common Hall has no control, and as the mayor is very rarely reëlected, any alderman not peculiarly objectionable is almost sure in time to reach his turn of service; so that the right to nominate is not of much value.

**The Lord Mayor.**

The real government of the City is vested in the Lord Mayor, the Court of Aldermen, and the Court of Common Council.[1] The Lord Mayor is the most ornamental figure in English municipal life, and by no means an inexpensive one, since he has the Mansion House for his residence, receives a salary of £10,000 a year, and spends a good deal more. As chief magistrate of the City, he does no small amount of judicial work, and this is in fact more important than his administrative duties; for although chairman of all the three courts or councils, and the titular holder

[1] On the constitution and actual working of the City Government see the evidence collected by the Com. on the Amal. of London, Com. Papers, 1894, XVII., 1, and XVIII., Apps. iii. and x.

of some other posts, his real share in the conduct of business does not appear to be large.

The Aldermen.

The aldermen, twenty-six in number, including the mayor, are elected for life by the voters of the wards;[1] and since the franchise is the same for all the municipal elections in the City, it may be well to describe it here. It is regulated by a private act of 1867, and extends to all resident householders, and all occupiers, without regard to residence, of any separate part of a building of the annual value of ten pounds.[2] As the tenants of dwelling-houses are not numerous, and the service franchise — that is qualification by occupation in virtue of employment — does not apply, the electorate consists mainly of the people who hire offices for business purposes. The aldermen so chosen have, like the mayor, judicial duties; but apart from this they possess, as a distinct body, few administrative functions beyond those still retained by the justices of the peace in the counties, notably the granting of licenses for the sale of liquor. They are, however, members of the Court of Common Council, which is the real centre of municipal government.[3]

The Common Council.

The common council consists of the mayor, aldermen and two hundred and six councillors, the latter elected afresh every year by the wards in numbers proportioned to their importance. As a matter of fact contests are infrequent, and are never conducted on party lines, the Conservatives forming, of course, an overwhelming majority of the electorate. Like all English municipal bodies the council works by means of committees, with the aid of a

[1] There are 26 wards, two of which unite in electing an alderman, but one member of the body is elected to represent the imaginary ward of Bridge Without, not now a part of the City.

[2] Sir John Evans in his evidence before the Com. on the Amal. of London, said that this act was cumulative, and did not exclude freemen already qualified by occupation of premises of less than £10 value, but that there were very few of these.

[3] Many of the most vital civic functions, such as the paving and care of the streets, were formerly delegated to the Committee of Sewers, but in 1897 they were transferred by statute to the common council.

corps of permanent officials, one of whom, the police commissioner, occupies an unusual position, for he has absolute authority to appoint his subordinates and all the members of the force.

**Powers of the City.** The City is more independent of superior authority than other parts of the metropolis. Unlike the rest of London it has a police force of its own, and it is exempt from many powers which the London County Council exercises over the rest of the county, such, for example, as the powers relating to bridges; traffic in, and improvement of, streets; coroners; asylums; reformatory schools; unhealthy areas; housing of the working-classes; offensive trades, and several others. But the City is not under the exclusive management of its own Corporation. It is subject to the authority of the County Council in a number of matters connected with main sewers, tramways, fire brigade, formation and width of streets, overhead wires, public education, and some others of smaller importance. By the Act of 1902 the City was also included in the jurisdiction of the new Metropolitan Water Board. But for the rest the Corporation of the City has all the powers of a county borough within its own area; and what is more it has a number of powers that extend beyond its boundaries. Thus by ancient charter it has, with a few exceptions, the exclusive right to keep any markets within seven miles, and by a later act it is the sanitary authority for the port of London. The City forms a poor-law union by itself, and elects a board of guardians for its management.

**Weight of Taxation.** One would imagine that the business centre of a great town, set off by itself as a district for local government, would have small expenses compared to its property, and that the taxation would be very light. In fact the ratable value of the City of London is more than one ninth of that of the whole administrative county. Yet the rates are not abnormally low, for in addition to its ordinary expenses the Corporation spends something for general educational and charitable objects, and what is more to the point the rates in the different parts of the county have been made more nearly equal than they otherwise would be by means of three funds created for the purpose. The funds are replenished partly from the national grants in aid of local taxation, partly by uniform rates throughout the county, and they are expended for the support of the poor, or distributed among the local districts on the basis of population.[1] The result is that in 1905–06 the rate in the City was 6*s.* 9½*d.*, as against an average of 7*s.* 5*d.* for the whole county.

**The London Boroughs.** In turning from the City of London to the rest of the metropolis we pass from the very old to the very new. The London Government Act of 1899 simplified in a measure the administration of the metropolitan area by substituting for the different vestries and local boards twenty-eight boroughs with uniform organisation and powers. No serious attempt was made to have these of the same size, and in fact at the time the Act was passed one of them was five times as populous as another. Subject to changes in boundaries, designed to make the areas of the new boroughs continuous in almost every case, seventeen of them were identical with the larger existing parishes or districts, half a dozen more were made out of parliamentary constituencies, and the rest were compiled out of a number of smaller parishes. Following the general pattern of the English boroughs and counties, the government of the new

[1] The first of these is the Common Poor Fund, established in 1867. It is raised by a uniform rate, and used to defray certain expenses relating to paupers, registration and vaccination, which are incurred far out of proportion to ratable value. Then, under the Local Govt. Act, 1888 (51–52 Vic., c. 41, § 43), other expenses of a similar nature are paid out of the Exchequer Contribution Account, which was created to relieve local taxation, and is made use of in London to equalize local burdens. Third, under the London (Equalization of Rates) Act, 1894, a rate of six pence in the pound is levied throughout the county of London, and distributed among the local districts on the basis of population for the maintenance of public health, lighting and streets. In 1903–04 these three funds had the effect of increasing the rates in the City by more than a shilling, and decreasing it in some parishes in other parts of the metropolis by more than two shillings.

metropolitan boroughs was placed in the hands of a single council consisting of mayor, aldermen, and councillors. But, as in the London County Council, the aldermen are one sixth, instead of one third, the number of the elected councillors; and to avoid their use by a party to perpetuate its majority they were forbidden, as in the case of all the county councils, to vote at elections of aldermen.[1] The electorates in London for the County Council, the borough councils and the boards of guardians, are now the same, and they comprise in substance all the persons who are entitled to vote under any existing franchise, parliamentary or municipal.[2] These provisions include married women, whose husbands have not already qualified by means of the same property; and in this connection it may be observed that the Act of 1899 was a grief of mind to some ardent suffragists. Women had been eligible to the London vestries, but in the act substituting therefor metropolitan boroughs the House of Lords inserted a provision excluding women from the councils, and to this the House of Commons ungallantly submitted. A few years later the abolition of the English school boards deprived them of another opportunity to serve the community,[3] and left almost no prominent public offices open to them, a disappointment to some of the more martial of the sex that lasted until an Act of 1907 opened to them the doors of all county and borough councils.[4]

The Franchise.

For the general reader it is needless to enumerate the functions conferred upon the metropolitan borough councils.

Powers of the Boroughs.

[1] Like the boroughs, but unlike the counties, the councillors were to retire one third each year, unless the Local Govt. Board should, at the request of any council, order all the councillors to retire together at the end of three years, a change which has curiously enough been made upon the almost unanimous request of the councils. As in the case of the provincial boroughs the elections take place on the first of November; and the triennial years began in 1900.

[2] London County Council Electors Qualification Act, 1900, 63–64 Vic., c. 29.

[3] Rogers on Elections, 17 Ed., III., 29, says they were legally ineligible to the school boards, but that was not the popular opinion, and they were in fact constantly elected.

[4] 7 Edw. VII., c. 33.

A thorough knowledge of these mysteries is the great source of power of the borough clerks, and it can be acquired only by patient research in many cryptic enactments. The new boroughs were given all the powers of the vestries and local boards which they superseded, with a few of those previously in the hands of the London County Council; and the Local Government Board has power to make transfers of authority between these bodies on the application of the County Council and a majority of the borough councils. In general it may be said that the boroughs are entrusted with the maintenance of the streets, of drainage (except main sewers) and of all the other matters in the charge of an ordinary borough, saving such as have been mentioned in an earlier paragraph as within the competence of the County Council.[1] In a few matters the two bodies have concurrent powers; the most important being the housing of the working-classes, for the greater part of the boroughs, as well as the County Council, have embarked to some extent on the policy of providing municipal dwellings. It may be added that the accounts of the metropolitan boroughs, like those of all the county councils, including that of London, but unlike those of the provincial boroughs, are subject to the audit of the Local Government Board.

**Increase in the Rates.**

The metropolitan boroughs have hardly been in existence long enough to draw conclusions about their efficiency, but there can be no doubt that the average rates for the whole of London have increased from 6*s*. 2.7*d*., in the year before the new boroughs were created, to 7*s*. 5*d*. in 1905–1906. About three shillings of the present rate, however, and more than one half of the increase, have been due to expenses incurred by the County Council.[2] Moreover, municipal rates have grown all over England, and they had been rising in London before the new borough councils

[1] In accordance with a provision of the Metropolis Management Act, 1855, 18–19 Vic., c. 120, § 183, which still applies to the existing authorities, loans by the metropolitan boroughs require the sanction of the London County Council.

[2] Including education, where the increase has been most rapid.

were formed. In some parts of the metropolis the increase has certainly been portentous. In Poplar, a working-class district in the east of London, the advance has amounted, since the creation of the borough council, to more than three shillings in the pound, and bad scandals have occurred there; but the extravagance exposed in Poplar was the work of the Board of Poor-law Guardians, not of the borough council. Nor can the increase of rates in London be laid wholly at the door of one party, for although it has been less rapid as a rule in boroughs where the Moderates have controlled the council, this has not always been true. Nevertheless the growth of taxation has had a political effect.

At the first elections for the new boroughs in 1900, which came at the time of the general election for Parliament during the excitement of the South African War, the Moderates obtained a majority in two thirds of the borough councils. In 1903 the parties were not unevenly balanced with a slight advantage in favour of the Progressives; but in 1906 the increase in rates, the scandals at Poplar, the ill-starred experiment of the London County Council with steamboats on the Thames, the dread of further municipal trading and of other socialistic tendencies, caused a sharp change in public opinion. A warlike tribe called "Municipal Reformers" appeared, and, absorbing the Moderate party, won a sweeping victory at the polls. They elected a majority of their members in twenty-three of the borough councils, while only three were left in the control of the Progressives.[1]

**Central Authorities.**

The central authorities, other than the London County Council, require for our purpose only a brief notice. The Metropolitan Asylums Board, eighteen of whose members are appointed by the Local Government Board, while the remaining fifty-five are chosen by the various boards of

[1] These were Battersea, Bethnal Green and Hammersmith, the last having up to that time been Moderate. In Stoke Newington, Independents alone were elected as before; while in Hackney they held the balance of power.

guardians, maintains hospitals for defectives and for contagious diseases, an ambulance service and a training ship. The members of the Thames and Lea Conservancy Boards, which have charge of the navigation of those rivers and their preservation from pollution, are appointed by various county councils, government departments and other associations and bodies, public and private, that have an interest in their operations.

**The Metropolitan Water Board.**

A much more recent institution of a similar type is the Metropolitan Water Board, created by an Act of 1902. Up to that time the water supply of London had been furnished by eight private companies; but it had not been satisfactory in the past, and, although much improved, there was a general feeling that it ought to be in the hands of a single public authority. The London County Council, or rather the Progressive majority in that body, was anxious to take it under its own control; but the Conservative government, disliking the radical tendencies of the council, decided to adopt a different plan. The Act established a board of sixty-five members, of whom fourteen are appointed by the London County Council, and the rest by the councils of the metropolitan boroughs and of the various counties, boroughs and districts outside of the administrative county, but within the area of supply.[1] Arbitrators were appointed to determine the price to be paid to the companies for their property and rights; and the Board is now furnishing water to more than six millions of people covering an area of over five hundred square miles.

[1] Metropolis Water Act, 1902, 2 Edw. VII., c. 41. The Board contains also representatives of the Thames and Lea Conservancy Boards.

# CHAPTER XLIII

## THE LONDON COUNTY COUNCIL

THE most interesting body in London, and one that has commanded universal attention throughout the world, is the County Council. In its organisation the principle of indirect election, which had been applied to the Metropolitan Board of Works, was abandoned, and, what is more, the existing areas of subordinate local government were wholly discarded as electoral units. For that purpose their irregularity and differences in size were too great, and in their stead were taken the parliamentary constituencies of the metropolis, which still remain the electoral divisions for the council. Each of the fifty-seven parliamentary boroughs elects two members and the City of London four, in each case twice the number of representatives in the House of Commons. The whole council is renewed at one time, the elections taking place every three years in March. The members, one hundred and eighteen in number, choose nineteen aldermen for six years, one half retiring every three years; and it became the custom after the first election to give some of these places to the party in the minority. They choose also a chairman, vice chairman and deputy chairman, who in practice are now changed every year. As in the case of the provincial boroughs, on which the county councils were modelled, the chairman, aldermen and elected councillors form a single chamber, which provides for its own internal organisation and procedure. Its standing orders are, in fact, as voluminous as the constitutions of the new states in America, and partly for the same reason. Organisation.

Powers. The powers of the London County Council have already been mentioned in speaking of the City and the metropolitan boroughs.[1] As originally granted they had a decidedly limited range, and although they have been constantly extended by a great number of special acts, these have dealt with particular matters, sometimes, as in the case of education, of great magnitude, but usually not in themselves of much consequence, and they have not built up any logical or comprehensive system. The Progressives, who had a majority in the council without a break until 1907, were anxious to make it the real centre of municipal life, and under their guidance it has expended a great part of its energy in striving for an enlargement of its authority, which the Conservative government was reluctant to concede.

Procedure. The organisation of the County Council, and its method of conducting business, are in their general outlines similar to those of the provincial boroughs. The chairman is, if anything, even less of a directing force than the mayor; and the real work is done in the same way by committees. Any one, indeed, who framed his idea of the council from the meetings at Spring Gardens would have a false impression, for the members who talk most freely in public are by no means always the ones that take the greatest part in shaping the work of the committees; nor are the subjects debated there with most energy those wherein the greatest good has been accomplished. The General Purposes Committee, composed of the chairmen and leaders of all the standing committees, was intended to act as a sort of cabinet, by reviewing the reports of the committees on the day before the council meets, effecting compromises, and agreeing upon the policy to be pursued; but it has not, in fact, filled that position, and thus the relation of the committees

[1] One important power that has not been mentioned is that of providing and managing parks and open spaces not already under the charge of some other authority; and the London County Council has done a great deal of good work in this respect.

to the council is not unlike that which prevails in the provincial towns. Instead of recapitulating, therefore, the general system of administration, it is better simply to indicate the points in which the practice differs from that of an ordinary borough.

Party in the Council.

One of the most marked differences to be observed between the London County Council and the governing body of a provincial borough lies in the greater prominence of party. In most of the provincial towns, party comes into the election of councillors, and often into the choice of mayor and aldermen, but has usually little or no connection with municipal administration. In London it persists more. The greater part of the business of the County Council, probably the most valuable part, is indeed transacted without regard to party; but there are a few subjects, like the water supply, street improvements, the works department, and some branches of municipal trading, where the parties have held opposite opinions strongly, and occasionally there is a strict party vote. In this respect the London County Council pursues a course between that of Parliament on one side, and an ordinary borough council on the other. It is not, as in the House of Commons, the function of the majority to stand together in support of their leaders on all questions, and of the Opposition to oppose; nor is it, as in most boroughs, possible to say that after November 9 party is forgotten. On the contrary, it has been the habit for each of the parties to have at all times a couple of whips, and also a committee of leading men to consider the attitude of the party on controversial subjects. With its organisation by committees, with the absence of a responsible executive, the County Council clearly belongs to the same general type of government as the borough councils; but in its work party has more importance, largely because London is like a sea, big enough to have a tide of its own. Local issues in the metropolis have a magnitude that fits them to be a basis for political division. The councillors of a provincial borough are usually elected on national issues, which have no real municipal significance; but in London, although the national and local lines very nearly coincide, the councillors are elected on a true municipal programme of their own.

Position of the Officials.

Another point in which the London County Council differs from the borough councils is the smaller influence of the permanent officials.[1] Succeeding as they did to the Metropolitan Board of Works, whose officials had been very influential and in some cases corrupt, the early members of the County Council, highly energetic men themselves, preferred to treat their experts as advisers rather than administrators. This condition seems to have been slowly changing, the relation of the officials to their political chiefs coming more into accord with the general English custom.

The Clerk of the Council.

A couple of examples will illustrate the nature of the change. When the council was first organised, the deputy chairman was given a salary, and placed at the head of the clerical staff. The Royal Commission on the Amalgamation of London in 1894 commented on this, expressing the opinion that it was a mistake, and urging that, as in the boroughs, a permanent clerk, instead of an elective member of the council, should fill that position.[2] The suggestion was adopted. In 1896 the salary of the deputy chairman was discontinued, and a clerk was appointed head of the staff, who in person, or by one of his assistants, attends the meetings of every committee.

Manager of Works.

A better known instance is that of the manager of the Works Department. The situation of the first manager does not seem to have been altogether comfortable, for although there is a conflict of evidence on the point, it is asserted that the committee interfered in the details of his work, and that members of the council both recommended

[1] Not wholly unconnected with this is the fact that the chairmen of committees have not been habitually reappointed, and hence have not acquired the same authority as in a borough council.

[2] Com. Papers, 1894, XVII., 1, p. 16.

workmen for employment and protected them against discharge. Falsification of accounts in the department, which came to light in 1896, brought a crisis. It was universally admitted that no money had been stolen, and that the sole object of the false entries was to make the Works Department appear more successful than it had really been, but the investigation that followed probed the defects in its administration. A new manager was appointed; the practice of recommending and protecting workmen became practically unknown, the foremen being given a free hand in regard to the men they employed; and before long the old Works Committee of twenty-five was replaced by a small committee which left the manager at liberty to carry out the details of the work entrusted to him as he thought best.

That the permanent officials have, in some cases at least, acquired a greater freedom in executive action, these examples suffice to show; but their influence on the policy to be adopted is still inferior to that of their brethren in provincial towns. How far a similar change has taken place in the case of the educational officers since their transfer from the school board to the council, will appear in a later chapter.

**Labour Policy.**

Another characteristic of the London County Council has been its policy in regard to labour. The Progressives on the council have unquestionably had in view not only good administration for the benefit of the whole community, but also indirectly an improvement in the condition of the working-classes. They have not intended to pay more than the men could earn in private employ, nor do they discriminate between union and non-union men, but they pay the rates, and adopt the terms, that the trade-unions succeed in procuring. Almost as soon as it was organised, the council began to force the same principle on contractors also, and in 1892 it adopted a standing order requiring all contractors to pay the rates of wages, and observe the hours of work, recognised and in practice obtained by the trade-unions. On the effect of this policy the committee of inquiry appointed by the council said in 1897: "Consequent upon the conditions of contract already set out, there has been a difficulty in obtaining responsible tenders, and sometimes those obtained have been at prices specially and largely enhanced by reason of the Council's conditions."[1]

The Works Department.

The council, finding at once a difficulty in getting satisfactory bids from good firms, determined to do a part of its construction and repairs itself. Acting on that motive, it executed some work directly in 1892, and at the end of that year established the Works Department on a permanent basis. With the early mishaps of the experiment, and with the remedies applied, we are already familiar.

By 1906 the department had done work amounting to more than two million pounds in value, and employed over three thousand men. It was treated as a privileged contractor, the ordinary mode of proceeding being as follows: The council's architect or engineer proposed plans, specifications and estimates of any piece of work to be done. These were then, as a rule, submitted to the Works Department, which, if satisfied with the estimates and if not already overcrowded, accepted the job. If not, bids were invited, and the work was given to a contractor. Under such conditions it is obviously impossible to compare accurately the results of the two processes. That the quality of the work executed by the department has been good, no one seems to deny, but on the question of cost opinions differ. The opponents of the department say that the expense is somewhat greater than the price paid to a contractor, while those who approve of it insist that the cost is about the same, and the work more certain to be good. The fair conclusion would seem to be that the expense is not very different; that the work costs the department more than it does the contractor, but that the council may perhaps save a part of his profits, the community as a whole losing the rest.

Municipal Trading.

The council has been active in the class of operations commonly known as municipal trading, although from the

[1] L.C.C. Rep. of Com. on the Works Dept. (1896–97), p. viii.

narrow range of its powers this has been confined to a few matters, notably housing, tramways and steamboats. The most successful kinds of trading undertaken by the British cities, the supply of gas and electricity, fall in London into the domain of the borough councils, and while the County Council has repeatedly sought from Parliament power to furnish electricity in bulk to the boroughs and other large consumers, it has not yet succeeded in obtaining it.

**Compulsory Housing.** The maintenance by municipal authorities of dwellings and lodging-houses for the working-classes is done in pursuance of four distinct statutory provisions. There is first a general principle, incorporated in most local acts, that whenever a public body, or a company, by the destruction of dwellings to make way for other buildings or improvements, displaces more than a certain number of working people, it must cause houses to be erected for them in the neighbourhood. In cutting through streets, opening tunnels and laying out embankments, the London County Council has displaced more than ten thousand people, for whom it has built new houses.

**Voluntary Housing.** The other three provisions that empower public authorities to supply dwellings are contained in the Housing of the Working Classes Act of 1890,[1] and its amendments. The Act is divided into three parts. The first provides for the taking by compulsory purchase of a whole unsanitary area, the demolition of the buildings upon it, and the sale of any part of it not needed for the purpose in hand.[2] When such an area is taken, houses for at least the number of people displaced must, as a rule, be built on or near the same spot, either by the local authority itself or by purchasers who buy the land with a contract to do so.[3] The

[1] The Act (53–54 Vic., c. 70) consolidated the Labouring Classes Lodging-houses Acts, 1851–1885; the Artisans Dwelling Acts, 1868–1885; and the Artisans and Labourers Dwellings Improvement Acts, 1875–1885.

[2] This is done by means of a scheme, on which is based a provisional order issued by the Local Govt. Board and confirmed by Parliament.

[3] In London the Local Govt. Board may dispense with this condition when equally convenient accommodation is furnished elsewhere. In other places the condition is not obligatory unless the Board requires it.

second part of the Act provides that by an order of court any single dwelling unfit for human habitation may be closed, and if necessary demolished. When this is done, rehousing of the people dispossessed is not obligatory, but the local authority may by means of a provisional order take the land and build new dwellings upon it. The third part of the Act enables local authorities, when of opinion that the supply of houses for the working-classes is insufficient — and irrespective of the existence of unhealthy conditions — to acquire land and build dwellings or lodging-houses.[1] In all these cases the local authority may assume the entire management of the houses that it has built.

**Extent of Housing in London.**

The London County Council has erected a number of dwellings under Part I. of the Act, and both the County Council and the borough councils under Parts II. and III.; under the last at an accelerating pace, for while the people rehoused under Parts I. and II. cannot be very much greater than those displaced, the provision of dwellings under Part III. is indefinite. The County Council has, indeed, gone into the business of housing on a large scale. At the end of March, 1905 it had already dwellings enough opened for thirty-one thousand people, with a gross rent of almost one hundred and thirty thousand pounds a year, and it had plans under way for the accommodation of nearly twice as many more.

**Financial Results.**

The results of the housing policy of the council may be considered from the financial and the social points of view. The accounts for the year 1904–1905 show that after deducting from the gross rents the expenses, the repairs and the charge for interest and sinking fund on the debt, there was a surplus of about five hundred pounds on the buildings which the council built of its own accord, and a loss three times as great in the few cases where, having destroyed

[1] If the owners are unwilling to sell, the land may be purchased compulsorily by means of a provisional order issued by the Local Govt. Board and confirmed by Parliament.

dwellings, it has been obliged to erect others because no purchasers could be found who would undertake to do so. In short, there was a net loss of about eleven hundred pounds on all the completed dwellings taken together. But in considering these figures two facts must be borne in mind. On the one hand, the sinking fund includes not only a charge which will cover the cost of the buildings in sixty years — probably not too large an allowance for depreciation — but also enough to cover the cost of the land in eighty years, although the site is more likely to rise than to fall in value. On the other hand, the County Council, unlike the provincial boroughs, habitually enters the land in its books, not at its actual cost, but at its fair value for the sole purpose of working-class dwellings, the difference being charged to the general expenditure of the county.[1]

**Social Effects.**

The social effect of the council's housing policy, which is far more difficult to measure, has been the subject of sharp differences of opinion; and so has the fundamental question why there should be a dearth of working-class dwellings in London. This last has been variously attributed to the difficulty of obtaining land; to the congested state of the metropolis, and the lack of cheap and rapid transit; to the condition of the building trade, and the small amount of capital now engaged in it. The advocates of municipal housing point to the number of dwellings built as at least a partial remedy for existing evils, while the opponents of the policy assert that the council has made the matter worse, because, by engaging in competition backed by the public purse, they have discouraged private enterprise.

**Failure to Reach the Poorest Class.**

If the direct results of a course of conduct are sometimes hard to follow, the indirect effects, often far more important, can rarely be traced with certainty. That the destruction and rebuilding of unsanitary areas has not abolished

[1] In the case of Reid's Brewery, Clerkenwell Road, for example — a site bought for rehousing in connection with the Holborn to Strand Improvement — the price paid for the land was £200,000, but for the purpose of housing the value was written down to £45,000.

the slums, must be admitted. The houses erected in such cases by the county have been well filled by tenants, for in 1904–1905, in spite of the fact that many of the buildings were just opened, the proportion of rooms vacant in all the council's dwellings was only 11.65 per cent, and in 1903–1904 it was only 5.30 per cent. But, as in almost every instance in England, the new tenants are of a more prosperous class than the ones displaced. Even in a case where the work was done by sections, so that all but the first set of people turned out were offered the new rooms at once, it was found that out of 5719 persons displaced only eleven went into the buildings erected for them.[1] The difficulty does not lie altogether with the grade of the tenements provided. They are mostly of two or three rooms apiece, with a few single rooms also. Nor does it lie wholly with the rent, although most of the dwellings seem to be above the reach of the very poor.

When a slum is broken up, the people dispossessed go to another place of the same kind. They want to reduce their rent by taking lodgers, a practice that cannot be permitted, because it involves the very overcrowding which the housing policy is designed to prevent. But apart from motives of that sort, the new buildings with modern appointments are evidently unattractive to people accustomed to the slums, and no doubt they find the regulations designed to secure orderliness and cleanliness irksome. In short, the experiments in municipal housing would seem to prove slum life very much a voluntary matter. That the tenants of the London County Council are in better circumstances than they were expected to be, is shown by the fact that, taking all the buildings together, the number of persons supposed to be provided for in 1904–1905 was 31,339, and, deducting the percentage of vacancies, the rooms occupied were roughly intended to hold 27,688, whereas the actual number of persons in them was only

[1] Rep. of Com. on Locomotion in London. Com. Papers, 1905, XXX., 533, p. 14.

19,335, or little more than two thirds as large. The tenants were, therefore, paying on the average a rent half as large again as the council estimated, and enjoying a corresponding amount of room. Moreover, the report of the housing manager for that year, in the list of occupations of the 4714 different tenants, returned only 592 as labourers. Leaving out of account the charwomen, and 118 whose occupation was given as "widow," the remainder, or four fifths of the whole number, were almost entirely artisans or other persons engaged in pursuits above that of the unskilled labourer.

**Magnitude of the Problem.**

If the public housing experiments in London fail to reach the very poor, and attract mainly the fairly comfortable working-classes, the policy of the council opens a very large problem. Great as the number of municipal tenants has become, it is insignificant in comparison with the vast multitude of people of this class in the metropolis. Unless, therefore, the council proposes to house the bulk of the workingmen in London, the matter must continue to be left to private enterprise, and in that case municipal housing is of no real value except so far as it affects the natural supply. The council does not, in fact, seem to have grasped the problem in its entirety. It appears to be dealing with symptoms rather than causes, and its action reminds one of the old-fashioned charities founded to support six poor maids. It has, no doubt, exerted itself to procure cheap workmen's trains on the railways, in order to diffuse the labouring classes over a wider area. It has also taken an active part in transportation; and this brings us to its policy in regard to the tramways.

**Tramways.**

Throughout Great Britain the development of tramways was hindered by two provisions in the Act of 1870; one giving the town a right to buy out a private company at the end of twenty-one years at the existing value of the structure, without allowance for the profits it could earn or the business it had built up;[1] the other requiring the

[1] 33–34 Vic., c. 78, § 43.

The Local Veto.

consent of the local authority, and of the road authority if any, within whose territory the tramway is to be built.[1] The second obstacle is greater in London than in the provincial towns, because the local and road authorities for this purpose are not the same; the County Council occupying the former position, and the borough and city councils the latter. Each of these bodies has, therefore, a veto, as it is called, upon a proposal for a tramway by a private company, while the boroughs have a veto on the construction of a line by the County Council. Now the power of veto has been used freely, and everybody agrees that it has been improperly used by everybody else. The borough councils have often used it to block the plans of the County Council; that body has used it consistently to prevent any new lines of private companies within the county limits; and the Court of Common Council has used it to keep tramways out of the old City altogether.[2]

Deficiency of Lines in London.

The result is that in the whole of greater London, with its six hundred and ninety-three square miles, and nearly seven millions of people, there were at the end of 1904 only two hundred and three route miles of tramways, of which one hundred and twenty miles were within the administrative county. Moreover, according to the report of the royal commission, in 1905, the lines inside the county belong to three systems, separated from each other by long intervals, without any connection. They are not operated in harmony with the lines outside of the county, even where a physical contact would make it possible; and there is no running of cars through, the passengers being obliged to alight at the county boundary and begin a fresh journey. In short, as the commission remark: "It will be

[1] *Ibid.*, § 4. Where a proposed tramway extends into the territory of more than one borough or district, the consent of the authorities in which two thirds of the line lies is enough (§ 5). The provision in terms covered only the grant of provisional orders, but a similar rule was shortly applied to the case of private bills by an amendment to the standing orders of both Houses of Parliament.

[2] On this whole subject, see the Rep. of Com. on Locomotion in London. Com. Papers, 1905, XXX., 533.

seen that, from every point of view, tramway accommodation is glaringly defective." [1]

Financial Results.

In 1896 the London County Council obtained from Parliament authority to operate tramways directly, and as fast as the leases to companies expired, it took control of the management. One half of the lines, almost all those south of the Thames, were acquired in this way in 1899, while the bulk of those on the north did not fall in until seven years later. With some trifling exceptions, the council now operates all the tramways within the county, and it has been substituting electricity for horses throughout the system. It might be supposed that short lines running through densely populated districts would be very profitable, and this was true at one time. In the first year after it was taken over, the southern system yielded a net profit of about forty thousand pounds; but the reduction in fares, the increase of wages, and the interest and sinking fund on the debt for electric installation, rapidly reduced the margin, until in 1903–1904 there was a loss on the system of eight thousand pounds. Since that time there has been a small profit. Under a provision in the lease for a share of the gross receipts, the northern system also made a large payment in 1899–1900, and in that year one hundred and ten thousand pounds were carried from tramway profits to the relief of rates. Smaller earnings on that system, and a growth of the general expenses of the council in connection with the tramways, have, however, cut down the yield so much that since 1903 nothing has been carried to the relief of rates, and the tramways as a whole have little more than paid their expenses. What will happen now that the lines are wholly operated by the council, remains to be seen.

The Council's Plans Inadequate.

Apart from equipping the existing lines with electricity, the County Council has not succeeded in making much progress in developing the tramways. This has been due in part to the veto of the local bodies, and in part to the

[1] Com. Papers, 1905, XXX., 533, p. 42.

reluctance of Parliament to permit the lines to cross the bridges over the river. But the council itself has not promoted any comprehensive scheme. The extensions it has planned have been small. Mr. Donald, in the London Manual for 1906, says that it has at various times proposed one hundred and thirty miles of new tramways; and remarks, not unjustly, that London, to be properly served, should have one thousand miles.

The Problem to be Solved.

The metropolis is undoubtedly overcrowded. According to the census of 1901, over one seventh of the inhabitants of the county were living with more than two people to a room, and as the Royal Commission pointed out in 1905, the experience of the railways in running workmen's trains shows that with appropriate transit the population can be spread over a much larger area. The London County Council is, indeed, building many of its houses for workingmen in the suburbs, but the proportion of the population who are benefited in this way is insignificant, and there is great need of better facilities for carrying vast numbers of people to and fro between the outskirts and the centre.

Need of Underground Transit.

Probably no surface lines alone can be adequate for the transport of passengers in a place so large as London. The speed cannot be great enough to take busy people far away from their work in the time they can afford to spend on the road. Rapid travel must be overhead or underground, where it is not delayed by the traffic in the streets; and elevated lines ruin the thoroughfares that they enter. The underground railways in London, valuable as they are, were built to connect the terminals of the different English roads, and run around the business centre rather than into it. The deep level tubes, on the other hand, begun a number of years ago, are being developed into an efficient system throughout the region within four miles of Charing Cross; but for the purpose of dispersing the population, they lack any connection, or any easy means of making a connection, with surface tramways beyond. For this object a continuous journey over surface lines in the suburbs and underground lines in the denser portions of the city is essential. In fact, the transit to suburban districts cannot be made in the time required without an express service that allows very few stops in the inner eight or ten miles, covering the distance in not more than twenty or thirty minutes. But an express service requires separate tracks parallel to, or between, or underneath, the other underground lines; and nothing of this kind has been attempted.

**Dispersion of the Middle Classes.**

Moreover, the mild efforts hitherto made to disperse the population have been aimed almost entirely at the working-class, whose removal to a distance presents the greatest difficulties. It may be suggested that the diffusion of the middle classes over a wide suburban area is both easier to accomplish and more effective. Their hours of work are shorter; they feel the cost of transportation less; they enjoy a small garden more; and their wives and children are not so anxious to live in the town, for they, too, can afford to pay the fare. Their dispersion is a more effective remedy for overcrowding, because one middle-class family removing from the denser part of the city makes as much room there as three or four families of the working-class would fill. To obtain the greatest relief from overcrowding, therefore, it would seem that rapidity and convenience of travel are questions as important as the fare; and that it is better to carry a moderate number of the middle class a long distance than many people a little way. It would seem, also, that a uniform charge over a great area is more effective than a very cheap one for short rides; and in fact the Royal Commission recommended a uniform two-penny fare underground;[1] whereas the London County Council, like other public bodies in Great Britain, has a scale of fares graded by the distance travelled, and running down as low as a half-penny.

An attempt to carry out a policy of this kind would

[1] Com. Papers, 1905, XXX., 533, p. 78.

involve the use of underground in connection with surface lines, because it requires a high rate of speed. Now the County Council, in trying to control the tramways of London, appears to have neglected that most vital factor of conveyance below the surface. It was, indeed, ready enough to ask for the privilege of purchasing all underground lines after sixty years at their structural value if successful;[1] but it had no idea of undertaking, or allowing any one else to undertake, the whole task of London transit above and below ground. Improvements in transportation alone may well be incapable of solving the question of overcrowding, but rapid transit is one element in the question, and as such it must be dealt with on a more comprehensive scale than heretofore. This would seem to be another case of a failure to grapple with a great problem in all its bearings.

**The Thames Steamboats.** The latest and least successful experiment of the London County Council in municipal trading has been that of steamboats on the river. The private company that had maintained passenger steamers on the Thames had given up the business, and the council, thinking it a pity that this means of conveyance should cease, undertook in 1905 to carry it on. During the summer the enterprise fared well enough, but the winter brought a loss so heavy that the service was thereafter discontinued at that season, and has since been abandoned altogether. This was a case of commercial miscalculation which involved a pecuniary loss to the county, and still more disastrous consequences to the Progressives, for it was one of the facts that contributed heavily to their defeat at the election of March, 1907.

**Political History of the County Council.** From the outset of its career the London County Council has been an object of widespread interest; and, especially in its early days, it attracted to itself many highly distinguished figures. The first council contained such men as Lord Rosebery, Sir John Lubbock (afterwards Lord Ave-

[1] Rep. of Com. on Electric and Cable Rys. (Metropolis), Com. Papers, 1892, XII., I., Qs. 416 *et seq.*, 629 *et seq.*, and App. B.

bury), Sir Thomas Farrer (afterwards Lord Farrer), Frederic Harrison, John Burns, Sidney Webb and others, some of whom have remained in it continuously. A number of these men were Progressives; and in fact it was to people of that stamp rather than to the Moderates, that the council seemed to offer the larger opportunity for usefulness, and hence the greatest attraction. It was no doubt partly for this reason that the first council had a Progressive majority at a time when, not only the House of Commons as a whole, but the members of Parliament from the boroughs that make up the County of London, were heavily Conservative.

Throughout the history of the council, London has, indeed, presented the extraordinary phenomenon of voting one way in national, and the opposite way in local, elections.[1] From 1889, when the first election for the council was held, until 1906, the greater part of the members of Parliament for the area included in the county were Conservative, while during the whole of that time the county chose a Progressive council, except in 1895, when the Progressives and Moderates elected were equal in number, the former, however, retaining their majority in consequence of the aldermen who held over. Curiously enough, if two lines be drawn, one showing the changes in the proportion of Conservative and Liberal members of Parliament from London, and the other the proportion of Moderates and Progressives elected to the County Council, these lines will be found to rise and fall roughly together from 1889 to 1905; and, in fact, for the first part of that period they are exactly parallel. Yet the Liberals never made gains enough among the members of Parliament for London, nor the Moderates among the members of the council, to obtain a majority.

[1] The only other case with which the writer is familiar where a similar condition has existed in anything like the same degree is in Canada. There it happened for several years after 1888 that while the Conservatives had a majority in the Dominion House of Commons, the Liberals controlled all but one of the local legislatures in which national party lines were drawn.

Several reasons have been given why London should have been continuously for fifteen years Conservative in national, and Progressive in local, matters. It has been suggested that this was due to the difference in franchise, the lodgers and the occupiers by virtue of service, who are believed to be strongly Conservative, not having at first been entitled to vote for the London County Council. But this was changed by the Electors' Qualification Act of 1900, and yet in the two following elections the Progressives were returned in as large proportions as ever before. A more satisfactory explanation has been that the capital of an empire is naturally imperialist; while in municipal affairs the people who take interest enough to vote, and especially the workingmen, are readily attracted by something that captivates their imagination, as the Progressive programme has done. Until they feel the burden, they like plans for expensive and magnificent administration. Now, although the Conservatives are in the main Moderates, and the Liberals are almost wholly Progressive, there is a certain resemblance between the national policy of the Tories and the local policy of the Progressives. Both believe in conducting their respective governments in a large and striking way, while the Liberals in Parliament and the Moderates in the London County Council profess to favour economy. It was not altogether a coincidence, therefore, that the year after the Liberals in 1906 carried the country, with a majority of two to one in the London constituencies, the Moderates, or rather their successors the Municipal Reformers, should have elected to the London County Council a majority about as great as the Progressives ever held there. This took place in March, 1907, and it was caused, as already pointed out, partly by the growth of local taxation throughout the metropolis, partly by a fear of socialism, partly by the scandals in Poplar, and partly by the luckless experiment with the steamboats.

# CHAPTER XLIV

## MUNICIPAL TRADING

WHEN the writer began to make a careful study of English institutions, he intended to discuss the problem of municipal trading at some length. The subject had then received far less attention than it deserved; but since that time much has been written upon it, much material accumulated, and it now requires a treatise by itself. It is, indeed, more controversial than any other English question not strictly a matter of party politics. It has even awakened deep interest in foreign lands, and books, articles and reports on the subject appear with great rapidity. Both the advocates and opponents of municipal trading are now so intrenched with arguments and statistics, so quick to attack any one who approaches their position, that the field can hardly be examined except by a reconnoissance in force, supported by a battery of figures. But there are certain broad, clearly marked features in the landscape that may be described even by a non-combatant.

**Meaning of Municipal Trade.**

The term "municipal trading" is commonly and properly applied only to those services for which public bodies make a charge to the persons benefited. It does not include work done gratuitously for the public, although this may have replaced a private agency that made a charge and even a profit. Free public roads and bridges, for example, have replaced the private turnpike roads and toll bridges. It is now assumed that these conveniences ought to be provided without charge to the wayfarer, and no one would think of calling the maintenance of roads municipal trading. In the same way, harbour improvements, parks, pleasure grounds, libraries, museums, hospitals, bands of music and many other delights, are now furnished in many places gratuitously at the public expense. The English elementary schools, which would not be classed as a branch of municipal trade, were not, indeed, at first free, but they are almost wholly free now; and it is, perhaps, the tendency of the age to treat in that way all education that is conducted by the state. This is generally true in the United States of secondary schools, and in a number of the state universities there is no fee, while in others it is trifling.

How far this principle should be carried, how far the comforts and conveniences of life should be furnished to the public without charge, is a question of expediency; and in the case of those things which do not ultimately contribute to the welfare of the whole community, but only to the pleasure of a part, there may be a question, also, how far it is fair that some taxpayers should pay for the recreation of others. The attempt to provide anything in this way is, in a sense, socialistic. In one sense it is more so than where the government sells commodities at their fair value; but the two things are not the same. The gratuitous supply of public needs by taxation is very different from engaging in self-supporting or remunerative trade. The question how far the former shall be carried is eternal, and its application will vary from one age to another. It is not, like municipal trading, an urgent question in England to-day.

**Distinction between Monopolies and Other Trades.**

In a discussion of municipal trade certain distinctions may be borne in mind. The first is between those occupations which from natural limitations, or by the law of increasing returns, or because of a privilege in the use of the public streets, are essentially monopolies, and those which are not. Among the former may be placed the supply of water, gas, electric light, telephones and transportation by tramways; while by virtue of a prevalent and long-established tradition, markets are also regarded in England as a species of monopoly. In the second class we must place such things as the provision of dwelling-houses for working-people, and the maintenance of baths and wash-houses. The question whether a dock, pier, ferry, race-course, theatre or golf links, is a monopoly or not, depends upon the physical nature of the locality, and the terms of the franchise granted by law.[1]

Between Trading for Profit, or Not.

The second distinction is between those undertakings which are conducted largely with a view to profit, and those which are not. This is obviously not a natural distinction, but one based upon the object for which any particular enterprise is actually carried on, and it may vary from place to place. Any service for which a fee is charged might be conducted for the sake of gain, or the fee might be so arranged as merely to secure the public from loss without yielding a profit. The distinction depends, therefore, on intent, but it affects very much the attitude of the governing body toward the undertaking. Now water, baths, wash-houses and working-class dwellings, are not, as a rule, maintained by the local authorities for the sake of gain; while markets, gas, electricity and tramways are not only usually conducted with a view to profit, but that is apparently the leading object in bringing them under public management. The fact that these things involve interference with the surface of the streets is commonly used as an argument for placing them entirely in the hands of the borough council; there are also advocates of municipal trading who are socialists on principle, or who are eager for the direct employment of labour; but in talking with many people of different kinds, one gets the impression that the popular motive force behind the direct management of undertakings of this sort is the desire to obtain for the public the profits that would otherwise flow into the pockets of capitalists. A race-course, theatre or golf links might be conducted either for profit or in order to

[1] These illustrations are, of course, taken from cases of municipal trading that have existed in British cities; but the national government has recently adopted the policy of treating the telephone, like the telegraph, as a national monopoly.

attract custom to the town, or merely for the general comfort and convenience, but in fact municipal activity in any of these last directions has been so uncommon that for the purpose of this chapter it is needless to consider them in detail.

Ensuing Classification.

These two distinctions give rise to four possible classes of municipal trading. Taking first the case where there is a monopoly and no profit, it is clear that since there is no gain to the town, no competition with private enterprise, and that a company can hardly expect to earn very large dividends where the alternative is public management with no profit at all, some of the strongest motives either for advocating or resisting public ownership are absent, and therefore feeling on the subject does not run high. A well-nigh universal feeling prevails, for example, in favour of the public management of the water supply; while in other matters, such as docks, which for one reason or another have prospered better in private or semi-private hands, there is no strong pressure for strict municipal control.

No Profit but a Monopoly.

Neither Profit nor Monopoly.

In the second case, that of no monopoly and no profit, the motive is again philanthropic, and here, if the business is not such as to compete with a considerable private trade, the public authorities who enter upon it are not unlikely to find it falling entirely into their own hands. In this field we find certainly the most harmless, and perhaps the most successful, forms of municipal trading; such, for example, as the provision of baths, and public laundries where the poorer classes can wash their clothes. But when the business does compete with a large private trade, especially if the trade is too great for the public authorities to absorb altogether, we have a case where the indirect effect on that trade is the most important matter, and hence we find the very gravest of all problems. This is true where a borough undertakes to build houses for the working-classes, or to distribute sterilised milk for babies.

In the third class of cases there is both a desire for municipal profit and a monopoly. Apart from markets, which are mainly a source of revenue with very little real trading, we get here the strongest motives for municipal trade, and at the same time a forcible opposition on the part of the private interests displaced thereby. Hence the greatest discussions have taken place over such matters as gas, electricity and tramways; and it is in these cases that the question of success or failure of municipal trading is being worked out in England at the present day.

Profit and Monopoly.

The fourth case, that of a profit and no monopoly, is so far practically confined to by-products, and to matters incidental to other trades, such as the manufacture of paving stones by dust destructors, the sale of tar, oil, etc., produced in making gas, the production and sale of ice in connection with the markets, the manufacture of stoves, fittings and the like to increase the use of gas and electricity, and omnibus lines run in connection with tramways. Of late years many attempts have been made by private bills to obtain authority to do things of this kind independently of any other form of trade, but Parliament has almost always refused to sanction them. If ever it begins to change its mind and to grant to towns the right to engage for profit in forms of business which are not natural monopolies, a new era in municipal trading will come with stronger feelings than ever, and a much longer step will be taken in the direction of municipal socialism.

Profit without a Monopoly.

For reasons that relate to the sequence of events and the nature of legislative policy, the various experiments in municipal trading will not here be taken up in their logical order under these four classes. Yet it is instructive to bear the distinctions in mind, and in giving a brief sketch of the principal forms of trade that have become common in the British towns, the main stress will be laid on the cases where there is both a monopoly and a desire to reap a profit for the local treasury. It does not follow, however, that because an undertaking is managed with a view to profit that the object is attained, or that when a profit is not sought there is neither gain nor loss. In the return of reproductive undertakings in England and Wales, compiled for the House of Commons in 1902,[1] it appeared that during the four years ending March 31 of that year, the municipal supply of electricity had, in the aggregate, resulted in a slight loss, and that this had been true to a much greater extent of all the kinds of trading — such as baths and wash-houses, burial grounds, working-class dwellings, piers and docks — which were not expected to yield a revenue, the only exception being waterworks, where the gain had been considerable.[2] It may be added that the gas works showed a large and the tramways and markets a substantial profit.

A number of municipal markets in England are ancient, but most of them have been established or acquired within the last two generations. Of late years, indeed, the towns, for motives of public health as well as a desire for profit, have been active in getting possession of them, until, according to the return of 1902, two thirds of the boroughs in England and Wales had done so. Except in the smaller places they are almost always profitable, yielding over and above the interest and sinking fund on the loans a revenue roughly in proportion to their size. From the return of 1902 it appears also that the gross income, before deducting interest and sinking-fund charges, amounted in the aggregate to about four and two thirds per cent on the capital invested. But markets involve, as already observed, very little real trading, even in the hundred towns that maintain slaughter-houses also. In some cases, no doubt, the borough manufactures ice for the benefit of the marketmen, and occasionally it sells the surplus to the public; but in the main its activity is confined in collecting tolls from those who

[1] Com. Papers, 1902, XCIV., 113.

[2] In some of these cases the results vary very much from place to place. In others they are nearly the same everywhere. Burial grounds, for example, sometimes involve a profit and sometimes a loss, and so do waterworks on a larger scale; while baths and wash-houses are almost always conducted at a loss which increases with their size.

make use of its property, a proceeding obviously very different from the production and distribution of commodities.

The industry in which the next largest number of towns have become engaged is the supply of water. According to the return of 1903 this had been taken up by one hundred and ninety-three boroughs in England and Wales, the capital outlay having been nearly fifty-seven millions of pounds, or almost one half of the total amount invested in municipal trading. Although not carried on, as a rule, with the object of gain, it is strictly a case of trading, and the aggregate yearly profits above interest and sinking-fund charges were at that time ninety thousand pounds; the gross income, after deducting the sum set apart for depreciation, but before deducting interest and sinking-fund charges, being three and a half per cent on the capital invested.[1] Water-works.

A dozen boroughs originally constructed their own supply, Southampton having begun to do so in 1250. The rest have bought out companies, in most cases by agreement, but sometimes by compulsory process. A few towns made the purchase more than fifty years ago. Manchester, for example, acquired her own waterworks in 1847. The greater part of the towns, however, undertook the supply of water in the second half of the nineteenth century, after its connection with infectious diseases was recognised. The growth in population, the increase in the use of water, and the importance of protecting the source of supply from contamination, have led the large towns to extend their works on a vast scale. In this they have shown enterprise and foresight. Glasgow takes its water from Loch Katrine, thirty-four miles away, and Manchester from Lake Thirlmere, while Liverpool and Birmingham use great tracts of hill country in Wales; Glasgow having spent four millions

[1] As the capital expenditure on waterworks is of a durable character, the sums laid aside for depreciation and sinking fund are much smaller than in most other kinds of municipal trading. The net profit is in some cases used in relief of rates, and in others accumulated as a fund for future expenses.

of pounds in the process, and the other towns six to eight millions apiece. It seems to be generally assumed that no private company would have undertaken such works as these, and in fact one hears little criticism of the administration of water supply by the borough councils.

Of all forms of trading, the water is the one best fitted for municipal management, for it offers the strongest inducements to good administration, with the smallest temptations to abuse. It is conducted with a view to public health and not to profit; the abundance and purity of the supply touch directly the whole population; after the works are completed, few persons are employed; the business is simple, hardly affected by new inventions; it does not compete with other industries, and breeds little desire to engage in collateral occupations.

Gas Works.

The kind of municipal trading that has yielded by far the greatest net profit, is gas light.[1] The difference of attitude towards gas and water is well illustrated by the often-quoted remark of Mr. Chamberlain in bringing before the town council of Birmingham his proposal to buy the gas works: "When the purchase of the Water Works comes before you," he said, "it will be a question concerning the health of the town; the acquisition of the Gas Works concerns the profits of the town." [2]

They were Acquired by Purchase.

Almost all the present municipal gas plants were started by private enterprise, and later bought by the public authorities. Manchester is the notable exception always referred to. There the police commissioners established in 1824 a plant, which in 1843 was transferred to the borough then recently incorporated. But although many gas works have been bought by the boroughs, the plants be-

[1] According to the return of 1902, ninety-seven boroughs in England and Wales managed their own gas works with a capital expenditure of £24,000,000. This does not include the urban districts, of which about an equal number owned their gas works, and the figures have, of course, grown since that time.

[2] N. M. Marris, "Joseph Chamberlain; the Man and the Statesman," p. 112.

longing to private companies are twice as numerous, and more than twice as great in value, as those owned by the municipal authorities; and some of the largest towns — such as Liverpool, Sheffield, Bristol, Newcastle and London itself — are still supplied in this way. The purchase of gas works by boroughs did not become common until the second half of the nineteenth century, when the business had become thoroughly established; and in fact only eight towns owned plants before 1850. The process then went on more rapidly, reaching its greatest activity in the seventies. Thereafter it slackened suddenly, in part, it is said, because the councils with a keen desire to acquire their gas had by that time done so, and in part for fear of competition from the newly invented electric light.

The private companies were of two kinds. First those authorised by Acts of Parliament, whose dividends under the Gas Works Clauses Act, 1847, were usually limited to ten per cent — a restriction for which in later provisional orders a sliding scale regulating the rate of dividends according to the price of gas was substituted. These companies were also usually compelled in issuing new stock to sell it at auction. On the other hand, they were protected by statute from competition by a local authority; nor was it the policy of Parliament to subject them to compulsory purchase,[1] although, of course, they might in some cases be badgered into a sale by hostility on the part of a borough council. The other class of companies, those without parliamentary authority, were not subject to these restrictions, but they were also less protected against both competition and compulsory purchase. As the charters of the statutory companies were perpetual, and contained no clause obliging

[1] Rep. of Com. on Mun. Trading, Com. Papers, 1900, VII., 183, App. A, pp. 349, 352. Under the Gas and Water Facilities Act of 1870, § 4, the consent of the local and road authorities, unless dispensed with by the Board of Trade, was required for the granting of a provisional order to a company; but most of the gas companies were established before the era of municipal trading, and the requirement of consent does not seem to have raised any serious obstacle.

them to transfer their rights to local authorities, the latter were obliged to offer such a sum as would induce the company to sell. But since the companies were conducting what had become a safe and profitable business, they naturally expected and obtained a premium upon their nominal capital. This was so large that in many cases, perhaps half of them, the town paid the company twice the par value of its shares. That such a price, though large, was hardly excessive may be presumed from the fact that the undertakings have been remunerative in the hands of the purchasers.[1]

**Profits Earned.** In all but a few places, and those small ones, the gas works yield a profit over and above the charges for both interest and sinking fund. In fact, according to the return of 1902, the gas works managed by boroughs in England and Wales, after deducting the sums set apart for depreciation, but before deducting interest and sinking-fund charges, were earning in the aggregate five and one third per cent on the total capital invested; the net revenue, after deducting all these charges, being greater than that from all the other profitable forms of municipal trading put together.

**Price charged for Gas.** A comparison between the prices charged for gas by municipalities and companies presents grave difficulties. Apart from economy in administration, the price must evidently be affected by the cost of coal in any particular town, and the value there of the residual products. Attempts have been made in Field's Analysis to take these matters into consideration in computing the normal cost of manufacture, but the results are not conclusive. The advocates of municipal trading point to the fact that the prices charged average a little higher in the case of companies than of local authorities;[2] but in answer it is said that the

[1] *Cf.* Hugo R. Meyer, "Municipal Ownership in Great Britain," p. 183.
[2] The "Municipal Year Book" for 1906, p. 379, gives the average price for local authorities at 2*s*. 8*d*., and for companies at 2*s*. 11¼*d*. per thousand cubic feet.

municipalities have, as a rule, bought the more prosperous concerns, and have shown little craving for the unprofitable ones.[1] Taking this into consideration, Sir Courtenay Boyle, late permanent under-secretary to the Board of Trade, told the committee on municipal trading in 1900 that the returns did not suggest, in like circumstances, any great balance of advantage to the consumer as regards the prices charged, in being supplied by a local authority instead of by a company.[2] A comparison of the prices of gas under public and private management in neighbouring towns, where the supply is about equal in quantity, seems to support this opinion. In short, when the experts disagree, and every one admits that the average prices are not very far apart, it is safe to assume, with Sir Courtenay Boyle, that up to this time the difference to the consumer between public and private ownership of gas plants has not been great.

The experience with gas works shows that an English borough can manage that kind of industry well, and make it profitable. Like water, it has some marked advantages, though to a far less extent. The supply affects almost everybody; the number of persons employed is not very large; the business is thoroughly established, comparatively simple, involves little risk, and is not likely to be revolutionised by inventions. The indirect disadvantages that a town may suffer from the public ownership of gas works will appear in the history of electric lighting.

Tramways.

Water and gas works developed before the era of municipal trading; and therefore while their purchase by the boroughs has furnished a test of the capacity of public authorities to conduct enterprises of this kind, it is to tramways and electric lighting that we must turn for illustrations of the full effect of a general system of municipal trade. The history of tramways in England has often been told. The earliest lines were laid down in the sixties with-

[1] Rep. of Com. on Mun. Trading, Com. Papers, 1900, VII., 183, Q. 621.
[2] *Ibid.*, Qs. 42–44.

out any authority from Parliament, and it was not until 1868 that the first private acts authorising tramways in Liverpool and a couple of other places were adopted. In the next year three private acts were passed authorising tramways in London. Private bills for the purpose then began to be introduced in such numbers that in 1870 the first general tramway law was enacted; and it remains in force to-day.[1]

The Act of 1870.

The Tramways Act of 1870 protected the interests of the municipalities. In the first place no provisional order under the Act could be granted by the Board of Trade except with the consent of the local and road authorities.[2] The restriction, of course, did not apply to private bills introduced directly into Parliament, but a couple of years later the standing orders of both houses were so amended as to require consent in that case also; and thus after 1872 companies could build tramways neither by provisional order nor by private bill without the approval of the local authorities. This has not only prevented the building of tramways altogether in a number of cases, as, for example, in London of late years, but it has enabled borough councils to annex to their consent conditions for the financial benefit of the town. A great deal of evidence on the subject was presented to the committee on municipal trading in 1900, and examples were given where the council had required the tramway company to pave the streets, contribute the whole or part of the cost of widening, pay rents, buy its electric power from the borough, and do other things which were by no means contemplated by the framers of the Act. Nor have the Board of Trade and private bill committees complete control over the matter, because even if the "agreed clauses," as they are termed, are struck out before the passage of a bill, yet being the consideration for which

The Local Veto.

[1] 33–34 Vic., c. 78.

[2] § 4; but by § 5 where a tramway was to traverse two or more local districts, the consent of the authorities in which two thirds of the line was to be built was enough.

the consent was granted, they are still looked upon as bargains binding in honour between the company and the town. For these reasons the so-called "veto" has provoked a great deal of discussion, but as yet it has not been changed.

The Purchase Clause.

Another provision was inserted with a direct view to public ownership. The era of municipal trading had begun, and the boroughs had no mind to be obliged, as they had been in the case of water and gas, to buy up at a very large premium the undertakings of companies working under perpetual charters. The private tramway acts passed in 1868–1869 had empowered the local authorities to buy out the company, after a certain period, at the structural value of the plant, with thirty per cent added for good-will. These terms the government thought so onerous as to make it impossible for the local authority to profit by them and the Act of 1870 therefore provided (§ 43) that the local authorities might purchase at the end of twenty-one years at the structural value alone. The purchase clause had an effect that became more marked as time went on.

Discouragement of Private Companies.

The tramway lines built under the Act of 1870 were for many years few and small. This has been attributed by the promoters of companies to the purchase clause, and to the right of veto with the conditions in the way of bargains for consent which arose therefrom. The Act seems, in fact, to have had a discouraging effect, for in introducing the bill Mr. Shaw-Lefevre stated that twenty-seven companies were asking for permission to build five hundred and fifteen miles of line, whereas by 1880 only three hundred and eighty-six miles had been built.[1]

Not only was the formation of tramway companies far from rapid, but the subsequent development of the lines proceeded more slowly still, for each year shortened the period of the charter, and hence gave less time for reaping profits before the time for purchase came. This was particularly felt in the matter of electric traction, an improve-

[1] Hans. 3 Ser. CXCIX., 1080; Meyer, "Municipal Ownership in Great Britain," p. 18.

ment that came into use only when the terms of the earlier companies were drawing to the end, and when the later ones chartered in the early eighties had exhausted nearly one half of their statutory period. The outlay required for the reconstruction of the line would not pay unless the period fixed by the charter were extended, and that the municipalities were rarely willing to concede. Dublin, indeed, was an exception. There an agreement was made for an extension of the time for purchase with a change in the price to be paid, and the company equipped the lines with electricity, giving what was at the time distinctly the best tramway service in the United Kingdom. Cases of the sort were uncommon, for the borough councils failed to see the importance to the urban population of a great immediate development of rapid transit, and, moreover, the desire for municipal ownership had begun. As the statutory period neared its end, any outlay by a tramway company was more and more avoided, and during the last few years a company naturally worked its lines as they stood for such profit as they could be made to yield.[1]

**Municipal Management.**

While private enterprise was thus failing to develop the tramways of England, the municipal authorities did not fill the gap, either by purchasing the companies' lines or by constructing new ones of their own. In fact, they were not as a rule allowed by law to operate tramways even where they owned them. The Act of 1870 permitted the local bodies to build tramways and to lease them, but not to work them.[2] A very few towns, indeed, ob-

[1] The relative development of tramways in the United Kingdom and the United States is shown by the following figures, taken from Com. Papers, 1880, LXIV., 441, p. 21; 1890, LXV., 1033, p. 19, and U. S. Census, 1890, Vol. VIII., "Transportation by Land," p. 692.

| | U. K. | U. S. |
|---|---|---|
| Miles of route, 1880 | 368 | 2050 |
| Miles of route, 1890 | 948 | 5783 |

[2] The crudity of the conception of tramway service at this time is shown in the provision authorising the municipalities to allow any one who chose to run cars on the tracks on paying toll: Tramways Act, 1870, 33–34 Vic., c. 78, § 19. It is hardly necessary to say that this power was never used.

tained working powers, perhaps by inadvertence. Glasgow, for example, and some other places, were enabled by private acts of 1870 to acquire the tramways at the end of twenty-one years, and "exercise the powers, rights and authorities of the companies in respect of the undertakings." It is under this provision that Glasgow is working now. Two or three more towns got similar privileges in the next two years. But in 1872 amendments to the standing orders were adopted by Parliament, forbidding wholly the grant of working powers to local authorities by private bills; and although the Act of 1870 did not expressly forbid the conferring of such rights by provisional order, the Board of Trade, following the policy of Parliament, refused to grant them.

Ten years later, in 1882, an exception became necessary. The hilly town of Huddersfield had built a tramway which no company would hire, and Parliament authorised the Board of Trade to allow that town to work its own lines, if it could not lease them on reasonable terms. For ten more years no other borough was treated in the same way; but in 1891 and 1892, as the leases and the statutory terms of the tramway companies were drawing to a close many towns sought such a power, and in the latter year Parliament amended the standing orders so far as to permit the insertion of the Huddersfield clause whenever it was asked for.

The pressure for municipal working soon grew so strong that in 1896 the provision against it was dropped from the standing orders altogether, and the period of municipal tramways began its full career. From that time the development of street railways became more rapid. Many town councils, taking the management into their own hands, constructed new lines or extended the old ones; while a few others, unable to do so, made agreements with companies for longer terms, or purchase at higher prices, than those provided in the Act of 1870. But in spite of the more rapid growth of the last ten years, tramways are still far less developed in England than in the United States, for although the urban population in the two countries is nearly the same, and is not unevenly massed in cities of the same size, there were in the United States 16,652 route miles of tramways in 1902, as against 2117 route miles in the United Kingdom in 1904–1905.[1]

Tramways in Glasgow.

There can be no doubt of the vast superiority of the municipal tramways as a whole, to those of private companies under the restrictions of the Act of 1870; and this has created in England a strong presumption in favour of municipal management. "But they, measuring themselves by themselves, and comparing themselves among themselves, are not wise." The example of Glasgow is typical. Having failed to agree with the company about an extension of time, the council took over the lines at the expiration of the lease in 1894; and failing again to agree with the company about the purchase of their cars, the council, strangely enough, proceeded to reëquip the line with horses, although that method of traction was rapidly disappearing in the United States. The Dublin companies having taken up electricity, Glasgow followed at first experimentally, and her tramways were not wholly electric before 1901. But even while horses were in use, the fares were at once reduced, and the service improved, until at the present day the Glasgow tramways are far superior in every way to the old ones under the company. Yet, as has often been pointed out, they are, as regards the profit reaped by the public treasury, the service rendered, and — except for very short distances — the fares charged, no less distinctly inferior to those in Boston which serve a population not far from the same size.[2]

[1] U. S. Census Bulletin, III., 1903; Com. Papers, 1905, LXX., 685, p. 33.

Glasgow and Boston.

[2] The profit to the public treasury is easily computed. Adding together the rates, the income tax, the payment towards sinking fund on the money borrowed and the contribution to the "common good," — which is a sort of compensation for the use of streets continued since the days of the old company, — the aggregate payments on public account by the Glasgow tramways in the year ending May 31, 1906, were as follows:—

Glasgow has made for herself the model municipal tramways, and what is true in her case is true of the English boroughs in general. The service rendered to the public by the town councils with their perpetual unhampered franchise is certainly better than that rendered by the old

| | | | |
|---|---|---|---|
| Rates | £ 43,924. | 4. | 7 |
| Income Tax | 12,422. | 14. | 1 |
| Sinking Fund | 48,327. | 0. | 5 |
| Payment to the Common Good | 35,000. | 0. | 0 |
| Total | £139,673. | 19. | 1 |

The Boston Elevated Railway Company, in addition to the rent of the subway and tunnels belonging to the city, paid in 1906:—

| | |
|---|---|
| Taxes on Real Estate and Capital Stock | $918,027.57 |
| Sinking Fund on Subway | 57,617.38 |
| Cost of street paving and interest on cost of paving previously laid | 316,857.56 |
| Compensation for use of streets | 115,986.77 |
| Total | $1,408,489.28 |

or more than twice as much.

The contrast between the services rendered is quite as marked. The Glasgow corporation has nearly 161 miles of single track; the Boston company 457 miles, of which more than twenty miles are in a subway or on an elevated structure, at a far greater cost to the company and giving much more rapid service in the crowded parts of the city. Glasgow owns 783 cars, against 3313 (passenger) cars in Boston; and the number of car miles run was 18,886,910 as against 50,056,608. Clearly the accommodation offered to the public is very much less in Glasgow, and this is the more evident when the actual number of people travelling is taken into consideration. It is, in fact, not very different in the two cases, the total number of passengers carried in Glasgow having been 208,059,833, and in Boston 262,267,240; so that the passengers per car mile were 11.02 in Glasgow and 5.24 in Boston. In other words, either the people in the Glasgow trams were more crowded, or they travelled shorter distances. This last is certainly the fact, and it has a bearing upon the question of fares.

The rates of fare are not easy to compare, because Boston has a uniform five-cent fare with transfers for distances running up in some cases to more than a dozen miles, while Glasgow charges as little as a half-penny for a half mile, and for longer rides at the rate of about a penny for every two and a quarter miles. The result is that Glasgow charges much less for short distances, and it is for this that her trams are chiefly used; 80 per cent of the passengers paying not over a penny, and therefore travelling not more than two and a quarter miles; 90 per cent paying not more than a penny and a half, and travelling not more than three miles and a half. In fact, the average fare paid per passenger is .94 of a penny. Boston, on the other hand, charges less for very long distances.

companies with their limited tenure and their liability to purchase. On the other hand, the municipal tramways are inferior to those constructed by American companies which are not subject to restrictions of a similar nature. An Englishman sometimes meets a comparison of

But so far as the working-classes are concerned, the fares should be measured not by the exchange value of gold, but by the earnings of the people, and for this purpose perhaps the wages of the conductors and motormen of the tramways themselves may be taken as a standard. Now the wages paid in Glasgow are almost exactly half of those paid in Boston.

GLASGOW TRAMWAYS

SCALE OF WAGES FOR MOTORMEN-CONDUCTORS

| | | *per day* | *per week* |
|---|---|---|---|
| 1st year | 1st 6 months | 4/ | 24/ |
| | 2d 6 months | 4/2 | 25/ |
| 2d year | 3d 6 months | 4/4 | 26/ |
| | 4th 6 months | 4/6 | 27/ |
| 3d year | 5th 6 months | 4/8 | 28/ |
| | 6th 6 months | 4/10 | 29/ |
| 4th year | | 5/ | 30/ |
| Thereafter | | 5/2 | 31/ |

BOSTON ELEVATED RAILWAY

SURFACE LINES

| *For Conductors and Motormen* | *per day* |
|---|---|
| During 1st and 2d year of service | $2.30 |
| During 3d, 4th and 5th years of continuous service | 2.35 |
| During 6th to 10th years inclusive continuous service | 2.40 |
| During 11th to 15th years inclusive continuous service | 2.45 |
| During 16th and later years inclusive continuous service | 2.50 |

Measured in this way a working-class passenger can travel from one end of Boston and its suburbs to the other for the same proportion of his wages that will carry him about two miles and a half in Glasgow.

It would seem that, with their system of graded fares, the tramways of Glasgow are not doing very effective work in spreading the population, and this impression is corroborated by the fact that at the census of 1901 48.3 per cent of the population of Glasgow were overcrowded at the rate of more than two to a room, the percentage having fallen from 59.6 in 1891, although the total number of persons overcrowded had increased slightly (Com. Papers, 1892, XCIV., 1, p. 331; 1902, CXXIX., 1133, p. 362). It is impossible to compare with this the condition of things in Boston accurately, because no statistics have been compiled on the same basis. From the report of the committee appointed by the mayor of Boston to investithis kind by virtually assuming that industrial enterprise in Great Britain cannot be expected to equal that of America. But England long led the world in engineering progress, and no general change has come over the national character that would make it impossible to-day.

Tramways running Beyond the Borough.

A difficult problem in the municipal management of tramways is presented by the constantly increasing need of extending the lines beyond the limits of the borough, a matter that has had in its turn a legislative history. The Board of Trade has never felt authorised to grant provisional orders enabling local councils to construct tramways outside of their areas;[1] but this was not important so long as those bodies had no right to operate the lines. As soon, however, as working powers began to be conferred on boroughs, the question forced itself upon public attention, for a tramway that is to be useful can rarely stop at the frontier of the town, and borough councils do not find it easy to make traffic agreements with independent outlying companies or suburban districts. The problem was especially obvious where a borough purchased under the Act of 1870 its share of a tramway that extended into the surrounding country. At the end of the eighties, therefore, power to construct or hire outside lines began to be sought. In the years from 1889 to 1895 eight private acts conferring such powers were passed,[2] and the next year Parliament took up a definite policy by adopting a standing order for

gate tenement-house conditions in 1904, it appears that in the 5232 tenement houses inspected — presumably the worst in the city — there were more rooms than occupants. Taking as a basis of overcrowding less than 300 cubic feet of air per adult, or 200 for a child, the committee found 623 (or about 12 per cent) of the tenements overcrowded. As these tenement houses include less than one fifth of the population of the city, the overcrowding on this estimate would be 2½ per cent of the population. It is clear that there is much less overcrowding in Boston than in Glasgow, and this in spite of the fact that Boston is built upon a series of peninsulas, naturally separated from its suburbs by broad stretches of water, and therefore little suited to expansion; while Glasgow has open available land on all sides.

[1] Rep. Com. on Mun. Trading, Com. Papers, 1900, VII., 183, Q. 125.

[2] *Ibid.*, App. III.

the grant of outside working powers whenever the conditions appeared to justify it. Thenceforward the private acts passed for the purpose were more numerous.

But the removal of legal impediments did not solve all questions about the terms on which lines outside the borough should be used. Mere traffic agreements between local authorities, each working its own lines, have been occasionally made. Such an arrangement was effected between Manchester and Salford, after the public had suffered serious inconvenience for a time. Contracts of this kind are, however, uncommon; while the plan of management by a joint board, appointed by the councils concerned, has met with little favour among local authorities, and seems to be applied in only one instance at the present day. The ordinary form of arrangement is either a lease by the suburb to the large city, or the direct construction and ownership by the latter of the lines outside its area. In the case of a lease it is not easy to fix a fair rent when the town that hires incurs a risk, but hopes to make a large profit; and where a borough builds and owns the outside lines, the old question arises of a right on the part of the suburban area to purchase the line after a certain period. In this connection it is noteworthy that the House of Commons in the Standing Order of 1896 (170 A) originally allowed a purchase after seven years, lengthening it in 1899 to twenty-one years after the analogy of private companies. But even this period was found by the boroughs too short, and it was increased in 1901 so as to authorise a maximum of forty-two years. Glasgow, moreover, which owns many more miles of track outside her area than any other borough, has always tried to obtain a perpetual franchise in such cases.[1]

Small Extent of Suburban Tramways.

With its large town population massed in places not far apart, Great Britain would seem to offer a paradise for

[1] Hans. 4 Ser. XCVII., 1251–52. Rep. Com. on Mun. Trading, Com. Papers, 1900, Q. 2825. Glasgow owns 48 miles of track outside her area, 44 of them in perpetuity, and 4 under the Clydebank order which entitles that burgh to purchase at the end of 42 years. The city has also a lease of 8½ miles of track in Govan, and running powers over 2 miles in Paisley.

suburban and interurban tramways, and yet it is precisely in this respect that the country compares least favourably with the United States.[1] Municipal enterprise does not appear to have proved favourable to tramways of that kind. The most extensive suburban systems are found in Glasgow, which operated in 1906 fifty-eight and a half miles of track outside of her area against one hundred and two miles within; and in Manchester and Salford, which operated between them in 1905, two hundred and seventeen miles of track in a region containing well over a million of people, the proportion of track outside of the two boroughs being apparently somewhat less than in the case of Glasgow.[2] The lines worked by other boroughs beyond their boundaries are of small extent.[3]

**Electric Lighting.**

The youngest of the great public utilities, and the last to be regulated by general law, is electric lighting. It did not become of practical use until the era of municipal trading was well under way, and hence the policy already adopted in the case of tramways was pursued. But the policy was followed under different conditions, for commercially

[1] *Cf.* Meyer, "Municipal Ownership in Great Britain," table on p. 87.

[2] The outside lines of Glasgow are mostly owned by that city; those of Manchester and Salford are held on lease.

**Light Railways.**

[3] In order to provide transportation for agricultural districts the Light Railway Act was passed in 1896. It created a Board of Commissioners empowered to issue provisional orders for building such railways, which became valid when confirmed by the Board of Trade without the need of parliamentary sanction.

Physically a light railway may be, and often is, simply a tramway under another name; but the Act does not require the consent of the local authorities, and contains no clause for compulsory purchase, although the commissioners have, as a rule, inserted a provision for purchase at the value of the railway as a going concern.

The Act appeared to remove some of the chief obstacles to private enterprise under the Tramways Act of 1870; for while the commissioners have refused to grant an order for a line wholly in one local area, a door would seem to be opened for suburban and interurban lines. To some extent this has been the case, and a large number of light railways have been built, but a line of that kind offers no alluring vision of profits unless it has access to a large town, or unless a favourable traffic agreement can be made with the tramways there. The former is not easy to obtain against the opposition of the town council, and as to the latter the councils have shown no signs of eagerness to coöperate with private companies.

electric light was still in an experimental and speculative stage when it came under the fostering care of Parliament. Both arc and incandescent lamps had been perfected, a number of small plants for supplying single establishments or a few neighbours had just been set up, and the industry was believed to have a great future before it, when the government in 1882 brought in a bill to permit the placing of wires in the streets.

The Act of 1882.

The object in view was to secure for the municipalities the benefit of the new invention so far as that could be done without discouraging private enterprise. The bill, therefore, provided that the local authority should have a right to purchase the plant for its existing structural value at the end of seven years. The select committee, to which the bill was referred, lengthened the term to fifteen, and the House of Lords to twenty-one, years, a compromise that was accepted by the Commons. On these conditions provisional orders could be issued by the Board of Trade. But the government had made a grave commercial miscalculation; for although the promoters felt that there was a chance of profit, and took out fifty-nine provisional orders within the next two years, the public was unwilling to invest its money. Only one of the orders was ever put into operation, and that not until 1889. During the four years from 1885 to 1888 a single order alone was granted to a company, and it was not used.[1] The business was regarded as too hazardous, and the terms too much in the nature of heads you win, tails I lose, to tempt capital. These conditions did not indeed apply to the boroughs themselves, and fourteen of them took out provisional orders, but they were not prepared to venture where companies feared to tread, and none of their orders were used until several years later when private enterprise had shown the way.

[1] The Board had power also to grant licenses for seven years. A number of them were issued, and two were put into operation. These, with a few unauthorised concerns that stretched their wires over housetops, were the only electric light plants that sold current in 1888, and none of them could work on more than a very small scale.

The Act of 1882 had apparently strangled the industry, and as the electric light was developing at a rapid pace in other countries, it was clear that something must be done. After various bills on the subject had been brought into Parliament without effect, the Act of 1888 was passed, which left the conditions of purchase unchanged, but lengthened the maximum period before it could take place from twenty-one to forty-two years. The Board of Trade was, however, empowered to vary the terms, and it has been not uncommon to fix a shorter period with a provision for the payment of a premium on purchase. The passage of this Act seems to have proved the purchase clause in the earlier statute to have been the decisive obstacle, because petitions for provisional orders began to be presented at once. In the three years following 1888, seventy-seven such orders were granted to companies, and the same number to local authorities. The latter, in fact, soon outstripped the private companies in the number of provisional orders obtained, although they were slower in making use of them.

The Act of 1888.

The Act of 1882 had required the consent of the local authority only in case of a license, but the Act of 1888 required it in case of a provisional order also, unless the Board, for special reasons, saw fit to dispense with it. That this checked the development of electric light is clear when one reflects that in the twelve years from 1890 to 1899, ninety-nine petitions for provisional orders were refused because the local authorities withheld their consent; and it is, of course, impossible to say how many more projects were nipped in the bud by the discovery that consent could not be obtained. The Board of Trade, indeed, never used its power of dispensation until 1899, when it did so in a couple of cases, a precedent that has been followed more freely of late years. The partial veto in the Act of 1888 did not ultimately prevent the introduction of electric light, for in almost all the cases where a provisional order was refused on that ground, the light was brought in later, usually by the borough itself; but the veto certainly caused delay.

The Local Veto.

Motives for refusing Consent.

The Committee on Municipal Trading in 1900 received a good deal of evidence to the effect that the motive for refusing consent was the possession by the local authority of a gas plant which it desired to protect from competition; and as specific instances were cited with quotations from statements or letters of local officials, there can be no doubt that this was sometimes true. But that it was not the general motive would seem to be proved by the fact that in by far the larger number of cases where a provisional order was refused for lack of consent, the local authority did not own a gas plant. The assertion has been often made, also, that the boroughs themselves applied for provisional orders, without intending to use them, simply in order to block the grant of an order to a company, and certainly many boroughs did not begin to supply electricity for several years after their orders were issued.[1] No doubt the boroughs in refusing consent, or applying for orders, were actuated by the ordinary commercial desire to secure for themselves any profit that the new venture might bring, instead of allowing it to go into the pockets of private companies; but it is needless to attribute to a deliberate purpose of abstaining from using the order a delay which may well have been due to business caution in embarking in a new venture.

The Electric Power Bills.

That boroughs in trade acquire the principles of trade, that they have the business instinct of striving to prevent competition, without always considering how it may affect the welfare of the community in other respects, is shown by the history of the electric power bills. The progress of electrical industry has made it possible to distribute power more cheaply over a large area from a central station, than it can be produced in smaller quantities on the spot; and in 1897 a company was formed to furnish power in the centre of England. But the bill to authorise this was opposed by the Association of Municipal Corporations and defeated in 1899. The next year the Lancashire Power Bill

[1] Rep. Com. on Mun. Trading, Com. Papers, 1900, VII., 183, App. J.

was opposed in the same way, although the company agreed not to supply electricity in the areas of any local authorities without their consent. It had been the policy of the Board of Trade to issue provisional electric lighting orders only for limited areas, to avoid competition therein and to give a preference to local authorities; and it was felt that the power bills involved a departure from that principle.[1] The Lancashire bill was, however, passed, together with four others affecting different parts of the country; and in the following years a large number of similar bills were enacted, but with provisions, at least in the earlier acts, to protect existing undertakings against serious competition.

**Results of Municipal Electric Light.**

According to the return of reproductive undertakings of the boroughs of England and Wales, laid before Parliament in 1902, there had been during the preceding years an aggregate annual loss on electric light of £11,707. This was due in large part to the fact that the industry was new, and in the next three years the conditions improved very much. Municipal ownership is now more common in the case of electricity than of gas, the capital outlay being also greater, and although the profit is not so large, the electric light undertakings of the boroughs were apparently earning on the average in 1905, above interest and sinking-fund charges, not far from three quarters of one per cent on the investment. The aggregate capital of the private companies is nearly equal to that of the municipal plants, and in spite of the disadvantages under which the companies labour, there has been much difference of opinion both about the relative efficiency, and the prices charged for current, under the two forms of management. The prices charged by the boroughs themselves vary, indeed, very much in different places, while in regard to efficiency one is always met by the eternal question of the method of keeping accounts. One often hears it said that the municipalities do not make sufficient allowance for the rapid deterioration of electrical

[1] Rep. Com. on Municipal Trading, Com. Papers, 1900, VII., 183, Qs. 65, 71–73.

machinery and the brief period in which it is made obsolete by improvements. To keep it in working order and abreast of the times, requires a large annual expenditure, but the ratio of working expenses to gross receipts, although varying a great deal in different boroughs, is usually low,[1] and in much more than half of them nothing was set aside for depreciation in 1905.[2]

Electric light has certainly made great progress in England since the Act of 1888, but the industry has not attained so large a development as in the United States, either in the proportion of towns supplied, or in the extent to which the light is used in those towns; and in the absence of any other sufficient cause it would seem that this must be attributed to the policy that has been pursued by Parliament and by the borough councils.

Housing.

There is one form of municipal trading not a monopoly, and only one, which has become so general as to provoke a sharp discussion, and that is the provision of dwellings for the working-classes. The subject has already been referred to in the chapter on London, and it is needless to deal with it here in detail, because the essential facts are much the same everywhere. The whole question bristles with difficulties which are constantly set forth in so many articles that even a bibliography of them would be out of date before it could appear in print.

The Problem and the Remedies.

The causes of the problem in the pressing form that it has recently assumed appear to be: a greater philanthropic interest in the welfare of the working-classes; the growth

[1] It is said to be the policy both of companies and of municipalities in England to spend less out of income for the renewal of electric light plants than is thought necessary in the United States.

[2] The fact that in Glasgow the expenses are only 34 per cent of the gross receipts is offset by the 28 per cent set aside for depreciation; but in Sheffield, where the working expenses are only 28 per cent and no allowance is made for depreciation, it would seem that the plant must be running down. As an illustration of the way the profits on one kind of trading can be used to help out another, it may be observed that cost of power for municipal tramways is almost always much greater where it is taken from the electric light plant of the borough, than when the tramway has a plant of its own.

in sanitary knowledge, with a recognition of the connection between bad housing and ill health; an increase in the cost of building and in local rates, which either checks the supply of houses or raises the rent; and finally the stringent building regulations that have raised, perhaps too suddenly, the standard for the houses of the poor. Parliament has sought to remedy the housing conditions in various ways. It has provided for closing, and if necessary demolishing, houses unfit for human habitation,[1] and some people believe that the wisest policy is a vigorous use of these provisions, trusting to the natural supply of new houses for the families gradually dispossessed in the process. In some places that has been done apparently with success, but for one reason or another it is not always easy to enforce the Act thoroughly, especially as no compensation is given to the landlord.

Then provision has been made in Part I. of the Housing of Working-classes Act of 1890, for clearing out whole unhealthy areas, or slums, by compulsory purchase. There has been a strong feeling, that in such a case overcrowding in a town would be actually increased unless the people displaced were rehoused, and rehoused in the neighbourhood of their work. Hence Parliament has laid down the general principle that when a municipality acts under this provision, or when a railroad or other great concern destroys many houses to enlarge its works, it shall see that accommodation is furnished near by for the people dispossessed. But land in a crowded district is usually worth more for other purposes than for working-men's houses, so that the proceeding commonly involves a loss. In that case the law has the effect of retaining workmen in a locality from which they would naturally remove, and since by keeping them it tends to keep employers also, shrewd people have urged that the whole policy

[1] Housing of the Working-classes Act, 1890, 53–54 Vic., c. 70, Part II. The powers conferred on local authorities by the three parts of this Act have been described in the chapter on London.

is a mistaken attempt to hinder a diffusion of the population away from the centre. All human progress, and perhaps, above all, improvement in the condition of the masses, involves temporary suffering to many individuals; and a too jealous effort to prevent that may sometimes impede a highly desirable change. Rehousing in clearing out a slum is not, indeed, obligatory on a provincial town unless required by the Local Government Board, and the celebrated improvement in the centre of Birmingham was made without providing for the people displaced.

Finally, provision has been made under Part III. of the Act for the construction of new dwellings or lodging-houses by local authorities, without regard to any destruction of houses, but solely to the sufficiency of the existing supply.

The Results of Housing.

Under Part I. or Part III. of the Act a large number of boroughs, and other local authorities mostly urban district councils,[1] have built houses of all kinds from rows of single cottages to large blocks of tenements; but, except for Gildart's Gardens and a few other buildings of a similar character in Liverpool, they have rarely, if ever, housed the poorest class, or any considerable proportion of the people displaced by clearing out unhealthy areas. A dozen towns, including London, have also built model lodging-houses, sometimes known as "poor man's hotels," although, save perhaps in the case of Glasgow, which has gone into the business on very much the largest scale, they are not occupied by very poor people.[2]

In short, throughout the country, as in the metropolis,

[1] Part I. of the Act does not apply to rural districts (§ 3); but Part III. may be adopted by them (§§ 54–55). The Allotment Acts, providing that local authorities may acquire rural land, and let it in allotments to labourers, have been little used.

[2] Glasgow has seven of these lodging-houses with room for 2166 men and 248 women, at a charge of three and a half to four and a half pence for the night. Glasgow has also a municipal family home for widowers with children. The lodging runs from *7s. 4d.* to *13s. 6d.* per week, according as there are from one to five children, and the board is *9½d.* per day for the father, nurses being provided without charge.

municipal housing does not furnish dwellings for the really poor, who are the class least likely to be decently housed by private enterprise, and the only class properly the subject of charity. The towns are therefore providing houses at about the current rents for a minute fraction of a large class that ought normally to be well housed without such help; and they are doing so in spite of the fact that in some of the boroughs, such as Glasgow, Manchester and Liverpool, many dwelling-houses have been lying vacant. As already pointed out in the case of London, apart from some obscure effect in promoting private enterprise — and there is some evidence that it has the opposite result — the building by a town of a few dwellings for people who earn fair wages, would not appear to be even a step toward the solution of the housing problem, unless the public authorities are proposing to go on and house the whole wage-earning class. But when one asks what the ultimate aim is, and whether or no such a gigantic idea has been contemplated, he is apt to find that the question is a surprise, that nothing is forecast beyond constructing a few more tenements. This would seem to be a case of meeting a great social problem by an immediate superficial palliative.[1] The people are insufficiently housed, *ergo*, build a few houses. It would seem to be a case of embarking on an undertaking of doubtful utility, and full of possible dangers, without a clear perception of the course to be pursued.

Leaving aside the question of policy, the management of municipal dwellings is sound. They are administered on business principles, while politics and favouritism appear to have been wholly excluded. Except for the loss involved in the obligation to rehouse in the same locality, they have generally paid their way, the net rents being more than

[1] Herein it differs from a recent statute that carries socialism, or in one aspect trading, very far — the act that provides for giving meals to school children, and charging the parents who can afford to pay for them. Education (Provision of Meals) Act, 1906, 6 Edw. VII., c. 57.

enough to defray the interest on the money borrowed. But, unlike gas, electricity and tramways, the commercial aspect of housing is not the most important one. The object being philanthropic, it is mainly as a solution of a social and philanthropic problem that the policy must be judged, and from that point of view it does not seem as yet to have had much success.

Docks. There is one other form of municipal trading which must be noticed, not on account of its actual magnitude, but because it has given rise to serious misapprehension in the United States; and that is the supply of docks. Almost all the large docks in Great Britain are either private property, like those in Cardiff, Southampton and London, or they are managed, like those in Glasgow and Liverpool, by a board, on which the town council is represented, but of which the members are mainly elected by ship-owners and other persons interested in the trade of the port. Liverpool, indeed, had charge of her own docks until 1858, when they were turned over to the Mersey Docks and Harbour Board. There are now in England only three places where the docks are managed by the town council, and in these three the undertaking is small or not very successful. They are Boston, Preston and Bristol. In Boston, a town of only sixteen thousand inhabitants, with no great commerce, the docks are said to have been highly profitable. In Preston this is certainly very far from being true, for they cost the town £36,000 a year, an amount equal to a rate of 1*s.* 10½*d.* in the pound, or more than one fifth of the whole local taxation for all purposes. In Bristol, where the docks are on a much larger scale, the result is not proportionately so bad, the amount paid from rates to meet expenses, including interest and sinking fund, having been £35,000 in the year ending April 30, 1906.[1] The commerce of the port has not developed very rapidly, and although this is, no doubt, due in large part to its situation, which is

[1] The amount of the sinking-fund charges was £28,172 2*s.* 1*d.*, so that the revenue did not even cover the interest on the debt.

not well adapted to modern needs, people whose opinions are entitled to weight, think it might have prospered better had the docks been in the hands of a company.

**Results of Municipal Trading.**

Experiments in municipal trading have hardly been conducted in England long enough to justify a forecast of their ultimate effects, but from the immediate results, some conclusions may be safely drawn. The first is that a simple routine business can be well conducted where there are, as in England, good permanent officials. Whether the community as a whole gains or loses by having it so managed depends, no doubt, very much upon the nature of the industry, and upon the control to be exercised over companies to which, as an alternative, the franchise would be granted.

Another fairly obvious conclusion is that municipalities do not, and cannot, speculate with the public funds, and hence are not suited for new and hazardous ventures. This involves the question how the local authorities are to acquire undertakings. Two methods have been tried in England; one in the case of water and gas, where the borough has, as a rule, bought at a premium a successful enterprise built up by a private company under a perpetual franchise; the other, applied to tramways and electric lighting, where the borough has been given an option of purchasing the undertaking at merely structural value after a certain number of years. It would seem that, in spite of the premiums paid, the former method has proved on the whole more profitable for the municipalities, and distinctly better for the public. In fact, a mistake in the period fixed for purchase stopped for a time the development of electric lighting altogether. Clearly the second method can be applied only to a new invention, not yet in general use, and in that case it is liable to check the growth of the industry, as happened in the case of both tramways and electric light. Perhaps some other plan of acquiring undertakings might be devised better than either of these; but we are concerned here only with the results of British experiments, not with the possibilities of municipal trading.

A third conclusion that may be drawn from English experience is that municipalities carry on trade in a business spirit. If they did not, they would certainly not succeed; but a part of the business spirit is a sharp eye to profit, and a dread of competition. It is commonly said that a private company is interested in dividends and a local council in the public welfare; yet the expert managers of both private and public industrial concerns think first neither of dividends nor of the public interest, but of the perfection of the enterprise. As often happens in human affairs, the end is largely obscured by the means.

Many examples besides those already mentioned could be cited to show how municipalities, like private companies, are averse to projects that threaten their own earnings,[1] and in this connection it is interesting to observe the great difficulty of coöperation in England between public and private bodies in any form of profitable trade. It is the more marked when compared with the large amount of coöperation that has taken place of late years between local authorities and endowed institutions in the matter of secondary education, although American experience shows that educational institutions are usually very jealous of their independence.

Causes of Municipal Trading.

The causes of municipal trading are threefold. One of them, and perhaps the one that most affects the bulk of the people, is the desire for profit. Another is the belief that a private company strives to get as much out of the public, and give as little in return, as it can. The old faith in the harmony of interests, boldly stated by the

[1] Major Darwin puts this forcibly when he says: "The difference between municipal and private traders is not that they are actuated by different motives; for both will always seek protection. Municipalities have, however, in many ways, greater powers and opportunities than private traders of checking competition, and they will take advantage of them exactly as private traders would do were they able." "Municipal Trade," p. 287.

Physiocrats, as well as by later French writers like Bastiat, and tacitly assumed by the classical English economists as the basis of the doctrine of *laissez faire*,[1] has lost its hold in England, and there is a growing feeling that the interests of capital are naturally inconsistent with those of the community. Curiously enough, this impression does not exist in regard to labour; but as applied to capital one meets with it continually, and it lies at the base of much of the strong popular inclination towards municipal trading.

A third cause of the extension of municipal enterprise in industrial fields comes from the same source as the efficiency of public management — from the presence of a corps of permanent professional officials. The officials, no less than the members of the borough councils, are anxious to magnify their office. Some opponents have suggested that they are actuated by a hope of increasing their salaries, but there is no good reason for ascribing to sordid motives an attitude resulting naturally from the universal and laudable desire to extend one's sphere of usefulness.

Herewith a subsidiary cause may also be noted. Before the private bill committees, where almost all new departures in municipal trading are made, the local public is unrepresented. The merit of the English system of private bill legislation lies in the fact that the proceedings are judicial rather than political; that the committee conducts something like an impartial trial between the parties interested. The Chairmen of Committees of the two Houses of Parliament have an eye to the general policy of innovations, and the central departments, which though favouring municipal trade are conservative in temper, submit their comments; but the burgess, who believes that the plan proposed

[1] It is characteristic that an explicit statement of the doctrine appears in Dumont's French edition of Bentham's "Treatise on Legislation"; but that in the English edition its place is taken by a long dissertation on criminal law.

is injurious to the welfare of the town, has no *locus standi* unless his private property is at stake. He is deemed to be represented by his borough council, or in other words it is not his affair. Now although the Chairmen and the departments may influence the private bill committee, or the House may reverse its action on the ground of public policy, the petition of the borough for authority to undertake some new function would seem to have a distinctly better chance of approval than it would if local ratepayers were allowed to present their case to the committee.

**Dangers of Municipal Trading.**

There is an objection to municipal trading arising from the difficulty of dealing with outside areas. The proper area for a tramway line, or the supply of electricity, does not naturally coincide with the proper boundaries of a borough; and, as we have seen, it has not been easy to regulate municipal trade satisfactorily in such cases. Joint boards are not liked, while a borough that trades beyond its limits is for the outside districts in the same position as a private company and actuated by similar motives. This is not only a difficulty, but a danger, for it may well result in shackling industrial and social progress.

Another danger arises from the enormous increase of debt, and that although the trading loans are in most cases offset by assets of at least equal value. The chief financial advantage of local authorities over companies lies in their ability to borrow at a lower rate of interest; but if in any town an important undertaking is unsuccessful, or if the bankers lose confidence in municipal operations, it may well be that the rate will rise, and then it will rise equally on all the loans made by the town for any purpose.[1] Now if one half of the debt of the town is incurred for trading, and in consequence of that the rate of interest should rise from three per cent to four per cent, the result would be the same as if the non-trading debt remained, as it would have done, at three per cent, and the loans for trading were placed at five per cent, a figure at which trading could

[1] Major Darwin refers to this, p. 242.

hardly be profitable. A little more rise still, and the effect on a town of its undertakings might easily be disastrous.

Then, again, there is the danger of checking industrial progress by a policy in favour of municipal trading, which fetters private enterprise in the initial stages, when public authorities will not, and ought not, to take the inevitable risks. This can involve consequences reaching far beyond the supply of public utilities in the towns, and many leading engineers are of opinion that the backwardness of England in the production of electrical machinery is due to the Tramways Act of 1870 and the Electrical Lighting Act of 1882.

Finally there is the great danger from an enormous number of municipal employees. These men may not as yet have combined to control elections to a serious extent, but human nature is not proof against temptation, and the attitude of the dockyard members in the House of Commons, together with the influence of the post-office clerks and telegraph operators there, shows that no elective body can be regarded as secure against the pressure of a large body of organised employees with votes. Whether the dangers inherent in municipal trading do or do not counterbalance its benefits, they cannot wisely be left out of account. But whether the evil or the good predominates, there can be no doubt of the popularity of the policy in England at the present day. In London it had a set-back at the last election, but over the country at large the tide is still on the flood.

## CHAPTER XLV

### OTHER LOCAL AUTHORITIES

The County.

THE political subdivision of the country for purposes of local government has been treated in an earlier chapter, and it will be remembered that the larger boroughs — in general those with more than fifty thousand people — were made counties by themselves. Since the administrative counties, therefore, do not include the county boroughs, an ancient geographical county may be large and rich, and yet a great part of the population and wealth may not be within the county so far as local government or local taxation are concerned.[1] On the other hand, it must be observed that all the non-county boroughs and urban districts are included in the county, with representatives on its council;[2] and thus the administrative counties are not necessarily rural in character, but may have a population in which the urban elements preponderate. Despite the fact that the great towns are taken out of the counties, and that some of the larger ancient shires have been divided into two or three parts, the administrative counties are still very unequal in size, running all the way from Rutland with 19,709 inhabitants and twenty-eight members in its council, to Lancashire with one hundred and forty members and 1,827,436 people. London is, of course, far larger still; but what is said in this chapter is intended only for the

[1] Except so far as they contribute to common objects under special arrangements.

[2] All non-county boroughs form a part of the administrative county; but those with more than ten thousand inhabitants retain the whole, and those with less a portion, of their municipal functions; while those which had a separate court of quarter sessions, or only a separate commission of the peace, enjoy certain privileges. Local Govt. Act, 1888, 51–52 Vic., c. 41, §§ 31–39; Redlich and Hirst, "Local Govt. in England," II., 104–15.

counties outside the metropolis, not for the London County Council which has already been described.

The County Council.

In creating a new governing body for the county the Local Government Act of 1888 followed the familiar pattern of the boroughs, with a few changes in detail.[1] It set up a single council to which the whole administration was entrusted, save that the licensing of publicans was left in the hands of the justices of the peace at brewster sessions, and the control of the police was vested in a joint standing committee of the council and the justices, the Lord Lieutenant and the Sheriff retaining by this time little or no administrative functions.[2] The burgess franchise was not only taken as the qualification for voting in all boroughs that elect representatives to the county council, but was also extended over the rest of the county;[3] although plural voting was expressly permitted by striking out the provision forbidding a person to vote in more than one electoral division.[4] As in the boroughs, the councillors are elected for a term of three years,[5] but instead of one third going out each year, they are all elected and retire together, an arrangement which was accompanied by the provision that each electoral division should have a single representative.[6]

Immediately after their own election the councillors proceed to choose a chairman and county aldermen. Again, following the example of the boroughs, the aldermen, who form an integral part of the council, are equal in number

[1] A legal difference is found in the fact that whereas the corporation of a borough consists of mayor, aldermen and burgesses, but can act only through its council, the county council, like other local authorities, is itself the corporate body. Local Govt. Act, 1888, § 79.

[2] By an Act of 1907 county associations can be formed for recruiting and organising the auxiliary forces.

[3] Local Govt. Act, 1888, § 2 (4).

[4] County Electors Act, 1888, 51 Vic., c. 10, § 7 (4).

[5] The qualifications for being elected are the same as those in the boroughs, except that clergymen are eligible, and so are peers and parliamentary voters who own land in the county but do not reside there. Local Govt. Act, 1888, § 2 (2).

[6] By the County Councils Election Act, 1891, 54–55 Vic., c. 68, the date of election was shifted from November 1 to the beginning of March, the elections coming in 1892, and every third year thereafter.

to one third of the councillors and serve for six years, one half retiring every three years; but in order to prevent a party that has secured less than half the elective seats from perpetuating its majority by means of aldermanic votes, as sometimes happens in the boroughs, it was provided that aldermen should not vote at elections for members of their class.[1]

Politics and Personnel.

Cities are, and always have been, the most favourable soil for political activity. One would, therefore, expect to find politics less prominent in rural than in town governments, and in fact the nomination of candidates for the council on party lines is much less common in the counties than in the boroughs. After election, party is almost completely forgotten in the work of the body, the divisions being mainly between different parts of the county, or between urban and rural districts, or between men of more or less progressive views, and all these cut across party lines. Not only does party politics run low, but the total number of seats contested for any reason is small, much smaller even than in the boroughs. At the very first election in 1889, for example, out of the 3240 seats in England and Wales only 1749 were contested; while at the election of 1901 out of 3349 the number contested sank to 433.[2] One might almost say that in spite of a democratic electorate, the counties are governed by common consent, or rather by a small number of people who take an active interest in the subject.

Apart from the general character of rural populations, there is a special reason why this should be true in England. Until 1888 the counties were governed by the justices of the peace, who belonged mainly to the land-owning gentry, and although these men were not free from the prejudices and interests of their class, their administration was honest, sound and not unpopular, while their possession of the land gave them a strong economic hold upon the whole

[1] Local Govt. Act, 1888, § 2 (2 c.).
[2] Ashley, "Local and Central Government," p. 25, note.

country-side. In the agricultural portions of the kingdom, that is in the greater part of the districts that elect councillors, men of this kind have retained their influence, and they are still the principal figures in most of the county councils. Occasionally they form a large majority of the council, and other people are considered so extraneous an element that one hears them referred to as "imported members." In other counties the landed gentry, although furnishing a large contingent, are a minority in the council, but in these cases they usually occupy the leading positions. It is only in heavily industrial shires, like Durham, that their influence is small; nor does it apparently tend to diminish. The councils contain also a number of tenant farmers; while the small boroughs and larger urban districts elect a good many professional men or tradesmen, and in the mining regions some workingmen. Agricultural labourers rarely appear, partly because they are not, like the workmen of the towns, highly organised in trade-unions, and partly because the long distances make attendance at the council and its committees expensive.[1]

The gentry appear to form, not unnaturally, an even larger proportion of the aldermen, and in fact these positions are conferred more often than in the boroughs upon men who are not councillors, the power of choosing outsiders being used not infrequently to retain a valuable member when he has failed of reëlection by the people. The most important difference in practice, however, between the counties and the boroughs consists in the well-nigh universal habit of reëlecting the chairman, who has thus an opportunity to acquire an authority that is quite without parallel in a borough.

**Committees.**

So far as the internal organisation of the borough councils is regulated by statute, it was adopted bodily for the counties by § 75 of the Act of 1888. Slight changes were, however,

[1] "Government by Horse and Trap," *Progressive Review*, May, 1897. Redlich and Hirst (II., 46) say that an agricultural labourer very often abstains from voting for fear of eviction.

made by other sections, mainly because it is difficult for the members of a county council to get together; and in fact they hold few more than the four statutory meetings a year. For this reason it was desirable to entrust the committees with some range of independent action, and the Act empowered the county council to delegate to them any of its functions, save the making of a rate or loan. Moreover, the committees are required by the Act only to report their proceedings, if excused by the council from submitting them for approval.[1]

The only committees prescribed by law are those on finance [2] and education,[3] the visiting committee on asylums,[4] and the joint standing committee for the management of the police composed of members appointed in equal numbers by the county council and the justices of the peace at quarter sessions.[5] Both the finance committee and the joint committee on police are given by statute certain powers which are not under the direct control of the county council. The finance committee is, indeed, placed in something akin to the position of a minister of the Crown in Parliament, for the council itself can make no order for the payment of money except on its recommendation, and, save for the expenses of the joint committee on police, no debt or liability above fifty pounds can be incurred until it has submitted an estimate. All other committees are purely creatures of the council, which can delegate powers to them it sees fit but is not obliged to do so.

Actual Working.

The standing orders are of the same nature as those of a borough council; in fact, the whole method of conducting business is very similar. An agenda containing the matters

[1] §§ 28 (2), (3); 82 (2). The council has authority to delegate its power on the same terms to a district council, § 28 (2), (3); or to a joint committee appointed in conjunction with another county council or with a court of quarter sessions, §§ 81, (1), (2), (3); 82 (3).

[2] Local Govt. Act, 1888, § 80 (3).

[3] Unless the council happens to have no elementary education in its charge. Educ. Act, 1902, 2 Edw. VII., c. 42, § 17.

[4] Lunacy Act, 1890, 53 Vic., c. 5, § 239.

[5] Local Govt. Act, 1888, § 30.

to be brought before the council, accompanied in most places by elaborate printed reports of committees, is sent to all the members before the meeting, and this is gone through in the same rapid way as in the boroughs, debate being concentrated upon a few points that provoke a difference of opinion. Almost the whole business comes from, or is at once referred to, a committee, and one may see the various chairmen seated around a table in the front of the hall presenting and defending their reports like ministers of state. In one respect, however, the actual working of a county council differs from that of its prototype in a borough. The person in whose hands the real influence lies varies much more in different places. The chairman of the council, like the mayor, is placed by the standing orders on every committee, and in his case that may mean a great deal. His time is not taken up by ceremonial duties, because they are much less numerous in a county than in a borough, and such as occur are performed by the Lord Lieutenant who is still the official head of the shire. What is more important, the chairman of the county council, unlike the mayor, is habitually reëlected, and his permanence gives him a large opportunity for power if he chooses to take advantage of it. His authority is not, indeed, the same everywhere, for while he is sometimes merely a presiding officer, in other cases he is the real mainspring of the whole county government.

The control over the committees by their own chairmen would also appear to be a more uncertain factor than in the boroughs, although it is usually of the same character — a statement that is not less true of the permanent officials.

**The Officials.** The county council always has a clerk, a chief constable, treasurer, surveyor, analyst, inspectors of various kinds, educational officers and coroners. It has usually a medical officer of health, often an accountant, and where it maintains a lunatic asylum there is a superintendent of that institution. Except for the first two, all these officers are appointed by the council. Apart from special provisions for certain counties, the clerk fills also the important post of clerk of the peace, and acting, therefore, on behalf of the justices of the peace as well as of the council, he is appointed by the joint standing committee of the two bodies;[1] while the chief constable who is under the immediate control of that committee is appointed in the same way. The council may create any other offices that it pleases; but since the duties it can undertake are very definitely prescribed by general law, other officers, not of a subordinate kind, are rarely appointed. As in almost all branches of English administration, the influence of the permanent officials is great, while the very size of the county tends to give them a free hand in current matters. The authority of the more purely professional men, like the surveyors, probably does not differ materially in boroughs and counties. Such officials, if strong men, have ordinarily much weight everywhere. It is with the clerk, who in a borough is almost always a directing and coördinating force, that the greatest variation in influence seems to occur. Sometimes, more particularly perhaps in Scotland, he is well-nigh the unseen ruler of the shire; but in others, where the chairman of the council combines long experience with personal vigour, the clerk occupies a position of less importance than in a borough.

**Powers of County Councils.**

The basis of the authority of the county council is the third section of the Act of 1888, which transfers to it the administrative powers of the justices of the peace in quarter sessions. The section goes on to enumerate those powers under sixteen heads, the most important being the raising, expending and borrowing of money; the care of county property, buildings, bridges, lunatic asylums, reformatory and industrial schools; the appointment and salary of administrative officers; the granting of certain licenses other than for the sale of liquor; the registration of scientific, charitable and religious societies; and the execution of various laws relating to animals, fish, birds

[1] Local Govt. Act, 1888, § 83.

and insects. The Act also gives the council charge of main roads,[1] makes it the protector of rivers from pollution, and grants it power to enact by-laws outside the limits of a borough; and finally the Act of 1902 made the council the general educational authority for the county, a matter that will be discussed in a later chapter. The control of the police had always been one of the most important functions of the justices of the peace, exercised as a part of their duties as magistrates, and instead of transferring this matter wholly to the new councils, a compromise was effected whereby the management of the police is vested in the joint standing committee of the justices and the county council.[2]

One of the objects aimed at in the creation of county councils was a decentralisation, which would relieve the national offices of a choking mass of detail, and free the local bodies from some of the red tape inseparable from a central department. For that purpose the county council was given by the Act of 1888 a voice in the union, division or change in boundaries of minor local areas, and its authority in the matter was much increased by the Local Government Act of 1894. Under this last statute it may also make provisional orders for the compulsory purchase of land by a parish council; its consent is needed for a loan by a parish; and if a district council fails to do its duty in regard to sanitation, or the obstruction of a public right of way, the county council may step in and do the work itself.[3] Originally, a much larger measure of decentralisation was contemplated, for the Act of 1888 (§ 10) authorised the Local Government Board to transfer to the county

[1] An urban district may retain the care of the main roads within its limits, and the council must make a contribution for the purpose. Local Govt. Act, 1888, § 11.

[2] Loc. Govt. Act, §§ 9, 30. The first of these sections reserves the right of the justices of the peace to give to the constables special orders in addition to their ordinary duties; but as the justices have no authority to incur expenses in so doing, the right is of limited importance. Redlich and Hirst, II., 71–72.

[3] Under the Allotments Act, 1890, 53–54 Vic., c. 65, § 2, it may do the same thing when a district council refuses improperly to provide allotments for labourers.

councils by provisional order the powers over local affairs of any department of state. But much as the boroughs and urban districts dislike the Local Government Board, their jealousy of the county councils is still stronger, and their hostility has hitherto prevented any action of importance under this provision, so that the tutelage of the councils is confined for the most part to rural bodies.

**Finance of County Councils.**

In speaking of the boroughs, attention was called to the Exchequer Contribution Account, or subvention from the national government to counties and county boroughs from the proceeds of the local license taxes, the additional duties on beer and spirits, and part of the proceeds of the probate duties. These sums are paid in lieu of former national grants in aid of local expenditure,[1] and must be applied to a number of definite objects, largely in the care of minor authorities. Such are vaccination, the education of pauper children, the support of pauper lunatics, the salaries of the officers of poor-law unions, one half of the salaries of medical officers of health, and one half of the pay and clothing of the police. The receipts, also, from certain additional duties on beer and spirits, commonly called "whiskey money," are expected, at least, to be used in aid of technical or secondary education. In fact, the county council is little more than a conduit pipe for most of these payments, because if anything is left after applying the money to the objects prescribed, it must be divided ratably among the different parts of the county. The Exchequer Contribution Account, therefore, helps chiefly the smaller local authorities.[2]

The county council itself receives small sums from tolls

[1] A further sum has been paid since 1896 to make up for the assessment of agricultural land at one half of its ratable value.

[2] A number of these subventions were originally granted to tempt local bodies to take up new duties, and to give the central government an effective control over their work. But this object has in most cases ceased, and the system of subsidies, which is unsound in principle, would very probably be abandoned or modified were it not that local rates are levied wholly on land and buildings, and the subsidies are virtually a contribution from other sources of taxation.

and rents, but obtains its income in the main from a county rate, assessed upon the parishes uniformly for general expenses, and on particular places for any special expenses incurred for their benefit. In order to insure a just apportionment of the burden among the parishes, the council may either accept the valuation of the parish overseers, or make an independent valuation of its own; but in any case the money is actually raised by means of a precept to the guardians of the union, the overseers in each parish collecting it with the other rates, and paying it over to the county treasurer.

A county council is subject to a good deal of financial control on the part of the national government. Its loans, which by the way are limited to one tenth of the ratable value [1] and must be repaid by annual instalments within thirty years, require, like all other local loans, the consent of the Local Government Board; and unlike a borough, but like all other local authorities, its accounts are subject to the audit of the board. In comparing the counties with the boroughs, we must also bear in mind the highly important fact that they have much less chance of enlarging their functions. The field of municipal trading is almost closed to them, for the Small Holdings Act of 1892 and the Light Railways Act of 1896 are almost, if not quite, the only general statutes that authorise them to undertake anything of this nature,[2] and until a few years ago they were cut off from the fruitful resource of private bill legislation by the provision which enabled them to oppose, but not to promote, bills in Parliament.[3]

**Urban District Councils.**

The title "urban district" would seem to imply a definite kind of community, one too small to be granted a borough charter, and yet of considerable density. This, however,

[1] Except in pursuance of a provisional order confirmed by Parliament. Local Govt. Act, 1888, § 68.

[2] Perhaps the power under the Small Dwellings Acquisition Act, 1899, 62–63 Vic., c. 44, of advancing money to tenants to help them buy houses, may be regarded as a species of municipal trading.

[3] Local Govt. Act, 1888, § 15. This was changed by 3 Edw. VII., c. 9.

is hardly the case, many very small places having received the organisation from which the present form is inherited at a time when it was the only means of obtaining any sanitary powers whatever, while a number of other districts have grown far beyond the size that would justify them in seeking to be made boroughs. The result is that urban districts vary much in population, the extremes, according to the Municipal Year Book for 1906, being Childwall in Lancashire with 218 inhabitants, and Willesden in Middlesex with 139,600. Yet they have the same form of government, and nominally, though not in reality, the same powers. Their present organisation, fixed by the Local Government Act of 1894, is based upon that of the boroughs, but differs from it in some essential points. In the first place, the voters are the parochial electors; that is, both the parliamentary and county-council voters registered in the parish;[1] and it is expressly provided that women otherwise qualified shall not be excluded on account of marriage.[2] Thus no woman is allowed to vote for Parliament, where national affairs are involved; a woman without a husband can vote for a county or borough council; and a married woman can vote on small things very near home. The councillors are elected for three years, one third, as in a borough, retiring every year; but the county council, upon a request of the district council passed by a two thirds vote, is authorised to direct that all the councillors shall retire together at the end of three years, and this has been done in a number of cases. The most marked contrast with the organisation of a borough council, however, lies in the fact that there are no aldermen.

In describing the boroughs it was pointed out that a very small part of their powers are conferred by the Municipal Corporations Act, that their functions came mainly from

[1] 56–57 Vic., c. 73, § 2 (1).

[2] § 43. But this does not allow husband and wife to qualify on the same property. Sex or marriage do not disqualify for being elected. § 23 (2). By the Act of 1907 they no longer disqualify for sitting on the council of a county or borough.

the Public Health and other acts, which treated them as the local sanitary authorities. In other words, the greater part of the duties of the boroughs comes from the fact that they are treated like urban district councils, and hence the latter have these same duties also.

They have the same functions as the boroughs in regard to drainage, water, nuisances, streets, lighting and the like; almost the only serious power that they lack being that of maintaining their own police force — a privilege of which boroughs with less than ten thousand people were deprived by the Act of 1888. The adoptive acts can be taken up by them, and they can, by provisional order or private bill, acquire the right to supply water, gas, electric light, tramways or houses for the working-classes. A great many of the larger ones have, in fact, done these things, so that in regard to functions, the line is far less broad between boroughs and urban districts as such, than between the places that have availed themselves fully of their opportunities, and those that have been reluctant to do so. The district councils are, however, under the care of the county councils in a few matters, such as alterations of boundaries, where a borough would be subject to the Local Government Board, and, unlike the boroughs, their accounts are audited by the Board.

It may be added that the method of conducting business in urban district councils is much the same as in the boroughs, and that the members are mainly tradesmen and persons of a similar class.

**Rural District Councils.**

Whereas the urban district councils, or their predecessors under other titles, were created for the purpose which they serve, sanitary powers in the rural parts of the country were at first entrusted to the poor-law guardians, a connection which in substance still persists. The Local Government Act of 1894 effected a great transformation in names. It provided that instead of the guardians acting as rural sanitary authorities, there should be set up for this work a new body of rural district councillors who should act as guardians, and so the bond between the two positions continues. Where the poor-law union and the rural district coincide in area, the guardians and the councillors are the same persons; where the district includes a parish not within the union, it will contain councillors from that parish who sit with another board of guardians, and in the same way a board of guardians may have members from a parish outside the district; but in any case the two bodies are legally distinct, holding separate meetings and keeping separate records. The Act of 1894 swept away the old method of election, and directed that the councillors should be chosen for a term of three years by the parochial electors in the different parishes. As in the case of urban districts, one third retire each year unless an order is made to the contrary, and there are no aldermen.

If in its powers an urban district is a somewhat reduced copy of a borough, with no little variation in different places, this may be said also of the relation of a rural to an urban district. It has very nearly the same authority of a purely sanitary nature in regard to such matters as drainage or nuisances, and every district council is required to appoint a medical health officer. It has even greater duties in regard to water, for it is directed by statute to see that every dwelling has a proper supply. It is also a highway authority, although it has not, like an urban council, a right to claim the care of main roads. But it has not the same powers in regard to such matters as lighting, watering and improving streets, regulating offensive trades, furnishing baths and wash-houses and clearing out unsanitary areas. The Local Government Board can, however, confer upon rural district councils any powers vested in urban districts by the Public Health Acts,[1] and orders of that kind are, in fact, constantly made. A rural district may also provide allotments and workingmen's houses; and may obtain provisional orders for electricity and tramways, although not, apparently, for gas. It is, moreover, under the control

[1] Public Health Act, 1875, § 276; Local Govt. Act, 1894, § 25.

of the county council to a somewhat greater extent than an urban district.

Unlike the county councils which are usually progressive in one way, as the boroughs and larger urban districts are in another, the rural district councils are largely in the hands of farmers who are afraid of increasing the rates. It appears to be difficult, also, to get good candidates to stand for them; but sometimes a man of higher position is elected, and then he is apt to obtain control.

**The Parish.** One of the aims of the Act of 1894 was to revive the rural parish. The urban parish had virtually ceased to be a factor in local government, and there was no object in trying to restore it; but men hoped that the rural parish might again be made a living thing. The Act, therefore, provided an elaborate machinery for a parish meeting of all the voters, with a council in parishes containing more than three hundred inhabitants. But one hears on every hand that the hopes entertained have not been realised, that the areas are too small, the powers conferred too insignificant, to excite interest, and that the parish as a centre of local public life has not been a success. As yet it remains, therefore, little more than a unit for the election of representatives and the collection of rates.

Except for the torpid parish, the local authorities hitherto described — the councils of the boroughs, counties, urban and rural districts — are based upon very much the same principles, and form very nearly a symmetrical system. Their organisation and their method of transacting business are essentially similar; and if we place in a line the borough councils, urban district councils and rural district councils, we have a series of bodies with similar but gradually diminishing functions, a series in which the control of the Local Government Board increases roughly in proportion to the diminution of power.

In the two eventful years 1834 and 1835, two rival systems of local government took their rise.[1] One found

[1] *Cf.* Redlich and Hirst, II., 204.

The Board of Guardians.

its expression in the Municipal Corporations Act of 1835, which gave diverse powers to a single body acting throughout a borough, and exercising those powers with much independence. The other was embodied in the Poor Law Amendment Act of 1834, which created new authorities, acting in new areas, for a single specific purpose, and carrying on a uniform administration in consequence of a minute power of regulation by a central department. For many years it seemed as if this second type was likely to prevail. From time to time new authorities with new areas were set up for specific objects, and although they were not so much under tutelage as the poor-law authorities, there was a tendency to subject them to more or less control by the national government. The upshot in the matter of central control will be discussed in the next chapter. But in regard to the multiplication of local bodies with special functions a strong reaction has set in. The principle of a single body ruling a given district with miscellaneous powers seems to have triumphed all along the line, the only remaining case of an *ad hoc* authority being the original one of the poor-law guardians.

As already pointed out, the elected guardians and district councillors for rural parishes are the same persons, though not necessarily combined in the same way into representative bodies, because the union may not coincide with the district. A parish, on the other hand, that lies in an urban district or a borough has no rural district councillors. In that case, the guardians are elected in exactly the same way that they are in rural parishes, but they have no other functions, and thus the board of a union that is partly rural and partly urban will contain the district councillors from the rural parishes, and members specially elected from the urban ones. The guardians in any union may add to their number two outside members, but these, like the chairman and vice-chairman when taken from outside the board, do not sit upon the district council; nor does the chairman of the district council, if taken from outside its members, sit upon the board of guardians.

The work of the guardians consists in giving poor relief in specific cases in accordance with general regulations laid down by the Local Government Board. How great the authority of that board is over the appointment and removal of officials, and even over the formal procedure of the guardians themselves, will be described in the following chapter. It is enough here to point out that the guardians have, in theory at least, very little discretion, being limited to the application of elaborate rules in particular cases. Their authority in matters other than poor relief is now very slight. Incidentally, they appoint the registrar of births and deaths, and enforce vaccination acts; but almost all the duties formerly imposed upon them in connection with public health or general local government were transferred in 1894 to the rural district councils. In local finance, however, they retain, in form at least, a wider importance. The support of the poor being for many years the chief local expenditure, the poor rate became the typical way of raising money; and when a new local authority was created, it was empowered to issue its precept to the guardians for the funds that it needed. Thus it has come about that almost all the local taxation of the present day is either added to the poor rate or assessed in the same way, the rates being collected in each parish by the overseer of the poor, who is elected therein for the purpose.

# CHAPTER XLVI

## CENTRAL CONTROL

Its Growth in the Last Century.

WITH the fall of the Star Chamber and the system of which it formed a part, administrative control of the local authorities by the central government came to an end; and during the eighteenth century the town councils and justices of the peace were singularly free, except from the strong hand of the courts of law when they exceeded the powers conferred on them by a vast mass of statutes. Now one of the most marked changes that the nineteenth century brought in local government, and one which has been very much discussed, was the introduction of central control of a highly developed kind.[1] Such a control may take various forms — a power to regulate the course of action, a power to compel action, a power to restrain action and a power to inspect. All these powers were combined, and more fully combined than anywhere else, in the Poor Law Amendment Act of 1834.

The Poor Law Act of 1834.

This Act which remodelled the poor law was the first great experiment in central control; and under the vigorous driving force of Edwin Chadwick the policy was carried at once almost to high-water mark. By the adoption under the stress of the times of unwise principles in giving relief, the poor law of England had become a means of creating, as well as supporting, paupers. In a number of counties a calculation was made of the sum required to sustain an

[1] Redlich and Hirst, II., Part VI., deal with this whole matter exceedingly well. The fullest treatment, however, is in Maltbie's "English Local Government of To-day," but as his sources are mainly the reports of the Local Government Board itself, he looks at the subject from the somewhat optimistic standpoint of that body.

agricultural labourer and his family, the difference between this and the amount he could earn being paid to him as relief, with the result that a large part of the rural population, though employed at current wages, was receiving aid from the poor rates. The need of reform was pressing, and in order that it might be uniform and thorough, a national poor-law commission was established to oversee the administration of the Act. This body, working at its task with relentless zeal, made enemies, who were the more dangerous because it had no spokesman in Parliament. In 1847, therefore, it was changed to a poor-law board with a minister at its head; and again in 1871 it was given a general supervision of local administration, and was reorganised under the name of Local Government Board.

**Authority of the Local Government Board over the Guardians.**

The commission was given, and the present board still retains, power to issue to all the poor-law guardians over the country general orders regulating their duties under the Act, or to send to one or more boards of guardians special orders affecting only the unions to which they are addressed. The orders may direct action of almost any kind, except the giving of relief in particular cases.[1] The general orders, indeed, cover almost every conceivable subject, such as the procedure at the meetings of the guardians themselves, the time when the paupers in workhouses shall get up in the morning, the kind and amount of food they shall receive, the conditions under which they may be allowed tobacco, and the places where they may smoke.[2] These orders, which go so much into details that they fill a stout volume, are intended to leave to the guardians little more than the application to individuals of rules that are minutely prescribed.

**Means of Enforcement.**

In order to see that these regulations are carried out, and that the work of the guardians is properly done, the Local Government Board appoints inspectors, who have a right not only to visit the workhouses, but also to attend

[1] 4–5 Will. IV., c. 76, §§ 15, 42.
[2] *Cf.* Maltbie, p. 28; Redlich and Hirst, II., 262–63.

and speak at the sittings of the guardians,[1] and this, in fact, they constantly do. The Local Government Board has also very effective means of enforcing its orders and regulations. It has a right to prescribe the qualifications, duties and salaries of the paid officers of the local boards; and although the appointments are made by the guardians, the officers may be removed by the Local Government Board, and cannot be dismissed without its consent.[2] The power of removal is, in fact, used often enough to make its existence a reality,[3] and naturally involves a great deal of control over the whole body of local poor-law officials. One must not suppose, however, that the Local Government Board accomplishes its objects chiefly by a resort to such means of compulsion. As in the case of its relations with local authorities on every other subject, most of its work is really persuasive, and consists in inducing the body to follow its advice by dint of much correspondence and of some labour on the part of inspectors, rather than by an appeal to sterner measures.

The Local Government Board has power to inspect, to regulate, to compel, and by the same token to restrain, the guardians. It has, indeed, special powers of restraint, for the general control conferred by the Act of 1834 over the sale of land and the making of loans,[4] crystallised into the requirement of a special sanction by the Board of each separate transaction.[5] Moreover, the accounts of the poor-law authorities are subject to the audit of the Board with the usual consequence that an expenditure may be disallowed, and surcharged personally against the guardians and officers of the union who are directly responsible therefor.

[1] Of course without a vote; 4–5 Will. IV., c. 76, § 21; 10–11 Vic., c. 109, § 20.

[2] 4–5 Will. IV., c. 76, §§ 46, 48.

[3] During the three years, 1902–1904, there were one hundred and fifteen such removals, and half as many more resignations forced by fear of removal.

[4] 4–5 Will. IV., c. 76, § 21.

[5] *Cf.* 5–6 Will. IV., c. 69, § 3; 5–6 Vic., c. 18, § 2; 32–33 Vic., c. 45, § 4.

In spite of all the regulations, absolute uniformity of practice is hardly intended to be attained. The rules, for example, forbid altogether the granting of outdoor relief to able-bodied paupers; but the conditions under which it shall be given to others must be left very much in the hands of the guardians, and the practice differs greatly. The proportion of the total expenditure used for outdoor relief ran in 1905 from thirty-five per cent in London to over eighty per cent in North Wales.[1] Nor is it impossible for the guardians to evade some of the best-laid plans of the board, as was shown by the recent example of Poplar, where they virtually used poor relief as a means of giving old-age pensions.

**Central Control over Public Health and Local Government.**

The system of central control set up by the Poor Law Amendment Act of 1834 was thorough, more complete than it has ever been in any other field, for although the same principles were later applied to a great extent in the matter of public health, this was not done in the same systematic way, in spite of all the zeal of Edwin Chadwick.

**Its History.**

The first general board of health was established in 1848; but Chadwick's energy was so unpopular that in 1854 the board was reorganised, and he was left out. Four years later the board, which had been created by temporary statutes, was allowed to die, and its powers were distributed among various other departments of state. A royal sanitary commission, however, appointed in 1869, urged strongly the need of a central sanitary authority to set local life in motion, and, in accordance with its recommendations, powers of that kind were granted in 1871 to the Poor Law Board under the new title of Local Government Board. So far as public health and local government are concerned, the powers of the Board over local authorities are based primarily upon the Public Health Act of 1875 and the Local Government Acts of 1888 and 1894; but every statute, and they are legion, which confers any power on a local body, is apt to contain some provision

[1] *Cf.* Com. Papers, 1905, XXXI., 1, pp. 464–67.

involving action by the Local Government Board, or at least contemplating its intervention, and thus the powers of the Board are scattered through innumerable statutes, and are constantly being enlarged.

Power to Make Regulations;

In regard to public health and administration at large the Local Government Board has no such general power to make regulations that it possesses in the case of poor relief. It has, indeed, some authority to make rules for district and parish elections; it can make regulations about vaccination,[1] or, in the case of epidemics, about interment, visitation, medical aid and disinfection.[2] Under certain statutes, also, it has power to make rules affecting a few special subjects, such as the prevention of disease,[3] and the provision of proper accommodation on canal boats.[4]

to Issue Orders;

Nor, except in such cases, does it usually have power to order acts done; although it can occasionally do so, as, for example, in directing a local authority to provide a mortuary or cemetery,[5] or to institute proceedings under the Rivers Pollution Act,[6] and in obliging an urban district to see that every house has a proper water supply.[7] Under this head also may, perhaps, be classed its power to make changes in the local areas, uniting and dividing them and altering their boundaries. But while its power to issue commands is very limited, it can sometimes oblige a local body to perform the duties expressly imposed by statute, especially where a complaint is made. This is true in the

[1] 34–35 Vic., c. 98, § 5; 37–38 Vic., c. 75.

[2] Public Health Acts, 1875, 38–39 Vic., c. 55, §§ 130, 134; 1896, 59–60 Vic., c. 19, § 1. The accounts of districts and parishes must be made up in such form as the Local Govt. Board prescribes. Local Govt. Act, 1894, 56–57 Vic., c. 73, § 58 (1).

[3] It can, for example, regulate cleanliness in dairies, and the protection of milk from contamination. Contagious Diseases (Animals) Acts, 1878, 41–42 Vic., c. 74, § 34; 1886, 49–50 Vic., c. 32, § 9.

[4] Canal Boats Act, 1877, 40–41 Vic., c. 60, § 2.

[5] Public Health Act, 1875, § 141; Public Health (Interments) Act, 1879, 42–43 Vic., c. 31.

[6] 39–40 Vic., c. 75, § 6.

[7] Public Health (Water) Act, 1888, 41–42 Vic., c. 25, § 11. This obligation is imposed upon rural districts by statute. *Ibid.*, § 3.

case of a failure to abate a nuisance,[1] to provide drainage or water,[2] to appoint analysts under the Food and Drug Acts,[3] and to execute the vaccination laws.[4] In such cases the Board can apply for a mandamus in the King's Bench Division, which orders the local authorities to act on pain of going to jail for contempt of court,[5] an alternative which the guardians of Leicester almost faced a few years ago rather than obey the vaccination laws. Instead of proceeding by mandamus the Board may sometimes appoint an officer of its own to carry out the work at the expense of the local body,[6] although this appears in fact to be rarely done.

**to Audit and Inspect.**

On the other hand, the power of the Board to inspect is very large. In the first place, it audits the accounts of all local authorities, except boroughs; and by refusing to sanction an illegal expenditure, can throw the cost upon the persons who ordered the payment. Then it can require accounts and returns on almost any subject connected with its work, and it is armed with special powers of inquiry in case of outbreaks of disease. It maintains also a body of inspectors, who do not indeed continually attend meetings of local bodies, as the poor-law inspectors do with the guardians, but who have a right to be present, except in the case of the borough councils.[7] The chief work of these officers, whether general inspectors or engineers, consists, however, in holding inquiries in cases where the sanction of the Board is asked for any local project. The activity of the Board is, indeed, principally displayed in the negative field of restraining action, if under this be included the many cases where its consent is required for any particular act, or where it can authorise a course of conduct. Thus the Board can confer on a rural district any of the powers of an

**Consent Required for Local Action.**

[1] Public Health Act, 1875, § 106. [2] *Ibid.*, § 299.
[3] 38–39 Vic., c. 63, § 10. [4] 34–35 Vic., c. 98, § 5.
[5] The Queen *vs.* Leicester Guardians (1899), 2 Q.B. 632.
[6] Public Health Act, 1875, §§ 106, 299; Local Government Act, 1894, § 16.
[7] Public Health Act, 1875, § 205.

urban one;[1] its sanction is required, among other things, for the supply of gas[2] and the purchase of waterworks,[3] for by-laws dealing with public health,[4] and for the raising of loans by all bodies,[5] including boroughs.[6] Now a borough can hardly undertake any important enterprise without borrowing money, and therefore it has to come to the Board for an approval which may be granted only subject to conditions.

Control through Provisional Orders.

Both the Local Government Board and the Board of Trade have also a great control over the whole field of municipal trading, whether in case of a borough or a local district, by virtue of the system whereby power to do these things is granted by provisional orders; for although either a borough or a district council may obtain the same privilege by private bill behind the back of the Board, that is a more expensive thing to do, and is not likely to be tried if the Board and the local body can easily come to terms. The result is that while the power of the Boards over these things is not absolute it is nevertheless very great.[7]

Control through National Grants.

In the case of public health and general local government, a means of control was adopted which had been little used in the administration of the poor law, and that was bringing the influence of the state to bear upon the local authority by an offer to assume a portion of its expenses. The Act of 1875 contains a general provision that where any part of the salary of a local officer is provided out of moneys voted by Parliament, the qualifications, conditions of appointment, duties, salary and tenure of

[1] Public Health Act, 1875, § 276.
[2] *Ibid.*, §§ 161–62.
[3] *Ibid.*, § 51.
[4] *Ibid.*, §§ 184, 187.
[5] *E.g.*, *Ibid.*, § 233; 41 Vic., c. 14, § 9; 55–56 Vic., c. 53, § 19; 56–57 Vic., c. 73, § 12.
[6] 45–46 Vic., c. 50, § 107; 51–52 Vic., c. 41, § 72.
[7] By the Acts of 1888 and 1894 some of the powers of control vested in the Local Government Board were, as we have already seen, transferred to the county councils, subject to appeal to the Local Government Board. Such were the power over the boundaries of rural sanitary districts, the power to grant provisional orders for compulsory purchase of the land by the same authorities, and the power to compel the performance of sanitary work by a rural district.

office, may be regulated by the Local Government Board.[1] This applies to the medical officers of health and inspectors of nuisances, and as the local authority habitually accepts the proffered sums, most of the officers of that kind are largely under the control of the Board.

Central Control over Police.

The policy of guiding by a subsidy has been carried much farther, and is, in fact, almost the sole basis of central control, in the case of police and of education. The modern organisation of the non-metropolitan police throughout the country dates from 1856, when it was made the duty of every county and large borough to maintain a police force, with a provision that if the Home Secretary certified that the police of a county or borough had been kept in a state of efficiency in point of numbers and discipline for the past year, the Treasury might defray one fourth of the cost of pay and clothing. It is astonishing how careful any public body will become not to forfeit a grant of this kind after becoming accustomed to receiving it. The proportion of the charge for pay and clothing borne by the national government has gradually been increased to one half, but with this change the system has been continued ever since and has proved a most effective means of pressure upon the local authorities. In 1888 the fixed Exchequer Contribution Account was substituted for the various grants in aid, but it was provided that a county or county borough whose police proved inefficient should pay to the Treasury a fine equal to one half of the cost of pay and clothing.[2] In fact, however, this almost never happens; and hence by the simple process of granting a subsidy, the police in every part of the land has been brought into good condition without any vexatious interference with local self-government.

[1] Public Health Act, 1875, § 191. Under the Local Govt. Act, 1888, § 24 (2), (c), this applies to officers whose salaries are paid in part by county councils from the Exchequer Contribution Account.

[2] If a non-county borough fails to earn its subsidy, the amount falls into the treasury of the county. On this subject, see Redlich and Hirst, II., 310–12.

Other Central Departments.

A couple of other departments of state have some control, direct or indirect, over the action of local bodies. Thus by-laws of counties and boroughs touching police regulation, or matters of general good order not of a sanitary nature, must be submitted to the Home Secretary, and may be disallowed by Order in Council within forty days.[1] Applications for provisional orders to supply electric light and build tramways or light railways are made to the Board of Trade; while the Board of Agriculture has among other functions that of making orders for the suppression of diseases in animals. These last must be carried out by the local authorities, and in case of refusal the Board has a right to empower some one else to do so.

Results of Central Control.

That the control of the national government over local affairs has been highly beneficial in some matters, no one would deny. The reforms of poor-law administration and of the police were certainly brought about in this way; but in other fields the results are more doubtful. In spite of requiring the sanction of the Local Government Board for loans, local debts have increased at a prodigious pace, and it is futile to speculate how much more they would have grown without that provision. Like all attempts to discover what would have occurred under different conditions, it is a case of postponed prophecy which depends greatly upon the preconceived opinions of the prophet. The audit of the Board has no doubt been useful, but of limited value as hitherto conducted. The Committee on Municipal Trading reported in 1903 that the auditors employed were not, as a rule, professional accountants, and were not properly qualified for the work they ought to do, while their duties were practically confined to the mere certification of figures and noting illegal items of expenditure.[2] No doubt the disallowance and surcharge of illegal items prevents a great many small payments that are not authorised

[1] Municipal Corp. Act, 1882, 45–46 Vic., c. 50, § 23; Local Govt. Act, 1888, § 16.
[2] Com. Papers, 1903, VII., 1.

by law; but, as the committee point out, the appeals to the dispensing power of the Board in these cases throw upon it an amount of work often out of proportion to the issue involved. In the great majority of instances the penalty is, in fact, remitted, and the item is allowed to stand. The committee recommended that the audit should be more comprehensive, so as to insure that the accounts show the real nature and effect of the transactions they cover.

In regard to the direct control of the Board over the local bodies by the power of giving or withholding consent to their plans, it is even more difficult to speak with confidence. The Board has faith in itself, and believes its work of great value; but from the local bodies one hears no little complaint of dilatoriness and red tape. The inspectors, who are not, like the engineers, of a strictly professional character, are said to be largely former military officers and others with a very imperfect knowledge of the subjects they investigate; while the permanent officials in the central office tend, not unnaturally, to follow precedent. They collate all the instances where a similar question has arisen before, and are loath to make a new departure. In short, they are said to suffer from some of the characteristic evils of bureaucracy. At the same time the corrective applied in other departments of the national government by means of questions in Parliament is less effective in the case of local government, because the whole subject of private and local bills and provisional orders, and with it the control of local bodies, lies to some extent outside the sphere of politics and cabinet responsibility. For a time the unpopularity of the Local Government Board prevented it from getting a much-needed addition to its clerical staff, so that its work fell into arrears, and matters became worse; but after the report of a departmental committee in 1898 [1] the appropriation was increased, and this source of delay was removed.

[1] Com. Papers, 1898, XL., 429.

On the whole, it must be said that the system of central control has done much good, and that the mere liability to inspection has no doubt prevented a certain amount of ill-management. But it must also be admitted that the system is not perfect; that it has been sometimes vexatious; and that a stranger is wise in refraining from any attempt to cast up the balance of profit and loss.

# PART IV.—EDUCATION

## CHAPTER XLVII

### PUBLIC ELEMENTARY EDUCATION

POPULAR education in England has been a slow growth, beset by enemies, or rather by friends who were so anxious to have the good work prosper in their own way that it has come near being torn in pieces of them. These dissensions, based upon religion, have been almost wholly confined to the question of public elementary instruction for the working-classes. They began before it existed, were renewed when it was still a very small thing, and have accompanied it ever since, neither antagonist being able to deal the other a fatal blow.

**The Early Grammar Schools.**

During the Middle Ages education was naturally in the hands of the Church, and largely in charge of the regular clergy; but when the dissolution of the monasteries brought this to an end, many schools were endowed, partly by the Crown and by men enriched from the spoils of the abbey lands. The change did not, however, secularise education, for while the laity had a share in the management of the new schools, they were, as a rule, still closely connected with the Church. The number of institutions founded under the impulse of the Reformation was large, and it is said that about one third of the existing grammar schools had their origin at that time. But although the endowed schools were not few, and were far more numerous in proportion to the population than they are now, they naturally did not reach the whole community. They came in time to be used mainly by the middle and upper strata of society to obtain an education above the primary grade, while the working-class was left with scanty opportunities for elementary instruction. It has been said that the need of this was met at first by apprenticeship, but that broke down with the introduction of the factory system, and primary schools were required to take its place; just as at the present day a higher grade of technical education is demanded in consequence of further changes in the method of recruiting labour in the industrial world.

**The National and British Societies.**

Elementary schools for the working-classes were started not long before the end of the eighteenth century by Joseph Lancaster and Andrew Bell. The question which of them invented the monitorial system — that is, the plan of having the instruction given to the younger children by the older ones — which lay at the base of their methods, has aroused keen controversy. But as it is now universally agreed that the system was very bad, the claim to priority is not important, except for the fact that a quarrel between these two men gave shape to a divergence of views that has prevailed ever since. Lancaster was a Quaker who believed in non-sectarian education. His schools prospered under the patronage of the Whigs, and in 1808 the British and Foreign School Society was founded to carry them on. Bell, a Scotchman, was convinced that education ought to be under the patronage of the Church, and in 1811 the National Society was formed to perpetuate his scheme. Thus these two rival bodies were organised nearly at the same time: the British and Foreign Society standing for non-sectarian schools; while the National Society stood for education by the Church, receiving children of every denomination, but teaching them all the Church catechism. Both bodies at the outset were maintained wholly by private contributions. At about the same time, Whitbread had, indeed, brought in a bill to establish parochial schools for the poor, to be supported by local rates; and the measure passed the House of Commons, but was rejected by the Lords. In 1820 Brougham tried to accomplish a similar object by means of a bill providing for a school rate to be administered by the justices of the peace. The teachers were to be Churchmen, although there was to be no religious instruction save the reading of the Bible. The plan, however, seems to have pleased nobody, and was abandoned by its author. Meanwhile he had been busy with a select committee on the education of the poor in London, which made in 1818 a suggestion destined to bear fruit. It recommended that in places where some aid from private subscriptions could be expected, but not on a scale large enough both to build and maintain schools, "a sum of money might be well employed in supplying this first want, leaving the charity of individuals to furnish the annual provision requisite for continuing the school." [1]

**The First Public Grants.** A dozen more years passed before any public aid was given to schools for the people, until in 1833 it came in the form of an appropriation by Parliament of £20,000 "for the erection of schoolhouses in aid of private subscriptions for that purpose." The sum was modest—the education vote in Prussia at this period being £600,000—and clearly it would not go very far. Nor had Parliament given any directions about its application. The Treasury, which had proposed the vote, was left free to administer it, and a minute of 1833 announced that the money would be applied to the building of schoolhouses on the recommendation of the two societies, provided that one half of the cost was met by voluntary contributions. At first the societies received equal amounts, but soon the British and Foreign Society was unable to raise the sums needed to claim its proportion, and hence the National Society obtained the lion's share.

**The Committee on Education.** On a small scale the state was thus helping voluntary associations to build schools, which they were to conduct thereafter in their own way. The policy was tentative, but it continued unchanged until 1839, when the government,

[1] Report of Com. on Educ. of the Lower Orders, Com. Papers, 1818, IV., 57.

in order to promote efficiency in the schools aided by public funds, created by Order in Council a Committee of the Privy Council on Education, and increased the annual grant from £20,000 to £30,000. The ministers had intended to establish for the training of teachers a state normal school, in which secular instruction was to be in common for all the students, while Churchmen and Dissenters were to be given religious instruction separately by persons of their own faith. But the education grant passed the Commons by a majority of only two votes, and the government was forced by the opposition of the Church to drop this part of its plan. The money intended for the purpose was divided between the National and British and Foreign Societies to be used in maintaining teachers' colleges of their own; and in fact no state normal school has ever been created to the present day.

**Inspectors and the Concordat.** Another project of the new Committee on Education was more successful, and in time wrought a marked improvement in the schools. The committee engaged a staff of educational officers with a secretary at their head, and appointed inspectors, making periodical inspection on their part a condition of aid in the building of a school. But as religious instruction was one of the subjects to be examined, a difficulty arose; for the National Society could hardly suffer inspection by men in whose orthodoxy it had no confidence. In 1840, therefore, an agreement, known as the Concordat, was made, whereby the inspectors were to be approved by the Archbishops of Canterbury and York; and a few years later the British and Foreign Society was given a veto on the inspectors of their schools.

The committee kept up the practice of grants to aid in the construction of schoolhouses, although these were no longer absolutely confined to the two original societies. Other bodies, however, could obtain a grant only by adopting a conscience clause, which permitted children to be withdrawn from the religious exercises — a precedent destined to be followed widely in later years.

Grants for Pupil Teachers.

So far the grants had been applied only to the erection and equipment of buildings; but the inspectors furnished a means of learning results, and their reports showed that the schools were sadly inefficient. One of them estimated that in the Midlands three quarters of the children left school unable to read the Scriptures with ease, one half without any instruction in penmanship whatever, and only five per cent with a mastery of the rule of three.[1] The defects were attributed to the monitorial system, which caused the infants to be taught by the other children, little older and less ignorant than themselves. The committee felt the crying need of competent teachers, and therefore by a minute of Dec. 21, 1846, it began a new departure. The master of a school was given a stipend for training one or more of the older children as pupil teachers for five years, while they were to receive sums rising from ten to twenty pounds a year during the period, with an opportunity of competing for a Queen's scholarship at one of the training colleges at the end of the time.[2] Teachers who had been educated at those colleges were also to receive augmentation grants in addition to their salaries from the schools. All this required money, but public interest in education had increased, and this year an appropriation of £100,000 was carried by a large majority.

Capitation Grants.

The national government had now helped to build schools, to inspect and improve them. It had entered upon a path in which it could not stop. But the schools were still far from adequate either in number or in quality. This was particularly true of the rural districts, which were poor in resources; and hence the committee, by a minute of April 2, 1853, granted a small sum to the managers of rural schools for every scholar who attended one hundred and ninety-two days, provided that at least three quarters of

[1] Com. Papers, 1845, XXXV., 337, pp. 242–43.

[2] How effective those scholarships were may be gathered from the fact that of the 2065 students in the 32 training colleges, 1676 were Queen's scholars in 1859. Rep. of Com. on Pub. Educ., Com. Papers, 1861, XXI., Part I., p. 115.

the children were presented to the inspector for examination, and that the school was in the charge of a certificated teacher — one who had received a certificate from the state in recognition of studies at a training college. The payment, called a "capitation grant," was extended three years later to urban districts also, and in this way the state entered on a general policy of direct contribution to the maintenance of schools.

**A Minister of Education.**

Of course the annual appropriations by Parliament were all the time increasing rapidly, but as yet their use was regulated by administrative minutes, not by legislation, and it was all the more important that some one in the House of Commons should directly represent the department. Historically, therefore, it was natural, though a little surprising, that the first statute on public elementary education was one providing in 1856 for a vice-president of the Committee of Council on Education, who should be eligible to the House and thus a responsible minister.

**The Commission of 1858.**

A number of bills to extend popular education by means of local taxation had been introduced from different quarters. Societies had been formed to promote different plans. People were well-nigh universally agreed that existing conditions were unsatisfactory; and in 1858 a strong commission of inquiry was appointed which presented an elaborate report in 1861.[1] From this it appeared that the Church of England possessed about nine tenths of the public elementary schools, with three quarters of the children; the British and Foreign Society had about ten per cent of the children; the Roman Catholic schools about five and a half per cent; the Wesleyans four per cent; and Congregationalists two per cent.[2] But of these children less than three fifths were in the schools assisted by government grants and inspected, the rest being in unassisted schools which were generally inferior, and which failed to obtain the grants chiefly on account of poverty, smallness

[1] Com. Papers, 1861, XXI., Part I.
[2] Report, *Ibid.*, pp. 55, 80.

of population and apathy.[1] In the assisted schools the annual cost was about thirty shillings a child, one quarter thereof being defrayed by the grants from the government, and from a quarter to a third from endowments and subscriptions, the burden of the latter in the Church schools being largely borne by the clergy. The rest of the cost was derived from the fees paid by the children;[2] for it must be remembered that public education was not at this time compulsory or gratuitous, and in fact the commission was of opinion that the country did not desire either. In regard to the efficiency of the schools, the commission reported that less than half the children registered attended during one hundred and fifty out of the two hundred and twenty days the schools were open. It added that a child of ten ought to be able to read with sufficient ease to be a pleasure, to write a legible and intelligent letter, to cipher well enough to make out a common shop bill, and to have some notion where the different countries of the world are; yet that in the very best schools two thirds of the pupils left without attaining this standard. The commission said that the assisted schools were within reach of half the children, but that three out of four of those who attend them "leave school with only such a smattering of education as they may have picked up in the lower classes," and hence "we are successfully educating one in eight of the class of children for which the schools were intended."[3] The report recommended that the national subsidy, which should be in the main a capitation grant on average attendance, ought to vary slightly according to the condition of the school, and ought to be supplemented by a grant from county rates given for each child passing an examination in reading, writing and arithmetic.[4]

The report was severely criticised on the ground that the statistics were inaccurate, and the statements about

[1] Com. Papers, 1861, XXI., Part I., pp. 229, 277–78.
[2] *Ibid.*, pp. 68, 71, 73, 77–78.
[3] *Ibid.*, pp. 172, 243–44, 246.
[4] *Ibid.*, pp. 328–33.

The Revised Code of 1861.

the results of the teaching unfair. Nor were the recommendations adopted in the form in which they were made, although they brought about a profound change in the method of administering the national grants. The minutes of the Committee on Education had been codified in 1860, the yearly edition of them being known ever since as "the code"; and in 1861 a revised code was issued. It provided that, in future, payments for maintenance should be made not to the teachers personally, but to the managers of the school, a change which increased the responsibility of the latter. The payments were to be made only on condition that the school buildings were approved, and the children were present a certain number of days. A more vital change was made in the method of giving aid. Except in the case of infants, where a capitation grant was to be made on attendance alone, a grant was to be awarded only for each child who passed before the inspector an examination in reading, writing and arithmetic. This last plan called "payment by results" provoked fierce opposition to the revised code. It was thought far too drastic, and the next year was so modified that four shillings was allowed for each child on average attendance and two shillings and eight pence for a pass in each of the three subjects. But even so, the total grants fell off for a few years, owing to the inability of the schools to win them. The method of payment by results was probably needed at the time to promote efficiency, yet it certainly involved the evil of fixing the attention of teacher and managers on earning grants, and cramming the largest possible number of children for examination in the three R's, without much regard for anything more. To counteract that effect, additional grants were offered from time to time for superior excellence, or proficiency in other subjects; but ultimately the system was found injurious, or had served its purpose, and was abandoned altogether.

That many children in the country should be unable to obtain the benefits conferred on others by the national

The Movement for Universal Education.

government out of general taxation, was an anomaly. It indicated a period of transition which could not endure, and a widespread demand arose for a universal system of popular education. Shortly before 1870 two associations were formed, representing the two views that had divided men since the days of Lancaster and Bell. The Education League, started at Birmingham in 1869, advocated free, compulsory, unsectarian education, conducted by local authorities by means of local rates. Among its leading spirits were Mr. Chamberlain, Mr. Harris and Mr. Schnadhorst, the men who organised the National Liberal Federation a few years later. The League had branches in many boroughs and drew its chief support from the Nonconformists and the more radical elements in the Liberal party. The other association was the Education Union, formed to urge a universal plan based upon the existing system of voluntary schools; that is, schools conducted by private bodies, most of which were in fact connected with the Church of England. The first great Education Act, adopted in 1870, although the work of the most powerful Liberal ministry of recent times, was in its essence a compromise between these two opposing views.[1]

The Bill of 1870.

As introduced on behalf of the government by Mr. Forster, the bill provided for the election of school boards in all places where the supply of schoolhouses should be insufficient one year thereafter, the voluntary societies being given a year to build sufficient schools, with the help, of course, of the usual grants from the Treasury. These boards were to be elected by the councils of boroughs and by the parish vestries in other places, and were to have power to raise money by local rates to carry on their work. They could either establish schools themselves or they could assist voluntary societies to do so; and in their own schools they could give such religious instruction as they pleased, subject to a provision that the children should not be compelled to attend it. They could pay the fees of children

[1] The Elementary Education Act, 1870, 33–34 Vic., c. 75.

in case of poverty, or make a school wholly free in a poor district; and finally they could, if they wished, make attendance at school compulsory. The League was much offended: because the bill did not provide that education must be compulsory and free; because of the year allowed to the voluntary societies to build denominational schools; because of the provisions about religious instruction; and because school boards were not to be universal, and were not elected directly by the people. On some of these points the government made important concessions. It agreed that school boards should not use their rates to assist voluntary schools; that a school board might be established in any district which applied for it, whether the supply of schools were sufficient or not; and that the boards should be elected directly by the voters. A provision for election by cumulative vote, which meant that each elector could cast for a single candidate, or distribute as he pleased, as many votes as there were places to be filled, was inserted for the protection of minorities, and especially of religious minorities. But like the minority representation in the three-cornered parliamentary boroughs which had been set up a couple of years earlier, it proved unsatisfactory and disappeared when the school boards were abolished in 1902. The concessions of greatest interest, however, and the ones around which the battle raged most fiercely, were those connected with religion. The government proposed and carried an amendment for a time-table conscience clause, as it was called, providing that in both voluntary and board schools the religious instruction should come at the beginning or end of the session, so that parents who did not approve of it could readily withdraw their children. But this was not enough, and during the debate Mr. Cowper-Temple, a Liberal, but the chairman of the Education Union, proposed that in the board schools no catechism or religious formulary distinctive of any particular denomination should be taught. The government accepted the suggestion, and although the League was so far from satisfied that in a couple of divisions a majority of the Liberals were opposed to the cabinet, the Cowper-Temple clause was incorporated in the Act. Some Churchmen still speak bitterly of Cowper-Temple, or school-board, religion; but throughout the controversies that have ensued the provision has remained a fixed principle of education in the board schools to the present day.[1]

The Act of 1870 did not substitute a new system of popular education for the old one. It merely supplemented it by providing schools managed by local authorities, and supported in part by local taxation, in places where enough voluntary schools did not exist, or could not be established at once. It created universal elementary education by placing side by side two sets of schools, each granted, under normal conditions, the same aid from the national Treasury; but one managed by private associations, teaching in most cases the creed of a church,[2] and receiving the balance of its revenue from voluntary contributions; the other managed by public authorities, obtaining support from local taxation, and forbidden to teach the formularies of any sect. The Act of 1870.

The Act provided that until the close of 1870 voluntary societies might apply for government aid in erecting schools, but that thereafter no more building grants should be made;[3] and that every school, whether voluntary or in charge of a school board, which fulfilled the conditions of a public elementary school, should receive an annual parliamentary grant for running expenses. This grant was to be made in accordance with the minutes of the Education Depart-

[1] That the religious teaching in the board schools under the Cowper-Temple clause, although entirely undenominational, is, as a rule, neither godless, radical, nor lacking in instruction in the Scriptures, any one may convince himself by looking at the return of the school programmes on the subject submitted by the Education Department to the House of Lords on June 13, 1906.

[2] This was not true of all voluntary schools; but it was true of those belonging to the Church of England which were by far the greatest in number, and also of the Roman Catholic schools.

[3] § 96.

ment,[1] but was not to exceed the amount received by the school from other sources.[2] In order, however, to prevent either a voluntary society or a school board from duplicating work done by the other, the Education Department was authorised to refuse grants to any new school that was not needed.[3] A public elementary school was declared to be one that observed the time-table conscience clause, was open to government inspection, was managed according to the conditions required for the parliamentary grant,[4] and did not charge fees of more than nine pence a week.[5]

For the purpose of creating school boards, the whole country was divided into districts, each borough forming a district by itself, and metropolitan London one great district, while elsewhere the parish was nominally a district, although the Education Department had power to combine parishes if it saw fit to do so.[6] The Department was to hold an inquiry, and order the formation of a school board in every district insufficiently supplied with schools. The board so created was obliged to provide sufficient schools, to conduct them according to the conditions required for public elementary schools, and to comply with the Cowper-Temple clause about religious instruction.[7] It was elected for a term of three years by cumulative voting, and had power to supplement the parliamentary grants and pupils' fees by means of local rates. On the petition of the council in a borough, or of the voters elsewhere, a board could also be set up by the Department in a district where

[1] This term is used throughout the Act as an abbreviation for the Committee of the Privy Council on Education.

[2] §§ 96, 97, 99. An additional grant in aid of board schools could be made where the district was so poor that a rate of 3*d*. in the pound produced less than a certain sum. § 97. The minutes of the Education Department were thereafter to be laid upon the tables of the Houses of Parliament for a month, and as this gave an opportunity of condemning them by resolution, they acquired a tacit parliamentary sanction. § 97.

[3] § 98.

[4] § 7. The inspectors were no longer to inquire into religious instruction.

[5] § 3.

[6] §§ 40–52.

[7] § 14. If a school board failed in any way to do its duty, the Education Department might order a new election, or itself appoint another board. §§ 6, 11, 16, 18, 32, 63–66.

no lack of schools was found[1]; but in that case, as the absence of a government grant made it impossible to maintain a school, the power of the board was practically confined to paying the fees of poor children, and making by-laws for compulsory attendance.

The Act in making elementary education universal did not attempt to make it gratuitous, but that was obviously necessary where the parents were unable to pay. School boards were, therefore, empowered to remit the fees in such cases,[2] or to pay the fees if the children were in voluntary schools.[3] They could, indeed, go farther, and provide wholly free schools in poor localities; but this was regarded as quite an exceptional condition, requiring the consent of the Department.[4] The government, moreover, did not feel that the country was ready for universal compulsory education, although willing to introduce it wherever the people wanted to do so; and hence the Act provided that a school board might, with the approval of the Department, make by-laws obliging children between the ages of five and thirteen to attend school, the fees being, of course, remitted or paid in case of poverty.[5]

**Effects of the Act.**

The Education League, together with some Nonconformists who did not belong to it, were displeased with the Act, and continued to urge fresh legislation. In fact, this measure was one cause of the lack of harmony in the Liberal ranks that helped to bring the Conservatives into power at the general elections of 1874. A few people went so far as to resist the payment of rates, but the country as a whole accepted the result as, for the time at least, a fair compromise of conflicting opinions.[6] Some of the British, Church of England, and other schools were transferred to the new boards, but most of the voluntary schools remained under their old management.[7] The vast majority of them were

[1] § 12. [2] § 17. [3] § 25. [4] § 26. [5] § 74.
[6] This is the view of Craik, "The State in its Relation to Education," Rev. Ed. (1896), 106–07.
[7] *Cf.* Com. Papers, 1875, LVIII., 459.

denominational, much the greater part belonging to the Established Church, a few to the Roman Catholics, and fewer still to the Wesleyans. For a time, indeed, the voluntary schools far exceeded those maintained by the boards, both in number and in the quantity of children attending. But the board schools gained rapidly on account of the supply of money from rates which enabled them to earn larger parliamentary grants; while the voluntary schools found it hard to increase their contributions, the more so because in many places the contributors were now burdened with rates to support board schools also. This gradually brought the voluntary schools into straits from which they sought relief in legislation.

**Further Progress.** The immediate problem, however, was to make education really universal by rendering it compulsory, and this almost of necessity involved making it ultimately free. The Act of 1870 had placed a school within the reach of every child, but had laid down no general rule obliging him to attend it; nor could any duty to attend be imposed except where a school board existed. Now public opinion on this subject grew so fast that in 1876 an act was passed requiring every council of a borough or urban district and every rural board of guardians, where there was no school board, to appoint a school attendance committee empowered to adopt by-laws for compulsory attendance.[1] Then the Education League dissolved on the ground that its object of securing the education of every child had been attained. But it had not really been attained, for neither the school boards nor the school attendance committees were obliged to make such by-laws, and many of them failed to do so. In 1880, indeed, only about three fifths of the population of England and Wales were subject to by-laws of this kind; and in that year another statute was enacted requiring the adoption of by-laws everywhere, thus at last making elementary education compulsory throughout the kingdom.[2] The process of making it free advanced more slowly, and cannot

[1] 39–40 Vic., c. 79.

[2] 43–44 Vic., c. 23.

be said to be entirely completed yet. The first attempt to abolish fees, except in cases of poverty, did not come until 1891, when Parliament decided to give to all public elementary schools an annual "fee grant" of ten shillings a head on the average attendance of children between the ages of three and fifteen. Schools which had not previously been charging higher fees than this were to charge nothing thereafter, except by special permission of the Department,[1] and the others were to charge only the excess above that sum.[2] The act did away with fees in most schools, and reduced them in all, but did not wholly extinguish them; and in fact even the Education Act of 1902 provided that voluntary schools which still made a charge might continue to do so, subject to a somewhat indefinite duty on the part of the local authorities to defray a portion of the dues.[3]

**Change of Policy in Grants.**

Meanwhile the method of distributing among the schools the grants from the national treasury was undergoing a great change. The revised code of 1861 had introduced the practice of payment by results, based upon the number of children who passed to the satisfaction of the government inspector an examination in reading, writing and arithmetic. To meet the criticism that this encouraged exclusive attention to the rudiments of education the Department began in 1868 to offer to the schools special grants for each child who passed an examination in a specific subject of higher grade, such as geography, history, algebra or languages. But examinations became a burden, and by a change of the code in 1875 grammar, geography, history and needlework were made "class subjects," that is, a grant was made to the school on average attendance if the class as a whole passed a creditable examination in these matters; additional grants being still made on the individual examination of pupils in more advanced studies, known as "specific subjects."

[1] Craik says this power was so freely used that in 1896 one seventh of the children in public elementary schools still paid fees. "The State in its Relation to Education," Rev. Ed. (1896), 134.

[2] 54–55 Vic., c. 56.

[3] 2 Edw. 7, § 14.

In 1882 a similar change was introduced for the three R's. Instead of a grant for each child who passed, there were substituted a fixed grant and a merit grant. The fixed grant depended upon average attendance, but was not really fixed, for it was reduced in proportion to the number of failures in the class; while the merit grant varied from one to three shillings a child, according to the report of the inspector on the general condition of the school. From time to time different studies were transferred to the group of "class" from that of "specific" subjects, the latter, however, being constantly enlarged by new studies for which grants could be obtained. By this elaborate process of grants the Department sought to direct the development of elementary education, and did so, for the schools could not live without the subventions from the national treasury, which supplied nearly one half of their revenue. But the system became excessively complicated. There was a fixed grant, a merit grant, a grant for discipline, class grants, grants for specific subjects and grants for pupil teachers, besides the fee grant and the grant to schools in poor districts. Moreover, working for grants, while a useful stimulus to sluggish bodies, is a hindrance to the best work in good schools; and that the schools of the country had improved greatly is shown by the very small number from which aid was withheld altogether, and the large proportion reported by the inspectors as worthy of full payment. In 1890, therefore, a principal grant of twelve shillings and six pence, or fourteen shillings, according to the report of the inspectors, was substituted for the fixed and merit grants; and by the code of 1900 all the grants mentioned above — except the fee grant and the aid to poor schools — were swept away to be replaced by a single sum.[1] Grants for specific subjects remained only for such matters as cooking, laundry and dairy work, gardening and manual training, which involve additional expense beyond the ordinary work of the school. The single sum, known as

[1] Com. Papers, 1900, XIX, 1, pp. 10–11.

the "block grant," was either twenty-one or twenty-two shillings a head, according to the efficiency of the school, the difference being deemed enough to cheer the managers without intoxicating them. After thirty-two years, therefore, payment by results was abandoned, the government relying for guidance of the schools solely upon the explicit requirements of the code.

**The Plight of the Voluntary Schools.**

The policy of payment by results told against the voluntary schools. Handicapped in their competition with the board schools by the larger resources derived by the latter from rates, they were unable to earn so much government aid, and thus they were at a double disadvantage. In 1900 they still had a slight superiority in the number of children in average attendance;[1] but whereas the average income per child from rates in the board schools had increased from 10*s.* ¾*d.* in 1872 to £1 5*s.* 6¼*d.* in 1900, the average contributions in the voluntary schools, after rising from 6*s.* 11¾*d.* in 1872 to 8*s.* 8¾*d.* in 1877, had fallen in 1900 to 6*s.* 4¾*d.*[2] The Church schools evidently could not keep up the pace without further help, and this had been evident for some time. In 1895 the Archbishop's Committee reported to Convocation, that as the board schools were

[1] The figures given in the report of the Education Department are as follows (Com. Papers, 1901, XIX, 1, pp. 358–59): —

| | Number of Schools | Average Attendance |
|---|---|---|
| National or Church of England Schools | 11,777 | 1,885,802 |
| Wesleyan Schools | 458 | 125,727 |
| Roman Catholic Schools | 1,045 | 255,036 |
| British and Other Schools | 1,079 | 220,032 |
| Total Voluntary Schools | 14,359 | 2,486,597 |
| Board Schools | 5,758 | 2,201,049 |
| Grand Total | 20,117 | 4,687,646 |

[2] Com. Papers, 1901, XIX, 1, p. 476. The voluntary schools received also about a shilling and a quarter a head from the income of endowments, and by this time they had the "aid grant," of which anon. The provision in the Act of 1870, that the national grant should not exceed the amount derived from other sources, had been repealed.

better equipped, and with higher salaries attracted better teachers, there was a distinct drifting of pupils to them; that a quarter of a million pounds was needed to make the buildings of the voluntary schools equal to those of their rivals; and that further public aid must be obtained either from the national exchequer or from local rates. The next year the Conservative government brought in a bill granting a larger subsidy from the treasury to the voluntary schools, providing that parents might insist on an opportunity for separate religious instruction for their children in any public elementary school, devolving upon county councils a part of the powers of the government, and changing in other ways the educational system of the country. But although the cabinet had a large majority on every division, the bill awoke no great enthusiasm. It attempted too many things, in an unsystematic way, and was finally dropped. In 1897 that part of the bill giving an additional subsidy to the voluntary schools was enacted in a separate statute, which provided for an "aid grant," not exceeding five shillings a head for all the children in these schools, to be distributed by the Education Department among the needy districts.[1]

The Aid Grant.

The Demand for more Help.

The aid grant of 1897 was only a partial relief, for whereas the expenditure per child had been nearly the same in the two classes of schools in 1872, by 1900 it had risen in the board schools to £2 17*s.* 7½*d.* as against £2 6*s.* 4½*d.* in the voluntary schools.[2] In the debate on the bill of 1896 Mr. Balfour had stated the position of the Churchmen clearly when he asked, "Do you mean to continue a system which will gradually, but inevitably, squeeze out of existence in a large part of the country every school which is by law permitted to teach denominational religion?"[3] Many people felt strongly that the only chance to instill religious principles into the children of the working-classes was in the public elementary schools, and that for this purpose

[1] Voluntary Schools Act, 1897, 60 Vic., c. 5.
[2] Com. Papers, 1901, XIX, 1, p. 480.
[3] Hans., 4 Ser., XL., 1247.

denominational religious teaching alone was of any value. They were determined, therefore, to maintain the existing voluntary schools, and believed that it could not be done permanently except with the aid of local rates. The Conservative ministry embodied this principle in the Act of 1902, which was carried at the end of a long fight, a stubborn opposition being overborne by a rigorous use of closure by compartments. In the course of its passage some concessions in details were made in the House of Commons; while the Lords demanded and obtained an amendment that reduced the expenditures to be met by voluntary contributions even below the point intended by the cabinet. Nevertheless as enacted the law conformed in its essential features to the government plan, which was extended to London by another statute in the following year.

**The Act of 1902.**

**Dissensions Thereon.**

Although touching a smaller number of sporadic matters than the bill of 1896, the Education Act of 1902 was quite as comprehensive, and the principles involved were carried out far more thoroughly. It had three main objects: the promotion of public secondary education; the abolition of the school boards, whose powers were transferred to the councils of the counties, boroughs and larger urban districts;[1] and the support of the voluntary schools from local rates. To the first object, as contained in Part II. of the Act, there was comparatively little opposition. To the second object there was more, but although the Liberals urged that a body selected for the express purpose of managing schools would do the work better than one chosen for totally different reasons, the existing method of electing school boards by cumulative voting was generally recognised as unfortunate, and in their bill of 1906 the Liberal ministers made no attempt to reverse in this respect the provisions of the Act of 1902.

[1] The same body was placed in control of both elementary and secondary education, except in the case of the non-county boroughs with more than 10,000 people, and the urban districts with more than 20,000, which were given charge of the elementary schools alone.

The real struggle was about the position accorded to the voluntary schools. This was fought over inch by inch from the beginning to the end; the difficulty, which arose, of course, from the fact that the voluntary schools were for the most part denominational, being mainly confined to elementary work. In the matter of education of a higher grade the local authorities were empowered either to provide institutions themselves or to assist those supplied by others, and the provisions about religion were simple. They were, in substance, that no formulary, distinctive of any denomination, should be taught at the public cost in a school provided by the local authority, but that religious bodies might be allowed to give instruction there at their own expense. The giving or not giving of any such instruction was not to be a condition of a grant of aid to an institution in private hands, and any institution receiving such aid was to have a time-table conscience clause.[1]

Elementary Education. How Organised.

The provisions of the Act of 1902 in regard to elementary education, as finally enacted, were as follows. The councils of counties, county boroughs, other boroughs with more than ten thousand people, and urban districts with more than twenty thousand were to be local education authorities, with all the powers hitherto possessed by school boards and school attendance committees.[2] The councils were to work through education committees, formed with the approval of the Education Department, under a scheme whereby, as a rule, a majority of the committee were to be members of the council, and the rest were to include women and persons experienced in education nominated by various bodies.[3] The grants paid by the national government to all the schools alike were maintained; but inasmuch as the local educational authorities were henceforth to support the

[1] 2 Edw. VII., c. 42, § 4.

[2] §§ 1, 5. When a non-county borough or urban district is a local authority for elementary education, its representatives on the county council cannot vote on any question of elementary education, because it does not affect their constituents. § 23 (3).

[3] § 17 and Sched. 1.

voluntary as well as the board schools out of local rates, the special aid grants to the former were discontinued, and a universal grant to the local authorities of four shillings a scholar was substituted therefor, the poorer authorities still receiving additional sums to enable them to keep their schools efficient.[1]

The Provided Schools.

The Act made it the duty of the local education authority to maintain and keep efficient all the public elementary schools; but a sharp distinction was drawn between those which it provided itself — the successors of the board schools — and those which it maintained but did not provide, in other words the voluntary schools. Over the former its power is absolute, for although a county council is required to establish for each school or group of schools a body of managers, of whom four only are to be appointed by the council itself and two by the small borough, urban district or rural parish in which the school is situated, yet those managers act wholly under the control of the council.[2]

The Non-Provided Schools.

A voluntary school has also a body of managers, of whom four are appointed in accordance with the original trust deed, one by the county council, and one by the small borough, urban district or rural parish, in which the school stands.[3] By this provision a concession was made to the principle that popular representation on the governing body ought to accompany support from public rates, while the majority was carefully retained in the hands of the religious or other association to which the school had belonged. The control of the local education authority over the managers of these schools is strictly limited by the Act.[4] It has power to give the managers directions

[1] § 10.

[2] *Cf.* §§ 6, 24 (2), Sched. 1 B (4). The number of managers could be increased, but the proportions were to be the same, § 6 (3 b). The council of a non-county borough or urban district might appoint similar bodies of managers if it pleased.

[3] §§ 6 (2), 11. Where the local education authority is a borough or urban district, so that there is no minor authority therein, the council of the borough or district appoints two managers.

[4] § 7.

about secular instruction, and about the number and educational qualifications of the teachers employed therefor, and those directions the managers must obey. It has power to inspect the school, and its consent is required for the appointment and dismissal of teachers, but that consent must not be withheld on religious grounds. In short, it does not manage the school, but can prescribe the course of secular study, the methods of instruction, and the qualifications of teachers, with a veto on the selection made. The object of the restrictions was, of course, to preserve the denominational character of the school, the religious instruction being given in accordance with the original deed of trust.

The rule laid down in 1870 that board schools should give no religious instruction distinctive of any denomination, and that voluntary schools should observe the time-table conscience clause, naturally remained in force. So long as the managers complied with the provisions of the Act, the local education authority must supply from rates the money needed to maintain the school, the managers being required only to provide the schoolhouse, with such alterations therein as might be required, and to make any repairs not due to wear and tear. By far the greater part of the burden hitherto borne by private subscribers was thus being lifted from their shoulders on to those of the ratepayers; but on the other hand it must be remembered that in a great part of rural England, where there were no board schools, the former subscribers were now called upon for the first time to pay school rates.

Effect of the Act on the Voluntary Schools.

The effect of the Act, so far as the voluntary schools are concerned, has been to transfer almost the whole cost of maintenance to public taxation, and to give to the local authorities the direction of secular education; but to leave in the hands of the proprietors of the school the entire control of religious instruction, the actual management of the school, and, subject to a veto on educational grounds, the selection of the teachers. The managers were given power to appoint assistant teachers without regard to creed; but they are under no obligation to do so, and therefore in a large part of the public elementary schools of the country, supported by taxation, attended, and often from the absence of any other school attended under legal compulsion, by children of different denominations, men and women who do not belong to the Church of England — and they form something like one half of the population — have no chance of appointment as teachers. This fact, and the enforced support by the ratepayers of denominational schools under private management, were felt as grievances by the Nonconformists and the Liberals who sympathised with their views. Many people with deep feelings, known as passive resisters, refused to pay the rates, and allowed their property to be seized, or went to gaol. A few local authorities, particularly in Wales where dissent is strong, declined to take steps to put the law in operation, and in 1904 an act was passed increasing the power of the Education Department to intervene in such cases.[1] Opposition to the enforcement of the statute slowly died down, but the determination to insist upon a change of the law remained unabated, and when a new resultant of the shifting political forces brought a Liberal ministry to power at the end of 1905, one of its first cares was to introduce the Education Bill of 1906.

**The Education Bill of 1906.** The chief objects of the bill were: to place all elementary schools aided by public funds under public management; to provide an undenominational school within reach of every child; to free the teachers in such schools wholly from religious tests; and nevertheless — for this bill, like its predecessors, was a compromise between opposing principles — to permit in some degree denominational religious teaching in schools where it had hitherto existed.[2]

[1] Education (Local Auth. Default) Act, 1904, 4 Edw. VII., c. 18.

[2] All this was contained in Part I. What was originally Part II., relating to educational endowments, was withdrawn during the passage of the bill through the House of Commons. Part III., which became Part II., pro-

Religious Teaching under the Bill.

The first clause virtually abolished the voluntary schools at a stroke by declaring that no public elementary school should in future be recognised as such unless provided by the local education authority. For this purpose the authority might make agreements with the owners for the use of a voluntary school building, the owners being at liberty, without expense for repairs, to use it out of school hours. Part of the bargain might be that facilities should be given for denominational religious instruction of a kind not allowed by the Cowper-Temple clause, and in that case children whose parents so desired might receive that instruction on two mornings in the week, provided that it must not be given by the regular teachers, and must not be paid for out of public funds. This privilege was known during the debate by the uncouth name of "ordinary facilities," because it was not the only opportunity of teaching a creed.

The Prime Minister said he had thought that the Cowper-Temple teaching of what he called the "common elements of Christianity with, no doubt, a flavour of Protestantism in them," would not be obnoxious to the Church of England, yet the bill had permitted in addition two mornings of special doctrinal instruction a week. But he recognised that the Roman Catholics, who had always demanded full control of schools from a religious point of view, were in a different position.[1] So a provision was made for "extended facilities," whereby, instead of Cowper-Temple teaching, the local authority might allow in a transferred voluntary school denominational instruction, to be given by the regular teachers, in any urban district of more than five thousand people,[2] if the parents of four fifths of the children wanted it and there was an undenominational school within reach. This clause provoked stronger opposition than anything else in

vided for the delegation of powers by county councils to lesser local bodies. Part III. as it passed the House created a separate Educational Council for Wales; while Part IV. contained sundry supplemental provisions.

[1] Hans., 4 Ser., CLIX., 838. [2] Including boroughs.

the bill. Nonconformists, with Dr. Clifford at their head, waited upon the ministers to protest against such an exception to the general principle of the bill. Churchmen complained bitterly of a privilege granted to Roman Catholics from which they did not derive an equal benefit; and in fact the provision affected all the Jewish schools and more than three quarters of the Roman Catholic schools, as against one quarter of those belonging to the Established Church.[1] Even the Irish members, who represented also the Roman Catholics of England and Wales, were dissatisfied, demanding a change in the figures of the clause, as well as an obligation on local authorities to act upon it;[2] and their discontent was so great that they voted against the third reading of the bill.

Confronted by such objections, the government made a concession which would have retained a strange anomaly in the educational system of the country. Having already provided for schools strictly under the Cowper-Temple clause, for schools with ordinary and schools with extended religious facilities, the amendment empowered the Education Department, in case a local authority refused extended facilities, to allow a school to remain under purely voluntary control and receive the parliamentary grants, but without any aid from local rates. This "contracting out," as it was called, would thus have left the school where it stood before the Act of 1902.

In order to free the teachers completely from all religious tests, the bill provided not only that they should never be required to subscribe to any creed, to attend any place of worship, or to give any religious instruction, but also that they should not be allowed to give any denominational instruction except where extended facilities were granted.

The Conservatives complained that the bill amounted

[1] The schools affected contained over ninety per cent of all the children in Roman Catholic schools, and fifty-six per cent of those in Church of England schools.

[2] An appeal could be made to the Education Department, but the effect of that might depend upon the policy of the party in power.

The Lords' Amendments.

to a confiscation of the voluntary schools, which, save for the "contracting out" amendment, were compelled to come to terms with the local authorities on pain of annihilation. They appealed also to the right — not recognised by the Act of 1902 — the natural and inalienable right of every parent to have his children brought up in and taught the religious faith that he himself professes.[1] Proceeding upon this last assumption, the House of Lords amended the bill very thoroughly. They retained the principle that all public elementary schools were to be transferred to the local authorities, except in the case of contracting out which under their amendments was a highly improbable event; and they left nearly untouched the provision that the denominational teaching was not to be given at the public expense.

But in other ways they made the religious character of the public schools more pronounced than it had ever been before. In the first clause of the bill they provided that in every public elementary school some part of each day must be set apart for religious instruction, so that the local authorities should be compelled, instead of permitted, to provide Cowper-Temple teaching. The next clause, which had left the local authorities free not to take over a voluntary school if no terms could be arranged satisfactory to them, was changed so that the commission appointed under the Act could compel them to take it on terms requiring ordinary facilities for denominational instruction. The amendments provided, moreover, that even where no condition had been made at the time of transfer, facilities of this kind could be demanded by the parents of a reasonable number of children in any transferred voluntary school, and must be allowed if they could not be obtained in another school conveniently near.

The right to claim extended facilities was also enlarged. Instead of being left in the discretion of the local authority, such facilities were made obligatory and were made so in all places, urban or rural, where the parents of two thirds

[1] *Cf.* Hans., 4 Ser., CLVI., 1027.

of the children demanded them. Nor was it necessary that there should be another school near by which the dissenting children could attend. It was enough if the religious teaching they preferred was offered in the school itself or elsewhere. In short, instruction in the tenets of the Established Church could still be given in almost every village school in England. The voluntary schools were to be transferred to the public, but on something very close to the principle of allowing each denomination to teach children its own creed at its own expense. This was a wide departure from the former practice, whereby a voluntary school belonged strictly to a single religious body. It was a clear recognition of a right of the parent to have his child educated in his own faith.

Another new feature introduced by the peers was the placing of denominational religious instruction under the control of a committee selected mainly by the parents. Finally the House of Lords provided that every teacher should be permitted to give denominational instruction, and that the teachers in schools with extended facilities must be qualified and willing to give the religious instruction required. In other words, the teachers in a large part of the schools must be Churchmen.

As these amendments struck at the very root of the bill, the House of Commons refused to consider them, and the measure perished. Had it passed, it would probably not have set the question of religion in the schools at rest; and having failed, the issue remains a burning one in politics. More, perhaps, in politics than in the country, for although the religious organisations, and many individuals, feel very strongly about the matter, the traveller is sometimes surprised to learn in a rural district, where he expects to find the greatest excitement, that people with children in the public schools are little stirred by hot speeches about the rights of parents, made in Parliament by men whose sons and daughters will never enter the schools established for the poor.

Public attention has been so concentrated on the religious

Other Effects of the Act of 1902.

aspects of the Act of 1902 as to obscure its other provisions. Yet these have had notable effects; not least by placing the control of both elementary and secondary education in the same hands, and thereby bringing about a more orderly and effective connection between different grades of schools.

Abolition of Cumulative Voting.

But aside from this, the Act improved the authorities that had charge of elementary education. People were almost universally of opinion that cumulative voting had not worked well. Not because it failed to accomplish its object of representing the minority, but because it did so too much. It enabled a small group of people to control at least one seat at the election, and hence in most cases the school board was made up of representatives of a number of minorities. This was not true in London, which is so large that the elections for the school board, like those for the County Council, turned on the large divisions of Progressive and Moderate. But in the provinces, where that was not the case, the school board was usually composed of representatives of the Church of England and the Nonconformists, often with a few Roman Catholics, one or more Labour members and a nominee of the teachers. The boards sometimes contained no considerable element that stood for the interests of the public at large, and too often the question whether a schoolhouse should be built in a particular place turned on the effect it would have upon a neighbouring voluntary school. Almost every one felt, therefore, that doing away with the cumulative system of voting was wise; but there was much difference of opinion about transferring the control of the schools from an authority elected for the purpose to one chosen for general county government. Incidentally, however, this has had a marked and apparently unexpected effect.

Effect on the Permanent Officials.

In the chapters on Local Government great stress has been laid upon the influence of the permanent officials, and its importance in promoting the efficiency of administration. Now it must have been evident to any one who had personal knowledge of school management before 1902, that as a rule the influence of the permanent officials was much less there than in other branches of local government. In an occasional town, indeed, a clerk of the board, or some other officer, was a real superintendent of education; but more commonly he was little more than a head clerical officer, the appointment of teachers and the management of schools being really done by the elected members of the board. This would seem to account in part for the long period that it took the schools to grow to maturity, even under the strong pressure of the Education Department. Here the Act of 1902 worked a great change, as any one travelling through the country a few years later could not fail to perceive. Owing to the fact that the members of the representative bodies who now control education are not selected for any special knowledge of the subject, and owing still more to the fact that they are busy with other affairs, the influence of the permanent officials in the schools has greatly increased, their position becoming much more like that of the officers in other branches of local government.

With many a hitch and start, over obstacles, around corners, through the cross-fire of warring forces, public elementary education in England has been slowly dragged along. In fifty years it has passed from somewhat feeble voluntary efforts, directed mainly by the parson, reaching only a part of the working-class children, and educating few of them, to a universal and efficient system, almost wholly gratuitous and guided in large measure by a corps of experts. It has become also an integral part of a still larger system, so that a child on finishing his elementary work can pass into technical training on one side, or secondary education on the other. The boy or girl who shows reasonable capacity in elementary studies can, indeed, often win a scholarship that will make further schooling possible, and thus there is now a path leading from the workman's home even to the university. A few words may therefore be said about public support of education above the elementary grade.

# CHAPTER XLVIII

## SECONDARY EDUCATION

History of Secondary Education.

Elementary education in England provokes strong political differences in regard to religious instruction, to the status of the voluntary schools, and perhaps, also, to the organisation of the local authorities. But from a purely educational point of view it has reached a firmly established position in which rapid changes are improbable. Popular secondary education, on the other hand, although free from political complications, is still in the making. Many agencies are at work, earnestly pushing forward, but as yet they are not welded into a complete system, and hence one must speak of tendencies rather than results.

The Great Public Schools.

Eton, Harrow, Rugby and the other great public schools stand in a class by themselves. They are boarding schools, national in character, drawing their pupils from all parts of the country, and filled with boys of the upper classes, or sons of men who have made money and want their children to achieve a place in society. The chief object of these schools is to fit for Oxford and Cambridge, although they send many boys into the Army and other careers. Except that in consequence of the report of a commission of 1861[1] they were to some extent remodelled by the Public Schools Act of 1868, they have been little affected by the recent development of secondary education.

The Grammar Schools.

Next in order on the score both of age and of the grade of instruction come the grammar schools. Many of them were founded more than three hundred years ago, after the dissolution of the monasteries had destroyed the medi-

[1] Com. Papers, 1864, XX., 1.

æval scheme of education. Some of them make provision for boarders; but in the main they are day schools, supplying the needs of their immediate neighbourhood. Until they were opened to a larger number of children from the working-classes, by the recent increase in scholarships carrying free tuition, they were used mostly by people of the middle ranks in life.

The Commission of 1864.

The grammar schools were examined by the Schools Inquiry Commission of 1864, which presented in 1867 an elaborate and luminous report,[1] recommending the formation of a complete network of central and local authorities for the promotion of secondary education, on something akin to the principles adopted a generation later. To only one part of the report did Parliament give immediate effect. It created an Endowed Schools Commission, with extensive powers of reconstructing educational foundations — powers subsequently transferred to the Charity Commissioners. Many endowed schools have been reformed in this way, and started on a new and more efficient life. But if the direct legislative results were small, the report helped to stimulate a much keener public interest in the subject, and led to the founding of new secondary schools, especially for girls, in whose case the supply had been peculiarly deficient.[2] One of the most successful agencies that sprang up was the Girls' Public Day School Company, which had in 1895 thirty-six schools scattered over England, with more than seven thousand pupils. These are what are known as proprietary schools, for they are not endowed, but owned by the company, and supported mainly by the fees of the children.[3]

The Science and Art Grants.

The great public schools and the grammar schools ministered almost exclusively to the wants of the upper and middle ranks of society. The first general attempt to supply

[1] Com. Papers, 1867–68, XXVIII., 1.
[2] *Cf.* Rep. of Com. on Secondary Educ., Com. Papers, 1895, XLIII., 1, p. 76.
[3] On the different kinds of proprietary schools, see the Report of 1895, p. 49.

instruction above the elementary grade to the children of working people came with the grants of the Department of Science and Art. These began in 1837, nearly as early as the grants to assist in the building of elementary schools. They were not originally made to maintain schools; but they came to be used to support classes and schools, held both in the daytime and the evening; and so far at least as science was concerned their real function was to furnish a special kind of secondary education for the working-classes.

In the case of elementary schools, the national government assisted voluntary effort by a system of grants for nearly forty years before local public authorities were empowered to deal with the matter, and a similar course was followed for a still longer period in regard to instruction in science and art. But there were two important differences between the methods pursued when local authorities were called into action. The religious question did not arise to at all the same extent in classes for science and art, and hence there has never been the sharp antithesis, one might almost say antagonism, between voluntary and public institutions; and instead of creating special *ad hoc* authorities for schools of science, their management was entrusted to bodies elected for general local administration.

**The Technical Instruction Act of 1889;**

About 1880 a conviction, which has grown stronger with the passing years, made itself felt, that the advance of England's industrial rivals was due to better technical education, and in 1881 a commission was appointed to study the need of it at home. The main report, presented in 1884, being as usual more far-reaching than Parliament would go, was carried out at the time only in part. It brought about, however, the Technical Instruction Act of 1889, which empowered the newly elected county councils, and also the council of any borough or urban district, to supply or aid the supply of technical or manual instruction by means of a local rate not exceeding one penny in the pound. The local authorities showed at first no great eagerness to tax themselves for the purpose, and some of them have not done so to the present day. But the next year a real impulse was given to the movement by placing at their disposition a subvention from revenues collected by the national government. The Local Taxation (Customs and Excise) Act of 1890 provided that out of the proceeds of the beer and spirit duties, commonly known as "whiskey money," three hundred thousand pounds should be paid for police pensions, and that the residue should be distributed among the counties and county boroughs, with power to use it for technical and manual instruction. They were at liberty to apply it for general purposes if they pleased, and thus reduce their rates; but in almost every case they gave at least a part of it to the object suggested in the act, so that at last technical education obtained real support and encouragement from the local authorities.[1]

and the Whiskey Money.

The Technical Instruction Act had defined the subjects of study for which aid might be given somewhat vaguely, leaving a more precise enumeration practically in the hands of the Department of Science and Art,[2] and this body in turn has been so liberal in its interpretation as to give rise to the saying that its grants may be used for anything but the teaching of Latin and Greek. At the outset the money was intended primarily for the benefit of the working-classes, and although the technical schools established or aided by the local authorities, were forbidden by statute to use it for teaching the practice of any trade, they taught the means of acquiring skill in trades. But they have gradually become more ambitious, seeking also to

The Scope of Technical Instruction.

[1] Rep. of Com. on Secondary Educ., Com. Papers, 1895, XLIII., 1, pp. 32, 37.

[2] The Act (52–53 Vic., c. 76, § 8) defined technical instruction as instruction in the principles of science and art applicable to industries, or the application of special branches of science and art to special industries. It said that the instruction should not include the practice of any trade, but that, save as aforesaid, it should include the branches of science and art for which grants are made by the Department, and any other form of instruction, including modern languages and commercial and agricultural subjects, which might be sanctioned by the Department. Manual instruction was defined as teaching the use of tools, the processes of agriculture and modelling.

prepare men for responsible positions in industrial life, in some cases even for the engineering professions. This may be seen in the case of the London polytechnics, which were in their early years something very near trade schools, but have by degrees been doing more and more advanced work, until by an arrangement with the University of London some of their teachers are recognised as instructors, and their pupils are students, in the university.[1] It may be seen also in the case of the Municipal Technical School of Manchester. That school grew out of a mechanics' institute founded in 1824, but did not succeed in giving effective teaching to the working-classes in the arts and industries until about 1884, when it was helped by the City and Guilds of London Institute. In 1892 it was transferred to the town council, which has rapidly enlarged it, adding higher grades of instruction. It is now the most highly developed technical school in the United Kingdom, and has recently formed a faculty of technology in common with the University of Manchester.[2]

Progress toward Aid of Secondary Schools.

Even in the years immediately following the Act of 1890, public aid was not strictly confined to technical education, for many of the counties made grants directly to the grammar schools. They were, indeed, given on account of technical instruction, and had in this way a tendency to modify the curricula by increasing the amount of science taught. Nevertheless they could hardly fail to strengthen the schools in all their work. In a number of cases the counties even founded general secondary schools, acting usually in conjunction with the Charity Commissioners, or with some endowed institution which was not restricted to technical instruction.[3]

The Science and Art Department, also, followed a policy

[1] Rep. Tech. Educ. Board of L. C. C., 1903–04, p. 26; Rep. Educ. Com. L. C. C., 1905, p. 41.

[2] Rep. of Educ. Com. of Manchester, 1904–05, p. 12; Calendar of the School, 1905–06, p. 24.

[3] Rep. of Com. on Secondary Educ., Com. Papers, 1895, XLIII., 1, pp. 32–35. All this was less true of the county boroughs. *Ibid.*, pp. 37–38.

of interpreting its functions broadly, for although its grants were made only on behalf of pupils belonging to the industrial classes,[1] the subjects for which they were given were comprehensive. They included such things as book-keeping, banking and commerce, political economy, seamanship, veterinary science, music and the art of teaching. Moreover, while the Department had no power to make grants for literary subjects as such, yet with a view to encourage them it reduced in 1895 the number of hours of scientific instruction required in an organized school of science, and made a part of the grant depend upon a general report of the inspector, based upon literary as well as technical work.[2]

**The Commission of 1894.**

The growing interest in secondary education gave rise to another royal commission, appointed in 1894, with Mr. Bryce at its head. Like its predecessor thirty years before it made an elaborate inquiry, and added one more to the great reports on English education.[3] Comparing the state of things it found with that which had existed in the sixties, the commission referred to the improvement in the endowed grammar schools, which it attributed in part to the larger resources that came from the abandonment of gratuitous instruction and the consequent increase in the revenue from fees. In the case of some of the larger foundations the number of pupils had grown three or four fold. Nevertheless many schools of this kind were still seriously crippled by lack of funds, or suffered from an unfortunate geographical position; and in fact the endowed schools alone were very far from supplying the need of secondary education. The report went on to state that the proprietary schools had done much to fill the gap, especially for girls; while the private schools, conducted for personal profit, differed a great deal in efficiency. Some of them were highly useful,

[1] "The definition of 'industrial' being the possession by the parent of an income not exceeding £400 (later £500) a year." *Ibid.*, p. 27.
[2] Com. Papers, 1895, XLIII., 1, p. 28; LXXVIII., 899.
[3] This is the report already referred to in Com. Papers, 1895, XLIII., 1.

but a large number were unsatisfactory, a state of things that persists to the present day.

Classification of Secondary Schools.

The Schools Inquiry Commission in their report of 1867 had divided secondary schools into three classes, according to the normal age of the pupils on completing the course. They placed in the first grade those schools which carry forward the instruction of the students to eighteen or nineteen, the time when a young man would go to Oxford or Cambridge. The second grade stops at sixteen or seventeen, at the point where the pupils would begin business life, or an apprenticeship in the less learned professions, or perhaps enter a provincial university. The third grade ends at fourteen or fifteen, when the pupils would naturally start in the lower branches of business, or take up one of the higher trades. Such a classification is valuable, in spite of the fact that the existing secondary schools are by no means separated into distinct groups of the kind.

Deficiencies in the Three Classes.

Accepting the three grades as a basis, the report of 1895 stated that there were, on the whole, enough schools of the first grade for boys; but not enough of the second and third grades, especially in rural districts where the farmers were apathetic about education. The higher grade elementary schools conducted by the school boards, and sometimes by the voluntary societies, had, indeed, done much to supply the lack in the third grade. These schools had classes beyond the seventh standard, the highest for which grants were made by the Education Department. In fact some of them took only children who had completed all but two years of the regular elementary course, and then kept them four years. Outside of London there were at the time no less than sixty higher grade board schools, but they did not exist in many places where they were sorely needed.

Strictures and Suggestions of the Commission.

The report pointed out the need of more free scholarships, to enable a promising child to pass from one rung of the educational ladder to another; and the lack of professionally trained teachers in the secondary schools. It complained also of the prevalent confusion of thought — unfortunately not confined either to England or to secondary education — between training the mind and teaching something of immediate practical utility, in one case, for example, shorthand being treated as an alternative to Latin and German. In the same vein the grants of the Science and Art Department were criticised on the ground that they encouraged too exclusive devotion to scientific subjects to the neglect of literary ones, and led to cramming in the effort of the schools to win the largest possible grants at the examinations. Above all the commission lamented the lack of effective organisation in secondary education, the want of a single central department, and of local representative authorities empowered to deal with the whole subject. Finally the report made a number of recommendations; and although these have not always been carried out in the form suggested, they have been followed to a great extent, with the result that the defects indicated are in process of removal.

**Creation of the Board of Education in 1899.**

In the very next year the Conservative government inserted provisions relating to secondary schools in the education bill, referred to in the preceding chapter, which it introduced but afterward dropped; and in 1899 it laid a real foundation for further progress in the Board of Education Act. Although political control of the whole educational work of the government had hitherto been concentrated in the hands of the Lord President of the Privy Council and the Vice-President of the Committee on the subject,[1] yet, except from 1873 to 1884, the Education Department, which dealt with elementary schools, and the Department of Science and Art, had been practically quite independent, each having a permanent secretary and staff of its own. Now the Act of 1899 substituted for the existing authorities a new Board of Education, or rather a single minister dressed in the garb of a board, and one man was then made permanent under-

[1] The relation of these two ministers to one another, and to the departments, was always somewhat undetermined.

secretary both at Whitehall and South Kensington. The entire supervision of education having thus been vested in a single department, the way was prepared for treating secondary education as a whole, and for adjusting its relation to the elementary schools.[1]

The Cockerton Decision.

Local authorities entitled to deal with the whole problem of secondary instruction were still wanting, and a decision rendered shortly after this date made the matter more pressing. By the Education Act of 1870 the school boards had been authorised to maintain only elementary schools. But many of them, as we have seen, went farther and established classes running beyond the limit of the grants given by the Education Department for elementary teaching. Now Mr. Cockerton, an auditor of the Local Government Board, disallowed certain payments made in London for instruction of this kind, and when the matter was brought before the courts the Queen's Bench Division, followed in 1901 by the Court of Appeal, held that such instruction was not elementary and hence was beyond the power of the school board. The decision would have destroyed a considerable part of the work, both of the higher grade elementary schools and of the evening continuation classes, and as this work was very valuable it was necessary to legalise it at once by statute. In 1901, therefore, the government, after withdrawing a comprehensive bill on secondary education which it had introduced, passed a brief measure giving the county councils a right to sanction the continuance of those schools on the old basis for a year.[2]

The Act of 1902.

The Act of 1901 was merely a stop gap to cover an emergency; and in the following session a permanent provision was made by Part II. of the Education Act of 1902. The

[1] The powers of the Charity Commissioners to reorganise endowed schools were not directly transferred by the Act to the new Board, but the Crown was authorised to transfer them by Order in Council (Board of Educ. Act, 1899, 62–63 Vic., c. 33, § 2). Another suggestion of the Commission on Secondary Education was carried out by a provision permitting the Board to inspect, with their consent, secondary schools not aided by the state.

[2] 1 Edw. VII., c. 11.

councils of counties and county boroughs were thereby empowered to take such steps as might be needed to supply, or aid the supply, of any education other than elementary, and to promote the coördination of all forms of education. In doing so they were to have regard to the existing supply of efficient schools and colleges.[1] In short they were authorised to establish or aid secondary or higher schools in any way they might see fit, but were cautioned not to squeeze out institutions under private management. In carrying out this object they had the use of the whiskey money, hitherto applicable only to science and art; and they could levy a rate up to a limit which was raised from a penny in the pound to twopence or such larger sum as the Local Government Board might approve.

It may be remembered that all boroughs and urban districts, as well as counties, had been given by the Technical Education Act of 1889 a right to take part in the supply of instruction in science and art, levying for the purpose a rate not exceeding one penny in the pound. In spite of the possible confusion from having more than one local authority dealing with the same subject, this power was left intact, the field of action being merely enlarged so as to include all secondary education. The arrangement, although historically a survival, has real merit, for the people in small boroughs and urban districts care far more about education than their rural neighbours, and are often willing to tax themselves for the purpose when the county as a whole is not.

Encouragement of Liberal Studies.

The provisions of Part II. of the Act of 1902 furnished machinery for the development of education of a general character above the elementary grade, and gave a stimulus to the movement, for which public opinion, especially in the cities, was beginning to be ripe. The Board of Educa-

[1] 2 Edw. VII., c. 42, § 2. § 4 contains the usual provisions about religious instruction. No formulary distinctive of any particular sect is to be taught in the schools maintained by the council; and no school receiving public aid is to require the attendance of a pupil at any religious exercise.

tion felt the need of a change of policy. Its report for 1904 stated that there was evidence of too early specialisation in the secondary schools; of a gradual loss in the cultivation of language and literature; and of a tendency to substitute a too exclusively scientific for a truly liberal education. Hitherto the Board had been making grants on two different scales to schools which it classed for the purpose as Divisions A and B. The former devoted a larger share of time to scientific and other utilitarian instruction, and received larger grants; while the latter paid more attention to general studies, and obtained less aid. This the report said was a survival from the time when the sole grants were made for classes in science and art. To counteract the tendency, which it deplored, the Board issued new regulations for 1904–05, designed to encourage a liberal curriculum by a change in the method of distributing grants.

The object of the new departure is clearly set forth in the preface to the more recent regulations, those issued in 1906, for example, in which the Board declares that the funds at its disposal can be most usefully applied by being concentrated upon a four years' course in approved secondary schools, and that in future no fresh grants in aid of science and art scholarships will be made. The preface goes on to emphasise the three essential points in the course of instruction which all recognised secondary schools are required to provide. The instruction must be general, exercising and developing all the faculties of the mind; it must be progressive; and it must be complete, so planned as to lead to a definite standard of acquirement. With this object in view the Board refused to make grants to any future schools which should specialise in applied science, or anything else, during the first two years of their four years' course.

The regulations themselves now provide that in any schools receiving a grant the course must include not less than a specified number of hours in English, in at least one other language, preferably Latin,[1] and in geography, history, mathematics, science, drawing, manual work and physical exercise. Finally, for the sake, no doubt, of retaining pupils during the whole course of four years, the grants for attendance are made to rise, by successive increments of twenty shillings, from two pounds for the first year to five pounds for the fourth.

Work of the Local Authorities.

The action of the county and borough councils has been less decided and more tentative. They perceive the need of general education on broad lines, but are loath to embark on a systematic programme. Moreover, the financial problem is a grave one. As a rule they are ready to use the whiskey money for secondary schools, but there is hesitation, especially on the part of rural counties, to tax themselves to the extent of the twopence in the pound allowed by the Act of 1902. Some of the councils have, in fact, levied no rate for the purpose at all. Nevertheless on the whole notable progress is being made. The direct work of the local authorities in promoting secondary education has taken three forms: maintenance of schools of their own; aiding endowed and other schools not under their management; and providing scholarships, whereby children who cannot afford to pay the fees can obtain schooling without charge.

Schools Managed Directly.

Although the local authorities in England have acquired and control a considerable number of schools giving a general secondary education, and their activity in that direction appears to be increasing, yet the institutions, other than elementary, now managed by them directly are still for the most part devoted primarily to instruction in science and art, to the kind of secondary teaching given in higher grade elementary schools, or to evening classes.[2]

[1] Regs. for Sec. Schools, 1906, ch. i., 4, "Where two languages other than English are taken, and Latin is not one of them, the Board will require to be satisfied that the omission of Latin is for the educational advantage of the school."

[2] From Table 61 in the Statistics of Public Education in England and Wales, issued by the Board of Education in 1906, it appears that of the 575

This is particularly true in London, where the County Council possessed in 1905 only one general secondary school of its own, and that was closely connected with the Shoreditch Technical Institute; while it had thirteen polytechnics or technical institutes, nearly fourscore higher grade elementary departments, and was helping to support some fifty secondary schools not under its own management.[1] In short, the secondary instruction conducted directly by the county and borough councils is as yet mainly of the lowest grade, or largely of a technical character.

Their Efficiency.

Of the results achieved in education of any grade an observer who has not made an exhaustive study of the subject must speak with diffidence. But it would seem that of the institutions managed directly by public authorities the schools of art are doing work of an excellent quality. The technical schools are also highly useful. Including evening classes the crowd of persons attending them is sometimes enormous, and they must do a vast deal of good in diffusing a familiarity with applied science, and still more in creating a widespread appreciation and respect for scientific knowledge. On the other hand the number of pupils who follow a continuous systematic course of any kind, either scientific or commercial, is very small. At the municipal technical school of Manchester, for example, the total roll of students in 1904–05 was 5757, and yet only twenty-two persons received the diploma given for a three years' course in the day school, and only two for the five years' course in the evening.[2] This appears to be true of the evening classes in many places. Most

secondary schools receiving grants from the Board on account of an approved four years' course, 123 were directly governed by a local authority, and of these 56 provided a four years' course of general instruction, with or without a special course in science also. Of the 452 not so governed 327 provided a general course of that kind. The figures are the more significant because they include only schools that obtain national grants. Obviously a very small part of the general secondary education of the country is as yet under the direct management of public bodies.

[1] Report L. C. C., Educ. Com., 1905, pp. 8, 14–15, 37.

[2] Rep. Manchester Educ. Com., 1904–05, pp. 6, 11.

of the students come to study some one subject, often of immediate practical utility, rather than to get an education; and there are complaints that others are merely reviving the elementary knowledge which they have lost since leaving school.

**The Spirit of Coöperation.**

Local authorities have not many schools of their own for general secondary education, and a large part of those that they do possess are not newly created by public funds, but older foundations transferred to them by the former managers who have found themselves in financial straits. Thus the Liverpool Institute, with its high and commercial schools, has recently been transferred to the city; and the education committee of the County of Durham has acquired, in return for its grants, a majority of members on the managing boards of a dozen schools scattered over different parts of the shire. Such transfers have not been forced by competition on the part of the public, for county and borough councils have no craving to set up new secondary schools of their own. They have, indeed, shown a most laudable absence of jealousy, an absence of any desire to rival existing institutions and drive them off the field. On the contrary there is a strong spirit of coöperation in a common public service. One sees it markedly at Birmingham, for example, where the city has avoided overlapping the instruction given at the King Edward's grammar schools. These are well endowed, and provide the more liberal education, while the city dovetails its work with theirs by maintaining three other secondary schools, one chiefly technical, and two that have both technical and business courses.

**Local Grants to Endowed Schools.**

With the increase in the cost of education many of the older foundations find it hard to pay their way, and the local authority frequently assists them from the resources at its command.[1] Sometimes the grants are still nominally made on account of scientific teaching; but since the Act

[1] This is, of course, not done in the case of private schools conducted for personal profit.

of 1902 they are often made for the general support of the school. In any case where aid is given the council of the county or borough appoints one or more members of the governing body, and in fact the Technical Instruction Act of 1889 provided for representation of a local authority in the proportion that the aid it gave bore to the other revenues of the school.[1] By this process the councils become partners in the schools, and a close coöperation is brought about in secondary education.

Local Grants for Scholarships.

The third way in which local authorities have been assisting secondary education is by providing scholarships whereby promising children in the elementary schools can continue their studies without charge. For it must be observed that secondary education in England is not gratuitous,[2] and would be almost inaccessible to the working-classes were it not that, by endowment or public aid, scholarships have been established entitling the holder to free tuition, and sometimes to a small additional sum. These open a door from below, while a means of going still higher is often provided by scholarships tenable at a university by graduates of the school.[3]

Now this matter of scholarships brings up a very interest-

[1] 52–53 Vic., c. 76, § 1 (e).

[2] This is true in most cases even of the kind of secondary education given in the higher grade elementary schools. Report of Com. on Secondary Educ., Com. Papers, 1895, XLIII., 1, p. 184.

Aid for Training Teachers.

[3] Indirectly the local authorities have been promoting secondary education by helping the training of teachers. Sometimes this takes the form of grants to training colleges; sometimes of maintaining centres where pupil teachers can practise teaching while pursuing their studies, for the old monitorial system, and its later substitute of pupil teachers, have left an enduring mark on English education. It is no longer enough, however, to serve an apprenticeship as a pupil teacher, and then go to a training college. The Board of Education now requires a good secondary education, and in schools of high grade one often finds a number of university graduates among the instructing staff.

The lack of professionally trained teachers for the secondary schools themselves was one of the matters on which the commission of 1894 laid stress; and, indeed, the supply of teachers for public schools of all grades is not superabundant. It would seem to be necessary either to pay larger salaries in order to attract a greater quantity of men into the career, or, as in the United States, to rely for instruction mainly upon women, an alternative that is not regarded with favour in England.

ing social problem. According to the old tradition, which is still very prevalent, the great national public schools and the ancient universities exist for the upper class, the grammar schools and the provincial universities for the middle class, the public elementary schools together with the technical courses in science and art for the working people; and it was partly because applied science was believed to be the proper form of secondary education for the latter that it secured so much encouragement and support from the central government. Middle-class children now attend public elementary schools somewhat more than they did formerly; but until after 1902, when school fees were in many cases abolished altogether by the county councils, those voluntary schools that charged a fee derived a certain advantage therefrom, because they were deemed socially a little more select. People of refinement not unnaturally object to sending their children to a school where they will acquire an uncultivated manner or accent; and the traveller observes that universal education in England has done little to break down local dialects, or to bring about a uniform pronunciation among all classes in any part of the country. Cockney, for example, instead of disappearing, tends to spread.

**Social Distinctions.**

The fact that the public elementary schools are used little except by the working-classes has two notable effects on higher education. The first is the large proportion of children in all secondary schools, not purely technical, who have come from private schools. This is very marked in institutions of the highest grade that prepare for the universities, but it is true of the ordinary grammar schools also. The second is the tender age at which these schools admit pupils. While the regular course of instruction may begin, let us say, at twelve years of age, children are very often taken into preparatory classes at seven or eight, and in extreme cases even at four. Although these things are due in part to a belief that different grades of education ought to be distinct from the start, they spring also from the strong social cleavage that has reserved the public elementary schools for the working-class.

Curiously enough the fact that the secondary schools are not gratuitous, but have a limited number of free scholarships, tends rather to break down, than to perpetuate, a separation of social classes in education. It admits a few picked children of the working-class at a later age than most of the others, without changing the character of the school, whereas if a school were wholly free the working-class children might come in such numbers as to drive out the rest. The present system thus tends to mix members of different classes gradually, and almost imperceptibly, together.

**Lack of Gradation of Schools.**

In a survey of English secondary schools one is struck by the lack, or, in order not to assume a doctrinal position, let us say by the absence, of precision in gradation and aims. The commissions of 1864 and 1894 divided secondary schools into three grades; but, except, perhaps, for the higher elementary schools, the existing instruction by no means conforms to that classification. Following the great example at Edinburgh the more advanced institutions are often called high schools, and the intermediate class grammar schools; but the nomenclature is as irregular as the gradation. Many schools have now both a classical and a modern side, the former being supposed to offer an appropriate preparation for the universities and the learned professions, the latter for other professions and for business. But in fact the pupils are not segregated according to their probable careers, either in different schools or in different departments of the same school. Apart from the great national public schools, such as Eton, Rugby, Harrow, and the rest, there are few if any places whose primary object is to fit for the universities. On the other hand, there are few schools of high grade that do not occasionally send boys to the university colleges, or even to Oxford or Cambridge, and few that do not send them into all sorts of business situations. Nor can any clear distinction be drawn at the other end of the scale between the modern sides of grammar schools and the commercial schools which are intended to give a cheaper education to a larger class of people. In short, the secondary schools do not conform to distinct types designed to prepare for definite kinds of occupations.[1]

Lack of Continuous Attendance.

A great deal can be said for and against such an absence of precision in aim; but there can be no doubt that the failure of pupils to remain at school throughout the four years' course is unfortunate. Professor Sadler, in his admirable reports upon secondary education in a number of English cities, prints diagrams showing the ages during which pupils stay at the various schools; and certainly the times of entering and leaving, together with the length of sojourn, are utterly irregular — a state of things that must interfere seriously with systematic instruction. We have seen that the Board of Education is trying by the arrangement of its grants to encourage attendance for four years, but the statistics it collects show that the number of scholars on the rolls falls off rapidly with each succeeding year of the course.[2]

Examining Bodies.

[1] Connected with the uncertainty of aim in secondary schools is the number of different bodies that inspect the schools and examine the pupils. In the schools that may desire it, examinations are held by Oxford or Cambridge; by the joint board of those two universities; by London University (the so-called matriculation examination); by the College of Preceptors (a purely voluntary body); by the City and Guilds of London Institute in technical subjects; by the London Chamber of Commerce in commercial ones; and by a number of other bodies under certain conditions. Some of these examinations are accepted by the General Medical Council, the Incorporated Law Society, the Institutes of Architects, Engineers, Actuaries and the like; while others provide merely a standard of efficiency for the satisfaction of the school or the pupil; and in fact many schools offer pupils for more than one of these local examinations.

No doubt all of these examinations have had an excellent effect in raising the standard among schools and keeping them up to the mark, but it may be doubted whether such a multiplicity of standards is wholly good to-day. One hears also complaints that, like the old method of payment by results in the elementary schools, they fix the attention of instructors too exclusively on preparation for examinations.

[2] Table 60 of the Statistics issued by the Board in 1906, for schools receiving its grants in England and Wales, gives the total number of scholars in each year of the approved four years' course as follows: first year, 27,770; second year, 17,563; third year, 10,178; fourth year, 4337.

The Tendency of Secondary Education.

At the beginning of this chapter it was pointed out that in English secondary education one must speak of tendencies rather than results. Three tendencies may be observed, or more properly a tendency with three aspects. One is in the direction of a more general public support of secondary education, another toward a broader or more liberal secondary education for the mass of the people, and the third is a gradual breaking down of class lines in secondary schools. The developments of the last dozen years, and especially since the Act of 1902, have involved a radical change in the policy of the state in giving public aid to education. That aid is no longer confined to the working-class. Nor could it be so confined when the state turned its attention to secondary instruction of a general character. The public elementary schools exist almost entirely for the working people, and although this is less strictly true than in the past, it will probably continue in the main to be the fact. But it cannot be true of general secondary schools. If it were, secondary education under state control would be narrow and technical, or a feeble thing. To be vigorous, it must include a large part at least of the classes that care most for it. The greatest obstacle to secondary education in England is the apathy of the people, their failure to grasp what it means for their own children; and by giving aid to schools filled mainly by the middle classes, and providing a number of free scholarships therein, the public seems to have taken the road that leads straightest to the goal.

# CHAPTER XLIX

## THE UNIVERSITIES

A TREATISE on the English universities would be out of place in a book on government; and yet a few words on the crowning point of the educational system, and on the part the state has recently taken in sustaining it, would seem a natural sequel to the story of public support to the elementary and secondary schools.

**Contrast with German Universities.**

English and German universities both sprang from the same great mediæval institution, which, with no little diversity of form, kept intellectual life awake, and prepared the world for the wider thought of later times. But their modern evolution presents a striking contrast. The German university developed into a group of four professional schools, under the faculties of theology, law, medicine and philosophy, the first three preparing for the careers of the same names, the latter mainly for the profession of scholarship or teaching, either in schools or universities. Meanwhile the life of the students as a community or group of communities has grown up independently of the authorities, and become a voluntary matter with which the governing body interferes little. In fact the relation of the university to its students is almost wholly that of instruction, either by lectures or by guiding individual research in seminars. Oxford and Cambridge moved on quite different lines. The halls formed to lodge the students were gradually superseded by more highly organised colleges with a vigorous common life which has long been the real vital force. In these colleges the student spends his time under constant supervision and discipline.[1]

[1] Each of the colleges, as well as the university itself, is a distinct corporation; and although in fact filled until recent years with clerical fellows, it is a lay corporation.

Oxford and Cambridge aim at Liberal Culture.

If the common life in separate colleges presents a strong contrast with the German universities, the difference has been no less marked in the aims and methods of instruction. The stress laid from an early period on the liberal arts at the English seats of learning grew stronger as time went on, and until a few years ago the professional objective was almost entirely absent there. The primary end in view has been the production of cultivated men, not of lawyers, physicians or even clergymen and scholars in a strictly professional sense. The curriculum, formerly based chiefly upon the classics and mathematics, has in later times been extended over the other fields of knowledge, but rather for the sake of their educational value than for any direct utility that the information acquired may have in a subsequent career. Some change has, indeed, come of late years. The faculties of law and medicine, for example, are very active; but the legal instruction does not fully prepare for practice, or avoid the need of reading at the Inns of Court; and no study of medicine at Oxford or Cambridge can take the place of clinical work in a hospital. An effort has been made, also, to recruit a large body of graduate students devoting themselves to advanced specialised subjects. As yet, however, the movement has not attained much size. The older practice whereby fellowships in the colleges were given to men who were not expected to teach or be taught, but to pursue their studies by themselves, is more in accord with the traditions of the place, and although subject to abuse has given rise to many notable productions.

The Methods of Instruction.

The mode of educating the undergraduate has been no less characteristic than the object aimed at. For a long time the university professors ceased to give instruction almost altogether. Their chief function was research and writing. This last is, no doubt, in theory true in Germany also; but formerly the English professor was not in practice required to impart the results of his work to the students, and did not do so. Although taught to some extent by the lecturers of their college, the students were in the main expected to study by themselves from books, under the guidance of a tutor appointed by the college or employed at their own expense. In that way they were prepared for an examination by officers of the university who conferred the degree. All this again has been modified of late, and the amount of direct instruction has increased very much, but the older methods still colour the whole system. They persist because, in spite of the fact that a small amount of research among original sources is now demanded of candidates for high honours, the principal work of all the students still consists in mastering standard authors. The process is not inappropriately called reading for an examination. The object is not so much a familiarity with the latest discoveries on any subject as a grasp of the ideas which, by passing through many minds, have been worn into shape, or have moulded the form of European civilisation. The examinations determine the nature of the course of study, and they are a test, not of minute information about many facts, but rather of a command of ideas and principles, coupled with a power of expression. In short, the university does not equip a man for an occupation, but aims at strengthening him to use any equipment he may afterwards acquire.

**Honour and Pass Degrees.**

At the opening of the nineteenth century the amount of study required for a degree had fallen so low, and the examinations had become so much a mere form, as to bring the universities into disrepute, when a change was made that has affected profoundly the attitude of the students. This was the institution of an honour degree, distinct from the ordinary or pass degree, and in later times based not only on greater excellence, but also to a large extent on a different course of study.[1] Besides the examinations

[1] In Oxford, honour degrees were first conferred in 1802, and the different schools were evolved from time to time. In Cambridge, the mathematical tripos began as far back as 1747–48, the civil law classes in 1815–16, the classical tripos in 1824, and the others later.

for matriculation in the university and for residence at a college, which, although deferred for a time, are really entrance examinations and are now taken more and more commonly at the preparatory school, there are as a rule two university examinations during a student's career. One, called in Oxford "moderations," and in Cambridge the "general examination" of the first part of a tripos, is taken part way through the course;[1] the other, which is more serious, comes at the time of going up for the bachelor's degree, and this is usually at the end of three or four years' residence.

The requirements both for a pass degree and for honours at each set of examinations are complex; but speaking generally, the essential difference between the two is that for a pass degree the latitude in the selection of subjects, although considerable, is not so great, and the candidate is usually required to read in more than one field; while for honours he chooses a single subject, known at Oxford as "a school" and in Cambridge as the subject of a tripos, and is examined in that alone. The subjects are classics,[2] law, history, natural science and a number of others, which have been constantly increased with the expansion of learning. For the higher grades of honours far greater attainment is required than for a pass degree; but in order, no doubt, not to discourage candidates, the standard for the lowest grade is often low — scarcely, if any, higher, it is said, than for the pass degree.

**Widespread Desire for Honours, and its Causes.**

The success of the universities in stimulating ambition to win honours and prizes has been so great that not far from half the students try for them. This is due to many causes. Foremost is the importance attached by the authorities themselves to the honour degree. The annual university calendar contains a list of all the men who have taken those

[1] In some subjects the whole examination in a tripos at Cambridge comes at one time at the end of the course.

[2] At Oxford known as *Literae Humaniores*, or commonly as "Greats"; it covers a wide range, including such matters as modern philosophy.

degrees since they were established, and in fact they seem to be the chief end of the instruction. In talking with the professors, one is struck by the fact that their interest is centred on this point. They can state at once the requirements for an honour degree, but are often unable to say what is the course of study for a pass. The English universities have impressed the significance of honour degrees so firmly on the public mind that they are held in high esteem throughout the land. A book for popular use, like "Who's Who," often gives the university honours a man obtained; and in the prospectus of a grammar school one may find stated the honours as well as the degrees taken by the instructing staff.

Then there is the rivalry between the different colleges. Some of them, like Balliol at Oxford and King's at Cambridge, admit only students who intend to read for honours; and the number of firsts taken by a college is mentioned with a pride not unlike that of having its boat at the head of the river.

More potent, however, than anything else in the mind of the undergraduate is the belief that honours of a high grade are both a precursor of success in life and a positive help in the initial steps of a career; and to any one who studies the early life of leading men in England, the belief is most certainly not without a solid foundation. That high honours are an assistance at the outset comes from the fact that older men share fully the conviction of the students; and that winning a first-class is a real indication of the qualities needed for success in life, is due in a peculiar degree to the nature of the examination itself. This does not measure the quantity of minute information possessed, and cannot be won by plodding study alone, however great, but is rather a test of native intellectual power, sharpened by reasonable diligence. It is a case where the race is to the swift, and while many a fox may go to sleep, the patient tortoise does not win.

The most characteristic feature of university life is, of

Social Structure of the Colleges.

course, the subdivision of the mass of undergraduates into colleges, each large enough to provide a goodly number of acquaintances, and not so large that the individual is lost or lonely in the crowd. It is the existence of these bodies — complete social communities in themselves, with common dining rooms, common traditions and collective ambitions, yet not so exclusive as to prevent friendships outside — it is these colleges that give to student days at Oxford and Cambridge the charm and the influence on character they possess. The danger that such a system will result in a segregation of men of diverse origin in different colleges, with a marked social gulf set between them, has been much lessened by the fact that by far the greater part of the students in the university belong to the same class in society. Many of them are not rich, or even well off; for although wealth in England affects social position to-day more than ever before, social lines are by no means based upon it. The custom of primogeniture, and the narrow incomes of clergymen, army officers and others, prevent that. In fact experience shows that one college is seldom regarded as distinctly inferior socially to another.

A few bright boys, born in different surroundings, have always found their way into the colleges by means of scholarships, yet there have never been enough of them to affect the fact that an overwhelming proportion of the college residents have been drawn from one social class. Of late years, indeed, the number of middle and working-class students has increased rapidly; but from motives of economy most of them have remained outside of any college, and are known as unattached or non-collegiate men. They profit by the education offered at the university, but miss much of the benefit of its social life.

The University of London.

Higher education for the middle classes in England is provided mainly by the University of London and the new provincial institutions. Formerly an examining body which conferred degrees but gave no instruction of its own, the University of London was remodelled in 1898 by the inclusion of a number of colleges and schools, such as University College, King's College, Bedford College for women, the London School of Economics, half a dozen divinity schools, and half a score of medical schools connected with the hospitals. Teaching became an essential part of its functions, and it became a true university in the modern sense. Even since its reorganisation, however, the University of London has remained very different from Oxford and Cambridge. It is doing an invaluable educational work, but it does not undertake to provide the common life so vital to the old seats of learning. It makes no attempt to house its students or supervise their conduct beyond its lecture rooms and laboratories, nor do the colleges and schools now forming part of it. At the most they have connected with them an occasional hostel for the convenience of the students.

**Provincial Universities.**

One of the most striking developments of the last half century has been the growth of universities and colleges in the great provincial towns. The cases of Manchester, Liverpool and Leeds may serve as types for the larger places. In 1851 Owens College was opened in Manchester and named after the testator who had founded it. Managed at first by the trustees under his will, it was later incorporated by statutes of 1870 and 1871. Gradually the institution grew. Gifts were made to it, and in 1872 a school of medicine was amalgamated with it. But a college has no power to confer degrees, and therefore Victoria University was founded at Manchester in 1880, with Owens College as the first institution under its wing. The charter, however, provided that other colleges might be admitted, and in 1884 this was done in the case of University College, Liverpool, which had been opened two years before. Then in 1887 Yorkshire College, Leeds, was included in the group. The triple alliance lasted until 1903, when it was broken up. University College was raised to the dignity of a separate University of Liverpool, Victoria University was reorganised under the title of Victoria University of Manchester with no constituent bodies in other places,[1] and the next year Yorkshire College in its turn became the University of Leeds.

There are now a considerable number of university colleges in the provincial towns, and in half a dozen of the largest places they have been turned into universities. As the latter alone can confer degrees, a distinct college must either form part of a provincial university, sometimes in conjunction with others in neighbouring boroughs, or it must prepare its students for the local examinations of London University, which still confers degrees upon persons who have studied elsewhere. The number of day students at the university colleges, and the provincial universities into which they have been transformed, runs from a couple of hundred to over a thousand; while the persons enrolled in the evening classes are often still more numerous. But it may be observed that the proportion, even of the day scholars, who follow a complete course and get a degree, is distinctly small.[2]

**Public Grants to Universities.**

In spite of their large endowments, Oxford and Cambridge are sorely in need of more funds, which they are trying with limited success to raise among their graduates. They receive no aid from public sources; but the provincial universities and university colleges, being intended to educate the mass of the people, are assisted both by the national government and by the local councils, and this although they are in some cases not without considerable endowments of their own. The grants from the national government are given partly by the Education Department, on account of scientific courses and the training of teachers; sometimes partly by the Agricultural Department also, on account of instruction in farming; and partly in the form of direct Treasury grants. These last run from £1000 to £4000 a year, being based in most cases on the income

[1] In the following year Owens College was wholly incorporated in the University by statute.

[2] *Cf.* Reports from Univ. Colleges for 1904, Com. Papers, 1905, XXV., 103.

of the institution from other sources.[1] The grants from local authorities are made under the provision in the Act of 1902 for assistance to any education not elementary, and as the clause is permissive, they vary much in size. They are made by the councils of the counties and boroughs where the university is situated, and in smaller sums by those of neighbouring places whose people profit by the instruction. The subventions given in this way are often large. Thus in 1905 the University of Liverpool received from the city £10,000, in addition to a special gift of a building and site valued at £30,000; while from other neighbouring councils it received £2300 more. In the same year the University of Leeds obtained annual grants of more than £15,000 from similar sources, Sheffield received a little more, Birmingham £7000 and Manchester about £6000.[2]

**Aims of the Provincial Universities.**

The provincial universities are quite unlike Oxford and Cambridge, both in aims and methods. In many ways they resemble more nearly the Scotch universities, and, no doubt from a similarity of conditions, the universities in America, especially the newer and smaller ones. In the first place, they are not collections of colleges, and do not undertake to foster the common life in an academic community which is the dominant note by the Isis and the Cam. The University of Durham, founded earlier than the others, was indeed originally framed on the pattern of Oxford, and still houses its academic students in a college and a hall; but the provincial universities as a class, while sometimes possessing or licensing hostels, seem to do so for the convenience of a few of the students, not in order to promote a collegiate life.

The standard of general education is not so high as at

[1] The University of London receives £8000 a year in addition to the Treasury grants to three of its constituent colleges.

[2] Sadler, Report on Sec. and Higher Educ. in Newcastle, 1905, p. 59. For the year ending March 31, 1904, the London County Council granted to the University of London £10,000, and to the colleges forming part of it £5762 10*s*. more. Rep. Tech. Educ. Board, 1903–04, p. 65.

Oxford or Cambridge, and there is a more prevalent tone of direct utility. The provincial universities are coeducational,[1] and in the department of arts, women form a large contingent, often heavily outnumbering the men. The other departments, such as law, medicine and applied science or engineering, are distinctly professional schools, and collectively they usually contain a much larger number of men than the department of arts.

**The Methods of Instruction.** Like Oxford and Cambridge, the provincial universities confer usually both an ordinary degree and an honour degree based upon higher and more specialised attainment. But in the methods of instruction one observes a significant tendency. In the ancient universities the examination is the important thing, and from the point of view of the undergraduate, at least, the lectures are a voluntary matter useful as a means of preparing for the final ordeal. At the provincial universities, on the other hand, the student is required to attend a certain number of courses; and while doing faithful work in these is not, as in Scotland and America, the essential requisite for a degree, but a separate examination is held in which professors from other places take part, yet there is evidently a tendency to base the degree, and especially, perhaps, the ordinary degree, on specific courses of instruction. In short, there seems to be a tendency to make teaching the important thing, and to examine on a course rather than a subject, a process that is likely to involve more detailed information and less general culture.

**Their Form of Government.** The method of government also shows traces of likeness to that found in Scotland and the United States. The legislative power in Oxford and Cambridge is vested in an assembly of those graduates who keep their names upon the register by the payment of a small fee. The executive control for current matters is virtually placed in the hands

[1] At Oxford and Cambridge there are colleges and halls for women, which have, however, no official connection with the university. Their members are admitted to most of the lectures and examinations, and if successful are given certificates, but not degrees.

of a smaller body chosen from certain categories of university and college officers. The Chancellor, nominally the head of the university, is usually a great nobleman, formerly valuable as its protector, but now an ornamental figure so far as the internal administration of the institution is concerned; while the Vice-Chancellor, who is entitled to exercise his powers in his absence, has really little authority, for he is changed frequently, and in fact the office passes by rotation among the heads of the different colleges. Now in the provincial universities and university colleges, the outward form of organisation is very much the same, except that the supreme power, instead of being vested in the graduates, is commonly entrusted to a court or council of governors—a numerous body whose members are selected by processes of every kind. Some of them are official personages, some are appointed for life in various ways, some are chosen to represent the instructing staff, the council of the borough and other bodies, and some are benefactors or annual subscribers. But as in the Scotch and American universities, and in the separate colleges of Oxford and Cambridge, there is a permanent executive head. This is the Vice-Chancellor or Principal, who by holding his post for an indefinite period is in a position to lay plans for the future, and thus acquire a really great influence on the destiny of the institution.

That the provincial universities should bear a resemblance to those of Scotland and America, is perhaps due to the fact that like them they serve the great mass of the people; and certainly they are an appropriate capping stone to the modern edifice of popular education in England.

# CHAPTER L

## EDUCATION IN SCOTLAND

THE continual need of distinct legislation for Scotland is well illustrated by the history of public schools on the two sides of the Tweed. The Scotch entered on the path of popular education a couple of centuries before the English, and during the changes of the last forty years they have kept ahead. What is more, their system from the outset has been national to a degree that in England has never yet been attained.

Earlier History of the Schools.

After the lands of the Church had been confiscated at the Reformation a number of attempts were made, especially by the clergy, to set up schools for the people throughout the kingdom. Statutes were, in fact, passed to authorise local taxation for the purpose, but the object was only partially accomplished before the Revolution. Finally in 1696 an act was passed which created the common school system of Scotland.[1] It directed the heritors, that is, the freeholders or landowners, together with the minister in every parish, to provide a schoolhouse and a salary for a schoolmaster, the expense to be defrayed by the levy of a local rate. By this means a school was in the end established in every parish in the land.

The Parish Schools.

In the parish schools provided under the Act of 1696 the schoolmaster was chosen by the heritors and minister; but according to a principle sanctioned by the Act of 1803 he was approved and supervised by the presbytery, that is,

[1] Craik, "The State in its Relation to Education," Ch. viii.; 2d Report of Com. on Schools in Scotland, Com. Papers, 1867, XXV., 1, pp. xxvi *et seq.* Both the second and third reports of this Commission contain a vast amount of information about Scotch education.

the ministers and elders of the churches in the district, and he was required to sign the Confession of Faith and the Formula of the Church of Scotland. The schools were therefore under the control of the Established Church, but there was very little friction on that ground. In 1829 the General Assembly of the Church directed the schoolmasters not to press on Roman Catholic children any instruction to which parents or priest might object, and the charters of schools founded by the Church itself contained a conscience clause.[1] The differences between the Presbyterian sects turned on such matters as the right to present to benefices, not on doctrine; and even when many denominational schools arose in the middle of the nineteenth century the choice of a school by the parents, including Episcopalians and Roman Catholics, was affected over most of the country very little by the denomination to which it belonged.[2]

The schoolmaster was appointed during good behaviour, *ad vitam aut culpam*, it was said; and while this did harm in protecting men who had become incompetent, it gave, as in the case of the parish clergy, a sense of security and proprietorship which must have had its value in the earlier times before teaching became a competitive profession.

**Their Nature.** The parish schools were by no means intended for the working people alone. In their second report the Commissioners on the Schools in Scotland said: "It is the peculiarity of the parish schools of Scotland that from their very foundation they have been frequented by persons of every order. . . . Upon their benches the children of every rank in life have met, and have contended for honours earned only by higher natural gifts or superior moral qualities."[3] Nor were these schools purely elementary. Many of the masters had studied at a university,[4] and took

[1] 2d Rep. of Com., Com. Papers, 1867, XXV., 1, p. xxx.
[2] *Ibid.*, pp. xix–xx, xxv–xxvi. [3] *Ibid.*, p. cv.
[4] This was always true. In 1901 twenty-two per cent of the masters in the public elementary schools were university graduates (Graham Balfour, "Educ. Systems of Great Britain and Ireland," 2d Ed., 278), and in view of

pride in preparing their brightest pupils to go there. Very few boys went from any one school, but in the aggregate the number of students at the universities from parish schools, and others of a similar character, was large. In fact, the commissioners found that in the sixties it was about one quarter of the whole student body.[1] A road to the highest education was always open to any lad, a road sometimes travelled by the sons of the poorest parents.

**Parish Schools Insufficient.**

A scheme of education which furnished only one school and one teacher in each parish became inadequate as population increased. This was true even in the lowland country districts, where the number of schools was very considerable, and in 1803 an attempt was made to improve matters by providing for a second or side school in any parish that needed it; but two schools were soon far from enough. In the western highlands, and still more in the islands off the coast, where the parishes covered a vast area, the supply was from the first wholly insufficient. Moreover, the Act of 1696 did not apply to the royal burghs; and although there the burgh schools supplied a good deal of elementary as well as secondary instruction, they supplied it almost exclusively to the middle class, and, at any rate in later times, did not reach the mass of the people.[2]

**Government Grants.**

Not long after the need of more schools became urgently felt, and while attempts to fill the gaps by voluntary effort were in active progress, the first grants were made by the national treasury to assist the building of schoolhouses. With the stimulus thus given the number of sectarian schools grew rapidly, the pace being soon quickened by the split in the Established Church, and the formation in 1843 of the Free Church which covered the land with schools of its own. By the middle of the century the denomina-

the large proportion of students at the Scotch universities who did not take a degree, the number of masters who had studied there must have been still greater.

[1] Com. Papers, 1867, XXV., 1, pp. cii–ciii.

[2] 3d Rep. of Com. on Schools in Scotland, Com. Papers, 1867–68, XXIX., 1, p. 156.

tional outnumbered the parish schools, while subscription, private and other schools were more numerous than either.[1] Still the supply was not large enough, especially in the cities and in the highlands and islands. On the whole, the schools were efficient, and the report of the Scotch commission presents on this score a marked contrast with that of the corresponding commission on popular education in England. But, as the commissioners point out, the policy of giving support to denominational schools depended on wholly different principles from a national system, and was not in harmony with Scotch ideas.[2]

**Effect of the Revised Code of 1861.**

The Revised Code of 1861, which introduced the principle of payment by results, made the differences between the English and Scotch methods so clear that they could not be ignored. It certainly did much good in keeping the schools up to a fixed standard of efficiency, but in two important respects it was inconsistent with Scotch traditions of national education. Under it the parliamentary grants were expressly made "to promote the education of children belonging to the classes who support themselves by manual labour." This was all very well in England, where the public elementary schools were filled by children of that kind alone; but in Scotland, where all the children from the country-side went to school together, an attempt to draw a line among them for the purpose of grants on any such basis was repellent and impracticable. Then the code provided that payments should be made only for passes in the elementary subjects, and hence it was alleged that the masters would be deterred from preparing the rare bright boy for the university — a service which had been the glory of their profession.[3] The complaints were so loud that, while the inspection under the code was retained, the basis of payment was not carried out.

Reviewing the whole matter, the Commission on Schools in Scotland recommended, in 1867, a plan for completing

[1] 2d Report of Com., *op. cit.*, App., Table II.
[2] *Ibid.*, pp. cvi *et seq.*
[3] *Ibid.*, pp. cii, cv.

The Act of 1872.

popular education, based as far as possible on the national system of parish schools; and a few years later this was adopted in the Act of 1872. The Scotch statute differed from the English one of two years before in several ways. It set up school boards everywhere. By transferring to them the parish schools, and giving them all future building grants, it entrusted them with the duty of completing popular education, instead of merely supplementing voluntary effort. As denominational teaching had caused no bitterness in Scotland, it allowed them to give such religious instruction as they pleased, subject to a time-table conscience clause. It established the principle, at least, of universal compulsory attendance, although the machinery for enforcement was for a time defective; and it gave to the school boards the control of secondary as well as of elementary education.

The kingdom was divided into districts corresponding in general with the parishes and burghs, and in each district a school board was elected by the owners and occupiers of four pounds annual value by cumulative voting. The boards were given charge not only of the parish and burgh schools and of such new ones as they might build, but also of any others that might be transferred to them. The last provision was by no means inoperative; for although the denominational as well as the board schools were entitled to parliamentary grants,[1] almost all of them, except those belonging to the Episcopalians and the Roman Catholics, were transferred to the school boards within a few years.[2]

[1] 35–36 Vic., c. 62, § 67.

[2] Balfour," Educational Systems," 2d Ed., pp. 127–28. In 1904 the number of schools of different kinds receiving annual grants was as follows (Com. Papers, 1905, XXIX., 1, p. 8): —

| | |
|---|---|
| School Board | 2834 |
| Church of Scotland | 18 |
| Free Church | 6 |
| Episcopal | 66 |
| Roman Catholic | 196 |
| Undenominational | 69 |
| | 3189 |

Improvements, especially in the direction of enforcing attendance at school, have been made by subsequent legislation; and by a series of measures beginning in 1889 Scotland's shares of the subvention from the Treasury for local government has been used to make elementary education wholly free. A change has also been made in the central authority. When the Act of 1872 was passed, a distinct committee of the Privy Council was established for Scotland, but the responsibility to Parliament remained with the English minister. In 1885, however, when a Secretary for Scotland was appointed, he was put at the head of the Scotch Education Department, and a separate secretary was appointed to take permanent charge of the work. The organisation effected by these measures remains substantially unchanged, and thus Scotland has returned to a truly national system of popular education in entire harmony with the spirit of her traditions.

**The Burgh Schools.**

The grammar schools of Scotland trace their history back to the Middle Ages, and by the care of the town councils they grew in strength after the Reformation. When the Commission made its report in 1867 the schools of this kind under the direct control of the town councils, together with public academies managed by trustees, often jointly with those councils, numbered eighty-six or eighty-seven, and they were so distributed that almost every burgh in Scotland had one or more such schools supplying education to the middle classes.[1] The quantity of pupils attending them was greater in proportion to population than in other countries of Europe, and they were said to be superior to the majority of English grammar schools.[2] Much of the instruction was, it is true, elementary in character, but most of them gave real secondary education to all who wanted it, and great as was the attendance they were large

[1] 3d Report, Com. Papers, 1867–68, XXIX., 1, pp. vii, lxxvii. All but twenty-seven of them appear to have been under the control of the town councils.

[2] *Ibid.*, pp. viii–xi.

enough to include more boys than applied for admission. The problem of secondary schools in the cities was therefore not a pressing one.

The Act of 1872 turned the burgh schools over to the new school boards, although it was not until 1878 that these bodies were given full power to maintain secondary education out of the proceeds of local school rates. In 1892, and again in 1896, acts were passed granting subventions from the national government to aid secondary schools. But it is unnecessary to follow these changes in detail; it is enough to point out that in Scotland, from the infant class to the university, the work of the last thirty-five years has been to complete a system already in vigorous existence, rather than to create anything new.

**The Universities.** The Scotch universities are an integral part of the system of popular instruction. They have long been attended by people of all classes, for the craving for education in Scotland is widespread. The middle-class burgh schools and academies, which might be supposed to be their natural feeders, furnished in the sixties less than half of their students,[1] while one quarter, as we have seen, came from the parish schools. The cost of a university education was, indeed, so small as to be within reach of the poor, and in fact the Commission of 1865 found that of the students in the arts departments of the four Scotch universities, the fathers of nineteen and a half per cent were artisans or labourers.[2] Under such conditions it was not unnatural that a part of the instruction should not have been above the secondary grade. With the introduction of examinations for matriculation this has disappeared, but there is still truth in the saying that the Scotch universities teach a man how to earn, and Oxford and Cambridge how to spend, £1000 a year.

Financially, the four Scotch universities have prospered of late years almost beyond the limits of frugal virtue.

[1] 3d Report of Com. on Schools in Scotland, p. 157.
[2] *Ibid.*, pp. 154–56.

Besides occasional grants for buildings, they now receive among them nearly £72,000 a year from the government, and in 1901 Mr. Carnegie put £2,000,000 in trust for them, the income to be used partly in paying students' fees and partly for scientific and general purposes. If with the smaller resources of the past they did not attain the standard of undergraduate scholarship in Oxford and Cambridge, they produced many distinguished men, and have had many eminent scholars in their chairs. Rich Scotchmen to-day send their sons to the great public schools and universities of England more than they did formerly; but for the rest of the people the Scotch universities remain what they have always been, national institutions and the fitting completion of a national plan of education.

# PART V. — THE CHURCH

## CHAPTER LI

### ORGANIZATION OF THE CHURCH

IF a treatise on the universities would be out of place in a work of this kind, an attempt to describe the manifold operations of the Church of England would be absurd; and yet American readers may well be so unfamiliar with the position of the Church as to misconceive its relation to public affairs. The following pages are written, therefore, with a stronger feeling than ever that they contain nothing of which an Englishman is not fully aware. No pretence is, of course, made here to discuss the merits and defects of the system, or to consider the proposals for a change. The object in view is merely to make clear the structure of the Church so far as that is necessary for an understanding of its connection with the public life of the nation; and the statements made relate to the legal and political, not the religious, aspects of the matter.

**Character of the Church.** The Church possesses organs so arranged and distributed as to imply a closely knit, if not a centralised, form of self-government; and yet those organs have so little power, either legislative or administrative, and the units are so independent, that for practical purposes the Church resembles a profession rather than an organisation. It has an assembly which can exert no authority over its structure, doctrine or ritual, and which cannot even discuss these matters, or offer advice upon them, without the consent of the Crown — a consent not given at all for the hundred and twenty years preceding the reign of Queen Victoria, and not given with entire freedom now. It has bishops and archbishops whom it does not select, whose right to give orders to the clergy is extremely small, and who cannot, as a rule, discipline, punish or remove a single parson, except by means of legal proceedings before lay judges, ending perchance in a court of appeal in the selection of whose members the Church has no voice. The parsons, indeed, forming the bulk of the working clergy, do not, in most cases, owe their livings to ecclesiastical appointment, or necessarily even to Churchmen; and so long as they obey the law, as laid down by Parliament and interpreted by the courts, they are virtually free from ecclesiastical control. The authority of the bishop over them is moral rather than legal, and is not always effective. What is more, the parson is independent of his own parishioners, no less than of everybody else, in regard to tenure of office, duties and emoluments. Such a condition could hardly exist if the rights and functions of every member of the body were not prescribed by law, and in fact the Church is rigidly bound in every direction by statutes, which can be changed only by Parliament, and are not often touched.

**Archbishops and Bishops.**

England is divided for the purposes of the Established Church into the two provinces of Canterbury and York, each with an archbishop at its head. The former, being very much the larger, is subdivided into twenty-seven sees with twenty-six bishops, the archbishop himself having direct charge of the diocese of Canterbury. The province of York is subdivided in the same way into ten sees and has nine bishops. In form, an archbishop or bishop is still elected by the dean and chapter; that is, by the dean and canons of the cathedral, but the *congé d'élire* from the Crown, which conveys the authority to elect, is accompanied by a letter missive, designating the person to be chosen, and they must choose him under the pains and penalties of a praemunire. The appointment is, therefore, really made by the Crown, or rather by the Prime Minister with the consent of the Crown. Like almost every officer in the Church, from the perpetual curate upward, the bishop enjoys a tenure for life. Formerly all the bishops sat in the House of Lords; but when new sees were created in the middle of the last century it was provided that the two archbishops, with the Bishops of London, Durham and Winchester, should always have seats, and only twenty-one of the others in the order of seniority of appointment; so that at present there are eleven bishops who do not sit among the peers.[1]

**Suffragan Bishops.**

In addition to the ordinary bishops, a suffragan bishop may be appointed for any such place as the Crown in Council may direct. His see lies within a regular diocese. He is selected by the Crown from two candidates nominated by the bishop, and he is, in fact, an assistant in the episcopal office. He performs such duties, including confirmation, ordination of priests and the like, as the bishop may charge him with; but he is not a member of the Upper House of Convocation, and has no seat in the House of Lords. There are now about a score of suffragan bishops, three of them within the diocese of London.

**Deans and Chapters.**

Next in order of dignity come the deans and canons of the cathedrals and of collegiate churches which, like Westminster Abbey, have a chapter without a bishop. The deans are, as a rule, appointed directly by the Crown; but in the case of canons there is much diversity, some of them being designated by the Crown and others by the bishops, while the chapter itself has sometimes a right to elect them. The position of the dean and canons has in the process of time become anomalous. They have no longer any connection with the administration of the diocese, and, on the other hand, they have the entire management of the cathedral, over which the bishop himself has really no more control than over the other churches in his see.

**Archdeacons and Rural Deans.**

The principal assistants of the bishop in his administration of local matters are the archdeacons and rural deans, both appointed, as a rule, by him. The diocese is divided into archdeaconries, and within each of these an arch-

[1] The bishop of Sodor and Man has a seat but no vote.

deacon performs the duty of visitation, with some small jurisdiction of his own. The archdeaconries are again subdivided into deaneries; but the rural dean, whose tenure of office is temporary, has power only to inspect and report.

The Clergy.

By far the greater part of the ministrations of the Church are conducted by the parish clergy. No one can be intrusted with a cure of souls until he has been ordained a priest by a bishop, who must be satisfied with his religious, moral and intellectual qualifications.[1] But ordination confers only a right to accept clerical employment, just as admission to the bar gives the capacity to hold a brief; and the employment comes, as a rule, not from any ecclesiastical body, whether clerical officer or congregation, but from a patron.

Advowsons.

Almost all the clergy in charge of parish churches hold benefices, or livings as they are commonly called, which lie in the gift of some person or body, the right to present to the living being legally termed an advowson. It is probable that from early times the founder of a church had occasionally a right to appoint to the living. It is certain that upon the dissolution of the monasteries and the granting away of their lands, many advowsons passed into lay hands, and at the present day about one half of the benefices in England are in the gift of lay patrons. The other half are in the gift of the Crown, the Lord Chancellor, the bishops, the deans and chapters, and the universities or their colleges, the bishops and the cathedral chapters having by far the largest share.[2] The owner of the advowson has not, indeed, an absolute right to appoint; he has only a right to present, and the bishop of the diocese may refuse institution if the candidate is unfit.[3] The ground

Presentment and Institution.

[1] A deacon is ordained in the same way. He can, it seems, perform all the offices of a priest, except consecrating the sacrament of the Lord's Supper and pronouncing the absolution, but he cannot hold any benefice. Phillimore, "Ecclesiastical Law," 2 Ed., I., 109–10.

[2] Elliot, "The State and the Church," 2 Ed., 121.

[3] In a few cases a patron had formerly a right to appoint without institution by the bishop. Such benefices were termed donative, but they were made presentative by the Benefices Act, 1898, 61–62 Vic., c. 48, § 12. Where the bishop himself possesses the advowson he naturally does not go through the form of presenting to himself, and is said to collate to the benefice.

of refusal, however, must be a personal one, based on the unfitness of the candidate to hold any benefice. It is not enough that, although a worthy man, he is wholly unsuited for the parish in question.[1] In fact, the right to refuse is not discretionary. The grounds of refusal must be legal, and in general they are much the same as in the case of ordination. For an improper refusal the candidate has a remedy by duplex querela in the ecclesiastical courts, and the patron by quare impedit in the civil tribunals. But the state of the law was felt to be unsatisfactory, and by the Benefices Act of 1898, a number of grounds for refusal were specified, with an appeal to a tribunal composed of the archbishop and a judge of the Supreme Court.[2] Refusals are, in fact, very rare.[3]

**Advowsons are Property.**

Religious institutions are proverbially conservative, and it is perhaps for this reason that the general tendency to regard every kind of public authority as a public trust has hardly touched advowsons. They are still treated as private property, which is inherited and can be sold like land. They may pass into the hands of Dissenters, Jews, Turks, infidels and heretics, who can nevertheless present to the living; for except in the case of Roman Catholics, where by statute the right to present is exercised by the universities, and of aliens where it is exercised by the Crown, there is no provision for the orthodoxy of a patron. The payment of money by a clergyman for his presentation to a living has, indeed, been treated throughout Christendom as a monstrous crime, known as simony, after Simon Magus

[1] But a lack of knowledge of Welsh is a good ground for refusing to admit to a benefice in Wales. Phillimore, "Ecclesiastical Law," 2 Ed., I., 325.

[2] The Act specified physical unfitness, pecuniary embarrassment, grave misconduct, neglect of clerical duty, and being privy to the purchase of the presentment for his own benefit. The appeal lies whenever a bishop refuses institution for any of these reasons, or on any other ground (lack of education, for example), except unsoundness in doctrine; and when the appeal is heard, the judge decides the law and fact, the archbishop whether the facts, if legally sufficient, constitute unfitness.

[3] During the five years 1899–1903 there were in all only four refusals under the Act. Com. Papers, 1900, LXIII., 527, p. 21; 1901, LIV., 901, p. 20; 1904, LXXIV., 507, p. 76.

its inventor. But in England the law was formerly evaded by various devices, and advertisements of livings for sale, public auctions and contracts of purchase through brokers, where the price was enhanced by the decrepitude of the incumbent, were everyday affairs. The Benefices Act of 1898 was designed to prevent the purchase of a particular appointment, and with that object forbade reconveyance immediately after presentment. But the Act made no attempt to restrict genuine sales of advowsons; it required merely that they should be registered, and in the very next year seventy-five transfers were recorded, which appears to be somewhat less than the usual number.[1]

**Motives for Presentment.**

The living attached to an estate was considered the birthright of a younger son; one in the gift of a college was the perquisite of a fellow. In fact, the idea of providing a living for some dependent formerly overshadowed the spiritual welfare of the parishioners. This is far less true to-day, and presentments are usually made with a conscientious regard to the moral and intellectual qualifications of the candidate. Still the special needs of the parish seem rarely to be taken into account. The college tries to select a deserving scholar, the official or lay patron an earnest man; but further than this there appears, as a rule, to be little if any attempt to consult the wishes, or heed the circumstances, of the parishioners. Such a system produces at the present day far better results than a stranger might expect; for the clergy, especially the high-church clergy, display great energy and devotion in parochial and social work.

**Absence of Desire for Selection by the Parish.**

Nor is there any general desire on the part of congregations to select their own pastors. The recent Commission on Ecclesiastical Discipline did, indeed, receive a memorial from a number of church wardens in Manchester, urging the advantage of requiring the consent of the vestry before the institution of a clergyman.[2] But such a feel-

[1] Com. Papers, 1900, LXIII., 527; 1901, LIV., 901; 1904, LXXIV., 507.
[2] Com. Papers, 1906, XXX., 1, p. 5.

ing is decidedly uncommon; and this is the more surprising because in Scotland, after the question of the right of a congregation to veto the appointment by the patron had, in 1843, brought about a breach and the formation of the Free Church, the objection to patronage became so general in the Established Church itself that it was abolished in 1874. Since that time the minister has been chosen by the communicants and adherents in the parish. In England the matter could not be arranged so simply. To make communicants alone the electing body would violate the principle that the English Church includes everybody, and in the few cases, notably in London, where the parishioners have enjoyed the privilege of choosing their own clergyman, the right has been exercised by the old parish vestry composed of all the ratepayers. This has not worked well, for since many of the ratepayers care nothing about the Church, and may even be Dissenters, efforts to obtain their votes by treating or other improper means have at times caused scandals. If a congregation has no voice in the selection of the clergyman, it is clearly necessary that the ritual should be fixed; and the very fact that it is fixed by law makes the choice of persons less important, especially as preaching is by no means so weighty a part of the functions of a clergyman in the Church of England as in most other Protestant bodies. But before speaking of the regulation of the ritual it may be well to describe the status of a settled clergyman.

**The Status of Incumbents.**

Holders of livings, or incumbents, are styled rectors, vicars or perpetual curates, the rector enjoying the whole, and the vicar a part, of the tithes, while the perpetual curate has a stipend in money.[1] But they are all alike in the fact that they have a life estate in their offices and revenues, of which they can be divested only by resignation or by the sentence of a court for clerical or moral miscon-

[1] This is not now the legal distinction, for by statute any incumbent who has power to solemnise marriages, baptisms, etc., is styled vicar. 31–32 Vic., c. 117.

duct.[1] They owe their appointment to the owner of the advowson, but once appointed they are not under his control or that of the parish, and possess the living in their own right as a freehold. About two thirds of the parish clergy in England are incumbents of livings, the rest being assistant curates, serving during the pleasure of the incumbent who appoints and pays them. Unlike the holders of livings, therefore, these curates have no permanent right to their positions, and they must obtain also from the bishop of the diocese a license which he can revoke for any cause that may seem to him sufficient.[2]

Uniformity in Ritual.

The doctrine and ritual of the Church of England were framed by Convocation and then sanctioned by statute, so that they can be changed only by Act of Parliament. The Thirty-Nine Articles, which embody the doctrines of the Church, were confirmed by statute in 1571;[3] the present Prayer Book was adopted by the Act of Uniformity of 1662;[4] while vestments are regulated by the advertisements of 1566, and church ornaments by the Ornaments Rubric and Edward the Sixth's Prayer Book of 1549.[5] Although so long a period has elapsed the only changes made in these matters have been those in the Acts of 1871, 1872 and 1880, which authorised the use of a different table of lessons, of shortened forms of service, and of departures from the regular liturgy for burial.[6] Most creeds have been framed to settle a doctrinal dispute, to brand a dogma as heretical, and hence to exclude, from the company of the faithful, men who claimed that their views were orthodox. But the design of the Thirty-Nine Articles was comprehensive; it was their aim to include a wide range of opinion. In the Prayer Book, on the other hand,

[1] When an incumbent is disabled by age or infirmity from performing his duties the bishop can, upon the report of a commission, require him to appoint and pay a curate; and indeed he can require it in any case where the parish needs the curate.

[2] Subject, however, to an appeal to the archbishop.

[3] 13 Eliz., c. 12. [4] 13–14 Car. II., c. 4. [5] 3–4 Edw. VI., c. 10.

[6] 34–35 Vic., c. 37; 35–36 Vic., c. 35; 43–44 Vic., c. 41.

although the latitude of belief is great, the ritual is very minutely prescribed. "The obligation to conform to the standard is rigid." "No omission and no addition can be permitted. The distinction between what is important and what appears to be trivial has been expressly and emphatically precluded." [1]

**Not Strictly Enforced.** The provisions of the Act of Uniformity have, in fact, never been strictly observed by the clergy, nor since the latter part of the seventeenth century has there been any systematic effort to enforce them. Until sixty or seventy years ago the departures from the prescribed forms were mainly in the nature of omissions, and in the direction of low-church ceremonial,[2] but about that time the ritualistic movement began, and the rites and vestments of Roman pattern, which it has brought in with increasing zeal, have of late years sorely troubled many people in the Church. The result has been a series of proceedings before ecclesiastical officers and courts to determine the legality of various practices; but they have neither produced uniformity nor banished discontent.

**Mode of Enforcing Discipline.** Assistant curates may have their licenses revoked by the bishop, and although this power is not always used where infringements of the ritual would seem to justify it,[3] the real difficulty comes, not in their case, but in that of permanent incumbents. The latter, save in a few cases such as engaging in trade or failure to reside in the parish, can be disturbed in the enjoyment of their benefices only by proceedings under one or other of three statutes. These are the Church Discipline Act, 1840, which applies to misconduct of all kinds; the Public Worship Regulation Act, 1874, which applies only to ritual and vestments; and the Clergy Discipline Act, 1892, which applies only to offences against morality. The forms of procedure are different under these Acts, but they have two points in common:

[1] Rep. of Com. on Eccles. Discipline, Com. Papers, 1906, pp. xxx, 1, 6–7.
[2] *Ibid.*, pp. 9, 54 *et seq.*
[3] *Ibid.*, p. 74.

first, that unless both complainant and defendant consent to submit to a final decision by the bishop in person, the trial takes place in the first instance, or on appeal, in an ecclesiastical court where the judge is a layman, and a final appeal lies to the Judicial Committee of the Privy Council;[1] second, that no proceedings can be instituted without the consent of the bishop. Both of these matters are important.

Objection to a Secular Court.

An incumbent is protected in the enjoyment of his benefice by law. He cannot be suspended, deprived or even admonished for alleged misconduct, except in accordance with the law as interpreted in the last instance by a purely secular court; for although the archbishops and bishops appoint the lay judges in their own ecclesiastical tribunals,[2] the members of the Judicial Committee of the Privy Council are selected by the Crown, and the bishops attend only as assessors with merely an advisory voice. But it follows that the doctrine a clergyman must profess, the ritual that he must observe, the vestments he may wear, and the ornaments he may use are determined by a secular tribunal. It has often been pointed out that the Judicial Committee does not pretend to decide what the doctrine or ritual of the Church ought to be, but merely to interpret the statutes which regulate them. Still the fact that such a power should be in the hands of secular judges, instead of in those of the Church itself, is felt as a grievance by a large and growing part of the clergy, many of whom go so far as to deny that they are bound to obey the decision rendered; and the recent Commission on Ecclesiastical Discipline has declared that under these conditions the judgments of the Judicial Committee cannot practically

[1] By the Clergy Discipline Act, 1892 (55–56 Vic., c. 32), where a clergyman is convicted of crime, or adjudged guilty of certain grave offences in a court of law, the bishop must declare his benefice vacant without further proceedings.

[2] By the Public Worship Regulation Act, 1874, 37–38 Vic., c. 85, § 7, the judge of the two provincial courts is the same person. He is appointed by the two archbishops, subject to confirmation by the Crown.

be enforced.[1] But the jurisdiction of a state court over these matters, if not inevitable, is a natural result of the existing constitution of the Established Church, and would seem, as already observed, particularly needed when the parishioners have no voice in the selection of their clergyman, or control over his method of conducting the service.

Effect of the Bishop's Veto.

Impressed by the repugnance to the tribunal, by the objection to penalties that turn conscientious offenders into martyrs, and by the fear of forcing differences of opinion to the breaking point, the bishops have been reluctant to allow prosecutions. They have preferred to rely on their influence with their clergy, and to seek a compromise instead of attempting to enforce the rubrics strictly. Every priest at his ordination promises to obey the lawful commands of his bishop, and although this has a moral rather than a legal sanction, it has weight, especially with the extreme high-churchmen whose practices are making trouble. But while the efforts of the bishops have, in fact, had some effect, they have by no means produced universal conformity to the law. The Commission on Ecclesiastical Discipline came to the conclusion that the law of public worship was too narrow for the present generation, and that the machinery for discipline had broken down. It recommended, therefore, greater latitude in unessential matters, and changes in procedure and discipline which would in its opinion render possible a rigorous suppression of graver transgressions.[2]

Convocation.

The nearest approach to a legislative body in the Church of England is found in the Convocations of Canterbury and York. Each of these consists of two houses, which do not, however, always sit apart. The upper house consists of the archbishop and bishops of the province. The lower contains the deans of cathedral and collegiate churches,

[1] Report of 1906, pp. 4, 66–67.

[2] It recommended that the bishop's veto should be abolished, and that where in the court of final appeal a question of doctrine or ritual was not governed by the plain language of statute, it should be virtually decided by an assembly of all the bishops. Report of 1906, p. 78.

one proctor elected by the chapter of each of those churches, the archdeacons, and two proctors elected by the beneficed clergy in each diocese, or in the province of York two proctors for every archdeaconry. Of late years a representative house of laymen has met also for consultation, but it has no authority, and is not legally a part of Convocation. The Church has thus an organ for legislation, but it is bound hand and foot, for it is summoned and prorogued by the Crown, cannot transact business not authorised by royal "letters of business," and cannot alter a canon without a previous license, and subsequent consent to promulgate, from the Crown. Moreover, the canon when passed cannot, without the sanction of Parliament, bind the laity or change the law of the land, which includes among other things every service and rubric in the Prayer Book.

## CHAPTER LII

### REVENUES OF THE CHURCH

Property owned not by the Church but by Incumbents.

UNTIL the reign of Queen Victoria the Church of England had as a body as little authority over its revenues and expenditure as over its doctrine and ritual or the appointment of its officers. Even now the property at its disposal is limited and can be applied only to specified objects; for the Church as a whole, not being a body corporate, cannot legally own any property at all, and the commissioners who hold estates in trust for it are created by statute for certain definite purposes. But while the Church itself has no legal corporate existence, it contains a vast number of separate bodies of that kind. Not only is the chapter of a cathedral or collegiate church a corporation, but every bishop, dean, rector and vicar is a corporation sole, and they are among the oldest corporations known to the English law. As such they hold the land and revenues of their benefices by a perpetual tenure. The rector or vicar, for example, owns in this way the glebe or parsonage, and the rents and tithes that belong to his living. He has also the freehold of the church and churchyard, although he holds these last for the use of the parishioners.

Tithes.

The revenues of incumbents in the Church are drawn mainly from the rent of lands and from tithes, the parish clergy deriving by far the greater part of their income from the latter source. Tithes were a tenth of the annual increase of the land, paid for the support of religion according to precepts of the Old Testament which were adopted by Christian custom and sanctioned by law. The tenth was levied on the gross produce both of crops and of domestic animals or fowls, and in some cases on the net profits of fishing and other labour. Now before the Reformation many of the monastic houses collected the tithes from a large district, supplying in return priests for the parish churches; and when the monasteries were dissolved the tithes, or a part of them, passed with the abbey lands to the new grantees.[1] As a rule only the greater tithes, those on hay, grain and wood, passed in this way; while the lesser ones, on the remaining crops, on animals and other things, were left to the incumbent of the parish, who in such case is called a vicar. By his enjoyment of the lesser tithes alone he is distinguished on one hand from a rector who receives all the tithes, and on the other from a perpetual curate who receives none, but is paid instead a money stipend. In 1836 the total annual value of tithes in England was a little over £4,000,000, of which three fifths belonged to the parish clergy, less than one fifth to lay impropriators, about one sixth to bishops, deans and chapters, and nearly £200,000 to colleges.[2] It may be observed that these tithes, and the money payments for which they have been commuted, cannot be regarded to-day as a state tax for the support of religion. They are a species of property of which nearly a quarter is neither paid to the Church nor used for its benefit.

**Commutation and Redemption of Tithes.**

Until 1836 a large part of the tithes were still paid in kind, but an act of that year provided in almost all cases for their commutation into a money payment called tithe rent-charge. This rises or falls annually according to the ratio which the average price of wheat, barley and oats for the preceding seven years bears to the price of those grains in 1837. By subsequent statutes, provision was made for the redemption of the rent-charges by the payment of a capital sum in money, but with the continual decline in the price of grain this has not been done to any great

[1] Tithes so acquired by a layman are said to be impropriated; those owned by a religious body other than the incumbent of the living are said to be appropriated.

[2] Com. Papers, 1892, XLVII., 355, Qs., 5–12.

extent.[1] The extension in the area of land under cultivation in the eighteenth century increased the income of the clergy; but the fall in the price of grain during the last sixty years, and the fact that profits from mines and manufactures and the rent of buildings, not being an increase from land, pay no tithes, has made the income of the Church smaller in proportion to the national wealth than it was formerly.[2]

Queen Anne's Bounty.

Two hundred years ago the income of many livings was miserably small, and Queen Anne granted to commissioners the first-fruits and tenths, which had been exacted by the Pope from the clergy, and annexed by Henry VIII. to the Crown. The fund thus formed, still known as Queen Anne's Bounty, is used to augment small livings. For eleven years, from 1809 to 1820, Parliament added to it £100,000 a year, and much has been accomplished in improving the lot of poor incumbents. But the provision was not designed, nor was it sufficient, to found new churches, and in fact the whole ecclesiastical system was singularly inelastic. It was adapted to the support of the clergy in an agricultural and unchanging community. This was especially felt after the middle of the eighteenth century, when the growth of manufactures, which paid no tithes, shifted the population about. Large towns grew up where the Established Church had only clergy and buildings enough for a rural village and possessed no effective means of increasing them. In such places the dissenting bodies, with their less rigid organisation, made rapid progress. To remedy this state of things, the Church Building Commission was created in 1818, and given by Parliament a million of pounds, increased later by half a million more.

Further action was brought about by the inquiries of

[1] The report of a commission in 1892 showed that only $\frac{1}{205}$ of the tithe rent-charge had been redeemed; adding the amount cancelled by merger it came to $\frac{1}{59}$. Com. Papers, 1892, XLVII., 341, p. vii.

[2] Elliot, "The State and the Church," 2 Ed., 85. In 1891 the total revenue of the Church from all sources was returned by the Ecclesiastical Commissioners as £57,753,557. Com. Papers, 1890–91, LXI., 59.

a commission appointed in 1835, which reported that the revenues of the bishoprics, and of some of the parish livings, were extremely unequal, and that those of cathedral and collegiate churches were excessive. In consequence of these reports the episcopal incomes were readjusted by statute, the revenues of cathedral and collegiate churches were cut down, and the surplus thus formed was placed in the charge of a board of Ecclesiastical Commissioners to be used in augmenting small livings and creating new ones.[1] By the original Act of 1836 the majority of the commissioners were laymen, but a few years later all the bishops were added, so that the administration of the fund is really in their hands. The powers of the Church Building Commission were afterward transferred to the same body, whose prudent management increased the revenue from the estates they manage; and thus, quite contrary to the earlier ecclesiastical system, the bishops now control a very large income which they apply in their discretion for the extension of parochial work.[2]

The Ecclesiastical Commission.

Early in the nineteenth century grants were made by Parliament to augment poor livings and build new churches, but nothing of that kind is done to-day. The funds for such purposes are now derived from a better application of ecclesiastical property, or from voluntary subscriptions. Parish churches also are no longer maintained by local taxation, for as already explained tithes cannot now be regarded as taxation, and church rates have been made voluntary. Until 1868 a rate was levied by the parish vestry for the repair of the church; but in that year an act was passed which provided, without formally abolishing the rate, that no proceeding of any kind should be taken

The Church is not Supported by Taxation.

[1] By later enactments all the estates and tithes of the bishoprics and cathedrals were transferred to the commissioners, who either reconveyed enough to produce the income fixed by law, or undertook to pay that income in money.

[2] In 1904 the net revenue of the commissioners above the sums paid to the bishops and cathedrals was about a million and a third of pounds. Com. Papers, 1905, XXIII., 713, pp. 6–7.

to enforce its payment. Hence it became in effect a free-will offering. If, therefore, we leave aside the vexed question of the voluntary schools, it may be stated that at the present day the Church is supported, not by taxation, but by the revenue from her own property and by the free gifts of her members.

**Disestablishment and Disendowment.**

It might seem that if the Church receives nothing from taxation, she would lose nothing by disestablishment; but this is by no means clear. When the Irish Church was disestablished the surplus revenue, above what was required for her proper support in the future and for compensation to persons injured by the change, was applied to charitable objects; and a similar course might be followed in England. Tithes, having become a private right to a rent-charge, could hardly be released, but the income of deans and canons, and a part of that of the bishops, might be considered unnecessary for a free church, and might be diverted into other channels; for although the revenues of the Church are not derived from taxation to-day, they might be regarded as in part at least national property, dedicated hitherto to one branch of the public service, the maintenance of a state church. The case of Ireland would certainly furnish a precedent for such a view.

The demand for disestablishment comes from two opposite quarters. It is heard as a loud cry from many Dissenters, and as a murmur from some of the high-church clergy who want the Church freed from the control of the state. The former complain of the presence of bishops in Parliament; they believe that religion should be a voluntary matter; and they object more particularly to the establishment of a church which has ceased to embody a national religion, which does not include a large part, perhaps not a majority, of the people, and does not include them. For Wales these claims have great force, because there Dissenters far outnumber the members of the Church of England, and in fact Welsh disestablishment has constantly figured in the programme of the National Liberal Federation. For the rest of the kingdom the question is more remote. Even those Churchmen who chafe under the civil power dread the fall in prestige and the possible reduction in revenue. They would like freedom from control without loss of privilege; but if disestablishment comes in the present generation, it will come from the other side. It will be the work of a Radical Parliament, and will not improbably be accompanied by some measure of disendowment.

**The Church as a Political Force.** With such a structure it is clear that the Church does not, and cannot, act in politics as an organised body. While the bishops are, of course, a force in the House of Lords, and there are voluntary political organisations of clergymen, the capacity of the Church as a whole for corporate action is very small. It is no doubt a real power in public life, but the power is that of a great profession with a strong sense of common interests. There are not a few Liberals among the clergy, but the vast bulk of men in orders feel that the welfare of the Church is in the keeping of the Conservative party, and for the time the bond has been drawn more tight by the struggle over the position of the voluntary schools. An established church which includes only a fraction of the nation has disadvantages; that it should be closely tied to one political party is a misfortune. Nevertheless the Church of England has given solidity to the political system. By reducing the emotional element in popular religion it has helped to discard fanaticism, and thus has had a steadying influence on the course of politics. Its missionary work among the poor, conducted with peculiar zeal by the high-church clergy, has contributed to the movement that has brought all classes into closer sympathy; while the very decentralisation of its structure has prevented it from assuming an official attitude that would tend to drive away those of its members, clerical and lay, who disagreed with its policy. In short the fact of establishment and the form of organisation have kept the Church from being politically a sect.

# CHAPTER LIII

## THE FREE CHURCH FEDERATION

DISSENTERS have been a great political force in England ever since the Reform Act of 1832 gave seats in Parliament to the new manufacturing towns in which their influence was great, and extended the franchise among the middle classes where their chief strength lay. Generally Liberals, and sometimes Radicals of an extreme type, they have played an important part in the history of the nineteenth century. But although in the main on the same side of public questions, and although their leading men, and even their ministers, have frequently thrown themselves warmly into political movements, the action has been that of individuals stirred by a common impulse rather than that of an organised host. The Nonconformists have, in fact, been separated into many religious bodies, often differing little if at all on doctrinal points, but quite distinct in history, in form of worship, and in church government. Such are the Congregationalists, the Baptists, the Presbyterians, the various kinds of Methodists, and the Quakers. Now these bodies, with a few others, have recently drawn closer together and formed a powerful organisation for the promotion of common aims.

Formation of the National Council.

Provoked in part by the aggressive attitude of the Church of England, there appeared in 1890 a suggestion for a Nonconformist church congress. The proposal bore fruit in a congress at Manchester in November, 1892, followed by another at Leeds in March, 1894, and when the latter separated a foundation had been fairly laid. A regular organisation had been adopted, and local councils comprising all the evangelical free churches of different denominations in a town or district had begun to be formed. These increased rapidly. In 1894 not more than a dozen of them were in existence; the next year there were one hundred and thirty; three years later five hundred; and so on until in 1906 they were only three short of nine hundred in number, and covered practically the whole of England and Wales. In fact, the Free Church Year Book for that year gives figures which show that there are almost as many communicants in the religious bodies belonging to the Federation as in the Church of England, while the sitting accommodation and number of Sunday-school scholars are decidedly larger.

Like other English associations the congress, later known as the National Council, holds a meeting every year in a different city. It is composed of the religious bodies already mentioned, with such other evangelical churches as the council may admit, and practically it includes all the evangelical Protestant churches in the country. In order, however, to emphasise the concord among the constituent elements, the delegates to the annual council do not represent the different churches, but the local councils, composed in their turn of all the free churches in their districts. Since there have been hitherto no serious differences of opinion in the Council it has not been necessary to prescribe in the constitution the number of delegates to which each local body shall be entitled, and in fact there are also many personal members of the Council, both ministers and laymen, who are entitled to take part in its work by virtue of an annual subscription. A president and other officers are chosen each year; and these, together with the ex-presidents, fifteen ministers and as many laymen elected by the Council, and a few coöpted members, form the executive committee. Through them the Federation maintains at Memorial Hall in London a permanent organisation, which issues publications, sends forth missioners like Gipsy Smith and Tolefree Parr, and acts as a stimulus to the whole Nonconformist body in the country.

Its Constitution.

The Local Councils.

More interesting even than the annual meeting, as a manifestation of the growing harmony among the Nonconformist churches, are the local councils. As we have already seen, these are now so universal as to include nearly the whole kingdom, and they bring together all the different evangelical denominations in a common effort to promote greater energy and avoid waste by overlapping. Where the plan is fully carried out, the area covered by the local council is divided into districts, one of which is allotted to each church to be worked as its especial parish. The church makes itself responsible so far as it can for the social and religious condition of that district, and for this purpose the minister and a corps of lay members conduct a house to house visitation of the inhabitants. The parochial system, as it is called, is an effective method of reaching all classes of people; but it implies complete mutual confidence and absence of jealousy among the churches. No attempt has been made to fuse the denominations together or to obliterate the differences between them, but merely to bring about a friendly coöperation; and the movement has certainly produced a more intimate fellowship among the churches, with a more frequent exchange of pulpits, than ever before. As the local councils increased, a need was felt of some intermediate link between them and the national association. District federations were therefore formed, composed for the most part of representatives from the local councils, with a president, executive committee and of course a secretary who is the mainspring of the machinery. England and Wales have been mapped out into fifty such federations, and thus the Free Churches have perfected for themselves an organisation of the type commonly adopted by other national voluntary associations in Great Britain.

Their Relation to Local Public Bodies.

Politics have a moral side and religion a practical application which are apt to come into contact, and in fact the formation of a Free Church Council in Birmingham in the early days of the movement was opposed on the ground that such bodies would be in danger of becoming "political and municipal caucuses."[1] That fear has certainly not been wholly justified, and yet from the very beginning the councils have taken an active part in elections for local representative bodies. In a manual entitled "The Work of a Free Church Council," issued by the secretary of the National Council, it is said to be "very desirable that every effort be made to put Free Church representatives on the various public bodies of a locality." A caution is indeed given "that we are not promoting any special political party, but are aiming to secure, first, the public good, and, secondly, that fair representation of Free Churchmanship which our numbers enable us to claim." Directions are given in the manual for the conduct of elections;[2] and in the annual reports of the national secretary frequent references are made to the effective work done at local elections by the councils and federations in different parts of the country.

**The Education Question and National Politics.**

Although in local elections the Free Church councils were naturally inclined to support Liberal candidates, their action was not conclusively partisan; but the struggle over the Education Act of 1902 drew the whole association definitely into the field of national party politics. After that Act was passed the annual councils demanded in effect the abolition of voluntary schools maintained by public taxation,[3] and the organisation was placed upon a war footing for the fight at the next general election of Parliament. The report for 1905 deprecated the necessity for so doing, saying that the Federation was a movement with spiritual objects and could take no part in ordinary politics, but that the situation was extraordinary and required extraordinary measures.[4] A special department for electoral work was therefore created; the local councils were spurred on to greater exertion; leaflets were issued;

[1] "The Free Church Federation Movement — A Historical Sketch," 20.
[2] pp. 70, 71, 120–24. [3] *E.g.*, Report for 1905, pp. 53–54.
[4] *Ibid.*, p. 61.

Nonconformists were urged to register; many of the more prominent of them were induced to become parliamentary candidates, and in not a few cases they were given aid by the National Council in defraying the expense of contesting a seat. In this way two hundred Free Churchmen were brought forward, who stood, of course, on the Liberal side, while other candidates were asked a series of questions, with the object of pledging them to support the educational policy of the council.

The Election of 1906.

No sooner did it become clear that a general election was close at hand than the officers of the National Council issued a manifesto, laying stress not only on education but also on temperance reform and Chinese indentured labour in South Africa. The document was not on its face an appeal in favour of the Liberal party, and one of the most pressing issues at stake, that of preferential tariffs, was not mentioned; but in effect the Free Church organisation made the Liberal cause in the election its own. It held great demonstrations in several provincial towns, and smaller gatherings throughout the land. Ministers took an active part in the fight, speaking at meetings both in the open air and under cover; while half a dozen of the most distinguished among them made tours of the country in motor cars, addressing enthusiastic audiences by the way. In fact, religion and politics went hand in hand. People were urged at prayer meetings to remember the general election, and at the political assemblies in some places they "broke out in fervent prayer."[1] The Education Act of 1902 had produced a sense of religious oppression, and Free Churchmen believed that they were fighting the battle of the Lord. When it was over they were convinced that their share in the combat had helped to win an overwhelming Liberal victory.

Political Prospects.

Throughout the struggle the National Council, although drawn into the political arena, felt that it was working for a religious, not a political end, and hoped that its connection

[1] Report for 1906, pp. 52, 58, 61.

with politics would be temporary. The report for 1906 said on the opening page: "It cannot be too often stated that the Federation Movement exists primarily and essentially for spiritual service. We are now hopeful that we shall have a cessation from the education conflict which was forced on us, and we rejoice in the confident belief that there are great and innumerable openings for spiritual and social work." But a national organisation can get into politics more easily than it can get out. Like the lion that has tasted blood, it is likely to acquire a lasting appetite. The education conflict is not over, and unless, when it passes away, politics should chance to turn on a great economic issue, there may well be other moral and religious questions on which Nonconformists will feel strongly. It is therefore by no means clear that the Federation will not play an active part in public life for many years to come.

# PART VI. — THE EMPIRE

## CHAPTER LIV

### COMPONENT PARTS OF THE EMPIRE

**Contrast with the Roman Empire.**

ENGLISH writers are fond of comparing the Roman Empire with their own, and in many ways the resemblance is striking. Beginning with a small country, each expanded over a huge domain, carrying with it an enlightened administration, respect for justice, more gradually its own conception of law,[1] and at length a peace and order which, in imitation of the Latin term, it has become the fashion to speak of in England as the *Pax Britannica.* But if the likeness is great, the differences are not less marked. The possessions of Rome were continuous, stretching in all directions from the shores of the Mediterranean. Her neighbours were at arm's length on the extreme edge of her frontier; no powerful state was interposed between the different portions of her empire. Moreover, the countries under her rule contained all the people most nearly akin to her in blood and civilisation, and they formed the bulk of her subjects, for she governed no vast population wholly different in race and colour. She was therefore enabled to stamp her own character indelibly upon a great part of her dominions.

**Geography of the British Empire.**

To all this the British Empire presents a strong contrast. The dependencies of England are scattered over the whole face of the earth in almost every habitable latitude, while there are scarcely ten consecutive degrees of longitude in which she does not have a foothold. Including Egypt, her six most important possessions lie in five different conti-

[1] *Cf.* Bryce, "The Extension of Roman and English Law" in "Studies in History and Jurisprudence."

nents with no means of communication between them but a long sea voyage. Outside of the British Isles with their hundred and twenty thousand square miles, she holds no land in Europe of other than a military significance; but she has nearly four millions of square miles in North America, as much more in Africa,[1] over three millions in Australasia, and nearly two millions in Asia, besides innumerable islands and small bits of coast dotting the map of the world.

Proportion of Races.

The population of the empire is as diverse as its geography. Only a small fraction of it is of European origin, and that fraction is far smaller than it was a hundred and fifty years ago, for by the annexation of huge territories the number of Asiatics and Africans under British rule has been multiplied enormously, while the people of European race in the dependencies are only about four times as many as they were at that time. In fact, the ratio of the people of European stock in the rest of the empire to those in the British Isles is little, if any, larger than it was in 1775. The revolt of the American colonies did not, as some people believed at the time, prevent England from building up a great empire, but it has so far prevented that empire from being in large part Anglo-Saxon. According to the last census, the British dominions, including Egypt and the Sudan, contained a total population of about four hundred and twenty millions; of which the people of European descent numbered about fifty-four millions; the natives of India over two hundred and ninety-five millions; African races of all kinds, from Egypt to the Cape, some sixty-two millions; the rest being Chinese, Singalese, Malays and aboriginal races of various kinds.

Distribution of the European Elements,

Of the fifty-four millions of people of European stock, forty-one and a half millions live in the United Kingdom, and only about twelve and a half millions elsewhere. Nor are these last gaining at such a rate of speed as to make it probable that they will soon overtake the mother country. If the rates of increase in the United Kingdom, in British

[1] Including Egypt and the Sudan.

North America and in Australasia, during the decade before the last census should continue, the European population of all the colonies combined would not be equal to that of the British Isles for some two centuries. Of course the rates of increase will not remain constant, and all such computations are valueless except to show that for an indefinite period the United Kingdom must outweigh all the other English-speaking commonwealths in the empire.

and of the English-speaking People.

Moreover, the twelve and a half millions of European origin in the colonies are by no means wholly of British extraction. Apart from streams of foreign immigrants who will soon become intermingled with and assimilated by the people among whom they live, there are certain old stocks, original settlers or ancient inhabitants, like the French Canadians, the Cape Dutch and the Maltese, who have not lost their language or their traditions. They number about two and a half millions, leaving not much more than ten millions of English-speaking subjects outside the British Isles. Except, perhaps, in South Africa, these stocks of foreign European race are not likely to give rise to serious political difficulties; but they are not likely to disappear. During the last few years an effort has, indeed, been made to bring English into more common use in Malta, and in a place which is essentially a British garrison the experiment may succeed. In Canada, on the other hand, nothing of the kind could be attempted. There the French, more than a million and a half in number, are for the most part massed together in the province of Quebec and comprise four fifths of its inhabitants. Forming a compact body, clinging strongly to their traditions, they are neither absorbed by, nor do they assimilate, their neighbours to any appreciable extent. Although more prolific than the English, they receive no accessions by immigration, while they wander over the border in large numbers to the manufacturing towns of New England, and thus they maintain to the English-speaking people in the Dominion a nearly constant ratio of three to seven.

In South Africa the discovery of gold and the Boer war have produced a condition such that for some years to come it will be impossible to predict what the relation of the races is likely to be. Taking the four colonies of the Transvaal, Orange River, Natal and Cape Colony together, the Dutch somewhat outnumber the English; but the races are geographically more intermingled, and marked off by religious differences less profound, than the English and French in Canada. Assimilation of one people by the other may not, therefore, be impossible. Now it would seem that in some parts of Europe, at least, the less cultivated race tends to gain at the expense of its rival, because it is more prolific, because it is more tenacious of its language and customs, and because mixed marriages turn out in its favour. If this should prove to be the case in South Africa, where permanent immigration on a large scale is improbable, it may in time affect seriously the proportions of the English and Dutch elements.

Unlike the outlying portions of most of the great empires in the past, the dependencies of England are not tributaries. Normally each colony, whether self-governing or not, is self-supporting. It contributes nothing to the imperial treasury, and the mother country defrays no part of the cost of its administration. India, for example, maintains the British troops stationed there, and pays both the salaries of English officials in her service and their retiring pensions after they leave; but although this may be an advantage to England, the money is spent solely on the government of India and in principle at least for her benefit. No more troops are, in fact, kept at the expense of the country than are deemed to be needed for its defence and for the preservation of order. Occasionally England advances money to one of the colonies to be repaid later, but she never extorts a loan from them. They do not even contribute to the common expenses, or regularly to the common defence, of the empire. Indian troops were, no doubt, used in Egypt both in 1882–1883 and in 1898, and Revenue.

English regiments were sent from India to South Africa in 1900. The self-governing colonies also sent volunteers to the South African war; but while in service all these troops were supported and paid by the English government. Of late years the self-governing colonies have, indeed, undertaken to maintain ships of war, but they are designed chiefly for the protection of their own coasts, and are insignificant in comparison with the cost of the British navy.

Commerce. The profit that England derives from her dependencies does not come in the form of tribute, but of enlarged opportunities for her citizens. Much discussion has taken place on the question whether trade follows the flag,[1] but whether it does so directly or not, there can be little doubt that the control of an immense empire has had an indirect effect in the past. If the war of 1870 helped to bring German scholarship to the attention of all mankind, the presence of a British flag in all parts of the world has been a productive advertisement of British manufactures. The trade of England has been promoted also by the ease of transport furnished by her mercantile marine, and this has been fostered by the extent of her over-sea possessions. It may well be true that trade follows the flag less than it did formerly, yet the flag prevents trade from being cut off, for at the present day almost every country whose commerce is worth having has either set up protective duties of its own, or has come under the control of some other state which strives by a hostile tariff to keep the commerce as much as possible to itself. England has not attempted to do this in her dependencies since she adopted the policy of free trade; but if she did not hold them, those that have not a predominant white population would almost certainly be under the control of some nation which would leave the door open much less wide to English merchants. So far from regulating trade during the last half century for her own benefit, England in granting self-government to her

[1] There is an interesting study of the question in Alleyne Ireland's "Tropical Colonisation."

larger white colonies allowed them to raise their revenues as they saw fit, and they have set up protective tariffs against her manufactures. Recently they have, indeed, given a preference in rates to English goods, although sometimes merely by raising their duties still more against other nations. Meanwhile the whole question of general preferential tariffs within the empire has been made by Mr. Chamberlain's vigorous propaganda a living issue in imperial politics. Such a plan, if adopted, might change seriously for good or evil the commercial relations of England with her colonies, and if it did so it could not fail to affect their political relations also.

**Forms of Colonial Government.**

There are now three distinct types of colonial government to be found in the British Empire: those of the self-governing colonies, the crown colonies, and what for want of a better generic term may be called the protectorates, that is, the states that are administered more or less completely by England through the form of advice to the native rulers. This is not wholly the official classification, because some of the dependencies are not under the Colonial Office, and hence are regarded as distinct from the rest. India, for example, being in charge of the India Office, is not called a colony, and yet the method of administration is essentially similar to that of a crown colony so far as the connection with the parent state is concerned. Egypt, also, is not classed as a colony at all, because nominally not a British possession, and practically administered by the Foreign Office. But if we disregard the question from which corner of the great building on Downing Street a dependency is ruled, and look merely to the actual forms of government, we find that they fall very comfortably under one or other of these three heads. In the following chapters each of the three types of government will be considered, not in regard to the domestic administration of the colony, but simply for the purpose of showing its relation to England.

## CHAPTER LV

### THE SELF-GOVERNING COLONIES

The North American Colonies.

EXCEPT for India, which was only beginning to be more than a collection of trading stations under the management of a chartered company, the foreign possessions of England in the middle of the eighteenth century consisted for the most part of the West Indian Islands and the colonies along the coast of North America. These dependencies differed much in origin, and not less in their early forms of government. In those on the mainland, which were destined to have the largest growth, the mother country took for a time little interest, and some of them conducted their affairs with great independence. This was notably the case with Massachusetts Bay, for by the transfer of the charter to America that colony came to be ruled almost from the start by its freemen, who elected their own legislature and governor without restraint. But as England grew more conscious of the importance of her transatlantic possessions, as she began with the Navigation Acts to develop a colonial policy in mercantile relations, and as her own internal strife subsided, she came to interfere with the colonies more. By proceedings in the Court of Chancery the old charter of Massachusetts Bay was annulled, and in 1691 another was granted which vested the appointment of the governor in the Crown. By the transfer to the Crown of the rights of the proprietors in some places, and by sundry other changes elsewhere, the forms under which the different colonies were administered became at last very much alike.

Before the eighteenth century was far advanced a single type of government had become prevalent in most of the important British colonies, both on the mainland of North

America and in the West Indies. It was that of a governor appointed by the Crown, and a legislature with a popular branch which was elected by the inhabitants of the colony and possessed the power of the purse. For any people with English political traditions that was the natural form to adopt. Where men of English stock were the predominant element in the population it was impossible to refuse them an elective assembly empowered to lay taxes and appropriate the proceeds; and, on the other hand, the governor must be appointed by the Crown if any real connection with the parent state was to be maintained. So far is this true that, as a matter of course, the same type of government has ordinarily been adopted by the United States for the administration of her territories and dependencies. **Appointed Governor and Elective Legislature the Prevalent Type of Government.**

As a temporary expedient, while a territory is too thinly inhabited to be admitted to statehood, the plan has worked well in the American republic; but as a permanent system in a community mature enough to have a will of its own the plan has grave defects. It involves inevitably dissensions between the ruling powers with no arbiter to whom both feel bound to submit; and in fact the history of the British colonies in the eighteenth century is full of bickerings between the governor and the legislature. In order to keep him under its control the assembly would refuse to grant his salary for more than a year at a time; it would vote appropriations and appoint officers of its own to expend them; or it would prevent his use of the veto by tacking a measure to a grant of supply.[1] These disputes harrowed the ground in which the seeds of the American Revolution were planted. But although it is now plain that the system was bad; although we can now see that the readiest means of acquiring popularity in a colony under such conditions is to attack the governor in the assembly, and to urge a policy which its advocates will never be called upon to carry out, and for which, therefore, they will never **Its Defects.**

[1] *Cf.* Greene, "The Provincial Governor"; Egerton, "Short History of British Colonial Policy."

be held to account by the people: although all this is now obvious, yet it is not clear what better plan could have been adopted at the time. Nor was any other found for many years to come, for after the loss of the American colonies British statesmen were long relieved from considering seriously the problem of ruling dependencies that wanted to manage their own affairs. But with the growth of a new colonial empire the problem arose again, and in its ultimate solution the old type has been replaced by one or other of two forms of administration known as those of the self-governing and the crown colonies. The former was evolved first in Canada.

Elective Assemblies in Canada.

The French possessions in North America, conquered in the Seven Years' War, were definitely ceded to England by the Treaty of Paris in 1763, and shortly afterward a proclamation directed the Governor of the new provinces to summon general assemblies like those in the other American colonies as soon as circumstances would permit. But the population of Canada at that time consisted of a few aggressive English Protestants amid a vast majority of French Catholics who were wholly unused to self-government. Hence it was decided, wisely no doubt, that circumstances did not permit the creation of representative institutions; and so the Quebec Act of 1774 set up instead a legislative council of persons appointed by the Crown. The arrangement, however, could not be permanent, especially after the outbreak of the American Revolution had brought a large immigration of British loyalists into Nova Scotia and what is now Ontario. In 1791, therefore, elective assemblies were granted to the British North American colonies, and to avoid friction between the races by separating them as far as possible, the chief province was divided into Upper and Lower Canada, the former wholly English, the latter mainly French.

The Rebellion of 1837.

For a time matters went smoothly, but before a score of years had run the French in Lower Canada learned to use the instrument placed in their hands. The Assembly in striving to increase its power came into collision with the Governor and with the English officials who carried on the administration. The struggle was embittered by the animosity of the races, and complicated by the economic dependence of Upper Canada on its neighbour lower down the river. In Upper Canada also a conflict of the old familiar kind broke out between the executive and the legislature. That province was unvexed by race questions, but the issue there was confused by widespread hostility to a small body of men who had concentrated political influence in their own hands, and who, from the personal ties connecting them, were known as the "family compact." As Professor Egerton remarks in his new edition of the introductory volume to Lucas's "Historical Geography of the British Colonies," Canadian "public life was a maze wherein all men and all parties had lost their way." [1] At last feeling grew so hot that in 1837 armed insurrection broke out in both Upper and Lower Canada. From a military point of view the risings were not serious, and they were quickly suppressed; but it was clear that things could not go on as they were. The English ministry, seeing that something must be done, suspended the constitution of the lower province, and sent out Lord Durham as High Commissioner to restore order and adjust the form of the future government in the colonies.

For his own peace of mind, Lord Durham's mission was not a success. His exiling of a couple of prominent agitators to Bermuda, without legal authority, drew upon him the censure of English statesmen, and finding that the ministers failed to defend him he resigned his position and went home. But his famous Report on the Affairs of British North America remains in several respects the most instructive public document on colonial administration that has ever been written.[2] Besides the general question of the

**Lord Durham's Report.**

[1] "Origin and Growth of the English Colonies," 168.

[2] It is printed in Com. Papers, 1839, XVII., 1; and it has recently been published by Methuen in 1902 and 1905.

form of government, which presented much the same difficulties in every province, he examined the political and social conditions of the country, and his observations in the case of Lower Canada upon the "two nations warring in the bosom of a single state," the "struggle, not of principles, but of races," contains things worthy of note to-day in many distant lands. His belief that the English would at last predominate in the province, and that the French could if treated wisely be assimilated by them, has, indeed, proved illusory; but that does not impair the value of his descriptions. Largely with a view to the absorption of the French, he proposed a union of Upper and Lower Canada, thereby placing the English in a majority in the united province. Unlike some of his other suggestions, this recommendation was at once carried out by the Reunion Act of 1840.

**His Condemnation of the Existing System.**

In regard to the form of government, Lord Durham's attitude was perfectly definite. Since the constitutions of all the provinces were similar, and all of them terminated in nearly the same result, he concluded that there must have been some defect common to all. There had, he tells us, been conflicts between the executive and the popular branch of the legislature in Upper and Lower Canada, Prince Edward Island, New Brunswick, Nova Scotia and Newfoundland. Such a condition was, in fact, so general as to lead him to remark "It may fairly be said, that the natural state of government in all these Colonies is that of collision between the executive and the representative body." [1] Speaking from the standpoint of an Englishman of his time, he asks what the result would be in England if the Crown were to retain a ministry in spite of a hostile majority in successive elections; and yet this had happened in every one of the provinces. "It is difficult," he declares, "to understand how any English statesmen could have imagined that representative and irresponsible government could be successfully combined." [2] It appears, he adds, "that the opposition of the Assembly to the Government was the un-

[1] Com. Papers, 1839, XVII., 1, p. 27. [2] *Ibid.*, p. 30.

avoidable result of a system which stinted the popular branch of the legislature of the necessary privileges of a representative body. . . . From the commencement, therefore, to the end of the disputes which mark the whole Parliamentary history of Lower Canada, I look on the conduct of the Assembly as a constant warfare with the executive, for the purpose of obtaining the powers inherent in a representative body by the very nature of representative government."[1] He notes the unhappy effect on the popular leaders. "The colonial demagogue bids high for popularity without the fear of future exposure . . . and thus the prominent places in the ranks of opposition are occupied for the most part by men of strong passions, and merely declamatory powers, who think but little of reforming the abuses which serve them as topics for exciting discontent."[2]

**He Urged Responsible Government.**

His remedy for these evils is ministerial responsibility on the English pattern; and he points out that it can be introduced, without legislation of any kind, by simply instructing the Governor to entrust the administration to such men as can command a majority in the Assembly, and giving him to understand that he can count on no aid from home in any dissension that does not involve directly the relations with the mother country. In the last point there lurks a difficulty the force of which he evidently did not fully perceive, for he says that England ought to control the constitution or form of government, foreign relations, trade with herself, with other colonies and with foreign nations, and the disposal of public lands. Perfect subordination in these matters would, he thought, be secured by the advantages resulting from the connection with the empire. Now subsequent events have shown that responsible government once granted, these attributes of overlordship could not be permanently retained. The control of trade and public lands has passed wholly into the hands of the colony; constitutional changes, while nominally made by Parliament, are in fact worked out in the colony itself before they

[1] Com. Papers, 1839, XVII., 1, pp. 30, 31. [2] *Ibid.*, p. 31.

are sent to Westminster for little more than a formal ratification; and although the control of the English government over foreign relations is much greater, it is far from absolute in commercial matters, nor can it be used in any case without a tactful regard for colonial opinion. But all these questions were still a long way off.

Responsible Government Introduced in 1848.

Lord Durham's suggestion of the grant of responsible government did not at once commend itself to the statesmen of his day. To them it seemed incompatible with the sovereignty of the mother country, a long step toward an independence which they did not indeed contemplate with abhorrence, but were by no means ready to hasten. Yet they were not inclined, on the other hand, to reject the suggestion conclusively. Lord John Russell took a somewhat non-committal attitude which was capable of misconstruction; but in fact the Governors of Canada for the next eight years did not treat their executive councils as responsible to the majority of the Assembly. It was left for Lord Elgin, the son-in-law of Lord Durham, who became Governor in 1847, to carry out the principle of the Report. He did so completely and under very trying conditions, for the appointment by him, in the year after his arrival, of a ministry from the French-Radical party that had obtained a majority in the Assembly led to a riot in which his own carriage was mobbed and the parliament house burned to the ground. But he persisted, was supported by the English government, and established the principle so firmly that it has never since been abandoned.

The Principle Generally Accepted.

Durham and Elgin were very far from regarding responsible government as a stage on the road to separation. Both were anxious to maintain the empire intact. But that feeling was not strong among most of their contemporaries. The ultimate independence of the colonies inhabited by men of European race was considered by many British statesmen as not improbable, and not necessarily a misfortune. The American Revolution seemed to point to such a result; and just at the time when responsible government was first introduced, the traditional motive for possessing colonies came to an end in England. For two hundred years a parent state had been expected to derive a substantial benefit from their commerce, and all nations had administered them with that object. Under the mercantile system their trade was confined more or less strictly to the mother country, and in return they were given privileges in her markets. Like other nations, England had pursued this course, but when she adopted free trade definitely in 1846 the commercial object in retaining her colonies seemed to be gone, and in fact her Navigation Laws, after a life of almost two centuries, were repealed in 1849. So completely did she abandon all idea of controlling the economic policy of her colonies for her own advantage that, after some hesitation, her government refused in 1858 to disallow a Canadian tariff which imposed duties on British manufactures.[1] Holding such opinions about the relations of the colonies to the mother country, it is not surprising that English statesmen were rapidly converted to the wisdom of granting to English subjects across the sea the political institutions which had become at home the keystone of the British Constitution.

**Responsible Government Granted to Other Colonies.**

The principle that in a dependency peopled by men fit for self-government the ministers ought to be responsible to the representative assembly soon became an axiom in English colonial policy. It was introduced in Nova Scotia and New Brunswick at about the same time as in Canada, and in the colonies elsewhere quite as early as they were prepared to use it. When the Assembly of New Zealand asked for responsible government in 1854 the English ministers replied that they had no objection whatever, and within two years it was obtained by New South Wales, Victoria, Tasmania, South Australia and Newfoundland; Queensland following in 1859. In Cape Colony the large

[1] Egerton, "Short History of British Colonial Policy," 335. The principle was definitely recognised in the case of the Canadian protective tariff of 1879. Egerton, 403; Hans. 3 Ser., CCXLIV., 1313.

native population, and the Kafir wars which involved the presence of British troops, delayed the change until 1872; while the newer settlements, Western Australia and Natal, received the privilege in 1890 and 1893, as soon as they attained sufficient size. Even in the case of the Transvaal and Orange River Colonies the terms of the Boer surrender on May 31, 1902, provided that military administration should at the earliest possible moment be succeeded by civil government, and that as soon as circumstances might permit representative institutions, leading up to self-government, should be introduced. This was promised, although it was at least doubtful whether the Boers lately in arms against England would not preponderate among the voters. Events marched faster than people expected. The Conservative cabinet, before its fall near the end of 1905, was already preparing a constitution for the Transvaal, and this, coupled with full responsibility of the colonial ministers to the Assembly, was put into effect by the Liberal ministry in December, 1906; to be followed six months later by a similar grant to the Orange River Colony.

Confederation in Canada and Australia.

A sequel to the granting of responsible ministries has been the formation of confederations in the two largest groups of self-governing colonies. In each case the initiative has come from the colonies themselves, the action of the mother country being almost entirely confined to embodying in an Act of Parliament the plans already agreed upon by them. The British North American Act of 1867 brought together in the Dominion of Canada the provinces of Ontario, Quebec, Nova Scotia and New Brunswick, with a provision for the admission of new members. Within a few years Manitoba, British Columbia and Prince Edward Island joined the union, and somewhat later the North West Territories were admitted to membership, so that the Dominion stretched across the whole continent and included all habitable British North America except Newfoundland. The progress of federation in Australia was less rapid. With no great neighbour to inspire distrust or stimulate ideas of national magnitude, local jealousies had more free play; and although there were no distinctions of race to keep the colonies apart, differences in economic policy had a similar effect, New South Wales holding strongly to free trade while Victoria was protectionist. The surprise, therefore, is not that federation was delayed, but rather that it came about so soon. In 1885 a Federal Council for Australia was created,[1] but its powers were very limited, and it did not accomplish much. It prepared the way, however, for a real federal constitution, which was ratified by popular vote in New South Wales, Victoria, South Australia, Queensland and Tasmania, and was then sanctioned by Parliament as the Commonwealth of Australia Act of 1900. Western Australia joined the Confederation before the Act went into effect, distant New Zealand, alone of the Australasian self-governing colonies, remaining apart.

**Its Effect on the Mother Country.**

The organisation and internal government of these confederations does not fall within the scope of this book; but it may be observed that their formation has not been without effect on the relation of the colonies to the mother country. Instead of dealing in Canada and Australia only with a dozen small communities, the very largest of which has scarcely more than a couple of million people, she deals with two confederations that contain some five millions of inhabitants apiece. She comes into contact mainly with national instead of provincial opinion, and this of itself tends to lessen the part she plays in the domestic affairs of the colonies. In Canada the change is magnified by the provision which confers upon the Governor General the appointment of the provincial governors[2] and the royal veto on provincial legislation, with other powers formerly exercised directly by the Crown in the different provinces;[3] and although by law the authority is in some cases vested

[1] Australia Federal Council Act, 1885, 48–49 Vic., c. 60.

[2] British North Amer. Act, 30–31 Vic., c. 3, § 58. They are styled Lieutenant Governors.

[3] *Ibid.*, § 90. By § 96 the provincial judges are also appointed by the Governor General.

in the Governor General in Council and in others in the Governor General alone, it is always exercised in accordance with the advice of the ministers of the Dominion. This is not true in the Commonwealth of Australia, where the governors of the component colonies, or as they are now termed "states," are still appointed directly by the Crown; but the creation of the Commonwealth had diminished very much the functions of the legislatures in the several states, while the growth of Australian national feeling and the natural tendency toward centralisation is likely to make imperial action in state affairs less and less frequent.

Control over the Self-governing Colonies.

The control of England over her self-governing colonies is now exerted through four channels: the royal Governor, the power to veto legislation, the control of foreign relations, and the appeals from the colonial courts to the Judicial Committee of the Privy Council.[1]

The Governor as the Representative of England.

The Governor in a self-governing colony has two functions. He is an officer of the mother country appointed to guard her rights and exercise a great part of the control which she still retains over the colony, and he is also the chief magistrate of the colony for its own internal government. In both he acts as the representative of the Crown, but, if one may use the expression, he acts in the former capacity for the Crown as titular sovereign of England or of the empire, in the latter for the Crown as titular sovereign of the colony. According to this distinction it is commonly said that in matters that affect other parts of the empire or foreign countries he must use his own discretion, or seek instructions from the Secretary of State in England; while

Colonial Agents.

[1] Almost every one of the self-governing colonies maintains an agent in England to watch over its interests; but with the growth of control over its own affairs, and the greater ease of direct communication by cable, his political functions have decreased. His duties are often rather those of a financial or commercial, and sometimes of a journalistic, agent. Whenever anything appeared in the press some years ago that reflected upon the economic or industrial conditions in one of the colonies, and might affect its credit or capacity for attracting investment, the agent felt bound to write to the papers at once and contradict it. As a bond of union, or as a political officer, it is hardly necessary now to dwell upon the agent.

in matters that affect only the internal affairs of the colony he must follow the advice of his ministers there. Neither branch of this statement is, however, perfectly accurate. A protective tariff, for example, affects most seriously both the rest of the empire and foreign nations, yet it is now well settled that the Governor cannot on that account refuse to give his assent to it; and the same thing is true of other legislative or administrative acts, such as an exclusion or detention of immigrants when no treaty is violated thereby.

**As Head of the Colonial Government.**

On the other hand, the Governor does not in matters of purely domestic concern always follow the advice of the colonial ministers. A generation or more ago the Governors were not infrequently in trouble with their ministers, or with the Secretary of State at home, in consequence of quarrels between the two branches of the legislature in the colony, or between the different parties there. This was especially true in Australia, for although that continent was settled by people from the British Isles, who might be supposed to have inherited the English political traditions, the course of public life did not at first run smoothly. In fact, for a couple of decades after the granting of responsible government most of the Australasian colonies had on the average a change of ministry almost every year. Dissensions arose that would not have occurred in England, where the conventions of parliamentary government are well recognised and consistently observed. Sometimes the Governor was asked to sanction an expenditure of money that had not been legally appropriated because the Legislative Council had refused its consent. Sometimes he was asked to dissolve the parliament, or make appointments, in cases which appeared to involve an abuse of authority for party purposes. On some of these occasions he refused and was able to carry the community with him, in others he came into collision with the majority of the elective chamber, and sometimes he yielded and was censured from Downing Street. With the reconstruction of several legislative councils, and a greater familiarity with the play of parties in a popular government, such difficulties have become less common, but it can hardly be said that they have wholly disappeared. One of the last cases occurred in Canada in 1896, when Sir Charles Tupper, the Conservative Premier, whose party had been defeated at the general elections, asked the Governor General, Lord Aberdeen, to fill a number of vacancies in the Senate of the Dominion with Conservatives before the new Liberal ministry came to power. As this would have hampered seriously the incoming cabinet Lord Aberdeen refused, and the incident aroused a good deal of discussion on the obligation of a Governor to comply with the advice of his ministers.

Similar constitutional questions might arise in England, but in fact they never do at the present day, and hence the colonial Governor is not in the same situation as the King. In spite of responsible government his position in regard to matters purely internal, as well as those which concern the rest of the world, is still a delicate one that may require much sound judgment and tact. His chief usefulness lies, however, rather in his moral influence than in his legal authority. Like the King his presence is important as a social and ornamental symbol of the empire, and in fact the growing experience in self-government, by reducing the occasions when he is called upon to exert his legal powers, has made the social attributes of greater consequence, and has thus brought a change in the quality of the Governors. Formerly these posts in most of the self-governing colonies, as well as in the crown colonies, formed steps in a lifelong career, which a man mounted one after another; but of late years there has been a strong tendency on the part of the self-governing colonies to prefer great English noblemen with distinguished names and ample fortunes, who will make Government House brilliant and attractive. In short, the Governor, although as yet at some distance, is taking more and more the position of the English King.

The Veto on Legislation.

Another means of control over the self-governing colonies lies in the right to refuse assent to their enactments. As in

England every statute requires for its validity the assent of the Crown, and according to the common practice, embodied in colonial constitutions,[1] the Governor can either assent to a bill on behalf of the Crown, or withhold its assent, or reserve the bill to await the King's pleasure; and even after an act had received his assent it may still be disallowed by the Crown within a certain time, usually one or two years. Now the veto is not, as in England, virtually obsolete, for in all the self-governing colonies taken together three or four acts on the average are killed in this way every year.[2] Nor is it used only to defeat measures prejudicial to other parts of the empire or to foreign countries, although that is, of course, its main object at the present day. An examination of the return made to Parliament of its use in recent years shows that in Newfoundland and Natal acts regulating elections and the franchise, which are certainly local matters, have been refused assent. But it may be observed that the extent to which the veto is used for bills relating chiefly to domestic affairs is inversely proportional to the size of the colony.

**Control of Foreign Relations.**

The actual relation of the United Kingdom to her self-governing colonies may not be easy to classify in the terms ordinarily used by publicists. But whether those colonies are dependencies or members of a confederation, whether sovereignty is really lodged in Parliament or divided, there is no doubt that as regards foreign nations the British Empire is treated as a single power, and that power is England. Diplomats are appointed, negotiations are conducted and treaties are made, on the advice of the English ministers. In order, however, to satisfy local opinion it is the habit when a really important question arises — between Canada and the United States, for example — to appoint a com-

[1] *E.g.*, British North Amer. Act, §§ 55–57; Comlth. of Austr. Const. Act, 63–64 Vic., c. 12, §§ 58–60.

[2] Com. Papers, 1901, XLVI., 7, gives a list of the recent cases where this has occurred. As the veto of acts passed by the provinces of Canada is in the hands of the Dominion government, the list covers only eleven colonies including those now united in the Commonwealth of Australia.

mission containing colonial members. But the situation is not wholly comfortable, and in fact the position of Canada is a little like that of a boy at school with a big brother. The state of the self-governing colonies in regard to foreign relations would no doubt be a much more difficult one, and give rise to no little friction, were it not that their remoteness saves them to a great extent from complications with other countries.

Judicial Appeals.

Finally a connection with England is maintained by the fact that appeals lie as a rule from the colonial courts to the Judicial Committee of the Privy Council. Centralisation in the administration of law is one of the most powerful of forces for political unification. It was one of the most effective instruments in the consolidation of the English monarchy. But it is not clear how much value there is in the mere right of appeal to a tribunal in London which is not the final court for England herself, particularly when appeals are costly and the cases are argued mainly by English barristers. The privilege is not entirely popular in the colonies. An attempt was made to restrict it by statute in Canada;[1] and the Act which created the Commonwealth of Australia provided that, save in the discretion of the colonial High Court established by the Act, no appeals should lie to England on constitutional questions, while appeals on other subjects might be cut off by subsequent legislation.[2] This was the only article of the draft constitution to which the English ministers objected, and it was modified slightly to meet their views, but on the main point they gave way.[3]

The events of the last hundred years have thus produced an entirely new form of government in those British colonies

[1] For the construction of the Act, and a discussion of the legality of cutting off appeals altogether, see *In re* Marois, 15 Moore, P.C. 189 (1862); Cushing *vs.* Dupuy, 5 App. Cas. 409 (1880).

[2] Comlth. of Austr. Const. Act, 1900, § 74.

[3] By the draft constitution there were to be no appeals from the High Court unless public interests of Her Majesty's dominions outside of Australia were involved, Com. Papers, 1900, LV., 1, p. 11; Hans. 4 Ser. LXXXIV., 342.

where the predominant population is of European stock. The American Revolution, and the later disturbances in Canada, made it clear that dependencies of that kind could not be ruled from London, and that elective assemblies in the colonies could not be combined with administration by a governor acting independently of the representative body. A solution of the difficulty was found in making the colonial ministers responsible to the elected legislature. In this way were evolved the self-governing colonies, in which the sovereign authority of the mother country has been reduced to little more than a control over foreign relations, and over some matters of imperial concern; while even that slender bond has become well-nigh voluntary, for it is generally assumed that if any of the larger colonies, at least, chose to sever their connection with England she would not attempt to restrain them by force. The system has now been extended to all the dependencies to which it seems likely to be applied. They are Canada and Newfoundland in North America; the Commonwealth of Australia and New Zealand in Australasia; and in South Africa, Cape Colony, Natal, the Transvaal and last of all the Orange River Colony.

**Summary of the Change in the Type of Government.**

If the grant and expansion of self-government has reduced greatly the political control of England over the colonies inhabited by people of her own race, it has also removed almost altogether the friction that existed formerly, and has thus allowed a strong imperial sentiment to grow up. The diminution of power has been followed by an increase of loyalty. Other conditions have promoted this feeling, not least among them a change of attitude toward the colonies in England itself. One hears nothing to-day on either side of the ocean about eventual independence. In its place one finds speculation about the possible means of drawing the empire closer together, a question that will be discussed in a later chapter.

**Effect of Self-government.**

## CHAPTER LVI

### THE CROWN COLONIES

THE old system of a governor appointed by the Crown coupled with a legislature elected by the people has disappeared also in most of the colonies whose inhabitants are not mainly of European origin, but in this case the evolution has proceeded in the opposite direction. And here it may be observed that in some colonies where the population was white a hundred years ago, it is no longer so now; not in consequence of any great change in the proportion of the races, but because however numerous the slaves might be, they were, until freed, of no political account. In this way most of the British West Indies, where formerly the Europeans were almost alone considered, are now filled with a teeming free population, of which the whites form a very small part.

History of Jamaica.

The history of Jamaica may serve to illustrate the transformations by which the earlier form of government has been turned into that of a modern crown colony. Captured from the Spaniards in 1655, the island was rapidly settled by Englishmen, and Lord Windsor, on his appointment as Governor in 1662, was instructed to call legislative assemblies according to the custom of the other colonies. Thus a government of the familiar type was created, with a royal governor, an appointed council, and an elected assembly. A score of years had not passed before friction with England began, and although in this instance matters were soon adjusted, troubles arose again later, and throughout the eighteenth century we find in a milder form quarrels, of the same nature as in the North American colonies, constantly breaking out between the Governor and the Assembly. That body refused for years to vote a permanent revenue, and made appropriations to be expended only by officers appointed by itself. In fact, by a series of local acts the collection and expenditure of the revenue was taken almost entirely out of the hands of the Governor, and transferred to commissioners who were really the members of the Assembly under another name. Had the island been inhabited only by Englishmen, these difficulties might eventually have led, as in Canada, to the grant of a responsible ministry, but the presence of slaves, ten times as numerous as the free whites, led in the nineteenth century to both economic and political upheavals.

**Abolition of Slavery and Distress in the Island.**

In 1807 Parliament forbade the slave trade, and this caused a scarcity of labour in Jamaica. In 1833 it went much farther, and against a protest of the Assembly denying its right to interfere in the internal affairs of the island, it abolished slavery, granting to the planters a compensation which they regarded as wholly inadequate. As the negroes in that climate could easily get a living from unoccupied lands, without working for wages, emancipation struck a severe blow at the industries of the colony. In 1838 Parliament again undertook to legislate about the domestic concerns of the island; this time by an act which took the regulation of prisons out of the hands of the local authorities. Whereupon the Assembly in consideration of "the aggressions which the British Parliament continue to make on the rights of the people" of the colony, resolved to "abstain from any legislative function, except such as may be necessary to preserve inviolate the faith of the island with the public creditor." [1] The English ministry then brought in a bill to suspend the constitution of Jamaica. This, however, was defeated in the House of Commons, causing the fall of Lord Melbourne's cabinet, and although Sir Robert Peel failed to form a ministry on account of the famous "Bedchamber Question," Mel-

[1] Quoted by Egerton, "Short History of British Colonial Policy," 329.

bourne on returning to power made no second attempt to pass the bill.[1]

The Constitution of 1854.

The planters must have felt that England was hounding them to their ruin, for in 1846 the foundations of their former prosperity were undermined still further by the adoption of free trade, and the removal of preferential tariffs in favour of sugar from the British West Indies. The Assembly, under the pressure of economic distress, passed retrenchment bills, which the appointed Council rejected as a breach of public faith, and the deadlock continued until, by the offer of a loan of half a million pounds, the Assembly was induced in 1854 to consent to a revision of its fundamental laws. The new constitution of that year enlarged the powers of the Governor in various ways; among others by transferring to him the functions hitherto exercised by the members of the Assembly when acting as commissioners for collecting and expending the revenue; and although he was to be assisted in the performance of his duties by an Executive Committee composed of three members of the Assembly and one of the Council, those members were to be selected by him.[2]

The Insurrection of 1865 and the Downfall of the Constitution.

For half a dozen years the new machinery worked well enough, but the opportunity for political deadlocks had by no means been removed, and in 1860 strife between the Governor and the Assembly began afresh. The first occasion therefor was a question about the responsibility of the Executive Committee for an over-expenditure; but the quarrel, as often happens, wandered off into other paths, and might have continued merrily on its way had not an alarming insurrection of the negroes broken out in 1865. Governor Eyre was accused of cruelty in suppressing it, but his action, which was vigorous and decisive,

[1] The provision in the Prisons Act for the regulation of prisons by the Governor was, for the most part, inoperative: Com. Papers, 1840, XXXV., 1, p. 79.

[2] About the same time a new electoral law admitted many negroes to the franchise, and before long the Assembly contained a number of colored members.

won the admiration of the white people. They had, in fact, been thoroughly frightened, and were ready to surrender their political rights for the sake of having a strong executive. At the close of 1866, therefore, the legislature of Jamaica authorised the Queen to create a new government for the island, and by an Act of Parliament the elective Assembly, after a life of two hundred years, came to an end.

The Constitutions of 1866 and 1884.

Under the constitution which went into effect in 1867, the island became a crown colony with a single Legislative Council, composed of six official and six unofficial members, all appointed by the Crown. The former were the principal officers of state in the island, such as the Colonial Secretary, the Attorney-General and the Commander of the Troops, while the Governor himself acted as chairman. But the political experiments in Jamaica were not yet over. After a few years the planters recovered from their fright, and longed to have the administration of public affairs once more in their own hands. In 1876 they sent a memorial to the House of Commons, asking that the inhabitants might have representatives in the Council and might control the revenues. The Secretary of State replied that a suggestion to alter the constitution so recently established could not be entertained. But when similar petitions were made in later years, the government yielded to the extent of permitting half of the seats in the Council to be elective. The change was made by the constitution of 1884, whereby the Council was to consist of the Governor, and of nine appointed,[1] and nine elected, members. Inasmuch as the Governor could control the appointed members, such an arrangement would appear to place a constant majority at his command, but this result was modified by a provision that a two thirds vote of the elective members on financial questions, or a unanimous vote of those members on any other subject, should be decisive, unless the Governor considered the matter of paramount public importance. In other words, he had power to override the elected members,

[1] Four of them official, and five unofficial.

but he was not intended to use that power for current affairs.

The Elective Members Overborne.

Except for a few changes that do not concern us here, the Constitution of 1884 remained unaltered until 1897, when the Council was enlarged in a way that must be described in order to make clear the present method of controlling that body. The elected members were increased from nine to fourteen, one for each of the parishes in the island. At the same time the official and appointed members were raised only to ten, or, including the Governor, to eleven, but he was empowered to add four more if a question of great importance made it necessary to do so. In short, he was normally in a minority in the Council, but as a last resort could transform his appointees into a majority. This he did a couple of years later, after a long series of altercations with the elected members, chiefly on the subject of the taxes. For some time insular finance had been perplexing. There had been deficits, and the Governor with the appointed members felt that the revenue must be made to balance the expenditure; while the elected members, suffering under the weight of the existing taxation, were loath to increase their burdens. Finally in 1899 the Governor proposed a tax on type-writers, sewing-machines, books and magazines, and when the elected members refused to vote for it, he made appointments to the four additional seats on the Council. The step was taken after a consultation with Mr. Chamberlain, then Secretary of State for the Colonies, and although the additional members resigned soon afterwards, on an undertaking by the elective councillors to vote for the tax,[1] their appointment showed that the home government was prepared in cases of serious disagreement to exert its authority by overpowering the elective element in the Council.

The history of Jamaica is the more instructive, because the government in its transition from the old type to its present form has passed through an unusual variety of

[1] Com. Papers, 1899, LIX., 219.

metamorphoses. It has had alongside of the Governor an Assembly wholly elected, a single Legislative Council wholly appointed, and a Council in which the elected members were, or could be made, a minority. Each of these forms is still found in the crown colonies, but save in a very few cases the first of them has disappeared, and the prevalent types are those in which the legislature is composed exclusively, or for the major part, of appointed members.

**The History of Malta.**

A more recent example of the tendency to do away with an elective assembly, where full responsible government cannot be granted, may be seen in the case of Malta. After its capture from the French in 1800 the island was at first under the sole authority of a Governor, who was often the Commander-in-Chief of the forces there; and in fact it is the great importance of Malta as a naval base that has prevented it from acquiring any large measure of self-government. Strategic considerations will not permit the people to govern themselves as they please, and yet the inhabitants, who enjoyed a representative assembly before the coming of the Knights of St. John, are so numerous that the post cannot be treated, like Gibraltar, simply as a garrison. But this peculiar condition, which has precluded government by responsible ministry on one side, and pure military rule on the other, does not make the political events in the island less valuable as an illustration of the difficulty of maintaining a semi-popular form of administration.

**Representative Assembly Granted.**

An advisory council was associated with the government of Malta in 1838–1839, but no trace of popular representation was introduced until 1849, when the Crown by Letters Patent created a Council of Government, composed of the Governor with nine appointed, and eight elected, members. This gave the people of the island a chance to make their opinions heard, but not to make them prevail, for the government always had a majority at its command, and at times used it so freely as to foster a strong desire to bring the local administration under real popular control.

The agitation continued for many years, and finally a plan for a new Council, based upon petitions by the Maltese themselves, was put into effect by Letters Patent of 1887. It reduced the appointed members to six, and increased the elected ones to fourteen, of whom ten were chosen by the ordinary voters, while the clergy, the nobility, the graduates of the university and the chamber of commerce had one representative apiece.[1] Thus the elected members preponderated heavily, and, what is more, on money bills their votes alone were to be counted.[2] On the other hand, the Crown had not only the usual veto and an exclusive right to initiate measures dealing with the revenue, but reserved to itself an ultimate power to legislate independently by Order in Council.

The Question of Language in the Courts,

The Maltese soon found that their actual control over the government was less than they had expected, and as early as 1891, after the elected members had resigned as a protest against the policy of the Governor, a riot was caused by the attempt of a mob to overawe the Council. Dissensions continued, with resignation as an occasional resource, but the popular party had no specific issue as a basis for opposition until 1898. In that year Colonel Hewson, a British army officer, who had given evidence in English as a witness, and was asked to sign a translation of it into Italian, the official language of the court, refused to do so on the ground that he could not read what he was required to sign. Thereupon he was committed for contempt of court; and although the Governor saved him from going to gaol, indignation was felt that a British officer should be ordered to prison by a British court for refusing to sign a statement in a foreign tongue that he did not understand. Mr. Chamberlain directed the Governor to lay before the Council ordinances making English

[1] The clergy were deprived of their representative in 1898 in consequence of their attempt to get control of the Council.

[2] Salaries, pensions and £1000 additional were, however, placed on the civil list and required no annual appropriation.

as well as Italian the official language of the courts, and when the Council rejected them, they were enacted by Order in Council in March, 1899. The elected members protested, resigned, were returned again without opposition, and then refused to pass money bills, which were in turn put in force by Order in Council.

The question of language involved a singular state of affairs. Italian, which had been substituted for Latin in the courts after the English occupation, was the tongue of the educated classes, but not of the great mass of the population, who speak Maltese, a dialect based upon Arabic. It could fairly be asserted, therefore, that English was quite as appropriate an official language as Italian. The question affected the schools as well as the courts. Some time before a plan had been put in force whereby the children were taught Maltese in the two youngest classes, and then the parents were allowed to choose whether they should study English or Italian, with the result that by far the greater part of them chose the former. But now the elected members of the Council, claiming that the choice of the parents was not really free, demanded that Italian should be the regular subject of study, and declined to pass some of the appropriations for the schools unless an ordinance for the purpose was adopted. In an interview with Mr. Chamberlain their delegates went much farther, asking for responsible government. Such a request was of course refused, with an intimation that the elected members did not fairly represent the people of the colony; and in view of the small proportion of voters, and the still smaller number who went to the polls, this may very well have been true. and in the Schools.

The leaders of the opposition to the government set on foot a vigorous agitation in the island; while in the Council they passed their ordinance for the schools, only to see it met by a veto. Thereupon they rejected appropriations, resigned, and were again reëlected. Clearly the constitution as it stood did not work. The popular element was The Constitution Withdrawn too strong or too weak to please any one; and finally in 1903 the gordian knot was cut by Letters Patent which abolished the Council, and substituted another composed, in addition to the Governor, of ten appointed, and only eight elected, members. The Governor was given also the sole right of initiating measures, and thus the Council was reduced to a consultative body where the representatives of the people can express their opinions, but have no means of putting them into effect. After an experience of seventeen years the Constitution of 1887 has been abandoned, and the conditions of 1849 have been restored. Nor was the result due to a change of party in England, for the Letters Patent of 1887 had been issued by a Conservative ministry. The constitution of that year was doomed to fail, because it created two independent forces that were almost certain to come into collision, without any power that could bring them into harmony. Parliamentary government avoids deadlocks by making the executive responsible to the legislature. Presidential government limits deadlocks, because all the organs of the state must ultimately submit to a superior tribunal, the electorate of the nation. But a legislature elected by the people, coupled with a Governor appointed by a distant power, is a contrivance for fomenting dissensions and making them perpetual.

**The existing Crown Colonies.**

The governments of Jamaica and Malta have been dwelt upon at some length because they illustrate a principle of universal application, which has been at work throughout the history of English colonisation in all parts of the earth. Nature is full of cases where extreme types prosper, while everything between them has been eliminated as unsuitable, and this has happened in the British dependencies. A colony can be governed by its own people, or it can be governed by the mother country, but under ordinary conditions it cannot be governed successfully by a combination of the two, and hence the English dominions over sea are sharply separated into two groups: one that of the self-governing colonies, which have tended towards more and more complete control of their own affairs; the other that of the crown colonies, which have tended to lose the remnants of self-government that they possessed. Of the old type, with an assembly wholly elected, and a governor whose ministers are not responsible to the legislature, only three examples remain. They are Bermuda, Bahamas and Barbados, the first and last having the oldest representative bodies in the British Empire except the House of Commons. The peculiar conditions in those islands, that have made possible the survival of institutions which have perished elsewhere, need not be examined in detail. Suffice it to say that they are peculiar, although not the same in each case.

**Different Types.**

The rest of the crown colonies may be divided into three classes. First, the Leeward Islands, British Guiana, Malta, Mauritius and Figi, where the legislative body includes elected members who are, however, in a minority.[1] Where the population contains any considerable number of Europeans, or other educated people, this has the advantage of bringing the Governor and his advisers into official contact with an enlightened local opinion which, in the absence of violent dissensions, is likely to have great weight. The second class of crown colonies is the most numerous of all, and consists of those where the legislative body is wholly appointed. This is true, for example, of the remaining British possessions in the West Indies and Central America, of Ceylon and of most of the colonies on the tropical coasts of Africa.[2] It is almost a necessity where the proportion

[1] British Guiana has a curious constitution derived from the Dutch. In the Court of Policy, which deals with ordinary legislation, the government has a bare majority; but the Combined Court that levies the taxes is formed by adding other elected members. For the method of controlling this body, see Ireland, "Tropical Colonisation," 45–51, 65–66.

Cyprus alone has a legislative body containing both elected and appointed members with the former in a majority. This is normally the case, as we have seen, in Jamaica also; but there the majority can be turned into a minority at any time.

[2] In Hong Kong and the Straits Settlements the Legislative Councils are wholly appointed, but in each case a couple of members are nominated by the chambers of commerce or other bodies.

of European residents is minute, or where they do not truly represent the local industries. Finally, in purely military stations like Gibraltar and St. Helena, and in half explored tracts like some of those in the interior of Africa, the Governor has no legislative council whatever.

The Public Officials.

Each of the colonies in the East — Ceylon, Hong Kong and the Straits Settlements (including the Federated Malay States) — has a distinct civil service of its own, but they are all recruited together by a competitive examination in London, held in common for these posts, the Indian Civil Service and the first-class clerkships in the English departments of state. The nature of that examination has already been explained,[1] and it has been pointed out that the successful candidates, in the order of their rank at the examination, are allowed to choose the service they will enter. Those assigned to these three colonies are known as the Eastern Cadets, and so far as there are vacancies to be filled, they can select the colony they prefer. They are then despatched forthwith to the East to learn the necessary Oriental languages. In general, it may be said that all the higher offices in the Eastern colonies, except those of Governor and of one or two of his subordinates, are reserved for the men recruited in this way; and the system, which is copied from the Indian Civil Service, works very well. Occasionally, no doubt, it produces a mere student who has no administrative faculty, but such cases appear to be rare, and no one to-day would seriously propose to give it up. On the other hand, it could hardly be extended generally to the British colonies elsewhere. Competitive examinations, either open or limited, are, indeed, used in a subsidiary way in some places, but there are grave obstacles to making them the basis of the civil service in all the crown colonies. Apart from the Eastern possessions, no one of the colonies is large enough by itself to support a service of this kind, and an attempt to group

[1] I., 162–65, *supra*. See also Lowell and Stephens, "Colonial Civil Service," 65–76.

them together for the purpose is well-nigh out of the question. In the West Indies, for example, the inhabitants of an island are quite capable of holding many of the offices. It would not be right, therefore, to fill these places by competitions in London open to all British subjects; and at the same time the West Indians have not usually breadth of view enough to be useful outside of their own colony. The system can probably be extended to some of the large possessions in Africa, but not to the great number of small crown colonies that dot the map of the world.

The Career of a Governor.

Nevertheless, public service in all the colonies is permanent and well paid. Above all, the positions of Governor and Colonial Secretary furnish a career, usually but not necessarily, for men born in the British Isles. Beginning, perhaps, in some subordinate post, a man obtains an appointment as Colonial Secretary in a small colony. If he does well, he is promoted to the same office in a larger place; then to be Governor of a little island; and so on up the ladder to the more important governorships. He does not stay many years in one place, and thus the Governor, although new to the particular colony over which he presides, has a wide experience of colonial problems. This is equally true in the exceptional cases where a man is sent out directly from service in the Colonial Office in London. In short, the Governor is in much the same situation as the minister at the head of an English department. He draws his knowledge of the immediate questions with which he has to deal from his subordinates on the spot, and brings to bear upon them the broader views of a man from a larger world. The increasing skill with which England conducts a vast and heterogeneous empire is, in fact, largely due to the great corps of men who, in the various dependencies or in the Colonial Office at home, have spent their lives in studying the subject from many sides.

# CHAPTER LVII

## INDIA AND THE PROTECTORATES

The East India Company.

BRITISH INDIA is an empire in itself, so marvellously complex that it can be described only in the kind of treatise whereof there are fortunately a number of good examples. But its relations with England are comparatively simple, because, as already observed, save for foreign affairs, the country is ruled mainly in India, not from London. This fortunate condition may perhaps be traced to the way in which the government came into the hands of the Crown. During the seventeenth and the first half of the eighteenth centuries the East India Company, which had charge of English interests in that part of the world, was a true commercial company holding trading stations, called factories, mainly near the coast. The struggle with France, whereby the Company became involved in the quarrels of the native princes, brought this state of things to a close, the turning points being Clive's victory at Plassey in 1757, and the grant to the Company by the Mogul emperor in 1765 of the diwan, or fiscal government, of Bengal. For a time the actual administration was left in the hands of the Nawab and the native rulers, but in 1771 the Company announced its determination to "stand forth as diwan," in other words to assume the direct administration, and from that time it was constantly extending its possessions over a greater and greater part of the peninsula.

It Becomes a Ruling, instead of a Trading, Concern.

A company with its offices in London could hardly be allowed to rule an Oriental empire free from interference by the British government, and in 1773 a Regulating Act provided for the management of its affairs, and ordained, among other things, that its civil and judicial officers should not trade on their own account. A few years later Pitt's India Act of 1784 created a Board of Control, to be appointed by the Crown alongside of, and in some respects above, the Court of Directors of the Company. Now by the Act of 1773 the charter expired in twenty years, and on each renewal for another term of the same length the privileges of the Company were curtailed, especially in the matter of trade, until it was gradually transformed from a mercantile to a purely governing body. In 1813 its commercial monopoly, except for the china and tea trade, was abolished; in 1833 it was deprived of its commercial functions altogether; and in 1853 the directors lost the right to appoint the recruits to the Indian Civil Service. Four years later came the Mutiny which brought about in 1858 the transfer of the government from the Company to the Crown. Thus the Crown took charge of an Asiatic empire that had been ruled for nearly a century by a private company acting under a general supervision by the ministers, and the traditions formed during that period seem to have coloured the methods of transacting public business to the present day. A series of statutes were passed to reorganise the government of India, but the last of them was enacted in 1861, and since that time Parliament has done little more than amend them in minor points;[1] while the internal administration of the country has been shaped in the main by the men who have acquired experience as Indian officials.

**Transfer of its Powers to the Crown.**

**The Viceroy.**

The Governor-General, or Viceroy, of India and the Czar of Russia are sometimes said to be the two great autocrats of the modern world. But, save in the case of a man of rare capacity and force, an autocrat, especially if like the Viceroy he comes for a few years to a strange land, must be largely under the influence of advisers who are thoroughly familiar with the work to be done; and this is the more true when those advisers, including his own private

[1] Ilbert, "The Government of India," 107. This is by far the best work on the public law of India.

secretary, belong to a great organisation with a strong *esprit de corps.* The Governors of Bombay and Madras, like the Viceroy himself, are English noblemen appointed directly by the Crown, but they must obey his orders, their legislative power is limited, and all laws made by them require his consent.[1] Hence their authority is not very great, and they, too, are surrounded by members of the civil service. The lieutenant-governors, or chief commissioners, at the head of the other provinces, are appointed by the Viceroy, and are regularly selected from the civil service; for which, indeed, by far the greater part of the administrative and judicial posts of higher grade in India are reserved.

The Civil Service of India.

Except for a number of seats in the high courts and in the councils of the various governors, and for special services, organised and recruited separately, like engineering, forestry, police and education, it may be said that almost all the offices of government involving any serious responsibility are held by members of the civil service of India.[2] From their ranks are taken the collector magistrates in the several districts,[3] who carry on the actual government throughout the country, and have charge of almost every branch of the administration, ruling, on the average, over nearly a million of people apiece. A few of the principal subordinates in the districts are also members of the service, the other offices, mainly of a lower grade, being filled by natives of the country. Thus the government of India is really in the hands of about eleven hundred Englishmen, of whom a couple of hundred are military officers or uncovenanted civilians, while all the rest belong to the great corps of the civil service.[4] With the mode of recruiting that service, we are already familiar. Its members go to India at not over

[1] Ilbert, 190–91, 221–22, 225.
[2] Ilbert, 126–28, 238–40, 276–77; Lowell and Stephens, "Colonial Civil Service," 50–53.
[3] The corresponding officer in the non-regulation provinces is styled Assistant Commissioner.
[4] Lowell and Stephens, 56–57.

twenty-four years of age, and after spending twenty-five years there they are entitled to retire with a liberal pension. Such a body of men, drawn for the most part from one source, nurtured by the English universities, spending their vigorous years in a common and highly responsible work in an Oriental land, are well fitted to develop traditions without bureaucratic rigidity. They do not conceive of their mission as ruling India for the benefit of England, and, in fact, without recognising any conflict of interest between the two, their first care is the welfare of India as they understand it.

A Trace of Representation.

The Indian Councils Act of 1892, or rather the regulations made thereunder, introduced a trace of representation into the general government of India. They provided that in the legislative councils of the chief provincial governors a part of the members should be appointed on the nomination of municipal and district councils, of landowners, manufacturers and tradesmen; others being appointed by the Governor "in such manner as shall in his opinion secure a fair representation of the different classes of the community." These members in each of the four provinces of Madras, Bombay, Bengal and the North West provinces, nominate one member for the legislative council of the Viceroy, while another is nominated by the Chamber of Commerce of Calcutta, and others again are selected with regard to a due representation of different classes.[1] Although the legislative councils so constituted have little actual power, they not only debate proposed changes in the laws, but can also discuss the annual financial statement, and ask questions after the manner practised in the House of Commons. All this gives serious native opinion some chance to make itself heard by the rulers, and provides a valuable means of obtaining information.[2]

If the trace of representation in India is very slight, the

[1] Ilbert, 110, 118–19, 121, 337–48.

[2] The Indian Congress, of which we have heard so much of late years, is an unofficial body.

Native Officials.

natives are employed largely in the government offices. The lower grades of the public service are reserved almost exclusively for them, and so are a certain number of the more responsible posts.[1] They can also compete at the regular examinations in London for the Civil Service of India, and four or five a year do so with success. In 1893, indeed, the House of Commons, in order to give the natives a fairer chance, passed a resolution in favour of holding the examinations in India, as well as in London where few of them can take part. But after collecting evidence on the subject the ministry decided not to make the change; partly from a fear of reducing the English element in the public service too much; partly because a competitive examination of a literary character, while suited for Englishmen, is not an effective way of selecting for office natives among whom a talent for absorbing information is great, but capacity for government is rare; and partly because such an examination would admit mainly Bengalis, to the exclusion of the Mohammedans who form a large part of the population and are distinctly better fitted to rule. In fact, the Mohammedans undoubtedly prefer the government of the British to that of the Bengali Babus, whom they would speedily overpower if the strong hand of England were removed; and this suggests one of the fundamental conditions of foreign supremacy in the peninsula.

India is not a Nation.

The people of India are not a nation, but a conglomerate of many different races and religions, often side by side in the same place, yet unmixed and sharply separate. It is this, as Seeley pointed out in his "Expansion of England," that has enabled the British to conquer and hold the country. If the inhabitants could act together, and were agreed in wanting independence, they could get it. In short, if they were capable of national self-government, the English would live on a volcano, and their occupation would be brief. The Mutiny was suppressed because it was not universal. The Sikhs helped to put down the Sepoys; and

[1] Lowell and Stephens, 54–61.

so long as large sections of the people distrust one another more than they do the English, disaffection has little chance of achieving any notable result.

**The Native States.**

The whole of India is not under direct British administration. Scattered all over the peninsula are tracts of country under native rulers, although subject to the overlordship of the English Crown. Fourteen years ago when Sir William Lee-Warner published his book on the "Protected Princes of India," there were six hundred and eighty-eight of them, with nearly six hundred and fifty thousand square miles of territory and sixty-seven millions of subjects, against a little less than a million square miles and about two hundred and twenty millions of people under direct British rule. The native states vary enormously in size, from that of the Nizam of Hyderabad with eighty-two thousand square miles and a population of eleven and a half millions, down to minute principalities. The relation of the English government to these states forms one of the most interesting, and least familiar, chapters in the management of dependencies. It has developed slowly, and although based to a great extent on treaties, it is not contained in any series of documents, but has grown up in large part through a customary policy and the gradual use of tactful pressure.

**Their Relation to the Government of India.**

Lee-Warner styles the relation one of subordinate union, and certainly it is very far from an international connection between sovereign states, because the government of India exercises in several ways a paramount authority, not only for its own security, but also for the protection of the native ruler's own subjects. Speaking generally, the native states are protected against both external foes and rebellion at home, and, on the other hand, their diplomatic intercourse with one another and with foreign powers is in the hands of the Indian government. They have military obligations, also, which vary a good deal according to the special treaties made with them. Sometimes they are obliged to maintain definite contingents under British officers, which act with the Indian Army; sometimes their assistance in war is rendered in other ways; but the strength of their forces is limited, and in any case they must allow the Indian troops to pass through their territory. Quite apart from military necessities, moreover, they must permit the construction of roads, railways, telegraphs and irrigation works within their limits; and, indeed, scattered as the native states are over the face of the country, communication between the different parts of British India would otherwise be extremely difficult. They are not suffered to employ Englishmen in martial or civil capacities without the consent of the Indian government, or any other men of European race at all, and all Europeans within their borders are subject to the jurisdiction of a British court.

The succession of the native princes' heir, by birth or adoption, is guaranteed, provided he is recognised by the government of India as a fit person to succeed. If not, some worthy relative is put in his place; for since the Mutiny it has not been the policy of the Crown to annex native states, even in case of forfeiture by the ruler for misconduct. The reigning prince may, however, be deposed for disloyalty or gross misrule, and this is the ultimate means of enforcing British authority. The Indian government can, in fact, intervene to suppress insurrection, grave misconduct of the ruler, inhuman practices or religious intolerance, and, if the case is very bad, deposition sometimes follows. In such a case it is an advantage to select a child for the successor, because the government of India has a right during a minority to administer the state and educate the minor, with the result that by the time he comes of age his dominions have been brought into order, and he is himself imbued with English conceptions of government. The instrument through which the control of the native states is carried on is the resident, whom the prince is bound to receive, and to whose advice he must listen. He need not always follow it, but the admonitions of the resident count for much in the long run. By pressure of this kind, and by intervention in flagrant cases, the bands of thugs, and barbarous customs like infanticide and suttee, have been abolished in the native states, which have indeed tended in many ways to follow at a distance the example of British India.

The Federated Malay States.

The policy of leaving the native ruler at the head of his state, but controlling him by means of a British resident, has recently been applied in two cases that appear to be among the most successful of experiments in the administration of dependencies. In these cases, indeed, the principle has been carried so far that the resident really governs the country in the name of the local prince. The first case is that of the Malay Peninsula, where a number of native principalities lay behind the Straits Settlements held by England upon the coast. Disquiet among the Malays was complicated by the presence of many Chinese immigrants, who came to work the rich tin mines of the country. As the two races quarrelled among themselves and with each other, neither the public revenue nor the operation of the mines was secure, and finally in 1874 the turbulence became so great as to threaten trade in the Straits Settlements. Then England intervened, and compelled the Sultans of Perak and Selangor to receive British residents. The next year the resident at Perak was murdered; but a punitive expedition was despatched, the murderers were hanged, the Sultan deposed, and his successor followed the resident's advice. Negri Sembilan and Pahang were brought under English control some years later, and in 1895 all four were united under the name of the Federated Malay States.

The government of each state is in the hands of a State Council, composed mainly of the Sultan and the principal Malay chiefs, but practically directed by the resident; the local administration, also, being really conducted by English officers who act under him in the different districts. For the Federation as a whole, there is a periodical Durbar, or Council, attended by the Sultans with their retainers; but here again the guiding spirit is the Resident General, who superintends the residents in the states, and is in turn responsible to the Governor of the Straits Settlements as High Commissioner for the Federation. The management of certain things is centralised for the whole Confederation. This is true, for example, of the railways, and of the police force, which is commanded by English officers and is composed in part of Sikhs from India. Both in the Confederation, therefore, and in the several states, the rank and nominal authority of the native chiefs have been preserved, and are useful in securing the obedience of their subjects, while the government is really in the hands of Englishmen selected and trained for the service. The conditions of the peninsula lent themselves singularly to such an arrangement. The mines, now yielding three quarters of the world's annual product of tin, were worked by Chinese, who were ready to pay heavily in return for protection; and in fact the export duty on tin supplies a large part of the total revenue. With the funds from this source the residents could guarantee to the native chiefs a personal income far greater than they enjoyed under their own inefficient rule. Assurance of rank and money consoled them for the loss of substantive power; and thus the existence of rich mines enabled the English, simply by restoring order, to bring contentment to both Malay rulers and Chinese. The advance in good order, in roads, railways, governmental work of all kinds, and in material prosperity, under British rule has been amazing. But it is not so clear that the ultimate welfare of the natives has been promoted, for the Chinese immigrants are now about as numerous as the Malays, who may be doomed to disappear before the influx of the more efficient race.

Egypt. The other recent example of preserving the local ruler and controlling him by means of an English adviser, that of Egypt, is better known. Although in theory the occupation by England is still temporary, Egypt is really her permanent possession, the gateway to the East which she cannot surrender. The government is organised as a protectorate, but the mechanism employed, with the nominal suzerainty of Turkey, the relics of rights in other Great Powers, the formal authority of the Khedive, and the actual government by England, is too intricate to be described here. In this connection it is enough to point out that although the ministers of state are Egyptians, behind each of them stands, as adviser or under-secretary, a British officer whose suggestions he must obey; while above them all, as adviser to the Khedive, the English Agent and Minister Plenipotentiary is the real ruler of the country. Considering the difficulties encountered, the various interests involved and the temporary nature of the first occupation, the administration of Egypt must be regarded, in spite of criticisms of detail, as one of the most signal achievements of English skill in the management of dependent states.

# CHAPTER LVIII

## IMPERIAL FEDERATION

The Desire for Closer Union.

No change of political sentiment in England within a generation has been more marked than that toward the colonies. The fatalistic indifference that was widespread fifty years ago has been replaced by an almost universal desire to draw closer the bonds that connect the mother country with her grown-up children, as orators are fond of calling them. Such a feeling springs from many causes, some of them, as often happens, quite unconscious. At the head of the list may be placed the progress of the self-governing colonies. Canada, Australia and the Cape of Good Hope attract the attention of the whole world and naturally of England herself, far more than they did when she bade them God-speed with the grant of responsible ministries. She appreciates their value and is proud of them. Then, England has ceased to be self-sustaining, and her dependence on other countries for food becomes more and more evident as time goes on. The greater size, also, of foreign powers has not been without effect. Italy and Germany have become nations, while the United States has developed rapidly, the two latter having surpassed the British Isles in population. Standing alone, England does not seem so large a member in the family of states as she did formerly. Moreover, the vast increase in the armaments of European countries has forced her to assume a burden borne almost entirely on her own shoulders, which she thinks her children old enough to share. The desire for federation has, no doubt, been stimulated also by its apparent success elsewhere. Half a century ago the United States was the sole example of federal government on a large scale, and its permanence seemed very doubtful. But since that time the American republic has proved its stability, Germany has become united in a similar form, Switzerland has prospered on those lines, and the two largest groups of British self-governing colonies have adopted the same structure to the advantage of their people.

Self-governing Colonies Alone Involved.

What imperial federation means is, therefore, an important matter for consideration; and first it may be observed that it can apply only to the self-governing colonies. Dependencies that do not govern themselves might be taxed for the support of general defence, but they can obviously take no part in the government of the empire. If they cannot rule themselves, they certainly cannot rule other people, and to go through the form of having them do so would be worse than illusory. If India, for example, or the West Indies, should appoint delegates to an imperial council, they would be merely agents of the English ministry, and would reduce the representatives of the self-governing colonies to an insignificant fragment of the body. India and the crown colonies must continue to be ruled by England, or, what is probably less desirable, by the federation as a whole, and they can take no real part in the united government. Nearly three hundred and seventy millions of British subjects can, therefore, have no active share in the federation, which would be confined to the United Kingdom with some forty-two millions of people, and British North America, Australasia and the Cape, with about thirteen millions among them. It would thus be a combination between one large state in Europe, and a number of small ones at great distances, containing in all only about one third of her population. These conditions must be borne in mind in discussing the possible forms of closer union; for while the ratio of inhabitants in different parts of the empire will, no doubt, change, a long time must elapse, as already observed, before the population of all self-governing colonies added together can equal that of the British Isles.

The Existing Connection.

As in the classic case of the Greeks, the tie that binds the self-governing colonies to the parent state is based mainly upon sentiment. It is fortified, also, by common citizenship, and by a naval protection on the part of England to which the colonies make only a trifling contribution.[1] So far the bond has proved effective, and it has grown distinctly stronger during the last three decades. But it has not been put to a severe strain, because, since the grant of responsible government, England has been engaged in no war with a great power that involved danger or suffering to the colonies; and what the result of such a strain might be is not perhaps perfectly clear. If the Venezuela question had led to war, and the United States had tried to recoup herself for damage to her defenceless coast towns, by seizing the wheat-growing region west of the Great Lakes, is it certain that Canada would not have sought to avert the danger by a proclamation of neutrality? In short, is it certain that the self-governing colonies would, at great loss to themselves, cling to England in a quarrel which was not of their making, and in which she could not fully protect them? The safety, and perchance the very existence, of the empire depends upon the ability of England to communicate with and defend its different parts, and that depends upon the control of the sea. Now although the situation of the self-governing colonies at a great distance is an obstacle to federation, the distribution of the empire is singularly favourable to sea power. England has, on almost every important line of communication, strongholds which keep the road open for her fleets, and sometimes close it for

[1] Bernard Holland, in his *Imperium et Libertas* (297–98), quotes figures compiled by the Imperial Federation Committee in 1899 to show that the self-governing colonies, with close upon one third of the population of the United Kingdom, and nearly one half as much revenue, contributed less than one hundredth of the cost of naval defence. According to the figures compiled for the Colonial Conference of 1902, the average naval expenditure per head of population in the self-governing colonies was 4*d*., while for the United Kingdom it was 15*s*. 1*d*. In the same way the military expenditure per head was 2*s*. 5*d*. against 14*s*. 1¾*d*. Com. Papers, 1902, LXVI., 451, p. 42.

those of her enemies, while many of her most distant possessions are large enough to furnish supplies and resist conquest by sea indefinitely. Moreover, Australia and the Cape, as well as the smaller islands, and practically we may add Egypt, are not exposed to an attack by land; and Canada borders only on a nation with which England is extremely unlikely to come to blows. While, therefore, the tie with the self-governing colonies might conceivably be put to a severe strain by war, that is highly improbable so long as England maintains a sufficient navy. But in spite of her wealth, the burden of holding the sea against all the world has grown so heavy as to make her want the colonies, for whose joint benefit she conceives that she carries it, to bear their share, and this cannot be done without giving them a real voice in the foreign policy which the navy may be used to enforce.

**Steps toward a Closer Union.**

The granting of responsible government was probably the only course that could have been pursued at the time, but although it did not lead, as some men then predicted, to separation, it was certainly not a step toward federal union. It placed the colonies in a position with which they do not seem to be dissatisfied.[1] They are substantially free to manage their own affairs as they please, while on foreign matters that affect them, their opinions have great weight, and they have the protection of England's name and navy almost without expense. To an outside observer it would seem that while England desires a closer political and financial connection, the colonies are interested mainly in strengthening commercial relations. In some directions tentative steps have already been taken. Steamship lines and submarine cables have been promoted, a general penny postage has been established, and preferential tariffs have been enacted by almost all the self-governing colonies.

As early as 1892 a resolution was adopted by Canada that when England gave a preference to her products, she

[1] They so voted, with only two dissentient voices, at the Colonial Conference of 1897. Com. Papers, 1897, LIX., 631, p. 15.

Preferential Tariffs.

would be ready to reciprocate.[1] England did not respond to the offer; but Canada, after increasing her protective duties in 1897, gave in the following year a preference of twenty-five per cent to British products, and increased it to thirty-three and a third per cent in 1900, a concession that has been maintained under her new tariff of 1907. In 1903, the South African colonies, following the Canadian lead, gave a preference of twenty-five per cent on many British goods, and in the same year New Zealand raised her tariff wall against all foreign countries, but not against England — an example which was substantially copied by Australia in 1907. Of course, these concessions are not made, and will not be maintained, to the detriment of protected interests in the colonies, for experience proves that even in the different parts of a single nation people do not act on tariff questions from unselfish motives. The colonies are willing to take from England, rather than elsewhere, such goods as they import, but they can hardly be expected to run counter to their policy of protecting native industries, and hence the benefit to England is likely to be limited. Some of them, notably Canada, would, no doubt, be glad to make a real sacrifice in return for preferential duties in favour of their own products. But the imports from the self-governing colonies are mainly raw materials and food-stuffs, and many people insist that a serious tax on such things would be severely felt by the labouring classes and manufacturers in England, while her compensating benefits could not be great, because the possible consumption of her wares in the colonies is as yet small in proportion to her exports to other countries. On this question which is still hotly discussed among Englishmen, the writer can express no opinion, but the general election of 1906 made it clear that such a proposal will not be entertained at present, and the English ministers said so distinctly at the Colonial Conference in 1907.

The only important steps toward a closer political con-

[1] Com. Papers, 1905, LIII., 441, p. 2.

nection have been the consultations with the colonial Premiers in London.[1] The first of these was held in 1887 on the occasion of the Queen's jubilee. Another followed ten years later, and subsequent ones in 1902 and 1907. At the last of these a permanent organisation was adopted, whereby meetings, to be styled Imperial Conferences, are to be held every four years. They are to consist of the English Prime Minister and Colonial Secretary, and of the Premiers and other delegates of the self-governing colonies, each community represented having one vote. The Conference is, of course, merely a means of consultation, and has no power by majority vote to bind the mother country or any colony without its own consent. It is in the nature of a congress of diplomats rather than an organ of government. Even so it has been, and is likely to be, of great value in promoting an interchange of views, mutual concessions, and a general accord in matters of common interest. Still it must be remembered that interests cannot always be made identical, and that government means not action by universal consent, but compulsory obedience to an ultimate authority. Such an authority is not easily created for the British Empire.

**Colonial Conferences.**

The parliamentary system is singularly flexible within its limits. It is highly elastic up to a certain point, but it cannot be stretched beyond that point. One of the chief merits, indeed, of the Constitution of the United States has been its capability of extension over an increasing number of new states; but the parliamentary form of government, as it has developed in England, does not lend itself to the same process. The case of Ireland is in point. Mr. Gladstone proposed in different stages of his Home Rule Bills to exclude Irish members from the House of Commons altogether, to admit them only for imperial questions, and to give them full rights of membership; yet, quite apart

**Difficulty in Framing a Federal Authority.**

**Representation in Parliament.**

[1] A subsidiary conference was held at Ottawa in 1894 to discuss submarine cables, mail service and trade relations between Great Britain, Canada and Australasia.

from the fundamental question of giving Ireland a legislature of her own, there were serious objections to each of those plans which apply to the colonies with no less force. To exclude the Irish altogether would deprive them of all share in imperial concerns, and that is the present position of the colonies. To admit colonial members to the House for all purposes would increase the obstacle to the smooth working of the parliamentary system that is now created by the presence of the Irish members. It would mean that the fate of an Education Bill, and of a ministry, might be decided by colonial votes against the opinion of the members from the British Isles, a condition that would be intolerable to England. To admit them for imperial purposes alone would mean that the ministry might have a majority to-day, lose it to-morrow, and get it again the day after, a state of things that would render the principle of cabinet responsibility almost unworkable. Nor would any proposal of this kind satisfy the colonies, for it would mean that such matters as were placed in the charge of the central power would be conducted by English ministers, over whose selection or policy they might have no substantial influence. In short, direct representation in the House of Commons would mean that the colonies would interfere with England, or England would rule the colonies, far too much. These objections to admitting colonial delegates to Parliament are, in fact, so patent that such a plan is hardly entertained by any one.

Objections to an Imperial Council.

On the other hand, the difficulties in creating any real imperial authority outside of Parliament are not less great. To just the extent of the powers vested in such a body, Parliament would become a subordinate legislature, and it is conceivable that the foreign relations of the empire might be conducted by men who were not in accord with the English ministers. In order to explain how that might happen, we must review the possible ways in which an imperial council might be made up. It can hardly be supposed that the colonies, with anything like their present population, would be given a majority of the seats. If they were, the suggestion that the imperial council might be out of harmony with the British cabinet would not improbably become a fact to a greater or less extent. If, on the contrary, the membership were in proportion to population, the colonies would have one quarter, and England three quarters, of the seats; and in that case it would be necessary to consider how the English delegates would be selected. If the Opposition were in any way represented, it might again well happen that the colonial members, with a minority of the English, could control the council contrary to the opinions of the leaders of the House of Commons. But if, as is more likely, the representatives of the United Kingdom were appointed by the Crown, that is, by the cabinet, then the colonial delegates would be in a permanent and hopeless minority. They would be free to express their views, and persuade the English ministers if they were able, but when it came to a vote, they would always be overborne. The self-governing colonies in such a case would be obliged to contribute to imperial expenses without any effective share in directing imperial policy. These difficulties might be reduced by some arrangement about the majority required for certain kinds of action, as is done in the case of the German Bundesrath, but such provisions would hardly work well in a confederation of popular governments, and they certainly would not remove the obstacles altogether.

**Difficulties about Revenue.**

Then there is the question of revenue. The history of the Germanic Confederation, and of the United States of America under the Articles of Confederation, shows the inherent weakness of a federal government that has no resources of its own, and must rely upon demands made upon its component states. Yet direct authority in an imperial council to tax England and her colonies would give rise to fierce dissensions. By far the most convenient, and probably the only practicable, means of raising money would be indirect taxation, and one can imagine the debates that would take place on the question of customs-duties within the empire and against foreign nations.

The Obstacles Underrated.

Political capacity is abundant in the English race, and the formation of an imperial federation may not be beyond the reach of British statesmanship. But to an outside observer, the public in England appear to underrate the difficulty of the task, to leave out of sight the fact that the formation, or closer union, of every confederation involves some surrender of powers with which communities are loath to part. They appear to forget that the present federal union in Switzerland followed the war of the Sonderbund; that in spite of strong national yearnings the German Empire was created, not by speeches and resolutions of majorities, but by blood and iron; and that, as John Quincy Adams said at the fiftieth anniversary of its adoption, the Constitution of the United States was "extorted from the grinding necessity of a reluctant nation."

# PART VII. — THE COURTS OF LAW

## CHAPTER LIX

### HISTORY OF THE COURTS

THE institutions of England being the subject of this book, those which are peculiar to Scotland and Ireland have been described only so far as they affect the working of the central government; and for that reason the present chapter deals with the English courts alone. It has been pointed out already that the Common Law of England extends over Ireland; while Scotland, like all the countries of continental Europe, having failed to produce a highly developed system of native law, adopted freely, after the Renaissance, the principles of the Civil or Roman Law. It is natural, therefore, that the Irish courts should bear a much closer resemblance to the English tribunals than do the Scotch courts [1]; and, in fact, a great deal of what follows about the distinction between Common Law and Equity, and about procedure, applies to Ireland and not to Scotland.[2]

Scope of the Chapter.

In a chapter of this kind it is impossible to do more than trace in outline the organisation of the courts, and

[1] The most important of the inferior courts of Scotland is that of the sheriff, who is appointed during good behaviour by the Crown, and whose jurisdiction corresponds to that of the English county courts in civil, and to that of quarter sessions in criminal, matters. The higher courts have either been substantially merged in the Court of Session, or have the same persons as judges. Some of the members of that court sit singly for criminal and civil business, being known in the latter case as the Outer House. The Inner House, which acts as a court of appeal, sits in two sections of four judges each, the Lord President presiding in one, and the Lord Justice Clerk in the other.

[2] The distinction between law and equity is practically unknown in Scotland.

the nature of the authority they wield; but even that can hardly be made clear to a reader unversed in English law without a short explanation of the origin of the different judicial bodies.

**The Three Ancient Courts of Common Law.**

By the middle of the thirteenth century there had been evolved from the *curia*, or lesser council, of the Norman kings, three courts of law. The oldest of these, later known as the Court of King's Bench, administered justice in matters affecting the Crown, and especially in criminal cases; the Court of Common Pleas decided suits between private parties; and the Court of Exchequer dealt with questions relating to the royal revenues. But the first and last of these courts, in order to enhance their own reputation, and for the sake of the fees that came to their officers, desired to acquire jurisdiction over ordinary civil suits; and this they did by means of fictions. Private claims could be recovered in the King's Bench against persons already in the custody of the royal officers on a charge of breach of the king's peace. Any one, therefore, who wished to bring a suit in that court, began with a sham process for the arrest of the defendant, and then proceeded against him, alleging that he was in the custody of the Marshall of the Marshalsea, an allegation which the court did not permit the defendant to contradict. The Court of Exchequer extended its authority in a similar way. It entertained private suits brought by the king's debtors, on the ground that the refusal of the defendant to satisfy the claim rendered the plaintiff less able to pay his debt to the Crown; and it did not suffer a statement that the plaintiff was the king's debtor to be denied.[1] Thus while each of these courts retained some jurisdiction peculiar to itself, all three dealt with ordinary

[1] A similar extension of the jurisdiction of the federal courts in the United States was made by their refusal to hear a denial that all the stockholders of a corporation are citizens of the State by which it is chartered; Louisville Railroad Co. *vs.* Letson, 2 How. 497, Marshall *vs.* Baltimore and Ohio Railroad Co., 16 How. 314, Covington Drawbridge Co. *vs.* Shepherd, 20 How. 227; and the first steps in a further extension of authority seem to be taking place through the process of receiverships.

civil suits.[1] Until 1830 each of them was composed of a chief justice and three *puisne* judges, the members of the Exchequer bearing the ancient titles of barons and chief baron.[2] Writs of error lay from each court to the members of the other two sitting together in what was known as the Exchequer Chamber;[3] and from there to the House of Lords.

Before 1846, when the new county courts were created, civil justice at Common Law was highly centralised, for the royal courts had superseded the old local ones, which had fallen almost entirely into disuse. The old county courts lingered with a nominal jurisdiction, in cases where the amount involved did not exceed forty shillings; and there were a few other tribunals which exercised a real, though limited, authority. Most of these were in chartered towns, or were small "courts of requests" established by statute to meet a special local need. But they covered only a fraction of the country, and it is not going too far to say that the administration of civil justice at Common Law was very nearly wholly in the hands of the three courts at Westminster. This did not mean that all the cases were tried there. Almost without interruption since the time of Henry II., royal officers have been commissioned to travel over the country holding court. In the course of time that duty became practically, although not formally, confined to the judges of the three courts, and a couple of those judges visited every part of England at least twice a year, to try, with the aid of local juries, civil and criminal cases that would otherwise come before the courts at Westminster. The judges in eyre were, in fact, the chief instrument in

**The Centralisation of Justice.**

**The Judges on Circuit.**

[1] The Common Pleas retained exclusive jurisdiction of real actions, and some matters that grew out of them. The Exchequer acquired also some jurisdiction in equity which was transferred to the Court of Chancery in 1841. 5 Vic., c. 5.

[2] They were not real barons, that is, they were not peers. In 1830 a fifth, and in 1868 a sixth judge was added to each court.

[3] Formerly errors from the Common Pleas went to the King's Bench, but this was changed by statute in 1830. 11 Geo. IV. and 1 Will. IV., c. 70.

breaking down the old local courts. It was they who made possible the centralisation of justice in the royal courts, and the growth of a truly national jurisprudence — the English Common Law.

The Court of Chancery.

Another system of justice arose later, and was still more centralised, because, having no connection with the practice of going on circuit, it was administered exclusively at Westminster.[1] As the Common Law developed, and became a real body of law, with greater precision, and more settled principles, it became at the same time more rigid. One of its maxims was that there is no wrong without a remedy, which came to mean that the existence of a remedy was the test of a wrong. Now the suits in the Common Law courts were based upon writs issued out of chancery, and in time these became fixed by precedent, so that redress was not readily obtained for a new class of injuries. Greater precision had made the law less elastic, and legislation had not reached the point where it could fill the gap caused by the failure of the courts to keep pace with the needs of a growing civilisation. But the King was still the fountain of justice. In creating the three great courts he had not yet exhausted his powers, and petitions were addressed to him for relief in cases where there was no remedy by the strict rules of the Common Law. When these related to private matters they were commonly referred to the Chancellor, to whom, indeed, the petitions themselves were in later times directly addressed. He did not in form reverse the decisions of the older courts, or in fact touch Common Law rights at all; but he forbade the possessors, on pain of imprisonment, to make use of them contrary to equity and good conscience.

In plain English there was superimposed upon the older system of law a new one known as Equity. A man continued to enjoy his Common Law rights, but he would

[1] Except for the courts of chancery in the counties palatine of which those of Lancashire and Durham still survive, *cf.* 11 Geo. IV. and 1 Will. IV., c. 70, §§ 13–14; 52–53 Vic., c. 47; 53–54 Vic., c. 23.

enjoy them in the chancery prison if he refused to obey the decree made by the Lord Chancellor. Equity, which affected chiefly the richer and more progressive part of the community, was used for two objects: to enforce rights quite unknown to the Common Law, and to give more effectual remedies for existing legal rights. As examples of the former, Equity enforced trusts, gave relief against frauds which were not recognised by the Common Law courts, and treated a mortgage as a security for debt instead of a pledge absolutely forfeited by non-fulfilment of the obligation. As examples of the latter it enjoined a man to perform a Common Law duty, or to abstain from committing a wrong; while the older courts could only award damages after the injury, and perhaps an irreparable one, had been done.

Later Courts of Equity.

Moving slowly from precedent to precedent, Equity, like the Common Law, evolved a vast mass of principles, and the Chancellor, who had many other duties to perform, cast some of his growing judicial work upon the Master of the Rolls. But the business of the court increased rapidly, for Equity furnished to the upper classes the means of tying up estates with elaborate provisions for the future, of securing property for married women against a husband and his creditors, and of doing many other things which they wanted to do. In the nineteenth century, therefore, one, and later three, Vice-Chancellors were created. From these, and from the Master of the Rolls an appeal lay to the Chancellor; but here again he was relieved in 1851 by the appointment of two Lords Justices of Appeal, from whose decision, as from that of the Chancellor himself, an appeal could be taken to the House of Lords. Now all these judges sat at Westminster alone, a state of things that would probably have been intolerable had not the Court of Chancery been a tribunal where the parties were in the main rich.

The earlier Chancellors were ecclesiastics bred in the Canon Law, which was based on Roman jurisprudence; and hence, in administering Equity they followed that law,

Procedure at Common Law.

rather than the practice of the older courts, both as to principles and forms. But the contrast between the procedure at Common Law and in Equity is due not only to a difference in legal conceptions and models, but also to the methods of trial. These have produced some notable effects. At Common Law trial was by judge and jury, the jury deciding the questions of fact, while the questions of law were decided by the judge, or referred in case of doubt to the full bench of the court in which the suit had been brought. Under these conditions it was natural that questions of law and fact should be carefully separated, and that the latter should be laid before the jury in as simple a form as possible. The system of pleading was well adapted to insure both of these results, although sometimes at the price of disabling a party from presenting fully his side of the case.

A civil suit began, as a rule, with a writ issued out of chancery which indicated the nature of the action and ordered the defendant to appear. Then followed the declaration stating briefly the basis of the claim. If the defendant wished to take the ground that the statement, even if true, furnished no good legal cause for recovery, he raised that question of law by a demurrer, which admitted the truth of the facts. If, on the other hand, he wished to deny the facts, or some part of the essential facts alleged, he filed a plea which traversed, as it was called, those facts, but admitted that, if true, they presented a good legal claim. If, in the third place, he wished to bring forward other facts that would afford a defence to the claim, he must set them up in a plea which admitted the truth of the declaration. This was known as a plea in confession and avoidance. The plaintiff in his turn might demur to such a plea, or by a replication either traverse it, or confess and avoid it by fresh allegations; and the pleading proceeded until either a demurrer or a traverse was reached. The demurrer raised the question whether, assuming all the statements of fact in the pleadings to be true, the plaintiff had in law set up a good claim; and that question went to the court for decision. The traverse raised a single and narrow issue of fact, which was tried before a jury.[1]

Procedure in Equity.

In Equity the judge sat without a jury, and hence there was no need of narrowing the issue, or of drawing a sharp line between law and facts. Greater elasticity was given at the very beginning of a suit, because the plaintiff was not confined to certain fixed forms of action, the writs issued out of chancery being used only off the premises. The procedure opened with a bill in the form of a petition for redress, stating fully the claim and the grounds on which the claim was based, and including much that at Common Law would be regarded as evidence. The defendant set up his defence in an answer equally full. If this introduced new matter, requiring additional statements to meet it, the plaintiff might amend his bill, the defendant having the same privilege for his answer; and each of the parties was required to prove every fact, and maintain every point of law essential to his case.

Rules of Evidence at Common Law.

Another result of trial by jury was the growth of elaborate rules of evidence. Jurymen being of necessity inexpert in weighing evidence, it was important to shut out from their consideration testimony that would have a greater tendency to bias or confuse them than to enable them to ascertain the truth. Hence, for example, the principle excluding hearsay. The rules became more and more strict and technical until, when Bentham attacked them in his "Rationale of Judicial Evidence," they had undoubtedly gone so far as to interfere seriously with justice. It is interesting to compare the rules of evidence of the English courts, which had trial by jury, with the rules of proof evolved by the

[1] The theory of pleading is stated in this simple form to make its principle clear, although in fact the parties were not conclusively limited to a single issue in law or fact so closely as a bare statement of the general system would indicate. A party beaten before the jury could still raise the questions of law presented on the pleadings by a motion for arrest of judgment, or for judgment *non obstante veredicto;* or if beaten on a demurrer he could move for leave to amend his pleading.

pre-revolutionary criminal courts on the Continent. These last, sitting without a jury, admitted evidence of every kind, but laid down minutely the weight to be attached to each kind, and the amount of each kind that would justify conviction for various classes of crimes.[1] The difference between rules of proof and rules of evidence is, indeed, largely responsible for the habitual use of torture to extract a confession among the nations that adopted the civil law, and its general absence in England.

In order to exclude improper evidence from the jury the court must know in advance what the nature of the testimony will be, and hence it is given only in the answer to questions asked by the counsel or the court.[2] Under such a method of introducing evidence has grown up the practice of examining and cross-examining witnesses; and an intelligent Japanese observer has rightly observed that the glory of Common Law trials consists not so much in the use of the jury as in the art of cross-examination. All this is in marked contrast with a trial under the French codes of procedure, which provide that a witness shall tell his story in his own way, and must not be interrupted until he has finished. In France the counsel for the prisoner in criminal cases has no right to cross-examine the witnesses directly, but only to propose questions to be asked of them by the president of the court; and this is true of both parties in civil suits.[3] Even at the present day each system is occasionally liable to result in a miscarriage of justice. It is safe to say that Dreyfus could not have been convicted by any court that applied the Common Law rules of evidence; and on the other hand in the case of Adolf Beck, which made a great stir in England in 1904, the prisoner was found guilty because the judge, by

[1] *Cf.* Esmein, *Histoire de la procédure criminelle en France*, Part II., Tit. 1, Ch. III.

[2] Before the Act of 1898 a prisoner in England, not being allowed to testify in his own defence, was permitted to make a general statement not under oath. But that was an illogical exception that mitigated the rigour of the rule.

[3] *Code d'Instruction Criminelle*, Art. 319. *Code de Procédure Civile*, Arts. 273, 276.

an erroneous exclusion of testimony, prevented him establishing his real defence — that of mistaken identity.[1]

The Court of Chancery, sitting like continental courts, without a jury, had not the same need of rules of evidence as the Common Law courts, and by itself would doubtless not have developed them. Its method of obtaining evidence was, in fact, very different from that used in jury trials. Each party could file interrogatories to be answered under oath by the other, and the testimony of third persons was taken in the form of depositions based upon written interrogatories answered in former times without the presence of the other party. The methods in Law and Equity drew in some matters farther and farther apart, until the Common Law courts refused to permit the parties to a suit to testify at all, on the ground that having an interest in the result they were biased and untrustworthy; while in Equity the sworn statements of the parties, with their answers to interrogatories, were the chief source of evidence. The divergence in practice was maintained by the fact that the judges in the two classes of courts, and for the most part the practitioners also, were distinct; but two such systems of law could not exist permanently side by side. In the process of time the gap became less insuperable, and a desire arose for a fusion of the two into a larger Common Law, enriched by the principles that Equity had drawn from Roman sources. Before the close of the nineteenth century the time was ripe for a long step in this direction, and it was taken when the old courts were recast by the Judicature Act of 1873. Evidence in Equity.

Before describing the reorganisation of the civil courts of Common Law and Equity, a word must be said about the other courts then existing; and first, of the criminal tribunals. Civil law relates to the maintenance of private claims, and the redress of private wrongs. Its object is to enable a person to enforce his rights, or obtain compensation for their violation; and, if he is not incompetent in the eye of Criminal Law.

[1] Rep. of Com. on the Beck Case, Com. Papers, 1905, LXII., 465, p. xii.

the law, no one else can enforce or release them. Criminal law deals with offences against the public, and their punishment on behalf of the community. In England any one may prosecute for such an offence, while the Crown can stop the proceedings and can pardon the offender. In many cases, no doubt, the wishes of the person who has suffered from a crime practically determine whether a prosecution shall be brought or not, but he has no legal rights in the matter. The same act may, no doubt, be both a public offence and a private wrong; but in England the criminal and civil proceedings that ensue are almost always entirely distinct, and the result in one has no legal effect upon the decision in the other. There is, however, a class of cases where the two kinds of law are deliberately confused; where the form of action is a civil suit, but the object is the punishment of a public offence. It is known in England as the penal action, and it takes the form of a suit by a person injured, or by a common informer, to recover a penalty which the statute makes payable to him. The penalty is not measured by the injury, and is not intended as a compensation therefor, but is meant in the interest of the community as a punishment that will act as a deterrent. The most famous example is that of the *Habeas Corpus* Act of 1679,[1] and there are many others, the object being to impose a fine which the Crown cannot remit, either by stopping the proceedings or by granting a pardon.

The Criminal Courts before 1875.

Before the creation of the county courts in 1846, civil justice at Common Law was highly centralised, and in Equity still more so; but criminal justice was administered by a large number of local tribunals, as well as by the judges on circuit. This was due not to the survival of early popular or feudal courts, for they had long faded into insignificance. It was due to the statutory authority of the justices of the peace. The criminal functions of these magistrates need not, however, be described in detail here, be-

[1] 31 Car. II., c. 2.

cause they remain to the present day, and will be mentioned hereafter in due course.[1] It is enough to point out that their powers were conferred, bit by bit, by a long series of statutes covering over more than six centuries; and that their jurisdiction extended from summary proceedings for trivial offences to the trial with a jury at quarter sessions of all but the gravest crimes. Above them stood the courts at Westminster, for although until 1907 the English law never provided a general system of appeals in criminal cases, a review of certain classes of questions was secured by various methods. In the first place, justices of the peace were kept from overstepping their authority by writs of *mandamus*, prohibition and *certiorari* brought before the King's Bench, of which more hereafter. Then for an error of law apparent on the record of any criminal case a writ of error lay to the King's Bench, and thence to the Exchequer Chamber and the House of Lords. Finally, upon a conviction, the presiding justice could reserve a question of law for decision, without further appeal, by the Court for Crown Cases Reserved. This last court, created in 1848, was composed of five members taken from among the judges of the three Common Law courts at Westminster.[2]

**The Ecclesiastical Courts.**

In former times the ecclesiastical courts touched the affairs of the ordinary citizen. They decided whether his marriage was valid, and they regulated the administration of his estate; but now their jurisdiction is practically confined to questions affecting the Established Church and its clergy. They are more appropriately treated, therefore, in connection with that Church than with the national courts of law. In 1857 their jurisdiction over the probate of wills, and the granting of letters of administration, was transferred to the Court of Probate; that over marriage to the Court for Divorce and Matrimonial Causes; both new

**Probate and Divorce.**

[1] Their administrative duties have been mainly transferred to elective local bodies, already dealt with under the head of Local Government. The justices of the peace had also a limited civil jurisdiction in a very few cases.

[2] 11–12 Vic., c. 78.

tribunals created for the purpose,[1] and both now united in a branch of the High Court of Justice.

The Court of Admiralty.

One other venerable tribunal has passed through sundry vicissitudes. The Lord High Admiral had jurisdiction over both crimes and civil wrongs done at sea. His court administered a justice based partly on the Civil Law, partly on the fiction that a ship is a person capable of moral responsibility and liable to be sold to make payment for its debts. In 1861[2] the criminal jurisdiction was virtually transferred to the ordinary criminal courts by a provision that offences committed at sea might be punished as though they had been committed on land. But meanwhile the judge of the Court of Admiralty himself went through some strange metamorphoses. For a time he was practically identified with the Dean of Arches, the most important ecclesiastical judge.[3] Then it was provided that upon the next vacancy he should be the same person as the judge of the Probate Court which had just been created,[4] and although the two offices were afterwards separated for a season, the tendency to regard wills, collisions and divorce as kindred matters to be dealt with by the same tribunal revived when the great reorganisation of the courts took place in 1873.

[1] 20–21 Vic., cc. 77 and 85. These two courts were distinct, but practically the same man was the ordinary judge in both, although in the second the Chancellor and a number of the Common Law judges were members also, and were called upon to sit in some special cases and on appeals from the ordinary judge. From the Court of Probate, and on petitions for dissolution of marriage, an appeal lay to the House of Lords.

The ecclesiastical courts could grant only a judicial separation. A complete divorce with a right to marry again had up to that time been confined to persons rich enough to promote a private bill in Parliament, but by this Act authority to decree a divorce was vested in the new court.

[2] 24–25 Vic., c. 97, § 72; c. 98, § 50; c. 99, § 68.

[3] *Cf.* 3–4 Vic., c. 65.

[4] 20–21 Vic., c. 77, §§ 10–11. Appeals in admiralty had formerly gone to the High Court of Delegates, but in 1832 they were transferred to the Crown in Council, which soon became the Judicial Committee of the Privy Council.

# CHAPTER LX

## THE EXISTING COURTS

THE courts at Westminster were completely remodelled in 1873. But before speaking of this it may be well to describe the inferior or local tribunals as they now exist. In their case the civil and criminal courts are entirely distinct, the former consisting of the new county courts together with a few older bodies that survive in some places, while the justices of the peace furnish the type for almost all the latter.

The present county courts were created in 1846. In spite of the title the area of their jurisdiction is not a county, but a district which is much smaller in extent and has no necessary relation to the county boundaries. The arrangement was a part of the habit — one can hardly call it policy — that prevailed during the middle of the nineteenth century, of parcelling the country for each new local object into fresh divisions regardless of those already in existence; the result being the geographical chaos from which England has of late been trying painfully to recover. The county court districts can be changed by order in council, and are now more than five hundred in number. They are, therefore, small in size, and while that is a convenience to suitors, the business in any one of them is not large enough to occupy the whole time of a judge. Hence they are grouped into circuits, in which a single judge usually does the work for all the districts. The judges are appointed, and can be removed, by the Lord Chancellor; but their salaries, like those of the higher judges, are charged upon the Consolidated Fund.

The County Courts.

Litigation in England is an expensive luxury, and the county courts were designed to supply justice cheaply in small matters. Their jurisdiction, although enlarged from time to time, is still very limited. With a few classes of actions, such as libel, slander and divorce, they are not competent to deal at all. In a few others, such as certain claims by workmen for injuries, and by farmers for improvements, their jurisdiction is exclusive; as a general rule, however, it is concurrent with that of the High Court in all matters of Common Law, Equity, Probate, Bankruptcy and Admiralty, up to a certain amount. That amount varies a great deal according to the subject involved, but in general it may be said that the ordinary limit for suits at Common Law in the county courts is a hundred pounds, and for those in Equity five hundred pounds.[1] The judge usually decides both law and fact, but, except where the sum involved is very small, either party has a right to a jury of eight persons.[2] On points of law an appeal lies to the High Court,[3] with whose consent it may go farther.

Besides the county courts there are a few local civil courts that are still active,[4] and a number of others that have practically ceased to do any business.

The Justices of the Peace.

Local criminal justice is administered by the justices of the peace, and by courts to which their powers in certain towns have been transferred. Geographically the area of their authority is normally the shire, and as a rule a separate commission of the peace is issued for each county; although in some cases it is issued for a smaller district. Thus there are separate commissions for each of the three ridings of Yorkshire, for each of the three parts of Lincolnshire, for a couple of special "liberties" that still remain, and

[1] *Cf.* County Courts Acts of 1888 and 1903, 51–52 Vic., c. 43, and 3 Edw. VII., c. 42.

[2] 3 Edw. VII., c. 42, § 4. Formerly the number was five. 51–52 Vic., c. 43, § 102.

[3] If the amount involved exceeds twenty pounds, or in any case with the leave of the judge. 51–52 Vic., c. 43, § 120.

[4] In most of these the Recorder acts as judge.

for many boroughs that have acquired the privilege. Formerly the office was confined to a small number of great landowners, assisted by a sprinkling of lawyers, but as the justices declined to accept their fees, the lawyers disappeared, while the service being honorary, the position became an honour coveted by more and more people. In many of the counties the lists now contain three or four hundred names, and in Lancashire there are about eight hundred, although some of these men never qualify as acting magistrates by taking the oaths prescribed, and the regular work is done by a comparatively small number of persons.[1] Except for privy councillors, judges, peers with their eldest sons, and some others whose station is deemed a guarantee of fitness, there was until a couple of years ago a property qualification consisting of the ownership of land, or the occupation of a dwelling-house, worth a hundred pounds a year. The justices are appointed and removed by the Crown, but for a couple of centuries removals have not been made for political motives. Mainly in consequence of the property qualification, however, the justices came to be overwhelmingly Conservative, and in order to prevent such a result, which was naturally a grievance to the Liberals,[2] the qualification was abolished altogether in 1906.[3]

**Their Criminal Jurisdiction.**

The work of the justices of the peace in the administration of criminal law is of three kinds. A single justice has the powers of a police magistrate. He can order the arrest of an offender, and except in a case of death, where the coroner's jury is called in, he conducts the preliminary investigation, and either releases the accused or commits him, with or without bail, for indictment by a grand jury. A single justice has also power to impose very small punishments for trivial violations of law. Then there is an extensive summary jurisdiction over minor offences vested in two or more justices, meeting in what is known as a petty

[1] Lists of the names of all the justices were published in Com. Papers, 1893, LXXIV., Part I., 229, 295.

[2] *Cf.* Hans. 4 Ser. CLVIII., 1079 *et seq.*

[3] 6 Edw. VII., c. 16.

session. They sit without a jury and are judges of both law and fact. As a rule, however, the accused, if sentenced to imprisonment, can by appeal obtain a new trial before the justices at quarter sessions,[1] and any person aggrieved can require the justices at the petty session to state a case, and so reserve for the High Court the questions of law that may have arisen.[2]

Finally all the justices of the peace for the county, or such of them as choose to attend, meet at least four times a year at quarter sessions. The criminal business done there consists: first, of the trial, without a jury, of cases appealed from the courts of summary jurisdiction; and second, of the trial, with a jury, and after indictment by a grand jury, of any offences not of a minor character, except crimes punishable by death or penal servitude for life and a few other grave offences which are reserved for the assizes — that is, for the judges from Westminster on their circuits. As a matter of fact a little less than one third of the indictable offences in the kingdom are tried at the assizes, and the rest at quarter sessions, including under that name the borough courts, to which in many places the functions of the justices of the peace have been transferred.

**The Control by the High Court.**

In case of conviction the justices may, if they think fit, state a question of law for the decision of the High Court[3]; but quite apart from this, the royal courts have maintained from of old a real control over the justices of the peace, and to some extent over ecclesiastical, military and other inferior or special tribunals. It is exerted by means of several Common Law writs, in form addressed to the tribunal itself: the writ of *mandamus*, ordering it to perform a duty; the writ of prohibition, forbidding it to act in a case not within its jurisdiction; and the writ of *certiorari*, directing it to transmit a case to the High Court in order that the proceedings may be quashed, or the trial take place there.

To draw up a list of all the rich men living in a county, and to allow those among them who happen to take interest

[1] 42–43 Vic., c. 49, § 19. [2] *Ibid.*, § 33. [3] 11–12 Vic., c. 78.

enough to be present, to form themselves into a court for the trial of offenders — and that without the least security that they have any knowledge of the law — may seem a strange method of selecting criminal judges. But in fact the justices of the peace have the qualifications of jurors rather than judges, and they are, as already observed in an earlier chapter, very much under the guidance of their clerk. He is a solicitor, and if not a highly trained lawyer is expected to be thoroughly familiar with the statutes under which the justices act, and with the interpretation that has been placed upon them by the courts. What is more, he knows the procedure and the traditions of the place, and the sentences that have been commonly imposed. For the whole county there is a Clerk of the Peace, the holder of an ancient office,[1] always present at quarter sessions, who has been well said to be the centre of the system,[2] and there is also a clerk for each petty session, who keeps the justices sitting there from errors and indiscretions.

**The Clerk of the Justices.**

The administration of criminal law by justices of the peace is a good deal modified in its application to the larger towns. The smallest boroughs have no separate commissions of the peace, and in that case they are treated for the purposes of criminal justice simply as parts of the counties in which they lie. The rest have separate commissions of the peace with or without quarter sessions. If they have no such sessions of their own, they come under the quarter sessions for the county; if they have separate quarter sessions, the work there is conducted not by ordinary justices of the peace, but solely by the Recorder, a barrister appointed to the office by the Crown, and paid a small salary by the borough. In either case the justices of the peace for the borough take no part in quarter sessions. Acting singly, they have the

**Borough Criminal Courts.**

[1] *Cf.* Statutes of the Realm, 12 Rich. II., c. 10, which provides for his compensation; and 37 Hen. VIII., c. 1, which directs that persons instructed in the laws of the realm shall be appointed to the office.

[2] Maitland, "Justice and Police," 92.

usual powers as magistrates, and sitting two or more together, they exercise the summary jurisdiction. The county justices can, indeed, perform the same duties, except in those boroughs that had acquired before 1835 the right to exclude them. In short, a separate commission of the peace does not mean quite what the name implies. It means merely that there is a distinct list of justices whose authority is confined to the lesser criminal business of the borough; while separate quarter sessions means that all the more important criminal jurisdiction is transferred from the justices of the peace to a single professional judge.

London.

In the City of London the mayor and aldermen are *ex officio* justices of the peace, with more than the usual powers; while the Recorder, the Common Sergeant, and the Judge of the City of London Court occupy an exceptional position, and try many criminal cases. But much more important is the metropolitan area outside the City, where the system of unpaid justices of the peace broke down more than a century ago, and was replaced by a salaried magistracy. At present the quarter sessions for the County of London are held twice a month and directed by a paid judge, the lesser judicial work being done by more than a score of salaried police magistrates, each of whom has the powers of two justices of the peace at petty sessions. Any provincial borough that chooses may have, for the same purpose, a stipendiary magistrate, as he is called; but only a part, even of the largest ones, have cared to do so. All such magistrates are appointed by the Crown; and in fact, if we leave out exceptional cases like those of the City of London, of the mayors of boroughs and chairmen of county and district councils who are *ex officio* justices of the peace, we may lay down the general rule that all local judges or justices, whether civil or criminal, are appointed, and can legally be removed, by the Crown or by the Lord Chancellor acting in its behalf.

Stipendiary Magistrates.

The Supreme Court of Judicature Act of 1873,[1] together

[1] 36–37 Vic., c. 66.

with the amending Act of 1875,[1] remodelled all the higher courts. Except for the House of Lords, whose appellate jurisdiction was according to the original plan abolished, they were all merged in a new organisation called the Supreme Court of Judicature, divided into two branches, a High Court of Justice, and above it a Court of Appeal. **Supreme Court of Judicature.**

To the High Court was transferred the jurisdiction of the courts which it replaced; and in fact it was made up of divisions that correspond very closely to those courts.[2] The Chancery Division took over the work of the courts of chancery. On the Common Law side there were at first three divisions, known as the Queen's Bench, Common Pleas and Exchequer. To these were transferred the duties of the old courts of the same names, together with those of the courts of pleas of Lancaster and Durham,[3] and after some vicissitudes, of the London Court of Bankruptcy also.[4] But, by an Order in Council of 1880,[5] issued under authority conferred in the Act, the Common Pleas and Exchequer Divisions were afterwards abolished, or rather consolidated with the Queen's (now King's) Bench Division. Finally the Probate, Divorce and Admiralty Division was given the functions of the courts dealing with those subjects. **The High Court and its Divisions.**

Each of the three existing divisions has a president. For the Chancery Division he is the Lord Chancellor; for the King's Bench the Chief Justice of England; while for the Division of Probate, Divorce and Admiralty, in default of a higher flight of imagination, he is called simply the President of that division. The amount of business in the three divisions is naturally very different, and hence the number of judges in each of them is not the same. At

[1] 38–39 Vic., c. 77. [2] 36–37 Vic., c. 66, §§ 31–36.

[3] The chancery courts of Lancaster and Durham were a convenience, and were allowed to remain. The courts of pleas there were not so great a convenience, because Common Law cases were tried in the county by the judges of the High Court on circuit.

[4] 36–37 Vic., c. 66, § 16; 38–39 Vic., c. 77, § 9; 46–47 Vic., c. 52, §§ 93, 94.

[5] Order of Dec. 16, 1880, Com. Papers, 1881, LXXVI., 409, 413.

present, including the presidents, there are in the Chancery Division seven judges; in the King's Bench Division, fifteen; and in the Probate, Divorce and Admiralty Division, only two.

Relation of Law and Equity

It might seem that so far as the two first divisions are concerned, the High Court was little more than a collective name for the older courts, but this is not entirely true, for the Act contains two important provisions. One of these allows a judge belonging to any division to sit in any other;[1] while the second declares that any equitable claim, defence or relief may be used in any division of the court, and that subject thereto every division shall give effect to Common Law rights.[2] In other words, equitable remedies and defences may be used at Common Law and *vice versa.* Apart from its immediate effect upon present practice, this provision may have a bearing on the future relations of Common Law and Equity. As yet, however, the two historic systems have made less progress toward fusion than was expected. Except for matters arising incidentally in a case, they are still administered in the main separately, and by judges reared in the traditions of their own system; while the counsel who practise in the two branches of the law are nearly as sharply divided as ever, and retain for each other's fields a sentiment not wholly of admiration. Nevertheless the two systems have been brought into closer contact, and the way has been paved for a possible ultimate fusion.

The Rules of Practice.

It may be observed, also, that the rules of practice of the new courts can be changed from time to time by the Chancellor and a majority of the judges, on condition that the rules so made must be laid on the tables of Parliament, and become void if within forty days either House adopts a resolution to that effect.[3] This is a most elastic and intelligent method of regulating judicial procedure, and it

[1] 36–37 Vic., c. 66, § 31.
[2] *Ibid.*, §§ 24, 25 (11).
[3] *Ibid.*, §§ 68–74; 38–39 Vic., c. 77, §§ 16–21, 24–25.

has had the effect of producing great simplicity and uniformity in pleading and practice both at Common Law and in Equity.[1]

Trial of Cases in the High Court.

The judges of the High Court do part of their work singly, and part of it in divisional courts. The ordinary trial of cases, that is, the hearing of evidence and giving judgment in the first instance, whether the case be civil or criminal, whether it be at Common Law or in Equity, whether with or without a jury, is done by a single judge. An Equity case is normally tried by a judge of the Chancery Division, sitting at the royal courts in the Strand,[2] without a jury; unless by leave of the court an issue is framed for a jury,[3] when it is usually placed on the list of cases to be tried by a judge of the King's Bench Division. In a civil case at Common Law, on the other hand, either party can, as a rule, claim a jury;[4] and whether this is done or not the case is normally tried by a judge of the King's Bench Division sitting with or without a jury as the case may be, either at the royal courts in the Strand or on circuit in the country.[5] Criminal cases that come before the High Court are tried almost wholly by the judges on their circuits, or at the Central Criminal Court in London.

Special Juries.

It may be interesting to note that there is more than one kind of jury. An ordinary jury is drawn from men having a small property qualification, the general basis being the occupation of land worth ten pounds a year. Service on an ordinary jury is thus less extended than the present parliamentary franchise, but it is by no means narrowly

[1] The practice has some features derived from Common Law and some from Equity. Each party may be called upon to prove his whole case, but the judge has power to split up a case which is too complicated for a jury. The mode of taking evidence has been derived mainly from the Common Law, supplemented by the equitable practice of interrogatories. *Cf.* Schedule to the Acts of 1873 and 1875.

[2] But it may be tried by a judge on circuit. 36–37 Vic., c. 66, § 29.

[3] *Cf. Ibid.*, §§ 56–57; *cf.* 38–39 Vic., c. 77, Order xxxvi., 26, 27.

[4] 38–39 Vic., c. 77, Order xxxvi., 2–4.

[5] A judge of one of the other divisions may be sent on circuit, *Ibid.*, § 37, but it is not usual.

restricted, and the compensation is only one shilling a day.[1] On the other hand, either party to a suit has a right to claim a special jury, drawn from persons who possess larger qualifications, and are paid, at the expense of the parties, a guinea a day. The category of men who can serve is limited to esquires and persons with a higher title; to bankers and merchants; and to those who occupy a house worth from fifty to a hundred pounds a year according to the size of the town, a farm worth three hundred pounds a year, or any other premises of an annual value of a hundred pounds.[2] That special juries are more satisfactory than ordinary ones, especially to defendants, is proved by the increasing use made of them of late years. In fact the statistics would seem to show that they are gaining not only upon ordinary juries, but also upon trials before a judge without a jury.[3]

The Circuits of Judges.

Of the commissions for the administration of justice on circuit there are three kinds. The commission of assize, which authorises the trial of civil cases pending before the High Court in the outlying counties; and the commissions of gaol delivery and *oyer et terminer*, for the trial of criminal cases. The commissions comprise many persons, but partly by statute, partly by the terms of the commissions themselves, and partly by custom, the real work is done by those judges of the High Court whose names are included; unless, as sometimes happens when the docket is crowded, a judge requests one of the King's Counsel, who is also included in the commission, to try some of the less important cases. The judges who go on circuit are almost always taken from the King's Bench Division, and when all three commissions are issued they travel in pairs, one attending to the civil and the other to the criminal business. This is not always the case, for the criminal commissions

[1] *Cf.* 6 Geo. IV., c. 50.
[2] 6 Geo. IV., c. 50, §§ 1, 30, 31; 33–34 Vic., c. 77, § 6.
[3] *Cf.* Judicial Statistics, Part II., Com. Papers, 1902, CXVII., 191, p. 22.

are issued for the whole country three times, and for some places four times a year, while for the greater part of the country the commissions of assize are issued only twice.

London is an exception. There civil cases come directly before the judges of the High Court without the need of any commission; and for criminal business a statutory standing commission makes the Central Criminal Court at the Old Bailey a continuous tribunal for the whole metropolis. The commission includes the judges of the courts of the City of London, who try the great bulk of the cases, as well as the judges of the High Court, one of whom tries the graver crimes. Apart from some alterations in nomenclature, the Judicature Acts made only one notable change in the system of circuits. It is that of allowing the judge of assize to determine all questions, and give final judgment in the cases before him[1] — a power always possessed under the criminal commissions.

**The Divisional Courts.**

So much for the duties of the judges acting singly. Sitting as a divisional court — which means merely two or more judges of the division sitting together without a jury — the High Court attends to those matters that are not committed to a single judge, its chief business being to hear appeals from inferior courts, motions for new trials in cases that have gone to a jury, questions reserved by a single judge for the purpose, and applications for writs of *mandamus*, prohibition and *certiorari*.[2] It will be observed that in spite of its name the whole of the High Court never meets as a court; and this is true also of the two largest of its divisions. The real function of each of these bodies is that of a judges' panel whose members are assigned singly or in groups to hold for various purposes "a court of the said High Court." The practice was not altogether

[1] This follows from 36–37 Vic., c. 66, § 29. In this connection it may be noted that instead of having writs in civil cases issued as of old only out of chancery, the summons and other process on which suits are based may be issued from district registries scattered over the country. *Cf. Ibid.*, §§ 60–66.

[2] Vic., c. 66, 36–37; §§ 40–46, 48.

new,[1] but its adoption as a general principle in the administration of justice by the High Court and the Court of Appeal was one of the great changes wrought by the Judicature Acts.

The Court of Appeal.

The regular working members of the Court of Appeal are the Master of the Rolls, who has now no other judicial duties,[2] and five Lords Justices appointed for the purpose;[3] but the presidents of the three divisions of the High Court are also members,[4] and ex-Chancellors can sit at the request of the Chancellor.[5] The Court does all its work in sections, commonly of three judges apiece, and it sits only in London. Its functions, which include those formerly vested in the Exchequer Chamber and the Lords Justices of Appeal in Chancery, consist mainly in hearing appeals from the High Court; but in some cases it hears appeals directly from other tribunals also, such as the chancery courts in Lancashire[6] and Durham,[7] and all courts having jurisdiction in lunacy.[8]

In the matter of appeals there is an important difference to be noted between civil and criminal cases. As a rule any civil case may be carried to the Court of Appeal, and thence to the House of Lords. Where there is no jury, and the judge has decided both law and fact, this is easily done, but a verdict by a jury cannot in itself be the subject of appeal. A dissatisfied party may, however, claim that, even if the verdict is right, the judgment is wrong in law; or he may ask to have the verdict set aside, and a new trial granted, on the ground that the judge misdirected the jury in a matter of law, or that he wrongly admitted or excluded evidence, or finally on the ground that the verdict was not such as a jury could reasonably have found upon the evidence. All these questions he can carry up to the higher courts, if his purse is long enough to defray the expense.

[1] *E.g.* 11 Geo. IV. and 1 Will. IV., c. 70, § 1.
[2] 44–45 Vic., c. 68, § 2.
[3] *Ibid.*, § 3.
[4] 36–37 Vic., c. 66, § 6; 38–39 Vic., c. 77, § 4; 44–45 Vic., c. 68, § 4.
[5] 54–55 Vic., c. 53.
[6] 36–37 Vic., c. 66, §§ 18, 77; 53–54 Vic., c. 23.
[7] 52–53 Vic., c. 47, § 11.
[8] 36–37 Vic., c. 66, § 18.

In criminal cases, on the other hand, there was until 1907 no general right of appeal. The judge who tried a case might upon conviction reserve a question of law,[1] which then went to the Court for Crown Cases Reserved, consisting of five judges of the High Court, where it was decided without further appeal.[2] Or a case might go up on error apparent on the record, which gave a chance to raise the question whether the indictment was bad or the sentence illegal. But misdirections to the jury, or wrong rulings about evidence do not appear upon the record; and hence some of the most vital questions that arose at the trial could not be brought before any court for revision.

The absence of a right of appeal in criminal cases may sometimes result in gross injustice. This happened recently in the case of Adolf Beck, who had no means of obtaining a judicial review of his trial, and could not for years provoke such an inquiry by the Home Office as to secure a pardon. The case aroused popular feeling very strongly, and helped to bring about in 1907 the creation of a general Court of Criminal Appeal composed of judges of the King's Bench Division. To this tribunal any person convicted may appeal on a question of law, or with the consent of the court itself, or of the judge who tried the case, on a question of fact also, and may show that the verdict was unreasonable.[3] But the system of appeals or exceptions in criminal cases has two sides. A prisoner convicted of a grave crime has everything to gain and nothing to lose by delay, and in America, at least, his counsel presses groundless exceptions to the last point. In that country, where such a system is given full play, we have seen witnesses kept in gaol a couple of years awaiting the decision of questions relating to the admissibility of evidence or the like; and the horrors of lynch law are not unconnected with delay in the administration of criminal justice.

[1] 11–12 Vic., c. 78.

[2] 36–37 Vic., c. 66, § 47. The High Court might grant a new trial after conviction for a misdemeanour, but not for a felony.

[3] 9 Edw. VII., c. 23.

The House of Lords.

The Act which reorganised the courts in 1873 abolished the appellate jurisdiction of the House of Lords altogether, and made provision for the presence in the Court of Appeal of judges from Scotland and Ireland.[1] But before this went into effect there came a change of heart, and a determination, instead of doing away with the House of Lords as a court of law, to strengthen it by the addition of legal members.

The Act of 1876, therefore, restored its appellate jurisdiction, and provided for the creation at first of two, and eventually of four, life peers, to be known as Lords of Appeal in Ordinary.[2] The Act declared that an appeal should lie to the House of Lords from any order or judgment of the Court of Appeal in England, and of those Scotch and Irish courts from which appeals had previously lain to the Lords.[3] In view of this jurisdiction over appeals from Scotland and Ireland it is customary to take one of the Lords of Appeal in Ordinary from each of those kingdoms.

The Lords of Appeal.

The position of the House of Lords as a court is anomalous. Legally, and in the form of procedure in giving opinions, it acts as a House. All its members have, therefore, a right to be present, and historic sentiment would be shocked if the peers who are not lawyers were excluded by statute; but common sense would be still more shocked if they actually took part in its judgments. No power could to-day prevent any peer from casting his vote on the decision of a case if he insisted on doing so. In 1845, indeed, when the legality of O'Connell's conviction came before the House, and a majority of the law lords were about to decide against the government, some of the other peers wanted to take part, but were dissuaded by the Chancellor, Lord Lyndhurst. The Act of 1876, however, while silent about the lay peers, does recognise the special functions of the law lords, and explains who they are. It provides that no appeal shall be heard unless three Lords of Appeal are present,[4] and it defines these as the Lord Chancellor, the

[1] 36–37 Vic., c. 66, §§ 6, 20; *cf.* 38–39 Vic., c. 77, § 2.
[2] 39–40 Vic., c. 59, §§ 6, 14. [3] *Ibid.*, § 3. [4] *Ibid.*, § 5.

Lords of Appeal in Ordinary, and any other peers who hold, or have held, high judicial office — a term further explained as meaning all the offices included in the Supreme Court of Judicature in England and in the courts of corresponding grade in Scotland and Ireland.[1] Curiously enough there is another clause which would, under certain conditions, have the effect of excluding the lay peers altogether. Formerly the House of Lords could not sit for any purpose while Parliament was dissolved. But it was irrational that a political event of that kind should arrest the regular administration of justice, and hence the Act contains a provision that during a dissolution the Lords of Appeal may sit and act in the name of the House.[2] The unwritten rule that only law lords shall sit when the House meets for judicial business is one of the conventions of the constitution that is most strictly observed, and yet it would seem that work of this kind is not absolutely confined to the Lords of Appeal as defined in the Act of 1876; for Lord James of Hereford has often taken part in the decision of cases in the House of Lords, and notably in that of the Free Church of Scotland in 1904. He was a barrister by profession, and had been Attorney-General, but he had never held high judicial office, and hence was not strictly a Lord of Appeal.

**The Judicial Committee of the Privy Council.**

**Jurisdiction.**

The House of Lords is not the only court of last resort in England. There is another with much the same personnel, but quite a different jurisdiction. This is the Judicial Committee of the Privy Council, which hears appeals from the ecclesiastical courts, from the Channel Islands and the Isle of Man, from the colonies and dependencies, and from English courts established by treaty in foreign lands. It is amazing that any one tribunal should be able to deal intelligently with the manifold systems of law that come before the Judicial Committee. Upon its docket one may find a case from Australia involving English Common Law or

[1] Former Lords of Appeal in Ordinary are specially included by 50–51 Vic., c. 70, §§ 2, 5.

[2] 39–40 Vic., c. 59, § 9.

Equity, another involving Roman French law from Canada, a third requiring a knowledge of the Roman Dutch law of Guiana or the Cape, still another that turns upon Hindoo or Mohammedan law in India, and so on through the long list of British possessions over the whole face of the earth. The capacity of the court to deal with all those questions is the more astonishing because its regular members are for the most part the same men who sit as judges in the House of Lords.

Member-ship.

Formerly the Judicial Committee was in fact as well as in law a very different body from the House of Lords sitting as a court, and its paid judges were wholly distinct; but, when salaried life peers were created, it was thought that they might be charged with the bulk of the work in both courts. At first two Lords of Appeal in Ordinary were appointed, with power to sit in the Judicial Committee; and a further provision was added that instead of filling any vacancies which occurred among the principal paid members of that Committee, a third and fourth Lord of Appeal in Ordinary should be appointed.[1] This has long since been done, with the result that a few years ago the Judicial Committee was made up of very nearly the same persons who did the judicial work of the House of Lords. All the latter, being privy councillors, were entitled to sit in the former, and almost all the members of the Judicial Committee were, in fact, Lords of Appeal. Of late, however, the desire to draw the bonds of the empire closer has led to giving places on the Committee to colonial judges, and this has increased the members of that Committee who do not sit in the House of Lords. Suggestions have been made from time to time that one great court of last resort should be created for the whole empire;[2] but at the present moment it seems less nearly a fact than it was a dozen years ago. The Judicial Committee is now composed of one or two former

[1] 39–40 Vic., c. 59, §§ 6, 14.
[2] *E.g.* Rep. of Com. of Lords on Appellate Jurisdiction, Com. Papers, 1872, VII., 193.

Indian judges appointed for the purpose, who receive eight hundred pounds a year between them;[1] of the Lords of Appeal in Ordinary; of all members of the Privy Council who hold, or have held, high judicial office in the United Kingdom,[2] or (not exceeding five in number) in the self-governing colonies;[3] and of two other members of the Privy Council if the Crown thinks fit to appoint them.[4]

**Decisions in the Lords and the Judicial Committee.**

Neither in the House of Lords, nor in the Judicial Committee is the form of giving a judgment that which is customary in courts of law. The law lords address the House one after another as if they were arguing a motion before the whole body of peers, and the action taken in the case is entered in the Journals of the House as a part of its proceedings. A decision of the Judicial Committee, on the other hand, takes the form of advising the Crown what ought to be done, with a full statement of the reasons therefor — advice which is, of course, invariably followed. There is another matter relating to the method of giving judgment that is more substantial. The usual custom, in courts that have derived their traditions from English sources, of publishing dissenting opinions may have a bad effect when the court is nearly evenly divided. The decision in such a case is not perfectly conclusive upon the point of law involved, for if some of the judges who made up the majority die or resign, and others are appointed in their stead, it may be possible to raise the question again, and perhaps with a different result. This difficulty is avoided by both of the British courts of last resort, although in different ways. The House of Lords now holds itself incompetent to overrule its own decisions;[5] and the Judicial Committee, which delivers a single collective opinion, is forbidden to make

[1] 3–4 Will. IV., c. 41; 50–51 Vic., c. 70, § 4. About half of the cases before the committee come from India.

[2] 50–51 Vic., c. 70, § 3.

[3] 58–59 Vic., c. 44.

[4] 3–4 Will. IV., c. 41, § 1. On ecclesiastical appeals certain archbishops and bishops have a right to sit, but since 1876 merely as assessors with an advisory voice. 39–40 Vic., c. 59, § 14.

[5] London Tramways Co. *vs.* London County Council, (1898) A. C. 375.

public any dissent or difference of views among its members.[1]

Barristers and Solicitors.

In the face of a legal education until recently very unsystematic, the excellence of English law as a body of jurisprudence has been promoted by the method of recruiting both the bar and the bench. As in most European countries, the practice of law is divided into two branches, that of the barristers, and that of the solicitors or attorneys. The solicitor or attorney alone comes into direct relations with the clients. He is their confidential adviser and friend; draws up their legal papers; carries on for them business of all sorts that may have only an incidental connection with law; does the preliminary work of preparing a case for trial; and can himself conduct the trial before inferior courts. A man is admitted by the court to practise as an attorney only after an apprenticeship and a series of examinations. These last are conducted by the Incorporated Law Society, an association composed of solicitors, which has done much to raise the standard of legal education in the profession. Other forces have, indeed, worked in the same direction; for in England, as elsewhere, the business side of law has grown in importance, and the great firms of solicitors have attained a position lucrative and dignified to a degree that would hardly have been thought possible a century ago.

The barrister gives the solicitor opinions on doubtful points of law; and has the exclusive privilege of conducting trials and making arguments before the higher courts. Unlike the solicitors, who are scattered over the country, the barristers are mainly concentrated in London.[2] Almost all those whose practice lies in chancery stay there permanently, while those who follow the Common Law courts at-

[1] Anson, "Law and Custom of the Constitution," 2 Edw. II., 471. In France the courts publish simply the decision, with a brief reference to the statutes, findings of fact and conclusions, but without an opinion containing anything in the nature of an argument or a statement of legal principles, and without any notice of dissent.

[2] There are, however, local bars in a few of the largest provincial cities.

tach themselves to one of the circuits. The more prominent members of the bar are created King's Counsel, an honour which carries with it a silk gown and a higher scale of fees, but involves giving up the class of work usually done by junior counsel, and hence does not always increase a man's income. The barristers have, in fact, a rigidly aristocratic organisation. They all belong to one or other of the four Inns of Court; the Inner Temple, the Middle Temple, Lincoln's Inn and Gray's Inn, each Inn being governed by a body of Benchers, who fill their own vacancies from the leading or senior men at the bar. Having almost uncontrolled power to admit or expel members of the Inns, the Benchers hold the keys to the profession; although in fact they very rarely refuse admission to any one who eats the dinners and passes the moderate examination required. An organisation of this kind, of which, by the way, the judges continue to be members, gives to the bar a great solidarity and capacity to maintain its traditions.

The late Lord Coleridge, Chief Justice of the Queen's Bench, expressed the opinion that the separation of the two branches of the profession was better for the development of law, while the American habit of combining them was probably better for the client. From the standpoint of perfecting the law the English system has two advantages. Instead of expending much of their time on business affairs, the counsel who assist the court by arguing cases have their minds engrossed by legal principles, and by the practice of law as a distinct art; and they are selected and retained by solicitors who are themselves lawyers by profession, instead of by clients with whom a business connection, a cheap notoriety, or engaging manners, may have more influence than a profound knowledge of the law.

**Salaries of Judges.**

The recruiting of the bench is certainly a matter of no less consequence. The judges are taken from among the barristers, and this is expressly required in most of the modern statutes. Moreover, for the higher courts they are habitually taken from the leading men at the bar.

At one time the appointments were mostly confined to friends of the party in power, but this is no longer true, except for the positions of Chancellor and Chief Justice, which are still regarded as political appointments.[1] In fact a barrister who achieves sufficient eminence in his profession can look forward with confidence to a seat on the bench, although he may wait for it longer if he belongs to the party out of power. It may be observed also that the salaries of the judges are large, so that judicial office is lucrative as well as highly honourable. Every successful practitioner is not, as in America, obliged to make a very heavy pecuniary sacrifice in accepting a judgeship. The salary of the Chancellor is £10,000, of which £6000 is regarded as a compensation for his purely judicial services. The Lord Chief Justice receives £8000; the Lords of Appeal in Ordinary, £6000; the judges of the High Court and Court of Appeal, £5000; the Recorder of the City of London, £4000; and even the County Court judges are paid £1500 apiece, a salary larger than that of the Circuit and District judges in the United States courts, whose jurisdiction is of the grade of that of the High Court in England.

[1] The Chancellor being a member of the cabinet must, of course, change with the ministry.

# CHAPTER LXI

## THE ENGLISH CONCEPTION OF LAW

LAW has played in many ways an unusually prominent part throughout the course of English history. First among the modern states of Europe to emerge from the confusion of the early middle ages, England solidified as a nation during the period when a legal tone of thought was dominant.[1] The foundation of her institutions was laid at that time, and they assumed more and more completely a legal form. Herein seems to have lain the real significance of Magna Carta, "for in brief it meant this, that the King is and shall be below the law." [2] The Charter has, indeed, been regarded as the turning point from the feudal state, universal in northwestern Europe, to the limited monarchy peculiar to England; [3] and although it is not the sole example of a document of that kind in the middle ages, it was followed in England, as in no other country, by the construction of legal machinery restricting permanently the royal power. King and Parliament came to express their will in formal statutes, which the national courts interpreted and enforced together with the Common Law evolved from their own decisions. Personal liberty, moreover, was based upon law, and for the most part not upon privileges of particular classes or places, but upon principles of universal application protected by the courts. All public life had, therefore, a legal tinge, which went so deep that it did not by any

**Influence of Law in English History.**

[1] *Cf.* Stubbs, "On the Characteristic Differences between Medieval and Modern History," in his "Lectures on Medieval and Modern History."

[2] Pollock and Maitland, "History of English Law," 1 Ed., I., 152.

[3] G. B. Adams, "Origin of the English Constitution," *Amer. Hist. Review*, Jan. 1908.

means wholly disappear when the transformation from mediæval to modern conditions called for the masterful hand of a strong government. It survived in England when the other states of Europe went through an era of autocratic rule; and after the discords of the seventeenth century had passed away it regained its hold upon the mind of the nation. In seeking to fortify their political claims men searched for precedents rather than abstract principles, and law resumed its place as the corner stone of English public life. For nearly two centuries since that time the national political system has, indeed, been developing by the growth of extra-legal custom instead of by the enactment of law; but, as pointed out in the Introductory Note on the Constitution, that has not detracted in the least from the strictness with which the law is enforced or legal forms are observed.

**English Law in America.**

Curiously enough the political evolution of America branched off from that of England early in the eighteenth century, nearly a couple of generations before the revolt of the colonies, and while the legal tone of thought was at its height. American institutions are still in some respects singularly like those of England at the death of Queen Anne, and not least in the power of legal tradition, which was rather intensified than weakened by its transfer to the new world. Thereafter the changes in the British Constitution found no echo on the other side of the Atlantic, largely no doubt because taking the form of custom, not of statute, they were not readily observed. Blackstone's Commentaries were of course read greedily across the water, but his political ideas had a strong legal cast and were quite behind the real conditions of his own time. It is indeed noteworthy that the United States has kept in far closer touch with the legal than with the political thought of the mother country. English decisions have never ceased to be cited as authorities in American courts, while Acts of Parliament have been copied with much less frequency, and political customs have scarcely been followed at all. The public institutions of the two countries are now very different, but their system of jurisprudence and their conceptions of law are essentially the same.

**Prominence of Lawyers in Public Life.**

A natural result of the political importance of law, and of the position in the community occupied by the bar, has been the prominence of lawyers in public life both in England and America. They are not, as sometimes happens in continental parliaments, declaimers who have attracted popular applause in a sensational criminal case, but in great part men who have made their mark by a thorough mastery of their profession. In England, as well as in the United States, the highest posts have long been open to them, and in fact a few of their members are always admitted to the ranks of the nobility, for the Lord Chancellor and the Lord Chief Justice are regularly created hereditary peers. Lawyers have thus had a considerable influence on the course of public affairs, and on the whole they have been distinctly a conservative force, or at least their presence has tended toward moderation and continuity of policy. The relation of law and lawyers to politics is closely connected with a principle of English jurisprudence that is interwoven with the whole political fabric.

**The Courts and the English Conception of Law.**

The historic position of the royal courts of justice has affected profoundly the English conception of law, and this has in turn influenced both the course of legislation and the authority of the courts themselves. To English speaking people, whether lawyers or not, law means a body of rules enforced by the courts. For this purpose it is unimportant whether the function of the courts be regarded as making or declaring law, because the question is not about the source or origin, but simply about the criterion of law. The essential point is that what the courts recognise and enforce is law, and what they refuse to recognise is not law. Such a definition of law is commonly assumed as an axiom,[1] and yet it is neither universally accepted in all countries,

[1] Professor Dicey, for example, in describing the distinction between

nor has it always been applicable even in England. One may be pardoned, therefore, for examining it in a very cursory way in relation to its historical development, its philosophical results, and its practical effects.

Historical Development.

The idea that English law is a body of rules enforced by the national courts may be traced to the centralising power of the Norman and Angevin kings, which was brought to bear upon the whole community mainly through their central courts of justice and their itinerant judges. These supplanted the local and feudal courts, and built up the conception of a Common Law for the whole realm, administered upon fixed principles by regular permanent tribunals.

Early Royal Justice.

But it was long before men felt that all law must be so administered; that there could be no law outside of that enforced by the regular courts. The Crown was still the fountain of justice, and the source had not yet run dry. Petitions were made both to the Crown, and in early times to Parliament, complaining of wrongs which the courts did

the law and the conventions of the constitution, says ("Law of the Constitution," 5 Ed., 23):

"The one set of rules are in the strictest sense 'laws,' since they are rules which . . . are enforced by the Courts."

"The other set of rules consist of conventions, understandings, habits, or practices which, though they may regulate the conduct of the several members of the sovereign power, of the Ministry, or of other officials, are not in reality laws at all since they are not enforced by the Courts."

In that book Professor Dicey expounds a principle of English government that seems to the writer more fundamental than even such matters as the composition of the legislature and its relation to the executive.

An excellent illustration of the different meanings attached to the conception of law by German and English jurists is furnished by Professor Hatschek's criticism of this passage from Professor Dicey's book, in his recent *Englisches Staatsrecht* (I., 546 n.). Even if it be true that a conventional rule is not a law unless recognised by a court, is not, he asks, the House of Commons a court? He argues that the conventions of the constitution are rules of law, because, as Professor Dicey points out, their violation will in the end lead to the breach of important rules of law, and such a sanction is, he contends, a true legal sanction. He insists, also, that many of the conventions are strict rules of law because the neglect of them will involve a conflict with parliamentary procedure, which he regards as customary law. He concludes (p. 557) that the parliamentary executive — in other words, the responsibility of ministers — is an institution established by law (*rechtsinstitut*), since by a failure to conform to it legal principles would either be violated or made superfluous.

not reach, and in such cases redress could be given in accordance with the general principles of justice. In civil cases petitions to the Crown came to be habitually referred to the Chancellor, who in dealing with them wrought out the rules of Equity. Criminal tribunals also emanated from the reserved justice of the Crown in Council. Such were the Star Chamber and the Court of High Commission; but under the early Stuarts these bodies were used for political and ecclesiastical objects to such an extent that, by casting discredit upon all extraordinary tribunals, they brought about the next step in the English conception of law.

Abolition of Extraordinary Tribunals.

The doctrine that there is no law save what is enforced by the regular courts resulted from the strife that filled the first half of the seventeenth century; and it involved a life and death struggle between the Civil and the Common Law, for the extraordinary tribunals were deeply impregnated with the principles of the Civil Law. It began with a conflict of jurisdiction over the right of the Common Law courts to issue writs of prohibition restraining the action of the extraordinary tribunals, Coke being the great champion of the former. It culminated in the Act of 1640,[1] which abolished the Star Chamber with the other courts exercising similar powers, and forbade the Privy Council or its members to exercise jurisdiction in English civil suits. This movement swept away all tribunals that had not firmly established their standing as regular courts. Even the Court of Requests, commonly called the poor man's court,[2] disappeared in the commotion of the times.[3]

Survival of Equity.

The Court of Chancery with its well-grounded principles was more solidly rooted. It filled a real need, and although vigorously attacked, it survived; but even long afterwards it was still regarded as having a somewhat extraordinary

[1] 16 Car. I., c. 10.

[2] Sir Thomas Smith, "The Commonwealth of England," Book III., Ch. vii.

[3] Selden Society, "Publication," XII.; Leadam, "Select Cases in the Court of Requests." Introd. p. 5.

character, for although the Crown could create a court of Common Law in a colony, the law officers were doubtful, as late as 1827, whether it could, without legislative authority, create a court of Equity there.[1] In England, however, the Court of Chancery maintained its position as a regular tribunal, and made the doctrines of Equity an essential part of the national jurisprudence.

**The Principle Established.** From the period of the Restoration the principle that law is the body of rules enforced by the ordinary courts may be regarded as definitely settled. For a time, indeed, the resort to extraordinary tribunals is replaced by an effort to use the regular judicial machinery for political purposes. But this in turn was checked in various ways, one of them being the penal action under the *Habeas Corpus* Act of 1679, which effectually prevented arbitrary imprisonment; and another the provision in the Act of Settlement giving the judges a tenure during good behaviour, which secured their freedom from political control. Thereafter the growth in the art of legislation, and the greater harmony between the Crown and the Houses, lessened the temptation on the part of the government to use courts of law as instruments for social or political objects. If a grievance was felt, if a change was wanted, if an obstacle blocked the way, the result desired could easily be brought about by a statute which was immediately enforced by the courts as a part of the law of the land. Thus in the eighteenth century the principle that law is that which is enforced by the courts thrived undisturbed, and attained its full maturity.

**Philosophical Results.** The practical maxim that the test of law is to be found in its recognition by the courts has coloured English juristic philosophy. It has limited the conception of law to positive law that can be enforced; to a definite set of rules, administered by tangible authorities. This theory, clearly stated

[1] *Cf. In re* Lord Bishop of Natal, 3 Moore, P. C. (N. S.) 115 at 152. Opinion of Scarlet and Tindal, Forsyth, "Cases on Constitutional Law," p. 172. Com. Dig. Prærog., D. 28. But *semble contra* Attorney-General Northey in 1703–4. Chalmers, "Opinions," I., 2 *et seq.*

by Hobbes,[1] was given its fullest systematic treatment by Austin,[2] and although his doctrine that the only source of law is a command of a definite political superior coupled with a sanction has been very generally discarded, his sharp distinction between that which is actually law and that which ought to be law has remained unshaken. The latter he classed, not as law, but merely as positive morality. Such a distinction is opposed to continental ideas, and above all to the doctrine of natural law, as taught by German jurists, which a man bred in the Common Law finds it hard to understand. To him it seems a confusion between what is and what ought to be, between law and ethics, between facts and aspirations, between the real and the imaginary. He is often a little puzzled to know whether public international law regulating the conduct of sovereign states, even so far as it is well settled by treaties and the universal observance of civilised nations, ought strictly to be classed as law, because there is no tribunal that has power to enforce it. To the continental jurist, on the other hand, such a view seems narrow. It substitutes a study of the enactments of men for that of scientific jurisprudence. It limits law to the *philosophie des positiven rechts,* to the exclusion of the broader *rechts philosophie;* and it leaves out of account the sense of justice, which, as every one must agree, does not always coincide with the actual provisions of law.[3]

**The Law of Nature in Rome.**

The doctrine of natural law, or the law of nature, has had a long and checkered history, from the ancient world,

[1] "Leviathan," Part II., Ch. xxvi.

[2] "Jurisprudence," Lect. I.

[3] In his recent work, Professor Hatschek speaks (*Englisches Staatsrecht,* I., 13) of the chasm in England, unbridged to the present day, between politics or jurisprudence on one hand and law on the other; and he adds that continental observers have made the great mistake of thinking that political philosophers, like Hobbes, Locke and the rest, were discussing English public law. Looking at the matter from a German point of view, he insists (p. 10) that, owing to her failure to adopt the Roman law, or to develop its study at the Universities, England has never had a true system of public law.

through the middle ages, down to modern times. Among the Roman jurists, who, like the English, had a practical turn of mind, it became closely blended with the *jus gentium*, which was conceived as the part of positive law common to all peoples. As such it could be enforced, and they applied it in practice to cases of persons who were not subject to the laws of Rome.[1]

In Germany.

To the philosopher or jurist in those countries that adopted the Civil Law, and especially in Germany, it meant something more complex. He thought of it as a system of jurisprudence, deduced by reason from the very nature of man, and existing outside, and quite independent of, positive law. It was a philosophical scheme of law, a set of principles, that ought to be in force, but was not necessarily so in fact. After the seventeenth century, natural law was carefully distinguished from morals or ethics, which deal with rules of conduct binding on the conscience of the individual without conferring rights on any one else, and which ought not to be made compulsory by public authority. But on the other hand, its relation to positive law is not always made perfectly clear. Positive law is sometimes described as the form that law happens to take at any one moment; but this is vague. If we render by "justice" the German "recht," which has no true analogue in English, it is often stated that justice is not the creature of positive law, and that the latter owes its force to its intrinsic justice. But positive law and justice do not always coincide, a fact that is one of the very reasons for the study of natural law, and hence it is important to know what force positive law has in such a case. The answer has not been the same at all times, and in fact it has been the subject of a gradual evolution, not unconnected with the growth of strong central governments in Germany.[2]

In the later middle ages natural law was regarded not only as the foundation on which the state was based, but as con-

[1] *Cf.* Bryce, "Studies in History and Jurisprudence," Essay XI.
[2] See the note at the end of this chapter.

ferring legal rights which were to some extent valid as against the positive law enacted by the ruler of the land. After the reception of the Roman law and the upheavals of the Thirty Years' War had recast the face of things in Germany, the conception of the law of nature as eternal and immutable remained, indeed, unshaken, but the idea of its relation to positive law was slowly modified. In spite of a repugnance to acknowledging that any power in the state could be entirely arbitrary, the restraints imposed by the law of nature came to be more and more regarded as ineffective when opposed to the will of the sovereign, until it came to be generally agreed that his command must in all cases be obeyed. Yet natural rights continued to be treated as real legal rights, although enforceable only so far as the state chose to make them so.

**Law and Justice.**

Now to an Anglo-Saxon a legal right that is not enforceable at law seems a contradiction in terms; and yet one must admit that a law may be unjust, and that an act may be immoral but not unjust; in short, that justice is not precisely the same thing as either morality or law. An analysis from this standpoint of the conception of justice is no doubt valuable, but to men trained in the Common Law it seems to lie within the domain of philosophy rather than jurisprudence; while an effort to deduce from that conception definite legal principles meets with very serious difficulties. Justice in any actual case depends very much upon the rules of positive law in view of which the acts that give rise to the question were performed, and therefore an attempt to construct a system of natural law in detail is apt to result, either in a somewhat transparent justification of existing institutions, or in deductions that appear fantastic. For this reason, such treatises are barren reading for a lawyer. The process is most likely to be fruitful when applied to a subject that has no existing positive law, and it is in such a field that its greatest service to mankind has been rendered — the creation of modern public international law by Hugo Grotius and his successors. The evolution of

German administrative law may, perhaps, be ascribed to a similar process.

The Law of Nature in England.

The idea of a law of nature has been neither unknown nor without influence in England, although it has commonly been called by other names.[1] It has been regarded, however, not as a set of principles to be excogitated by jurists apart from positive law, but as a general sense of justice in the court to guide it in the decision of doubtful cases. Under such expressions as *malum in se* and *malum prohibitum*, the distinction between an act which was wrong by nature, and one which was arbitrarily made so by statute, has been clearly recognised. Natural justice was not distinct from that which was administered by the courts. On the contrary, the law that grew up at Westminster was considered a product of reason, although, as Coke said to James I., a somewhat artificial reason. In fact, under the name of common right and reason, natural justice was thought to be embodied in the Common Law; while under the name of equity and good conscience the Chancellors felt that it was the very foundation of their principles.

Its Relation to Statutes.

Obviously statute law could not be traced to the same source, and the courts at one time talked loosely about their authority to disregard an Act of Parliament if contrary to natural equity, or common right and reason; because, in the words of Hobart, in 1615, "*jura naturae sunt immutabilia*, and they are *leges legum*."[2] The doctrine that a statute is void if contrary to natural law, which had been often stated in the middle ages, was put into philosophical form for the English people by Locke,[3] and finds a hollow echo even in the pages of Blackstone.[4] With the growth, however, of the doctrine of the omnipotence of Parliament,

[1] Pollock, "History of the Law of Nature," Journal Soc. of Comp. Leg., 1900, No. 3; 1901, No. 2. *Ibid.*, Columbia Law Review, January, 1901; March, 1902; *cf.* Hatschek, I., 154.

[2] Day *vs.* Savadge, Hobart, 85, at 87. *Cf.* "Doctor and Student," Ch. vi.; Calvin's Case, 7 Rep. 1, at 13b and 14a; Bonham's Case, 8 Rep. 114a; City of London *vs.* Wood, 12 Mod. 669, at 687.

[3] "Treatises of Government," Book II., Ch. ii.

[4] "Commentaries," Introd. § 2, 41.

it vanished from the courts early in the eighteenth century; but this was the point where the stream of political thought in the American colonies separated from that of the mother country, and the doctrine not only contributed indirectly to the evolution of constitutional law in the United States, but has been occasionally repeated in express terms by American judges.

Enactment of Natural Law.

Curiously enough, although English courts have ceased to discourse much about natural law, by whatever name it be called, the idea that it is, or may be, enforced as positive law has not altogether disappeared, for we find recent directions to the courts in British dependencies to apply, in default of positive law, the principles of justice, equity and good conscience,[1] or to apply native or other laws if not repugnant to natural justice.[2] But here, again, as throughout English juridical thought, natural justice means not a body of abstract principles, but practical maxims to be applied by the court in the decision of actual cases.

## NOTE ON THE HISTORY OF THE RELATION OF THE LAW OF NATURE TO POSITIVE LAW IN GERMANY

The history of the theory of natural law from this point of view can hardly be sketched better than by an epitome of what Gierke has said in his book on Althusius.[3] When the middle ages began to theorise, he tells us, the old German conception of the legally constructed state, which exists only by and through law, became insufficient; and the idea that the state created law was generally accepted. But mediæval thought never lost a belief in the intrinsic and original force of law on which the state itself is based. The contradiction between the creation of law by the state,

[1] Ilbert, "Government of India," 21, 362, 378, 394.

[2] Order in Council for Southern Rhodesia, Oct. 20, 1898, § 50, Com. Papers, 1899, LXIII., 157.

[3] *Johannes Althusius und die Entwicklung der naturrechtlichen Staatstheorien*, 2 Ed., 264–320.

and of the state by the law, was met by drawing a distinction between positive and natural law. There was a long controversy over the whereabouts of sovereignty in the state, but it was generally agreed that the sovereign power was not restrained by the provisions of positive law, for the sovereign, having created that law, could change it. Natural law, on the other hand, was outside of and above the state or any other earthly power, and was a true and completely binding law. It could be amplified and modified, though not destroyed, by positive law. Thus legal restraints were imposed by natural law upon the authority of the sovereign; but there was a difference of opinion about the effect of violating them. The earlier opinion, never wholly abandoned, treated acts that transcended these limits as null, and devoid of binding force on anybody. With the evolution in the conception of the sovereign, however, a doctrine grew up that he was formally omnipotent in the field of law, so that his commands were outwardly binding, and could at most be resisted passively. Practically, therefore, the restraints on his power were only claims upon his sense of justice; yet they were regarded as legal, and not merely moral, restraints. A man who, in following them, disobeyed the ruler and suffered the consequences was thought to be doing his legal duty.

The development of juristic thought after the sixteenth century followed the same lines. The distinction between positive and natural law continued, and more and more the view prevailed that the real source of positive law was the will of the sovereign; but his will was regarded as bound up with the dictates of natural law, and efforts were made to avoid the conception of any "*potestas legibus soluta.*" Many fine distinctions were drawn, and many theories worked out, which do not concern us here. It is enough to point out that after the sixteenth century the theory of natural law had for its central doctrine the position of that law as the foundation, end and limiting principle of the state. As in the later middle ages, natural law was considered the legal basis of all political authority, outwardly binding, preëxisting and unalterable by any power on earth. It still imposed legal restraints upon the sovereign, for the maxim about a "*potestas legibus soluta*" applied only to positive law; and although the opinion grew stronger and stronger that natural law contained only a "*vis directiva,*" and not a "*vis coactiva,*" and thus acted only on the conscience of the ruler, nevertheless the restraint, if not one that could be politically enforced, was still conceived as distinctly legal in its nature. In accordance with this view, subjective natural rights were almost universally regarded by German writers as real legal rights. In England, indeed, Hobbes discarded natural law as furnishing of itself a basis for legal rights, but he had few disciples on the Continent. His ideas provoked general aversion there, and Puffendorf, one of the great leaders of German juristic thought, combated his theory, contending for the legal character of natural law, and its binding force upon the sovereign. But Puffendorf admitted that it was an incomplete law, depending for actual enforcement on a sanction by the sovereign upon whom it laid only an "*obligatio imperfecta.*" Tomasius took the same ground, although for the first time he drew a sharp distinction between natural law on one side, and morals or politics on the other, and his views were commonly accepted by his countrymen.

Late in the eighteenth century two tendencies became prominent; one that of evolving from pure reason an all-embracing system of law; the other that of regarding the function of the state as limited to putting such a system into effect, its activity being thus confined to purely legal objects. Kant carried both of these conceptions to their highest point. He gave up the division of law into natural and positive, and admitted only a single law of reason unchangeable by the state. But like his predecessors he declared that this law could come into force by the act of the state alone, that is by voluntary legislation; and he denied the possibility of any external guarantee against an improper exercise of authority.

This brief sketch may, perhaps, be supplemented by examples from two or three of the leaders of German thought on the subject. Puffendorf, whose book, *De Jure Naturae*, was published in 1672,[1] defines a law in the common way as a command of the sovereign, and natural law as the command of God which may be known by human reason as well as by Revelation.[2] Through the greater part of a bulky volume he treats of various kinds of rights from the standpoint of natural law, sometimes going into great detail, in discussing, for example, contracts, marriage and the transfer and lease of property. At the close of his work he takes up the formation and constitution of civil societies or states. Like other writers of his time, he founds these upon a social compact,[3] and in every state he finds a supreme power which cannot be called to account by any man and is above all human laws.[4] Intellectually cautious, and shunning the horns of a logical dilemma, Puffendorf approaches the question of resistance to the commands of a sovereign as if he disliked to make a sharp statement of principle. A subject, he says, has rights, and is capable of being injured by the sovereign; but even when threatened with the worst evils, it is better for him to flee than to resist. Again, he tells us that if a prince commands an act which cannot be performed without guilt, he has made himself an enemy, and is supposed to have remitted the obligation of obedience; yet the subject in such a case ought to avoid danger by flight, and if he cannot escape, he ought rather to be killed than to kill.[5] When it comes to the direct relation between the laws of nature and positive law, he evades the issue more completely. Disagreeing with Hobbes — the German juristic philoso-

[1] Translated into English in 1729, and edited with notes by Barbeyrac. The references given here are to this translation.

[2] Book I., Ch. vi., § 4.

[3] Book VII., Ch. ii., §§ 6–8.

[4] Book VII., Ch. vi., §§ 1–3.

[5] Book VII., Ch. viii., §§ 2, 5.

phers of this period spent a great part of their energy in refuting Hobbes — he holds that the definition of crimes is not left arbitrarily to the civil laws, and that justice and injustice existed before civil governments. The laws of nature, he insists, are of universal application, but it is the civil power that gives them the force of laws in civil courts, and determines what crimes shall be punished. It is possible, therefore, he admits, that a civil law might be made in opposition to the law of nature, but he adds, no man in his wits would ever attempt to make such a law unless he were resolved to ruin and overturn the whole commonwealth.[1]

A generation later came Christian Tomasius, who made a distinct contribution to the science of jurisprudence by placing for the first time the distinction between natural law and morality upon an enduring philosophic basis. Like his master, Puffendorf, he treated law as the command of a superior, and God as the author of natural law, which is, in fact, the divine law written in the hearts of men, obliging them to do those things which accord with, and avoid those repugnant to, the nature of rational man. It follows, he says, that natural law is immutable and cannot be dispensed with, because that is true of human reason itself.[2] But although the law of nature is unchangeable, it does not follow that this is true of the consequences of that law, for he draws a distinction between the law itself[3] and the rights[4] to which it gives rise. The former, in the case of laws of nature, is unchangeable; but the right and the obligation attached thereto can be changed by the will of a political superior.[5] From the very definition of law as the command of a superior, he derives the first practical principle of jurisprudence, that the ruler must be

[1] Book VIII., Ch. i., §§ 2–3, 5.

[2] *Institutionum Jurisprudentiæ Divinæ Libri Tres*, 7 Ed., 1730; Lib. I., Cap. ii., §§ 97, 98.

[3] *Jus. Pro Lege.*

[4] *Jus. Pro Attributo Personæ.*

[5] Lib. I., Cap. i., §§ 81, 82, 131, 132, 139–141.

obeyed.[1] This principle he applies very strictly, for after speaking in the usual way of sovereignty as the supreme power of directing the actions of the citizens, exercised subject to no human superior and above all human laws, he goes on to quote with apparent approval the statement that to resist its legitimate commands is not only wrong, but that its severities must be patiently borne, and the most atrocious injury suffered without resistance.[2] In short, he believes like the rest in an immutable natural law, which loses all practical effect, but does not cease to be valid, when it conflicts with positive law and cannot be enforced.

Kant is another great landmark in German juristic philosophy, and he speaks of intrinsic justice with greater emphasis, while at the same time denying its practical efficiency even more distinctly, than most of his predecessors. He discusses the inherent right to liberty, equality and the free expression of opinion on public affairs, maintains in opposition to Hobbes that the citizens retain certain indestructible rights, and stigmatises as horrible Hobbes's doctrine that the sovereign can do no injustice to the subject. But these rights, he says, are not enforceable, and depend for their exercise upon the good-will of the sovereign. Going more into detail, he explains why privileges cannot rightly be hereditary, or existing religious creeds be made perpetual. A provision for this last purpose in the original compact of civil society would, he declares, be null and void, and a law to that effect could not express the real will of a monarch. Nevertheless, if passed, it could not be opposed; and in fact nothing can justify resistance to the sovereign, who ought in all cases to be obeyed.[3]

As an example of the legal thought of a much later

[1] Lib. I., Cap. iii., §§ 33–37. [2] Lib. III., Cap. vi., § 119.

[3] *Cf. Rechtslehre; Algemeine Anmerkungen A;* but the most definite statement of his views on these questions is to be found in the second of his essays on the proverb, "*Das mag in der Theorie richtig sein taugt aber nicht für die Praxis.*"

period, Gierke's own views on the question are interesting, and they are given concisely at the end of his historical description of the theories of natural law, in his work on Althusius.[1] Law, he tells us, is completed and secured only by force, although neither the state nor any political power creates it. Law is not the result of a common will that a thing shall be, but of a common conviction that it is; and this conviction is manifested by usage, or declared by an organ of state. When the common will orders that a legal right shall be enforced, it does not create, but merely secures that right; and although it can be enforced only by means of the state, yet a law that has no sanction is a law when there is a common conviction that a sanction, if imposed, would be right. In short, a law may be truly a law even if the state and the courts refuse to recognise or enforce it; and he admits, of course, the possibility of a conflict between the material or theoretical and the formal or practical law.

Just as the German juristic writers in the seventeenth and eighteenth centuries agree that there is a body of natural law, which is not necessarily enforceable, or identical with the actual law of the state, so the English political philosophers are really agreed in regarding law as the body of rules which are really enforced. Much as Hobbes and Locke differ, they agree in the principle that law means positive law alone. Hobbes was unconsciously imbued with the English conception with which the German jurists were not familiar, and he virtually takes the ground that natural law cannot be enforced, and is therefore not law, while Locke, starting with the same assumption, maintains that it is law, and therefore can be enforced.

The English conception has, perhaps, never been put in a more striking way than by Hume, in his essay on the Origin of Government: "Man, born in a family," he says, is "compelled to maintain society, from necessity, from natural inclination, and from habit. The same creature,

[1] 2 Ed., pp. 318–20.

in his farther progress, is engaged to establish political society, in order to administer justice; without which there can be no peace among them, nor safety, nor mutual intercourse. We are, therefore, to look upon all the vast apparatus of our government, as having ultimately no other object or purpose but the distribution of justice, or, in other words, the support of the twelve judges. Kings and parliaments, fleets and armies, officers of the court and revenue, ambassadors, ministers, and privy-counsellors, are all subordinate in their end to this part of administration."

# CHAPTER LXII

## EFFECTS OF THE CONCEPTION OF LAW

Judge-made Law.

IT is hardly fanciful to believe that the study of natural law in continental Europe as a thing independent of positive law, while no such distinction has been drawn in England, is closely connected with the fact that judge-made law is a peculiarly important factor in English jurisprudence. On the Continent the principles of justice are excogitated by the jurist in his study, and are merely applied by the judge; or in more recent times they have been embodied in codes whose text binds the judge very closely in deciding the cases before him. But in England these principles are worked out by the court in the actual decision of cases, and enunciated in the opinions rendered which become the authoritative sources of legal principles. Another effect of the different way of regarding law on the two sides of the Channel can be traced with greater certainty, and has left more tangible marks upon existing public life.

Absence of Administrative Courts.

The English conception of law has made the monarchy what Gneist, a most penetrating although biassed student of the comparative history of British and continental institutions, called a *Rechtsstaat*, or commonwealth based upon law. The parliamentary government of England is, he said, a government according to law and by means of law,[1] a proposition most fully expounded in Professor Dicey's "Law of the Constitution."[2] One result of this has been the absence of a body of administrative law, with peculiar

[1] Preface to *Verwaltung, Justiz, Rechtsweg.*

[2] My friend, Mr. Edmund M. Parker, to whom I am indebted for much information about French administrative law, has criticised Professor Dicey's statements on that subject in an article in the *Harvard Law Review* for March, 1906.

principles of its own, enforced by special tribunals distinct from the ordinary courts. Such a system of law exists in most of the large states of Europe; and, as Gneist was fond of pointing out, something very similar was developed in England by the Star Chamber, but it disappeared with the fall of the extraordinary tribunals, and from that time the action of the courts in matters of administration assumed more and more strictly the character of judicial decisions based upon the ordinary principles of law.[1] Nor has the great increase in the nineteenth century of central control over local government brought any real approach to administrative law of the continental type. Boards with judicial functions, such as the Railway Commission, have, indeed, been created, but they do not stand in at all the position of the administrative courts, for they afford no protection to public officials, and by means of writs of prohibition the ordinary courts determine the limits of their power.[2]

**The Liability of Officials**

There is a maxim in England so often repeated as to be commonplace, that no man is above the law; that, save the sovereign alone, every man, whether public officer or private citizen, from the ministers of state down, may be sued or prosecuted in the ordinary courts, under the Common Law of the land. To the rule there are some few exceptions, real or apparent;[3] but the general principles

[1] Gneist, *Englisches Verwaltungsrecht*, I., 389–90. Gneist himself thought the change unfortunate. More than any other man he was the founder of the modern German system of administrative law, and one of the chief objects of his many works was to show the need of such a system, and enforce it by examples from English history. One feels, however, that he never perceived correctly the underlying current of English legal thought.

[2] Shortt, "Informations," 433–34.

[3] The immunity of the Lord Lieutenant of Ireland from suit in that country while he holds the office is an exception. In other cases, however, it is not always clear whether an exemption from suit should be ascribed to official privilege or to the discretionary nature of the authority conferred; for it is a general principle that where an official is given by law any latitude of action, his authority within those limits is regarded as discretionary and free from judicial control. Members of Parliament, for example, and judges are, on one ground or the other, exempt from liability for acts done in the exercise of their functions.

of English law in regard to the liability of officials, and of the state, may be broadly stated.

Beginning with the liability of officials for positive wrongful acts or torts, it may be said that any person, whether a private citizen or an official, may be sued for a tort, and must show in defence that his act was authorised by law. If, for example, a man takes my cattle, I may sue him, and he may set up that he holds them under a lien, or distrained them damage feasant, or found them at large on the highway and impounded them. Now the right to do those things may be conferred by law upon any person, or only upon a public official; but either the private man or the official, as the case may be, must, if sued, prove in an ordinary court that authority to take the cattle was actually conferred upon him by law. The mere fact that a man was acting in an official capacity is in itself neither a ground for liability nor a defence. That a wrong has been done by a subordinate who is subject to the orders of a superior, and for whose conduct that superior is politically responsible, does not render the superior liable for damages unless it appears affirmatively that he personally directed, or took part in, the act.[1] Nor are the holding of an office, the orders of a superior, or the exigencies of state, any excuse for a wrong.[2] The defendant must prove that he was authorised by law to do what he did, or that his superior had a right to issue the command.[3] When the colonel gives an order to fire on a mob, the soldier may conceivably have to choose between obeying and being hanged for murder, or disobeying and being court-martialled and shot. That is one of the risks of the business. for Torts;

[1] Raleigh *vs.* Goschen (1898), 1, Ch., 73.

[2] "With respect to the argument of state necessity, or a distinction which has been aimed at between state offences and others, the Common Law does not understand that kind of reasoning, nor do our books take notice of any such distinctions." Entick *vs.* Carrington, 19 State Trials, 1030, at 1073.

[3] Here, again, there are exceptions, such as that of sheriffs and constables who are held harmless for the service of process fair on its face, although actually issued without authority. But even in that case the officer must show to the satisfaction of the court that the process was fair on its face.

The only question for the court is whether an act falls within the authority conferred by law; and hence an attempt is made to define the powers of a public official as closely as possible. Where they cannot be exactly prescribed, where he is given any latitude of choice, his powers within the limits laid down are regarded as discretionary, and the court will not, as a rule, inquire whether the discretion was used wisely or foolishly, whether the motives were in fact good or bad, or even whether it was used for the purpose for which it was given or not.[1] In some cases the exercise of the discretion must, indeed, be reasonable, in other words, the authority extends only within reasonable limits, but that is a general maxim of law in private as well as public matters. The principle is the same whether it be applied to a military commander dispersing a mob, to a city by-law regulating the use of vehicles, or to a private citizen who injures a thief in defending his property. In each case the court, aided by the prejudices of twelve impartial men, must decide whether under all the circumstances the act is such as a reasonable man actuated by proper motives would have done.[2]

**for Neglect of Official Duty.**

So much for the liability of officials for acts which, if done without authority, would be tortious. Their liability to persons injured by a neglect of official duties depends to some extent upon similar principles. In a suit for tort the only question is upon the authority to do the act, for the court cannot ordinarily inquire whether the authority has been wisely used or not; and on the same ground an official cannot, as a rule, be held liable for a failure to use it at all. Where the exercise of a power is left discretionary, the court cannot substitute its discretion for that of the

[1] This also is not altogether without exception. A justice of the peace is liable in certain cases only for nominal damages, unless he acted with malice, *e.g.*, under 43 Geo. III., c. 141.

[2] The liability of officials to criminal prosecution for offences at Common Law is based upon the same principles as their liability to suits for civil wrongs. But as officials can be prosecuted for crimes only before the ordinary courts in almost all countries to-day, it is not necessary to dwell on the subject.

official; and even where the duty is exactly prescribed, so that he is given no option, the general rule in England is that the duty is owed to the Crown alone, and the courts cannot enforce it, unless it can be shown, as often happens, to be a public duty imposed for the benefit of the individual members of the community.[1] It may be added that where a duty is so imposed, the King's Bench Division can, in its discretion, issue a *mandamus* ordering the performance of the duty, instead of waiting until the injury has occurred and a suit is brought for damages.

**Liability of the State.** In England the state can be sued only by a proceeding against the King, and he cannot be sued without his own consent. Strictly speaking, therefore, no one has a right to sue the state for any cause; but in practice an action is brought in the form of a petition of right,[2] and to this the royal assent is always given where the purpose is to obtain restitution of, or compensation for, private property that has found its way into the possession of the Crown, or where the claim is based upon contract. In cases of that kind the state is virtually liable in damages, but the remedy does not extend to tortious acts done by officials.[3] For these an action lies only against the official himself who may be unable to pay. In cases of contract, therefore, a person injured may obtain compensation from the state, but cannot proceed against the official;[4] while for

[1] Gidley *vs.* Palmerston, 3 B. & B., 284. Kinloch *vs.* Sec. of State, 7 App. Cases, 619. *In re* Nathan, 12 Q.B.D., 461. Reg. *vs.* Comrs., 21 Q.B.D., 313. Queen *vs.* Sec. of State for War (1891), 2 Q.B., 326. In the United States there is a tendency to hold that the courts can compel the performance of all purely ministerial duties, that is, duties which are absolute and not discretionary. *Cf.* Mechem, "Law of Public Offices," §§ 610, 635, 643, 647, 657–59, 947. Wyman, "Administrative Law," § 38.

[2] *Cf.* 23–24 Vic., c. 34.

[3] Tobin *vs.* The Queen, 16 C.B.N.S., 310; and see Feather *vs.* The Queen, 6 B. & S., 293; Windsor & Annapolis Ry. Co. *vs.* The Queen, 11 App. Cases, 615. The remedy has been extended to torts in some of the colonies. *Cf.* Anson, 2 Ed., II., 476.

[4] Like any other agent who contracts in the name of his principal, an official is not personally liable on a contract which he has made on behalf of the state. *Cf.* Gidley *vs.* Lord Palmerston, 3 B. & B., 284.

torts he has no certainty of pecuniary redress, but can wreak his vengeance on the offender.

Besides the direct proceedings against the state and its officials, the courts exert indirectly a powerful control over the administration. Their assistance by means of a writ of *mandamus*, or some other proceeding, is often required for the enforcement of the law; and what is more, if a question about the legality of any act of the public authorities, the validity, let us say, of the regulations made by some department, arises incidentally in a suit between two private persons, and the court is of opinion that the act is not legal, that will ordinarily be treated by the government as decisive; because it is perfectly clear that if not, some one in interest will shortly bring suit against the officials concerned, and the courts will follow the precedent they have already set.[1]

**Administrative Law in France.**

The great countries of continental Europe, whose jurisprudence is based upon the Roman Law, have solved these problems in a very different way. In France, where administrative law is older and more fully developed than elsewhere, acts done by public officers of the state are classified as personal acts, acts of administration and acts of government.

**Liability of Officials.**

Personal acts are such as involve grave personal misconduct on the part of the official. They are not defined with precision in the books;[2] but if, with the temerity of ignorance, the writer were to suggest a definition, it would be, acts which no reasonable official, guided by right motives, could suppose that he was justified in doing. They include not only wrongs committed by the official without authority, for which he would be liable in England, but also an abuse of the powers legally vested in

[1] Gneist, looking at English institutions from a continental standpoint, was impressed by the importance of this fact, *Englische Verwaltungsrecht der Gegenwart*, I., 380.

[2] *Cf.* Aucoc, *Conferences*, I., § 426. Laferrière, *Traité*, I., Liv. III., Ch. vii., § 2. Block, *Dictionnaire*, Sub. Tit., *Fonctionnaires*, § 83. Simonet, *Traité*, § 356. Hauriou, *Précis*, Part II., Liv. I., § 1.

him,[1] and gross negligence in the exercise of those powers.[2] On the other hand, all wrongs committed in excess of authority are not personal acts. If done in good faith in the public interest, they are acts of administration; and the orders of a superior are presumptive, although not absolutely conclusive,[3] evidence of this. Now for personal acts, and for personal acts alone, an official is liable to a civil suit for damages in the ordinary courts. For administrative acts, however illegal, he is not personally liable for damages in any court; and while he can be prosecuted criminally in the ordinary courts for offences committed in the conduct of his office,[4] the proceedings in such a case are entirely under the control of the government. Moreover, the ordinary courts have not final power of determining whether any act is administrative or personal, such a question going, in case of dispute, before the tribunal of conflicts,[5]

[1] Thus, although it is the duty of a mayor to report upon the character of another official, a statement intentionally false, calumnious, or made in bad faith, would be a personal act: *Bourges*, Feb. 10, 1879; Dalloz, *Recueil Periodique* (cited as D.P.), 1879, 2, 164 (Colas *c.* Tissier). A similar case is Lalande *c.* Peynaud, D.P., 1899, 3, 93. So, where a mayor, in order to prevent a civil interment, closed the gates of the cemetery so that the bier had to be carried through a breach in the wall, it was held a personal act, because an abuse of his authority to maintain order in such cases. Court of Cass., Aug. 4, 1880, D.P., 1881, 1, 454 (Delcassé *c.* Mérie-Nègre).

[2] For example, in constructing a bridge, in failure to deliver a letter, or in a mistake in a telegram. (Aucoc, *Conf.*, I., § 426.)

[3] For example, the orders of the Minister of the Interior will not justify a prefect in seizing a political circular contrary to the provisions of the Code of Criminal Procedure. Usannaz-Joris *c.* Préfet de la Savoiè, D.P., 1890, 3, 65, 66.

[4] This is not true in all cases. See a discussion of the subject in Dalloz 1881, 3, 17 note.

[5] Composed of three members of the Court of Cassation, the highest ordinary court, three members of the Section of the Council of State, the highest administrative court, and the Minister of Justice. If the ordinary court is of opinion that the act is merely personal, and that it is therefore at liberty to proceed, the conflict, as it is called, can only be raised by the prefect on behalf of the government; and when it is raised, proceedings must cease, and the question must go before the Tribunal of Conflicts. The Constitution of the year, VIII., provided that officials should not be sued or prosecuted without the consent of the government. During the excitement following the fall of Napoleon III., this was repealed by a decree of Dec. 19, 1870. But that decree produced little change, because the Tri-

which determines the limits of authority between the ordinary and the administrative courts.

Liability of the State. Acts of Administration.

Although acts of administration do not give rise to suits for damages against the officials concerned, the person injured is by no means always without remedy; for the pecuniary liability of the state for the acts of its agents is based upon a principle not recognised by the Common Law of England, and by no means confined to cases of contract.[1] All acts of administration are not, however, treated alike. A distinction is drawn in continental countries between what may be called the exercise by the state of political authority over its citizens, and its business dealings with them. In the latter case the state is commonly liable not only on contracts, but also for torts and even for bad service on the part of the officials. In Germany the state in such cases is said to be sued as *Fiscus*, and the suits against it can be brought in the ordinary courts.[2]

*Actes de Gestion.*

In France the same distinction is made. Acts done in the course of the administration of the public services being termed, according to the latest nomenclature, *actes de gestion*, and those done in the exercise of the political right of the state to issue commands to the citizen *actes d'authorité.*

bunal of Conflicts held that it applied only to the personal protection of officials, and did not affect the principle of the separation of powers, which, as understood in France, forbids the ordinary judges to determine the legality of administrative acts. (July 30, 1873, *Pelletier;* D.P., 1874, 3, 5.) The decree did not, therefore, enlarge the jurisdiction of the ordinary courts, but merely enabled them to entertain civil suits against officials for personal acts without the consent of the government, which in the past had not been given freely. (Aucoc, *Conf.*, I., § 424.) In criminal cases it gave the courts the right to proceed without the formal consent of the government; but that is unimportant as the public prosecutor does not act without its approval.

[1] Hatschek (*Englisches Staatsrecht*, I., 79–81) attributes the absence of such a liability in England to the fact that the conception of the state as a corporation never developed there, so that the state itself never became the subject of rights and duties. Its separate organs had rights and duties toward each other and toward individuals, but as the state itself had not, no antagonism arose between public and private law.

[2] *Cf.* Goodnow, "Comparative Administrative Law," II., Book VI., Ch. ii., § 1, and Ch. vii.

Although the form of the action and its results are different for these two classes of acts, all proceedings based upon either of them must, as a rule, be brought in the administrative courts. It is, indeed, a general principle of French law that the ordinary courts cannot pass upon the legality of any administrative conduct, whether the question arises in a suit against the official or in any other way. This principle is not, indeed, strictly followed out. In the first place, matters arising in the management of the *domaine de l'état*, or private property of the state, fall within the jurisdiction of the ordinary courts.[1] Then, questions of indirect taxes, and those relating to the lesser highways, come before these courts; while those arising under direct taxes, or relating to the greater highways, come before the administrative tribunals.[2] Moreover, there is at the present day a general rule that the arrest of an offender, and the other preliminaries of a criminal case, are judicial matters, and therefore in a suit for false imprisonment it is the ordinary, and not the administrative, courts that pass upon the legality of the arrest.[3] Wherever, also, the government seeks the aid of the ordinary courts in giving effect to its orders, as, for example, in a proceeding to recover a fine for the violation of an administrative regulation, the court can refuse its aid if the order is not legally made.[4]

Now, it must be observed that while the jurisdiction of the administrative courts rests in part upon statute, the administrative law, unlike the civil law, has never been codified, and, indeed, codification would destroy the element of discretion, which is one reason for its existence. So far as it is not contained in statutes and ordinances, it

[1] Laferrière, *Cours*, I., 553–70; Aucoc, *Conf.*, § 214.

[2] Laferrière, *Traité*, *passim*.

[3] Laferrière, *Traité*, I., 486, 529; Hauriou, *Précis*, 5 Ed., 260; and see a recent case decided Jan. 28, 1904, Favre *c.* Mas, Pilot et Perrin, D.P. 1904, 2, 321. Whenever administrative officials act under the provisions of the Code of Criminal Procedure, they are acting as judicial police, and their conduct falls within the jurisdiction of the ordinary courts. Dufeuille *c.* Préfet de Police, D.P. 1890, 3, 65.

[4] Aucoc, *Conf.*, I., § 171; Ducrocq, *Cours*, I., § 652.

has developed, like the English Common Law, by decision and precedent; and hence the sources for studying it are the reported cases and the writings of jurists. This fact has given to the administrative law an elasticity and power of growth that are readily perceived in the expansion of its principles during the last century, and that justify us in speaking of the tendency of the law no less than of the law itself.

In the case of *actes de gestion* there has been a decided expansion of the law; and there is a general tendency to hold the state liable for all injuries arising from acts of this kind, unless they are mere personal acts — that is, the gross personal fault of an official.[1] Any one injured thereby in his property or legal rights can bring suit in the administrative courts both for relief against the act complained of and for compensation for his loss; and he can do so not only when the act has been performed wholly without legal authority, but when it involves an abuse of that authority — a matter that will be referred to again — and also when it is the result of negligence, as, for example, where a merchantman has been damaged by collision with a man-of-war.[2]

*Actes d'Authorité.*

Acts of authority, on the other hand, do not ordinarily give rise to a liability on the part of the state for damages; but they may be annulled by means of a special procedure brought directly before the Council of State, or rather before that section of it which acts as the highest administrative court. This is open both to persons who are injured in their property or legal rights by the order or regulation complained of, and also to those who are merely interested in having it set aside. Acts of administration are thus divided into two classes, *actes de gestion* and *actes d'authorité*, for both of which, remedies against the state are provided. The proceedings in the case of *actes de gestion*,

[1] See the interesting discussion on this subject in the recent work of Hauriou, *La Gestion Administrative.*

[2] 15 February, 1892, Valéry c. l'État, D.P. 1873, 3, 57. Jan. 17, 1874, Hoirs Ferrandini et Ribetti c. Valéry, D.P. 1875, 3, 2.

open only to those persons whose legal rights have been invaded, are brought first in the lower administrative courts, and result principally in damages. The proceedings in the cases of acts of authority, open to any one whose interest is involved, are brought directly before the Council of State, and seek primarily the annulling of the order complained of.

Although the remedy in the case of acts of authority is termed "*recours pour excès de pouvoir,*" it is not limited to cases where the order exceeds the power of the official and is therefore strictly illegal, but may be used also where there has been merely an abuse of legal authority. This principle, which in any such form is unknown to the Common Law, is based upon what is called "*détournement de pouvoir*" — that is, the use of power for a purpose other than that for which it was conferred.[1] It runs all through the French administrative law, and is applied to the personal acts of officials, to *actes de gestion,* and to acts of authority. The most striking case in which this principle was recognised occurred in 1874, and is known by the name of the complainant, Laumonnier-Carriol. The government had decided to set up in its own hands a monopoly of the manufacture of matches, and to buy for that purpose all existing factories. But in order not to expend more than was necessary for this purpose, it directed the prefects, under their power to stop unhealthy trades, to close all the factories operated without a license. The Council of State, however, without considering whether the factory could have been properly closed as unhealthy, annulled the order closing it, on the ground that the power had been used for an object other than that for which it was granted.[2] The complainant then sued the Minister of Finance and the prefect in the civil courts, but the conflict being raised, the Tribunal of Conflicts held that, although annulled, the

Abuse of Power.

[1] *Cf.* Aucoc, *Conf.*, I., § 298.

[2] The decree annulling the prefect's order was made Nov. 26, 1875, D.P. 1876, 3, 41.

order in this case was an administrative, not a personal, act, and hence damages could be recovered, if at all, only against the state in the administrative courts.[1] On a proceeding of that nature the Council of State decided that while an abuse of the police powers did not usually give rise to pecuniary liability on the part of the state, yet in this instance the order was made in the financial interest of the state, which was, therefore, liable for the loss suffered during the time the factory was closed.[2]

Acts of Government.

Finally, acts of government, that is, acts done for reasons of state with a view to the public safety, whether within the legal power of the government or not, lie beyond the jurisdiction both of the ordinary and of the administrative courts, and can neither be annulled by any judicial process nor create a claim for compensation against the state or its officials. Not unnaturally the kind of acts that have been regarded as falling within this class has not always been the same. Under the Second Empire, the arbitrary suppression of a newspaper,[3] and the confiscation of the proof-sheets of a book written by the Duc d'Aumale about the princes of his house,[4] were held to be acts of government; while under the Third Republic, in cases closely similar to the latter, and in a case involving the seizure of a political circular in favour of the monarchy, the decisions were the other way.[5] The prevailing opinion at present is that the exemption afforded by this principle covers only measures taken to secure external safety or to carry on a war, decrees creating the state of siege, with perhaps some matters of sanitary police,[6] and does not cover other steps taken by the government for the preservation of order.[7]

[1] May 5, 1877, D.P. 1878, 3, 13. [2] Dec. 5, 1879, D.P. 1880, 3, 41.

[3] June 10, 1856 (Dautreville), D.P. 1856, 3, 57.

[4] May 9, 1867 (Duc d'Aumale), D.P. 1867, 3, 49.

[5] March 25, 1889, Dufeuille *c.* Préfet de Police, D.P. 1890, 3, 65 *et seq.*; and see April 2, 1886 (Fontenaud), D.P. 1886, 34, 8. May 20, 1887 (Duc d'Aumale), etc., D.P. 1888, 3, 105.

[6] In 1857 a decree forbidding the distillation of cereals was held to be an act of government, Feb. 26, 1857 (Cohen), D.P. 3, 81.

[7] Laferrière, *Traité*, II., Liv. IV., Ch. ii.; Hauriou, *Précis*, 5 Ed., 274–81.

**Growth of Administrative Law.**

It may be observed that throughout continental Europe administrative law is getting a firmer and firmer foothold. The number of treatises upon it have increased rapidly; and it has assumed the character of a real system of jurisprudence with a regular judicial procedure. This is in fact a somewhat recent matter. Until 1831 the Council of State in France did not give public hearings upon the cases submitted to it; and except for three years from 1849 to 1852 it had, until 1872, only power to advise the head of the state. It would, indeed, appear that its opinions were always carried out by him,[1] but any one who studies its decisions can hardly fail to note a greater degree of independence as against the government in later years. In Germany the administrative courts are of even more recent origin. The first regular tribunal of the kind there was established by Baden in 1863; the next by Prussia in 1872; then followed Wurtemburg in 1876, and Bavaria in 1878. Austria did the same in 1875.

**Relative Advantages of the Two Systems.**

Advocates of administrative courts urge that under the continental system an individual can obtain redress in many cases where he cannot do so in England; in cases, for example, where an official has been guilty of a neglect of duty for which he would not be liable in England, or where the power that the official undoubtedly possesses by law has been abused. They urge, also, that he has a much more effective means of getting reparation, because the suit can often be brought against the state in cases where in England it can be brought only against an official who may be quite unable to pay the damages awarded. All this is undoubtedly true, and is so far a merit of the French system; but it is not so great a one as it might at first appear, because the administration in England is much more decentralised than it is in France, and the local bodies are liable in damages for many of the things for which the state is liable in France.

The advocates of administrative courts claim further

[1] Laferrière, *Cours de Droit Public*, 5 Ed., I., 181.

that tribunals composed of administrative officials are more competent to deal with the law governing administrative questions than are the judges of the ordinary courts. They say that the latter are likely either to delay and hamper the necessary work of administration,[1] or, for fear of doing so, to be timid in maintaining the rights of the individual. This would, no doubt, be a very real danger if the judges of the ordinary courts in England had a mere academic education. But, in fact, there are always a number of them who are well acquainted with public life. A certain sprinkling, indeed, of judges with political experience is needed to enable the courts to deal intelligently with questions that touch the administration of the state. This is one of many cases where the efficiency of public bodies depends upon the presence in small quantities of what in large doses would be a poison.

It may very well be true that the English system of law gives a less effective pecuniary redress to the sufferer, but it does, undoubtedly, secure a more strict adherence to law; first, because the judges of the ordinary courts adhere more strictly to legal rules, and, in fact, that is one of the very reasons on the Continent for putting administrative cases into the hands of administrative tribunals; second, because there are no questions of high state policy in which the government has a free hand apart from the control of the courts; and, third, because the direct remedy against an official, although less remunerative to the complainant, is more sure to hold him within limits of his authority, than an ultimate right of redress against the state either by way of damages or of annulling an illegal order.[2] The French system at the present day is based upon the idea of giving

[1] This has, in fact, made it difficult for the Board of Trade to carry out provisions of the law preventing the sailing of unseaworthy ships. Dicey, "Law of the Const.," 5 Ed., 329–30.

[2] Hatschek (*Englisches Staatsrecht*, I., 93) notes as one advantage of the personal liability of officials in England, that it prevents every policeman or tax collector from feeling himself an incarnation of the idea of the state; and thus, he says, the individualism of the people is preserved.

to the individual the greatest protection against pecuniary loss that is compatible with the freedom of the government to take measures for public order and safety. The English system is based on legal traditions. It aims not primarily to make good private loss, but to maintain the law and prevent arbitrary violations of it; and in doing so it has prevented the conflict between the ideas of order and progress which has exercised the minds of statesmen in other countries, for it has made liberty dependent upon law.

It is a great mistake to suppose that the government in France commonly extorts a favourable judgment from the administrative courts. This was shown in a case in 1895 which became politically famous. The Minister of the Interior and the railroads disagreed about the interpretation of a statute relating to the state guaranty of interest on the securities of the roads. The matter was brought before the Council of State which decided in favour of the railroads,[1] whereupon the Minister of the Interior resigned, while the rest of the cabinet felt bound to abide by the decision. A debate was, however, raised in the Chamber of Deputies, where the ministers were blamed for taking action which made it possible to bring the matter before the Council of State. A hostile order adopted in the chamber caused the fall of the cabinet, and this, as it happened, became the occasion of the resignation of Casimir-Perier, the President of the Republic.

There have been many other cases where the courts have decided against the wishes of the government; and sometimes — like those already referred to in regard to the princes of the House of Orleans — where politics were involved. Still, one may ask himself how great the independence of the administrative courts would be in face of a really important political question. In 1880 the government issued decrees for the suppression of all monastic orders not authorised by law. There seemed to be grave

[1] 11 Jan., 1895, Paris-Lyons-Med.; 12 Jan., 1895, Orleans et Midi; all in D.P., 1896, 3, 12.

doubt about the legality of the decrees, and the persons evicted brought suits in the ordinary courts in several parts of France. Many of these courts held that they were authorized to entertain the suits, and in some cases restored the complainants to possession pending trial.[1] The Tribunal of Conflicts, however, decided that the ordinary courts were not competent to deal with the matter;[2] and it is a significant fact that the complainants did not bring the question of the legality of the decrees before the Council of State.

[1] See a number of these cases in Dalloz, 1880, III., 57–62, 80.
[2] Dalloz, 1880, 3, 121–32; 1881, 3, 21–22, 81–82, etc.

# PART VIII. — REFLECTIONS

## CHAPTER LXIII

### ARISTOCRACY AND DEMOCRACY

Politics not an Exact Science.

SITTING down after long study of a government to crystallise in print general reflections about it, one feels like exclaiming with Taine in his work on the history of French institutions: So far I have discovered only one political principle, so simple that I hardly dare to mention it. It is contained entirely in the remark that a human society, and especially a modern society, is a vast and complex thing.[1] An attempt to unravel the skein of human actions, to follow the line of any one thread, to trace the relation of cause and effect among the institutions, the traditions and the current impulses that make up the fabric of political life, involves difficulties not lightly overcome; and the more the pattern is examined the more perplexing it becomes. Dealing, as political economy does, mainly with a single motive, that of commercial profit, an object which men contrive to keep distinct in their minds more completely, perhaps, than any other, economists are enabled to reason about causes and results with considerable success. They have even ventured to apply mathematical processes, to treat, for example, the amount of a commodity sold as a function of the price, and have obtained thereby results approximate enough to be of value. But such methods can hardly be of much use in the more intricate phenomena of politics. Their validity depends upon the assumption which lies at the base of physical science, the doctrine of the conservation of energy with its corollary the parallelogram of forces.

[1] *Origines de la France contemporaine: La Révolution*, Vol. II. Pref.

It depends upon the assumption that each force acts independently of every other, so that its effects can be isolated, studied by themselves, and then combined. But this is not true in politics, where forces react upon one another in such a way that two institutions or two motives, each of which working alone would tend in a certain direction, may together produce exactly the opposite result. Politics, therefore, must forever remain an inexact science, and the only conclusion one can draw with certainty is that in a given environment a certain combination of causes produces the consequences that we observe. We can detect the factors that are essential in the public life of a country, and we can feel sure that without the presence of all of them the result would not be what it is, but we cannot predict that even the whole of those factors would reproduce exactly the same conditions elsewhere.

**Comparisons of Corruption in England and America.**

No better illustration of the difficulty and danger of making generalisations can be given than by the question one is often asked, why there is so much more corruption in the United States than in England; and perhaps the question affords as good a peg as any other to hang a discourse upon. But an endeavour to answer it, like any statement of general reflections upon the English government, must of necessity involve a repetition of much that has gone before, because the aim is to bring together in a new relation conclusions already reached in the study of various branches of the subject. Now, in the first place, the difference in the extent of corruption, in the case at least of the national governments, would appear to be somewhat exaggerated in the eyes of the public[1]; and herein the attitude towards political life is unlike in the two countries. A score of years ago cultivated Americans took pleasure in decrying their government, and the habit has not wholly disappeared. It arose partly from the small number of their friends who were actively engaged in affairs of state, partly from the

[1] The recent report of the Royal Commission on War Stores in South Africa (Com. Papers, 1906, LVII., 1) shows that British administration has not always been spotless.

contrast between their lofty ideals and the sordid realities about them, and partly from the gratification of self-righteousness that comes from finding fault with others. Such a temper of mind led them to credit and repeat any charge of misconduct, until a spotted surface seemed wholly dark.

**Pride of Englishmen in their Government.**

In Great Britain one is impressed by the opposite tone of mind in regard to public life. Englishmen dwell upon their industrial defects. They insist so constantly upon the lack of commercial enterprise and progress among their people that an observer who surveys the prosperity of the nation, suspects exaggeration here also, and is inclined to think that industry, when not too much hampered by the state and by trade-unions, is by no means so backward as such statements would imply. On the other hand, the typical Englishman believes that his government is incomparably the best in the world. It is the thing above all others that he is proud of. He does not, of course, always agree with the course of policy pursued; that will depend largely upon whether the party to which he belongs is at the moment sitting at the right or left hand of the Speaker in the House of Commons. If a Liberal, he may feel at one time that the Tories are misguiding the nation, or that the House of Lords is putting a yoke upon its neck; if a Conservative, he may feel at another that the Radicals are ruining the country; but he is certain that the general form of government is well-nigh perfect, and he has an unshaken confidence in the personal integrity of statesmen. On this point he lays to heart the text: Thou shalt not speak evil of the ruler of thy people. Such a frame of mind has an excellent effect upon the rising generation, for it makes them regard a lack of probity in public affairs as the unpardonable sin which no respectable person ever commits; and respectability is among the cardinal virtues in England. In spite of occasional abuses, such as the common habit of taking secret business commissions, which provoked much discussion a few years ago, one is, indeed, struck by the honesty of the English people, not only in their dealings with a stranger, but still more by their confidence in him, by the general assumption that everybody speaks the truth. There is an absence of admiration for the mere cleverness that consists in getting the better of others by one's wits.

The Rule of a Class.

Then the fact that the national government is still mainly in the hands of the upper class is not without effect upon the standard of political integrity. The rule of an aristocracy is not proverbial for a high moral tone or scrupulous honesty; and Ferrero, in his recent history, portrays a decline in the public virtues of the Roman nobility accompanying the enlargement of the basis of political power, the advent of commercial wealth, and the extension of the empire. But in England a course of events not wholly dissimilar in appearance has been followed by a very different result. Corruption that was rife and open in the eighteenth century is now mentioned with abhorrence. The fact is that the upper classes in England rule to-day, not by means of political privileges which they retain, but by the sufferance of the great mass of the people, and as trustees for its benefit. Their leadership is highly popular with the masses, but it depends upon keeping the respect of the nation by a generally unstained reputation for probity of character; for if that reputation were seriously impaired the ruling class would soon be swept from power. Now although such a motive for integrity may be largely unconscious it is none the less effective. It makes the men in public life highly sensitive in avoiding dubious conduct, while it also causes them to discredit scandalous reports and repel insinuations against members of their own order. It has thus the double consequence of preventing lapses from the recognised standard of political ethics, and of sustaining a reputation for unblemished purity. Moreover, most of the men who play the leading parts in the game of politics, as trustees for the people under the public eye, have fought together in the sports of schools and colleges, and are constantly meeting in the society of London. This in itself tends to make them play the game fairly, and observe the conventional rules of honour of the day.

Nature of the Class.

The condition is one to which Professor Burgess alludes as "government of the people, for the people, by the best of the people." [1] Without discussing in what sense they are the best of the people, it is clear that most of the seats in the House of Commons are still held by the members of a distinct social class. The elements are not, indeed, precisely the same as those that made up the aristocracy of a century ago. The old landed gentry are less numerous, and the representatives of commercial wealth more prominent, than they were then; but the English aristocracy has never been a closed body. Its doors have always been open to achievement, success and wealth. Its composition has always been changing, and probably on the average as large a proportion as ever of members of the House of Commons frequent the drawing-rooms of London. The connection of fashionable society with politics is still very close, perhaps on the whole not less close than at other times.[2]

Society in England is a national institution. It is not a collection of separate groups in different places, but a single body with ramifications all over the country, and a central meeting ground in London during the season. Unlike the other classes in the community, which are local, society is universal. Its members have an extraordinarily wide acquaintance with one another from one end of the land to the other. They are connected by marriage, by early association at the public schools and at Oxford or Cambridge, and they are brought constantly together by entertainments in the capital, and visits at country houses. Such a constitution gives to society great solidity and great influence, without the narrowness and rigidity that attends a purely hereditary caste.

Why Class Rule Persists.

It has already been pointed out that the mass of the people prefer to be represented by men of social position, and the

[1] "Political Science and Constitutional Law," II., 4.

[2] Redlich comments on the importance of this aspect of English public life ("The Procedure of the House of Commons," Eng. Ed., II., 125 *et seq.*); and Sidney Low devotes an excellent chapter to it ("The Governance of England," Ch. x.).

higher his social position the better they like a candidate; provided, of course, that the party to which he belongs is prepared to carry out their wishes — a condition, as we shall see, that the parties are only too ready to fulfil. There is an almost complete absence of the passion for equality and the class jealousy so common in some other countries. On the contrary, the sentiment of deference, or snobbishness, becomes, if anything, stronger as the social scale descends. The workingman, when not provoked by an acute grievance to vote for a trade-union candidate, prefers a man with a title, and thus the latest extensions of the franchise have rather strengthened than weakened the hold of the governing class upon public life.

The general habit of electing non-residents has also given an advantage to men of means and position. It enables them to come forward as candidates with an excellent prospect of success in every constituency in the kingdom; whereas a man who is not well off, who has been brought up in modest surroundings, would find it almost impossible to win an election away from his home, unless he had already become distinguished. Even in his native town the absence of a graded series of public offices, of a recognised political ladder leading up to Parliament makes it hard for him to climb into the House of Commons.

**The Cost of a Seat in Parliament.**

The popular sentiment which helps to maintain the political leadership of the upper class is reinforced by the direct effect of wealth; for the influence of money in politics is, as a rule, very different in England and America. In the latter it is not seldom used to procure favours from a legislature or city council, and more frequently to obtain fair treatment or ward off unprincipled attacks. Direct bribery of legislators tends, indeed, to become more rare, and money is more commonly employed in the form of subscriptions to campaign funds, paid to the boss in places where he exists. A contribution of that kind, although not a purchase of a definite service, gives a claim to gratitude and consideration in the future. In England, on the other hand, public office is rarely, if ever, used as a means of assisting wealth, but wealth is used freely to procure office. Members of Parliament are unpaid, the regular expenses of registration and election are usually heavy, and, except in the case of labour men supported by trade-unions, fall mainly upon the candidate, while the additional cost of nursing the constituency adds no small sum to his outlay. The result is that a seat in the House of Commons is a luxury enjoyed mainly by the only class in the community that can afford it.

**Attraction of Public Life for that Class.**

All these things tend to place the management of national affairs in the hands of the richer portion of the community, and at the same time public life exerts upon that class an almost irresistible attraction. The desire to take part in politics appears to be more general among English men of leisure than in the corresponding social element in any other country in the world. The pleasures to be found are, on the whole, greater, and the drawbacks less, than anywhere else. If the House of Commons is no longer the best club in London, it is a very pleasant place and the gateway to much that is agreeable. Parliament sits during the fashionable season in the capital of the empire, where the society from the whole British Isles meets, and everything of moment in the world passes under review. To that society the aristocratic representative of a provincial borough, with most of his fellow-members, belongs, and there he is an object of interest and attention. One cannot help wondering how different things might be, if with the payment of members a large proportion of men of different antecedents came into the House, and if on the principle of geographical centre of gravity, so strangely in vogue in the United States, Parliament were to sit at Nottingham.

Moreover, the process of getting into the House of Commons involves little that repels a candidate. He is not obliged to undergo a long apprenticeship in public work on a smaller scale. He does not receive many rough buffets from men of less fastidious temperament, or suffer from the personal abuse too common in English municipal elections and in political contests of all kinds in other lands. Finally, Parliament is the easiest road to distinction, or to honours of any kind, and almost the only road to the greatest power and highest rank the nation can bestow; for although private members have individually little influence now on the course of public affairs, a follower of the dominant party without marked talent, if faithful and rich, is often rewarded by a baronetcy or even by a peerage, and it is only through Parliament that a seat in the cabinet can be reached. There is, probably, no other career in which a man of birth and means, with good abilities and moderate exertion, is so likely to win fame as in English politics. Nor does he run the risk, so great in other democratic countries, of falling back into oblivion without serious fault of his own after he has achieved a high position. Once a leader always a leader is very nearly true in England, for a former cabinet minister who is still vigorous is almost certain of a seat in the next cabinet of his party, or if not, he can, if a man of wealth, claim the consolation of a peerage. President Roosevelt's advice to young Americans who consulted him about politics as a career, that to go into politics was an excellent thing, but to regard it as a career involved temptations which could hardly be escaped, could not be given in England. It is not surprising, therefore, that a seat in Parliament should have a strong fascination for young men born in the governing class.

The Ruling Class and the Cabinet.

The men who move in the fashionable society of London preponderate, as Sidney Low observes, even more in the cabinet than in the House of Commons.[1] This he attributes partly to the well-known fact that a man has a far better chance of reaching the cabinet if he has begun his experience in the House of Commons young; and no one can do so unless he is saved by hereditary wealth from the need of earning his living. He lays still greater stress on the fact that men of that class are selected for places in the ministry

[1] "The Governance of England," 184 *et seq.*

because they are known to the leaders by constant social intercourse, and by ties of blood or friendship; while, apart from a few marked personalities or the representatives of prominent opinions, "the public is not specially concerned in asserting the claims of one member of the House of Commons, rather than another, to Cabinet office. It has done its duty at the polls by practically appointing A and his party to the government, in preference to B and his following; and it is quite content to leave the constitution of the executive committee, and the allocation of the posts in it, to the leader and his advisers." The popular indifference to the selection of many of the cabinet ministers is, indeed, a little extraordinary.

In this connection the gradual change whereby the cabinet has been gaining in political weight at the expense of the House of Commons is of importance, for it is precisely in the cabinet that the governing class is most strongly intrenched. Such a condition may not be permanent, but all the prophecies of the levelling effects of democracy in Great Britain have so far proved fallacious. Where political class jealousy is weak, social ambition and social cohesion are among the strongest forces in human nature, and in a society as centralised and powerfully constructed as that of England they are not likely to fade quickly into the background. All this is far more true of the Conservative, than of the Liberal, party; but even among the Liberals social influence is a power, and a power that does not seem likely to pass away.

## CHAPTER LXIV

### PUBLIC, PRIVATE AND LOCAL INTERESTS

Reasons for the Prominence of Public Issues.

THE comparative absence in English political life, not only of corruption in its grosser shapes, but also of the pressure for patronage, the insistence on private and local interests and the log-rolling that vex many states, is largely due to the fact that politics turn almost wholly on public questions. Private and local affairs play a very subordinate part, and scarcely affect the really vital matter, the tenure of office of the ministry. The same result has by no means always been attained in other countries where the parliamentary form of government has been adopted, and hence it cannot be ascribed solely to the responsibility of the cabinet, although in England that is, no doubt, an essential element in the problem. It must be attributed to a number of other factors that relieve both ministers and representatives from the exactions to which they are commonly subjected elsewhere. Most of these have already been mentioned in a similar connection in earlier chapters, but it may not be out of place to review them here.

The Permanent Civil Service.

At the head of the list may be placed the existence of a permanent civil service, covering not only inferior and clerical positions, but also those which involve responsible work of a high grade; in fact all the government offices below the rank of minister. Every one of this great mass of public servants retains his post without regard to a change of the party in power, and almost all vacancies that occur are filled without regard to political connections. In most of the departments, indeed, the holders of all but a few of the very highest positions in the permanent service are selected by open competitive examination followed by promotion. Such a system, which constitutes, perhaps, the most essential difference between the English and American governments, prevents the use of public office as party spoils and keeps politics out of the civil service. It promotes consecutive, businesslike administration, and renders possible party changes without dislocation of public functions. It leaves ministers and representatives free to devote their attention to national questions, without being distracted by the need of satisfying a horde of applicants or rewarding faithful retainers; and it eliminates geographical considerations altogether. The idea that appointments to public office ought to be distributed among the different parts of the country in proportion to population would seem ludicrous to an Englishman. In their reports on the result of competitions for the first-class clerkships, for example, the Civil Service Commissioners state the universities at which the successful candidates have studied, and sometimes the occupations of their parents, but never the counties where they reside. No one inquires whether Scotland or Yorkshire or London have won more places than Wales, the Midlands or East Anglia; nor would a greater degree of success, where every one can compete on the same terms, be regarded as a grievance.

The filling of responsible positions by competition could hardly be successful except by the method the English have employed; that is, the selection of a large number of very young men by an examination testing their general education and ability, and then the promotion to higher posts of those among them who show the qualities required. No examination can measure administrative capacity; that depends upon personal aptitudes which lie to a great extent outside the field of scholarly attainment. On the other hand, as the chapter on the Permanent Civil Service points out, familiarity with the work to be done, immediate fitness for employment, essential as it is when the office is to be held for a short time, is of little importance in selecting young men for a life-long career. What is more, to require it actually drives away many of the best applicants by obliging them to devote a great deal of time to learning things that will be quite useless to them if unsuccessful in the ordeal. For this reason Macaulay's commission laid down the principle that the examination should include only subjects which candidates would naturally have studied as a part of their general education, and the principle has since been extended to the lower branches of the English civil service. The opposite practice, of an examination bearing upon technical preparation, was tried in Holland for admission to the colonial service in Java, but after an experience of many years it was abandoned for the very reasons that Macaulay had adduced.[1]

Now an examination of a literary character, like that for the first-class clerkships, could hardly be maintained were it not that rank in the studies of the universities is generally believed to be a trustworthy measure of intellectual power. In America, where the value of education is commonly deemed to lie in the utility of the information acquired, such a test of ability would not readily be accepted; and in fact while examinations for fitness have been largely used there to remove subordinate and clerical positions from politics, very little progress has been made in the case of offices of a responsible nature. Yet it is in these that the greatest merit of the English system consists. Only by taking them out of the sphere of party action has personal patronage been eliminated from public life.

Free Trade.

If the organisation of the permanent civil service has discarded many personal questions, the pressure of private and local interests has been much lessened in other ways. Whatever may be thought of the economic effects of protection, whatever its necessity may be in developing the industries of a new land, there can be no doubt that the policy of free trade in England has taken out of the

[1] Lowell and Stephens, "Colonial Civil Service," 144 *et seq.*

political arena a subject full of conflicts between different parts of the country and different occupations. However men may talk about a scientific tariff, the adjustment of the schedule in a legislative chamber involves in practice concessions among the various forms of industry, each of which urges its own claims to the utmost of its power.

**Absence of Local Improvements by the State.**

A second thing that has helped to keep local interests out of politics is the tradition forbidding the use of national resources for the benefit of particular places. The government is, of course, obliged to maintain dockyards in a number of seaports, and the dockyard members have become a byword in politics. But except in such cases it spends no money upon harbours; the gigantic improvements in Liverpool, Glasgow and other places having been carried out by the people of those towns at their own expense. Post-offices it must have, no doubt, but it has them everywhere. It constructs no canals, no roads; and although it has made large grants for local police, education and other services, it has done so by general rules which apply equally to all parts of the country. To the relief both of the members and of public business, this cuts off a source of activity on behalf of local interests that has a baneful influence elsewhere.

**Private Bill Legislation.**

Another fruitful source of private and local pressure is cut off by the English method of dealing with private bills. By the quasi-judicial procedure before small impartial committees to which such bills are subjected, the opportunities of members to push the measures desired by their constituents or their friends are taken away, and the occasions when they can effectively oppose private bills that their constituents do not want are very much reduced. The representative whose aim during the session is so riveted on putting through a water bill, for which his town is clamouring, that he is willing to trade his vote on other measures for support on this, is unknown; and without being consciously lacking in a sense of public duty, such a man is a demoralising element in a legislative body. In one sense a Member of Parliament no doubt uses his vote on one measure as a means of carrying another, for he is always voting with his party in matters on which he has no decided opinions in order to keep them in power for objects that interest him deeply. The principle of cabinet responsibility obliges him to follow the whips with singular fidelity, but this relates to public not private or local affairs.

The Strength of Party.

The strictness with which party lines are drawn in the House of Commons is, indeed, both a cause and a result of the prominence of public questions as compared with private and local ones. The two front benches wage an unceasing war, while the whole nation looks on. Every one is interested in watching the battle. Every one thinks he understands the issues involved, because the fight itself is perfectly clear. It is between two permanent bands of warriors, always on opposite sides, contending for a definite stake, which of them shall rule the country. There is no confusion of aims, no cross division among the leaders. These conditions force the front benches to take their stand on matters of public interest, and they compel the other members of the House to support one side or the other. A member of the dominant party who votes against his leaders runs the risk of turning them out in favour of a ministry of the Opposition; and in the dissolution that will certainly follow he is likely to find scant sympathy among his constituents. They are concerned with the main question of party victory which overshadows everything else. In a presidential form of government representatives cannot be whipped into line, because they cannot be threatened with a dissolution or a change of ministry, and hence both their personal convictions and their demands on behalf of friends and constituents have greater weight. In the parliamentary government of France the same thing is true, because the fall of a cabinet does not mean a real change of party. But in England the ministers lead and the majority must follow them. The conflict is so plain, and absorbs public attention so thoroughly, that the ministers are not obliged to purchase support by giving personal or local favours. They can afford to rely on their public programme alone, and it is for their interest and comfort to do so. In fact they refrain almost altogether from interfering with the class of matters that fall within the province of private bill legislation. To repeat, therefore, the conclusion reached in an earlier chapter, the English political parties under their responsible parliamentary chiefs are unusually potent factors in directing legislation, but they are concerned almost entirely with matters of national consequence.

That politics turn on public, not on private or local, questions has manifest advantages. It lessens the temptation to seek for personal benefits, to form secret combinations, which if not corrupt are demoralising and have gone far to bring popular legislative bodies into disrepute. But it involves also dangers not unconnected with a phenomenon of world-wide significance, the modern revival of paternalism.

# CHAPTER LXV

## THE GROWTH OF PATERNALISM

*Laissez-Faire.*

THE readjustment from an older state of things to modern industrial and social conditions brought about, between the middle of the eighteenth and the middle of the nineteenth centuries, many changes of laws and institutions. Rules devised for needs that had passed away were so often worse than useless, an actual hindrance to progress, that men began to look on all regulations as presumptively bad, and on their ancestors as guilty of an almost malign stupidity in framing them. Rousseau, indeed, made the comprehensive discovery that civilisation itself had been a blunder from the start. In France the new spirit, unchained by the Revolution, swept before it all the more obvious portions of the old constitution; and while in England a conservative sentiment and dislike of upheavals impeded the spread of subversive doctrines in the political field, on economic questions highly radical theories came to be very widely held. That this should have been the case in England was, no doubt, because the theory of reducing government interference to the lowest possible point coincided with the immediate needs of the day. Manufactures in Great Britain had developed very rapidly, and one object of legislation in the second quarter of the last century was the removal of obstacles to their expansion. The grave problems they would raise, the abuses they would create, were not at first fully perceived. Labour, also, was not sufficiently organised to make its voice effectively heard, for the extension of the suffrage had enfranchised mainly the middle classes, who were primarily interested in the growth of industry and the production of wealth. Moreover, the prophets of the new era believed that all men must ultimately share in the benefits conferred by wealth, that each man in pursuing his own interest contributed thereby to the greatest welfare of the community. The doctrine of *laissez-faire* propounded by the classical economists, and carried into practical politics by the Manchester School, was in fact founded upon the assumption that the enlightened self-interest of each individual must be in general harmony with that of everybody else; and the more ardent spirits looked forward to a state of universal prosperity based upon universal selfishness.

**Change of Theory.**

Every political theory contains the seeds of its own destruction, because it must be to some extent inaccurate, and the more thoroughly it is put into practice the more fully its defects appear. The result is that when a principle seems to be generally accepted, when it has become acknowledged as the spirit of the age, the time of its overthrow is usually close at hand. Human progress is like beating to windward, a tack to starboard and then a tack to port, for mankind, unable to discern absolute truth in shaping its course, moves forward by over-accentuating one principle at a time. The doctrine of *laissez-faire* was no exception to the rule. Managers of the new industries, intent on building up their business, unrestrained by statute, employed labour on the terms fixed by the law of demand and supply with too little thought for the well-being of their operatives, and hence the rapid growth of industrial life led to misery among the lowest class of working people, especially among women and children in factories and mines. When these evils were brought into general notice, they gave rise to factory legislation. Gradually the employment of child labour was limited, hours of work were regulated, sanitary conditions were improved, dangerous machinery was guarded, compulsory education of children was enforced, and employers were made liable for injuries to their workmen. Laws of this kind began long before the doctrine of *laissez-faire* had reached high-water mark in public favour, and they have ever since been enacted at increasing speed. They involve an admission that enlightened self-interest of employers or employed is not a sufficient safeguard against oppression.[1]

The Tinge of Socialism.

The factory acts made a breach in the tenets of *laissez-faire* which has been constantly growing wider, until there is not enough of the doctrine left to offer a formidable resistance to legislation purporting to be philanthropic. Economists have been busy with it, showing its defects and limitations. It has also been undermined by socialistic theories based upon exactly the opposite principle, and although these are not accepted as a creed by any large part of the English people, they have leavened public opinion among all classes. They proceed upon the premise that the interests of men are essentially discordant, and that the state must intervene to regulate conflicting forces and prevent abuse of power. In fact the theory in its most complete form would place all industry in the hands of the government, and deny to private individuals the conduct of business altogether. The extent to which a belief in the natural discord of human interests may be carried is seen in a couple of the vivid fables of H. G. Wells, for fiction sometimes exhibits opinion quite as clearly as any formal treatise. In "The Time Machine," where he projects himself into the world many thousand years hence, he finds mankind divided into two parts, of which the more vigorous preserves the other for food. In "The War of the Worlds," the creatures, far superior to men, who invade the Earth from Mars, live by sucking the blood of the people they find here. These tales are written with a purpose, and it is not merely as a literary fantasy that the unfettered course of selfish evolution is portrayed as ending in cannibalism. They show the extreme swing of the pendulum away from the fundamental conceptions of *laissez-faire*. While Englishmen are certainly not inclined

[1] On this whole subject see the luminous work of Prof. A. V. Dicey in "Law and Opinion in England."

to accept any theory of necessary discord in human interests, they have faith no longer in any essential harmony, and when a present grievance is pointed out they are quite ready to apply a remedy, instead of waiting with a blind confidence that the natural course of events will make things right.

The Growth of Humanitarian Sentiment.

The new seed fell into ground prepared for it by the growth of humanitarian ideas. Civilisation may, perhaps, be measured by the breadth of human sympathy. At first men have a fellow-feeling only for members of their own family, tribe or clan. All other people are natural enemies to be destroyed or enslaved. Then the conception of common ties extends to a larger body, a city, a state, or even a whole race speaking the same language or worshipping the same gods; but still the limits are narrow. Even in the classic times in Greece the slaves were to a great extent regarded as a means to the perfection of a superior caste, rather than as beings whose happiness was of itself important. The idea that all mankind, of every colour, race or creed, is entitled to friendship and help is comparatively new as a popular belief, and even now finds it hard to maintain itself in the stress of actual life. Finally, animals have aroused pity as never before, until people feel that every creature capable of joy or suffering has a right to the sympathy of man.

If an advance in civilisation may be measured by the broadening of sympathy, the forward movement begun in Europe in the middle of the eighteenth century has continued at an increasing rate. The rapid growth of all agencies, public and private, for alleviating suffering and improving the comfort and prospects of the poor, the settlement work, the general interest in all philanthropic movements, furnish evidence enough of this. The efforts may not always be wisely directed, but the sentiment behind them is strong and genuine. One sees it at every turn. A few years ago the writer was told of an old gentleman who said that when he went to London as a youth the cats ran away from you, but now they came up to be stroked; and the remark covers a chapter in human progress. Bear-baiting is certainly not forbidden in England to-day because it gives pleasure to the spectator. The popular amusements of the time, like professional cricket and foot-ball matches, may be unedifying forms of distraction, but except, curiously enough, among the upper classes, sport is not cruel, and nowhere is it brutalising either to the participant or the spectator.

Decrease of Brutality.

In spite of the cases of wife-beating and other outrages of which one still hears, brutality among the English masses appears to have lessened very much; and in fact the judicial statistics show a steady decrease in crimes of violence.[1] An observer does not see the constant street brawls of men and boys that Dickens described. Drink is, of course, a plague, especially in Scotland, where the amount of drunkenness and the disregard with which it is treated are amazing. But according to the returns of the Commissioners of Inland Revenue the consumption of alcohol has been diminishing during the last few years;[2] and certainly the love of street fighting for the mere fun of it has largely died out.[3] Even more striking, perhaps, is the attitude of the government toward crime, as set forth in the court-house recently erected on the site of the Old Bailey, by the spot where Newgate prison stood with its long story of retribution and suffering. Over the new building is carved the motto: "Thou shalt protect the children of the poor, and punish the wrong-doer."

Loss of Stolidity.

The increase in humanitarian feeling, with the change in national disposition that it implies, is not unconnected with the growth of cities. By residence the English are now mainly an urban people, and in their qualities they are perhaps still more essentially so, for urban characteristics in the past have been chiefly due to the constant intercourse with others that came in city life. The townsman was quick to receive and impart ideas. He became

[1] Com. Papers, 1905, XCIX., 1, pp. 32–33.

[2] *Cf.* Com. Papers, 1895, XXVI., 443, p. 14; 1905, XXIV., 1, p. 38.

[3] On a higher social plane the same change of spirit is shown not less markedly in the disappearance of the barbarity connected with fagging in the great public schools.

alert, responsive, impressionable, ready to act in concert with his fellows; while the rustic was slow, meditative, and self-dependent. But the ease of travel, the rapidity of communication, the post-office and the daily press, have revolutionised country life all the world over, and nowhere, perhaps, so much as in England. The whole kingdom has become, in a sense, suburban. Now with the growth in urban life, and the great advance in a spirit of humanity, there has been loss as well as gain. Something of the old stolidity has passed away to be replaced by greater impulsiveness. This was particularly marked during the South African war, when popular excitement was excessive, especially after British victories, when it was sometimes almost hysterical. Any one who happened to be in London at the time of the relief of Mafeking will not readily forget the pandemonium in the streets on the evening the news arrived, or the exuberance of the next day. It was clearly spontaneous, and all the more instructive. The conditions were, of course, abnormal, yet the display of emotion expressed, in a grossly exaggerated form, a real change that has crept over the national character. The typical John Bull, stolid, inflexible, who did not begin a struggle until he could not help it, and then kept on doggedly, who preferred the ways of his fathers to any new-fangled improvements, has certainly not disappeared altogether, but with the decay of agricultural prosperity he has become far less common. In social problems the Englishman of to-day is sanguine, impatient, eager to attack the evils he perceives, and very willing to try experiments in the process. If there is overcrowding in the cities, he builds at once a few dwelling-houses. If the agricultural labourers are not well off, he passes a law whereby some of them may be furnished with plots of land. If neither of these things proves to be a serious remedy, he builds a few more houses, and makes some ineffective amendment to the Allotment Act. If the mortality among babies is large, he has in some boroughs even provided a supply of municipal milk.

In short, he no longer takes the discomforts of life, either in his own case or that of others, as part of the inevitable order of nature to be endured with patience, but he wants to do something about them and do it now.

Attitude toward Economic Problems.

The decay of the doctrine of *laissez-faire*, coupled with the growth of humanitarian feelings and some change in national temperament, has thus brought about a different attitude towards social and economic questions. The old belief that if riches increased every one would be a gainer has been replaced by solicitude for the condition of the less prosperous people; and this has been made more pronounced by the extension of the franchise. The fact that the bulk of the voters now belong to the classes who possess little property and depend for their living upon wages, has made all men in public life keenly attentive to the wants of the workingman. In striking contrast, therefore, with the ideas dominant threescore years ago, political interest in England at the present day seems to be greater in the distribution than in the production of wealth, and this in spite of the many business men in the House of Commons. Perhaps it would be less true were it not that a large proportion of the people who live upon their income draw a part at least of their revenues from investments in foreign lands, but that is a minor matter, not one of the chief factors in the situation.

Increase of Paternal Legislation.

All these causes have produced a great deal of paternal, perhaps even grandmotherly, legislation. Such a tendency is, of course, by no means confined to England. It has been at work everywhere; and, indeed, to some extent it might have been expected, for unless one adopts the principles of *laissez-faire* in their most absolute form, more or less regulation of economic and social relations is always necessary. Naturally the first step in the transition from one industrial condition to another is the repeal of laws that have become vexatious, and then follows the enactment of the new rules required by a different state of affairs. But although the process has gone on everywhere it has been particularly marked in England, because of the contrast with earlier theories, and because in some directions it has been carried far. Without going into the matter deeply any one can see that this is true by running through the statute book even for the few years of this century. The Factory and Workshop Act of 1901,[1] mainly a consolidation of earlier laws, prescribes the sanitary condition of factories and workshops, the number of people who may work in a certain space, the fencing of machinery, fire-escapes, the conduct of trades dangerous to health, the limit of humidity in textile mills, and the hours of work of women and children; a force of inspectors being kept busy to see that these provisions are carried out. The Merchant Shipping Act of 1906,[2] which extends to foreign vessels a series of existing statutes, regulates the load line, the cargo, the equipment, and the accommodation and food of both passengers and crew. Another series of statutes, ending in the Agricultural Holdings Act of the same year,[3] gives to the tenant farmer, without regard to the terms of any future lease, compensation for improvements he has made and for damage done by game that he is not permitted to kill, allows him to crop the land as he pleases, and gives him compensation also for the termination of his tenancy without good and sufficient cause although his lease may have expired. A Workmen's Compensation Act [4] consolidates and enlarges still another line of enactments, and provides that up to a certain amount employers of every kind shall be liable for accidental injuries to their employees, whether caused by the negligence of fellow-servants or by the carelessness of the person injured, unless the accident is due to his serious and wilful misconduct, and does not result in his death or permanent disablement. In this, as in other cases, the rights granted by the Act cannot be reduced by contract between the parties concerned.[5]

[1] 1 Edw. VII., c. 22.
[2] 6 Edw. VII., c. 48.
[3] 6 Edw. VII., c. 56.
[4] 6 Edw. VII., c. 58.
[5] Except by an arrangement for a scheme affording an equally large compensation: *Ibid.*, § 3.

Old-age pensions, such as exist in Germany, have been talked of seriously for some years, but they have not been established; and in fact the expense of the South African war placed the question for a time beyond the range of practical politics.

In addition to legislation of this kind there is a great deal of work of a paternal character carried on by means of local authorities. The Allotment Acts, for example, provide for the purchase of land to be let for small gardens to labourers; and the Housing of the Working Classes Acts for the construction of dwellings and lodging-houses to be occupied by working people not necessarily poor. There is also the great field of true municipal trading, already discussed in an earlier chapter; the gas works, electric light, tramways and other industries, owned and managed by public bodies. Of a truly paternal nature is the recent statute which empowers local authorities to order shops closed at such hours as they may prescribe.[1] Finally, an act of 1906[2] allows them to furnish meals to school children and recover the cost from parents who can afford to pay, or, if the children are unable for lack of food to take full advantage of the instruction, the meals may be supplied at public expense without involving pauperism.

Tendency to Treat Symptoms.

Beneficial as much of this legislation certainly is, it involves dangers that are not lessened by the English form of government. The scientific tone of thought at the present day leads men to rely upon an inductive rather than a deductive process of reasoning, to judge of theories by their effects rather than by some inherent rational quality.[3] The most important question that can be asked about a policy is not, why is it sound? but how does it work? Hence there is a tendency in the modern world, especially in countries that have long enjoyed free institutions, to magnify efficiency as compared with abstract principles.

[1] 4 Edw. VII., c. 31.

[2] 6 Edw. VII., c. 57.

[3] The Benthamite doctrine of utility has fortified this attitude in England.

This is well, but like all good things it may be overdone. Man has wrought such marvels by his growing control over the forces of nature that he tends to look on all evils as curable and curable quickly. The modern world is in a hurry. Not only does it measure the wisdom of a course of action by the results, but it wants to see those results. It demands of men and of policies rapid success. Conversely it is not content, when something is wrong, to see whether matters will not right themselves in the natural course of events, or even to wait until the subject has been thoroughly studied. It seeks an immediate remedy and often grasps at the first plausible suggestion. Nor does it look far ahead for the signs of future trouble, because it is busy; its hands are filled by the work of the day. In short, the world is prone to deal only with the things that are pressing and obvious, and therefore to treat symptoms rather than causes.

**Particularly Strong in England.**

The habit of dealing with immediate needs instead of seeking for ultimate causes is particularly strong where the cabinet, with its virtual control over the House of Commons, has all the powers of the state in its hands, and is expected to rectify anything that is wrong. The ministers must take steps for the relief of every acute ailment, or convince the public that to act at all would be unwise — not by any means an easy thing to do. On the other hand, with all the cares of the nation on their shoulders, they are not inclined to add to their burdens by trying to deal with matters which do not appear to be urgent and in which the public is not much interested. Mr. Gladstone, in many ways a typical product of the British parliamentary system, confessed that he had never been "able sufficiently to adjust the proper conditions of handling any difficult question, until the question itself was at the door."[1] That expresses very well the habitual attitude of the British cabinet. But it means a tendency to take

[1] "Gleanings of Past Years," VII., 133.

short views, and crowd out the far-sighted policy that looks for results in the remote future. With the prevailing tone of thought and the rapid changes of party in popular governments, such a tendency to deal with symptoms rather than causes is a characteristic of modern democracies; but owing to the concentration of power in the hands of the ministry it is especially pronounced in the case of England.

## CHAPTER LXVI

### PARTY AND CLASS LEGISLATION

The Demand for Privilege.

WHILE modern humanitarianism inclines people to relieve distress at once, while modern thought requires immediate results, and modern government tends toward the treatment of superficial rather than fundamental problems, universal suffrage enables all the different classes in the community to urge forcibly their own particular interests. A hundred years ago many demands of this kind took the form of asking for the removal of privileges or restrictions imposed by earlier legislation, and hence they were marshalled under the banner of liberty and equality. But with the abolition of old restraints, and the evolution of a new system of regulations based upon present industrial conditions, the character of the demands has changed, and the classes that ask for positive legislation are apt to seek something that is essentially in the nature of privilege. Whether it be landowners and farmers who want their rates assessed at a lower figure than other people, Churchmen who want grants for their schools, manufacturers who want protection against foreign competition or a fairer chance in foreign markets, workingmen who want a limitation of the hours of labour, or trade-unions that want exemption from liability, the demands are really for special rights that will confer benefits on the classes affected, although they appear, of course, to their advocates as the plain dictates of justice.

The Position of the Ministers.

Men who hold or aspire to public office must carry elections in order to give effect to their opinions. To succeed they must, so far as their conscience will permit, win the votes of the various elements in the electorate, and especially they must try to obtain the support of a part at least of the working-classes who form the largest mass of voters in the nation. Now the pressure to do this is especially great in the English parliamentary government, because the cabinet can be held responsible at any moment for the whole state of legislation, both for the statutes it enacts and for those it neglects to propose. In countries where power is divided among a number of bodies, or hidden away in committees, responsibility is intangible. Every one can throw it off his own shoulders, and it may become the subject of a game of hide-and-seek. Amid the confused issues of politics the voters cannot readily hold a man or a party to account for a failure to enact a measure, which may never have come out of the committee room; and hence the support of powerful individuals, secured by methods good or bad, may have more influence on the political future of a representative than his attitude toward a bill of public importance. Where, moreover, as in the American state legislatures, party lines are not often strictly drawn, a member will vote according to his own opinions or those of his constituents, with little regard to the effect his vote may have upon the prospects of the party in other places. Under these circumstances, it is obviously very difficult to hold a party responsible for the fate of public measures.

But in England responsibility is perfectly definite, for the cabinet can almost always control the party, and every voter knows that in casting his ballot at a general election he is voting for or against the policy of the ministers. They virtually appeal to the country on a legislative programme which they have power under ordinary conditions to carry out, and if they fail to do so the nation will pass judgment on that failure at the next election. They receive all the credit and all the blame for what the House of Commons has done and left undone, so far as public measures are concerned; and it must be remembered that class legislation of the kind we are considering belongs in the category of public matters for which the cabinet is responsible. For it they are held to strict account by the voters, and there is no distribution of private benefits or local concessions to affect the result. Since the party under the lead of the ministers acts as a unit on all important matters, any class of voters can with confidence support or oppose it as a whole on its record of what it has done, and on what it promises to do, for them. The very fact, therefore, that politics in England turn, not upon private or local affairs, but upon public questions on which party lines are drawn, strengthens the motives for winning over the various classes in the community by yielding to their wishes. Under the late Conservative administrations complaints were made of doles to the landowners, the Church of England and the publicans; now, under the Liberals, of concessions to Nonconformists and to the trade-unions. In short, there is a peculiarly strong temptation at Westminster to procure political support for the party, not by granting favours to individuals or localities, but by conciliating large classes of voters.

**Parties not Divided on Class Lines.**

The greatest possible evil in this connection, that of a division of parties into rich and poor fighting over the distribution of property, has been predicted,[1] but as yet it has certainly not come. Grave as the danger might seem, it is contrary to the course of English history. On the Continent, from the middle ages to the present day, parties have often been divided on class lines; a fact that explains in great part the growth and continuance in the past of arbitrary monarchical power, for tyranny is preferable to class war. But in England such a division of classes has been uncommon, the lines of political cleavage being habitually vertical rather than horizontal. So far as the result at the present day may be traced to any deliberate plan, it is the work of Disraeli, who in spite of much levity, and perhaps even charlatanry, in the use of means, kept

[1] *Cf.* G. Lowes Dickinson, "The Development of Parliament during the Nineteenth Century," 163.

the harmony of classes steadily in view throughout his career. In early life he was interested in the fantastic Young England movement, designed to promote the object by social gatherings of rich and poor at country seats. Later he aimed at converting his Tory following into a national party comprising people of all grades, and in that effort he persisted with ultimate success. Believing that workingmen are by nature largely Conservative, he led his reluctant party to accept an extension of the franchise to them in 1867, and he prepared the way for the policy of legislating in their interest, afterwards known as Tory Democracy.[1] Thanks to his efforts, or to the "sublime instincts of an ancient people," parties in England are by no means divided on class lines, and unless the Labour Party should grow in a way that seems unlikely, there is no probability that they will be so divided in the near future.

Each Party Bids for Working-Class Votes.

The result at present is that each of the two great parties contains members of the working-classes, and each of them tries to enlist their support by concessions to their claims. The latest example is that of the Trade Disputes Act of 1906,[2] which forbids any suit for tort against a trade-union, and thus, while permitting those bodies to use their benefit funds to carry on a strike, exempts them from all liability for tortious injuries that they may commit in so doing. The Act confers a privilege quite foreign to the fundamental principles of the Common Law, contrary to the report of the royal commission appointed to inquire into the subject, which was unanimous on this point,[3] and contrary to the original intention of the government. Yet in deference to the strong electoral pressure of the trade-unions it was accepted by the Liberal cabinet, and passed by the Conservative House of Lords without a division, except on

[1] This is the opinion commonly held; but Lord Rosebery maintains that Disraeli never "became seriously responsible for any form of Tory Democracy," which in his view involves a contradiction in terms. ("Lord Randolph Churchill," xi., xii.)

[2] 6 Edw. VII., c. 47.

[3] Com. Papers, 1906, LVI., 1, pp. 8, 71, 120.

subsidiary amendments relating to picketing and to interests in land.

It might be supposed that the people as a whole would be most concerned about the interests of the public as a whole, but that is true only in part. The community is made up of many elements, each of which is usually more intent upon its own objects than upon the general welfare. Democracy, therefore, while changing the nature of class legislation, has by no means abolished its dangers. They exist in all popular governments at the present day, and in one form or another they are inseparable from government of any kind; but they would seem to be especially great in the English parliamentary system. In short the peril in England is not personal corruption, or the pressure of local interests, or again the turning of the representative into a delegate of his constituents which has created so much apprehension, but the bidding for support of whole classes of voters by legislation for their benefit. This presents probably the most serious menace to which British institutions are exposed.

Correctives in the English System.

If there is grave danger from class legislation in England, there are also forces at work that tend to limit it. There is the great difficulty in passing laws, the small number of acts that can be placed upon the statute book in a session, and the new doctrine that Parliament ought not to adopt any far-reaching measure without a mandate from the nation. These matters have been discussed before, and their effect in causing delay and giving time for reflection is of some value. There is also the fact that as a rule a cabinet can legislate to-day only with the consent of substantially the whole body of its followers in the House of Commons; and in this connection there is an important difference between the parties in England and in most of the other states in Europe. On the Continent a party is usually a collection of men holding a definite political principle or body of doctrine, and therefore while its adherents may differ on a particular measure which does not affect that principle, they can hardly abandon the party without apostasy. Under these circumstances the party is likely to be directed by the more active portion of its members, by those who have the strongest convictions and are most aggressive; in short by the extremists. Thus it has often happened that politics has been a battle between the extreme opinions, the moderate elements, which may really represent the great mass of the people, having a disproportionately small share in the government of the country. But in England, where the parties are not separated by any profound divergence in political creed, but are essentially instruments of government contending over concrete issues, a man will cling to his party so long as its policy on the whole accords with his views better than the policy of its rival, and when it ceases to do so he will cross over to the other side. Now the voters who pass most readily to the Opposition are those who stand nearest to it, and hence their opinions have peculiar weight. Under normal conditions, therefore, when England is divided into two camps, the parties tend to be very much influenced by their moderate elements, and thus, to use a continental expression, the nation is ruled mainly by the centre rather than by the extreme right and left. This certainly conduces to safety and is a healthy political condition. It does not obstruct progress, but prevents the movement from being too rapid, and avoids violent changes, or conflicts that are perilously acute.

The fact that the government is in the hands of a small upper class, while the electorate is mainly composed of workingmen, has also a noteworthy effect. Although the men who sit in Parliament and in the cabinet are constrained to follow the wishes of the mass of the voters, and even to bid against one another for popular support, they cannot divest themselves altogether of the opinions derived from their education and environment. They are for the most part men of social position and wealth, who cannot lead a class war or a general assault on property;

and in fact the Socialist-Labour organisations complain bitterly that both of the great parties are capitalist at heart. The parliamentary leaders may go a long way in socialistic legislation, but they cannot move very fast, and there is a limit to the distance they will go. To entrust a man of conservative traditions with the execution of a radical programme is a safe and sometimes a wise proceeding. Such a condition does not obviate pressure for democratic class legislation, or prevent it from being effective, but it does act as a moderating force.

**Centres of Political and Social Gravity.**

This may be put in another way. All government involves compulsion, and is therefore based ultimately on power. But power among men has many sources, of which numbers is only one. Another is wealth, another the capacity for organisation, another intelligence, and in fact it would be easy to mention many more without exhausting the possible list. Taking all the various sources of power together and ascribing to each its real weight, we could find what might be called the actual centre of gravity of a community. It would not be the same in all countries or at all times. It would be affected by such matters as the distribution of property, and the prevalent intellectual and moral convictions, for ideas are an essential element in the problem. A priesthood, for example, might have great power at one time, and none at another. But it would be theoretically possible to ascertain the actual centre of gravity in any community at a certain time. The political centre of gravity is quite a different thing. Nominally it depends upon the distribution of political power, or in a popular government upon the extension of the franchise. Practically it may be determined in other ways. Now these two centres of gravity can never long remain very far apart. What we have called the actual centre of power will assert itself, peacefully if it can, forcibly if it must. A government that is seriously out of accord with it will provoke resistance, unless it yields. When numbers are insufficiently represented there may be violent outbreaks. With other forces the pressure is more commonly exerted steadily, silently and often without attracting attention. This has been true in all ages of the world, and not least in recent years. We live in a period of democracy where every man's vote has equal weight, but in spite of the great force that organisation has placed in the hands of masses of men, numbers are still not the only source of power. Education and wealth are still strong and they make themselves felt, sometimes by a natural leadership with the voters, sometimes unfortunately by corrupt means. In England the balance between numbers and the other forces in the state would seem to be brought about largely by the fact that the electorate comprises almost the whole community, while the immediate direction of affairs is still mainly in the hands of a smaller governing class.

# CHAPTER LXVII

## CONCLUSION

Writers who have studied the British government profoundly have often been impressed by the nice adjustment of the forces that maintain its equilibrium, and they have commonly felt that any disturbance of those forces would upset a balance that could not be restored. Hence they have tended to be conservative and deprecate any radical change. This was eminently true of Bagehot, the most penetrating of observers, who dreaded the effect of the extension of the suffrage in 1867. But their fears have not been wholly justified, for when the old equilibrium has been destroyed it has been replaced by a new one not very different in character. In attempting to describe the play of forces as they exist at the present day, the writer has no idea that they will remain unaltered. Constant change is the law of life, in institutions as well as in animals; but in England the process of change is not in all ways the same as in some other countries.

A written constitution permits wide variation in action without a lasting modification of structure. The President of the United States may exert far greater power at one time than at another without affecting permanently the institutions of the country. At one moment a brilliant writer like Woodrow Wilson may even depict him as almost completely subordinate to congressional action, and a score of years later his authority may overshadow that of Congress. Where the constitution is in writing it is natural to look for the source of authority to the document itself, which thus tends to prevent a loss by disuse of legal powers that are not, like those of the Electoral College, wholly inappropriate. In fact there is a tendency, after a departure from the prevailing usage, to revert to the normal type. In England, on the other hand, where the exercise of power depends, not upon legal provisions, but mainly upon the conventions of the constitution, custom is the basis of authority. Hence changes of practice, jealously watched, develop slowly, and there is no tendency to revert. A change once made is likely to be permanent. In short, in the United States a sharp distinction can be drawn between the structure and functions of the organs of state. But in the English Constitution, as in the Gulf Stream or a whirlwind, functions and structure are the same thing.

Changes in the British government will therefore take place, but they will come slowly, the organism constantly adjusting itself to a new equilibrium, and the only safe prediction is that each fresh balance of forces will probably be as intricate, as nicely adjusted, and as worthy of study, as the ones that have gone before.

# INDEX

Bei Fragen zur Produktsicherheit wenden Sie sich bitte an:
If you have any questions regarding product safety,
please contact:

Walter de Gruyter GmbH
Genthiner Straße 13
10785 Berlin
productsafety@degruyterbrill.com